THE POLITICS OF THE EIGHTH CENTRAL COMMITTEE

OF THE

COMMUNIST PARTY OF CHINA

This volume is the fourteenth of a number in which are being published the results of research carried on by the faculty and research scholars working at Yale University in the field of Foreign Area Studies. In 1953 there was published *The Multi-State System of Ancient China* by Richard A. Walker, and in 1954 there were published *The Russian Hexameter* by Richard T. Burgi and *China's March Toward The Tropics* by Herold J. Wiens. This was followed in 1960 by the *Index To Ch'ing Tai Ch'ou Pan I Wu Shih Mo* edited by David Nelson Rowe. In 1961 was published *Britain's Imperial Role in the Red Sea Area 1800-1878* by Thomas E. Marston, and *What China Policy?* by Vladimir Petrov. In 1964 there was published *United States Foreign Policy Toward South Africa 1948-1963* by Leon M. S. Slawecki, and in 1965, *Taiwan in China's Foreign Relations 1836-1874* by Sophia Su-fei Yen, and *Index To Su-Lien Yin-Mou Wen-Cheng* edited by David Nelson Rowe and Sophia Su-fei Yen. In 1968 were published *The Opening of Korea: A Study in Chinese Diplomacy, 1876-1885* by Frederick Foo Chien, and *The Filipino Reaction To American Rule, 1901-1913* by Bonifacio S. Salamanca, and *New Nations: A Student Handbook* edited by David Nelson Rowe. In 1971 was published *French Policy Towards The Chinese in Madagascar* by Leon M. S. Slawecki. Subsequent volumes will include studies in the various disciplines, both Humanities and Social Sciences, in respect to Foreign Area Studies.

David Nelson Rowe
Chairman, Editorial Committee
Professor of Political Science

THE POLITICS OF THE EIGHTH CENTRAL COMMITTEE OF THE COMMUNIST PARTY OF CHINA

BY
PETER R. MOODY, Jr.

The Shoe String Press, Inc.   1973

62418

Library of Congress Cataloging in Publication Data

Moody, Peter R.
 The politics of the Eighth Central Committee of the Communist Party of China.

 Bibliography: p.
 1. Chung-kuo kung ch'an tang. Chung yang wei yüan hui. 2. China (People's Republic of China, 1949-   ) —Politics and government. I. Title.
 JQ1519.A5M66   329.9'51   73-4308
 ISBN 0-208-01328-8

© Copyright 1973 by The Shoe String Press, Inc.
Hamden, Connecticut 06514
All rights reserved

Printed in the United States of America

*To my wife,
and to the memory of
my mother*

CONTENTS

Foreword ix

Major Abbreviations xi

I. The Failure of Political Development 1
   The Thermidor Syndrome, 2; Thermidor and Bureaucracy, 3;
   Bureaucracy and Political Development, 5; The Power Struggle
   Hypothesis, 9; Political Opportunities in China: The Two Roads, 16;
   Summary Hypotheses, 27

II. The Central Committee as a Political Institution 29
    Career Patterns of Central Committee Members, 30;
    The Structure of the Party Center, 32; The CC as a Policy-Making
    Body, 47; Party, State, Army: The Problem of Party Autonomy
    and Party Control, 48

III. Political Groupings on the Central Committee and the
     Nature of the Purge 56
     Determining Group Membership, 57; Nature of the Groupings:
     An Overview, 61; Characteristics of the Groups, 74; The Incidence
     of the Purge, 83

IV. The Role of the "Party" Under the Eighth Central
    Committee 88
    The Eighth Congress—Institutionalized Party Control and
    Thermidor, 88; The Maoist Counter-Attack on the Party, 91;
    The Triumph of the Party, 96; The Cult of Mao Prior to the Rise
    of Lin Piao, 101; The Party on the Capitalist Road, 104; The
    Evolution of the Role of the Army, 106; The Humiliation of the
    Party, 110; Appendix: The Apparatchik-Commissars, 112

V. Political Relations Within the CC Prior to the Cultural
   Revolution 114
   Politics of the Eighth Congress, 114; A Hundred Flowers
   Bloom, 116; The Politics of Anti-Localism, 120; Economic
   Radicalism, 125; The Retirement of Mao and the First
   Moderation of the Leap, 133; P'eng Te-huai Is Dismissed From
   Office, 139; Moving Toward the Capitalist Road: 1959-1960, 146;
   A Walk on the Capitalist Road, 151; Deadlock, 157

| VI. | The Center Does Not Hold: The Destruction of the Party Center | 167 |

Factional Play Prior to the Purge of P'eng Chen, 169; The Purge of P'eng Chen, 176; The Purge of Liu Shao-ch'i and Teng Hsiao-p'ing, 180; The Purge of T'ao Chu, 186; The New Order, 189

| VII. | Conclusions | 193 |

Notes by Chapter 201

Appendix 263

Bibliography 275

Index 333

FOREWORD

This study was begun in a seminar on Comparative Government at Yale University, continued and expanded thereafter, and brought to final development through intensive research in archives available in The Republic of China.

It constitutes one of the few studies of the complicated internal politics of Communist China, based upon original sources from that country and which investigates in all their intricacy and inter-meshed relationships the real factors leading to and conditioning the various shifts in power inside the higher echelons of Chinese Communist government.

Particularly in its emphasis upon what we may justifiably term the "real" factors in internal Chinese Communist politics at this level, the study makes a valuable contribution. Flowing from this approach, usually emphasized policy differences or ideological disagreements are seen to have been much less important as bases for power shifts among top leaders of the Chinese Communist regime than has usually been held to be the case.

In fact it is not too much to say that as seen in this study, Chinese Communist politics at the higher levels, while influenced by extraneous factors, continues to be substantially in conformity with the norms of traditional Chinese political struggle, where the basic presupposition was always that, since there was only personal politics and it was carried out through conspiracy, powerful individuals were always successful conspirators. Since by its nature, conspiracy involves very intense interpersonal relationships, politics is always a struggle of cliques. The important thing is, always, skill and assiduity in clique politics. Therefore politics consists for the most part of an inevitably destructive process of liquidation—advancement of liquidators—counter liquidation. (Liquidation is not always defined in purely physical terms.) Total tyranny of successful liquidators over would-be claimants to power is a necessary adjunct to this process, given its presuppositions and procedural norms.

The above are just a few of the significant factors emerging from this study, which is recommended to students of comparative politics everywhere.

David Nelson Rowe
Professor of Political Science
Yale University

MAJOR ABBREVIATIONS

CB—*Current Background*
CC—Central Committee (中央委員會)
CEL—Chou En-lai Group
CNA—*China News Analysis*
CPC—Communist Party of China (中國共產党)
CR—Cultural Revolution Group
CQ—*China Quarterly*
CY—*China Youth* (中國青年)
DSJP—*Daily Summary of the Japanese Press*
GPD—General Political Department (總政治部)
HL—Ho Lung Group
KMD—*Kuang Ming Daily* (光明日報)
LAD—*Liberation Army Daily* (解放軍報)
LP—Lin Piao Group
LT—Liu-Teng Group
MAC—Military Affairs Commission (軍事委員會)
NCHM—*New China Half-Monthly* (新華半月刊)
PBSC—Politburo Standing Committee (政治局常務委員會)
PC—P'eng Chen Group
PD—*People's Daily* (人民日報)
PHB—*People's Handbook* (人民手冊)
PLA—People's Liberation Army (人民解放軍)
PTH—P'eng Te-huai Group
SCMP—*Survey of the China Mainland Press*
SD—*Southern Daily* (南方日報)
TC—T'ao Chu Group
TMTT—Thought of Mao Tse-tung (毛澤東思想)
URI—Union Research Institute
WB—*Work Bulletins* (工作通訊)

I

THE FAILURE OF POLITICAL DEVELOPMENT

Among many possible definitions of that vague term "political development" one might refer to an increase in the capacity of a government to govern.[1] This would make political development a rather rare attribute of those countries we like to call the "developing nations." Perhaps this is not too surprising. We live, we are told, in revolutionary times, blown by the winds of change. These are times of shaking and breaking, not building.

Yes the most skilled of the shakers and breakers, the communist parties in the Leninist tradition, have also proved to be skilled at restoring order and political stability to the systems they govern. As Samuel P. Huntington notes, Communist parties "may not provide liberty, but they do provide authority; they do create governments that can govern."[2] Or so it seemed before 1966, when events in mainland China began to call even this into question. This study will attempt to explain the failure of China to attain political stability during the years of the rule of the Eighth Central Committee (CC) of the Communist Party of China (CPC).

It is argued in this first chapter that at times during the tenure of the Eighth Central Committee the Chinese revolution was moving toward its "Thermidor," but that by the mid-1960's the revolution had failed to attain Thermidor. The political manifestation of Thermidor is seen as the growth of institutional patterns of authority; institutional patterns of authority are contrasted with what in this study are called "charismatic patterns" of authority. The focus of this study is an examination of the politics of the CC in an attempt to determine why China after 1956 failed to transcend the charismatic pattern, and, specifically, why the professional Party workers, the "apparatchiks," failed to institutionalize the authority of the organized party, as occurred, for example, in the Soviet Union. It is hypothesized that an explanation for this revolves around the nature of the power struggle, that the nature of political or social changes can be understood in part as a function of who benefits from these changes, and how the beneficiaries come to realize their desires. "Political opportunities" in China, it is argued, were shaped by two long-enduring thems in Chinese Communist history, one stressing the institutional authority of the Party, the other stressing the personal authority of the leader of the Party. The development of these two themes prior to 1956 is sketched briefly; and the "Maoist" alternative to institutional authority, as enunciated during the more extreme phases of the Cultural Revolution, is outlined.

1. THE THERMIDOR SYNDROME[3]

Students of revolution have long noted a pattern of phenomena they term "Thermidor," from the name of the French revolutionary month which witnessed the overthrow of Robespierre and the end of the Jacobin terror. Crane Brinton, using the metaphor of an illness, calls Thermidor the "convalescence from the fever of revolution."[4] Thermidor entails a kind of "return to normalcy" for the society, as revolutionary pressure against the common man is relaxed:

> As time goes on, the pressures of the terror applied to ordinary men are relaxed... The taste and habit of political violence live on in *coups d'etat,* in purges, in well-staged trials. But John Jones, Jaques Dupont, Ivan Ivanovich, the man in the street is no longer included in the cast — he is now left to his normal role as spectator or supernumerary.[5]

The old revolutionary ardor has gone out of style:

> The new ruling class settles down to do as good a job as it can. But it clearly intends to enjoy life, to possess the privileges and wealth a ruling class has hitherto always had... It is quite content with the stratification system that has worked itself out in the revolution.[6]

During the early 1960's similar attitudes were held to have developed among segments of the ruling elite of China, and the Cultural Revolution may be seen in part as a reaction against these tendencies. The various cow devils and snake spirits, black gangsters, and power holders on the capitalist road were supposed to have lost any ardor and idealism they might once have had. Liu Shao-ch'i had "as many as five wives whom he married legally."[7] His current wife was "a woman of dubious reputation," a "harlot."[8] T'ao Chu, a former First Secretary of the Central South Regional Bureau, used to hold private showings of pornographic movies imported from the United States and Hong Kong.[9] Secretary General Teng Hsiao-p'ing liked to play bridge. "So addicted to his bridge games was Teng Hsiao-p'ing that he was not to be bothered with official business while he was playing."[10] Ho Lung, a former marshal, a member of the Politburo, and Vice-Premier of the State Council, was "once a big bandit," and has "lived a life tinged with a bourgeois odor." Among other sins, he liked animals. "He is indeed no different from the big capitalists of the 'free' world in the West, who do practically nothing all day long except play with their pets."[11]

Behind all of these attacks, of course, was more than a disgust with hedonistic degeneracy. We might consider the following critique of the Three Family Village (三家村), a group of satirists active during the early 1960's under the patronage of the Peking Party Committee:

> The main interests of the Three Family Village, aside from secretly plotting anti-Party anti-socialist activities, were eating, drinking, and fooling around; exalting landlords, cracking jokes, playing with antiques, playing mahjong, wheeling and dealing, pandering to Soviet revisionists and intellectuals. These were the interests of the Three Family Village.[12]

Thermidor was thus seen as a political threat to the Maoist order: the bad men liked to "plot." The thermidorians seem to have recognized certain positive aspects of the "old" society, especially imperial society. They also seem to have felt that politics were not the end-all and be-all of human life. Thermidorian periods in history seem generally to have a bad press. But the Chinese Thermidor, such as it was, may have contained the seeds for the development of a more humane, more effective, and, in the long run, perhaps even a more democratic polity in China.[13]

2. THERMIDOR AND BUREAUCRACY

Brinton conceives of Thermidor as a social phenomenon—men become tired of revolution. Marxist writers take another approach—they see Thermidor as the result of the bureaucratization of the instruments of rule. According to Leon Trotsky, under Stalin the bureaucracy came to constitute a "new commanding caste."[14] "The leaden rump of the bureaucracy outweights the head of the revolution. That is the secret of Stalin's Thermidor."[15] Trotsky worried mainly about the growth of the influence of the state bureaucracy *vis á vis* the Communist Party. Milovan Djilas traces Thermidorian results to the bureaucratization of the Party itself: "Membership in the Communist Party before the revolution meant sacrifice... Now that the Party has consolidated its power, membership means that one belongs to a privileged class. And at the core of the Party are the all-powerful exploiters and masters."[16] His famous "new class" is identified as "the bureaucracy, or more accurately, the political bureaucracy."[17] These men are "unconcerned with great ideals, and concerned only with the everyday pleasures of life."[18]

This cooling of revolutionary ardor and concentration of power in the bureaucracy seems to be a result of processes initiated by the revolutionaries themselves. Communist parties in general have come to power in relatively backward countries, and one of their main goals has been rapid modernization. They have also desired to control and shape the resulting social system to their own liking. Under these circumstances the elites have adopted what A.F.K. Organsky calls "Stalinist politics." This pattern is marked by a narrow concentration of authority, with increasing popular participation in the process of economic development without any increase in popular control of the government.[19]

A strict hierarchy—a bureaucracy—is required to carry out a program of increased production, low consumption, and thorough social control. The ruling group will also need to employ technical experts. For these men and for the bureaucrats supervising them the revolutionary ideology, too vague to provide any detailed guide to day to day problem solving, will become increasingly irrelevant. As David Apter overstates the case, "At its widest limits the modernization process is the confrontation of the ideologue and the scientist, not because their respective ethics are antagonistic but because of the changes that occur in the modernization process itself."[20]

Thermidorian tendencies are implicit in the nature of bureaucracy. Robert Michels, like Trotsky and Djilas a disillusioned leftist intellectual, writes "The bureaucratic spirit corrupts character and engenders moral poverty."[21] Even bureaucrats from the "exploited classes" do not escape this corruption: "Their own social revolution has already been effected."[22] The bureaucracy tends to acquire its own vested interests. Eisenstadt notes of bureaucratic empires: "The bureaucratic administrators tended to develop some specific organizational characteristics of their own. The most important of these was the tendency to emphasize internal organizational and professional autonomy."[23]

This does not mean, of course, that the bureaucrats in the Party and state cease to believe in the doctrine; they will probably hold to it with unshakeable, closed conviction.[24] But the *élan* is gone out of the ideology, and its mundane relevance has become unclear. In Leninist ideology the Party, as vanguard of the proletariat, should supervise the government, and the Party should provide the *élan*. However, in order to supervise the government effectively the Party tends to develop a bureaucracy of its own,[25] and this bureaucracy will tend to share the characteristics common to other bureaucracies. We might expect that the Party apparatus will tend to show on the whole fewer thermidorian characteristics than the state bureaucracy. But as the supervisors come to be judged according to the performance of those they supervise, that part of the ideology with no day to day relation to production and the exaction of obedience will tend to fade, and the Party will come to feel the impact of the forces making for Thermidor.

In its rhetoric at any rate, the Cultural Revolution can be seen as an abortion of Thermidor. Some of the utterances of the Maoists echo those of Trotsky and Djilas. The following is from Lin Piao:

> The Party-building line of Liu and Teng is a revisionist one, it is the root of a privileged stratum in our country. . . It promotes economic privileges of cadres, raising their salaries and giving them special material treatment. . . In the last analysis, it aims at protecting the system of exploitation. This leads to a decline of the fighting will of the cadres, causing them to be content with the *status quo*. . . It breeds a sense of superiority in them, making them give up thought reform, lead a life of laxity, and divorce themselves from the masses.[26]

3. BUREAUCRACY AND POLITICAL DEVELOPMENT

"Political power," says the Chairman, "grows out of the barrel of a gun."[27] Behind all effective government above the level of roving bands we should expect to find some basis of coercion. But over an extended area and period of time, power must "grow into" something else. Thus, Mao adds that the Party must control the gun, not the gun the Party.[28] That is, there is need for authority—coercion plus the "ability to evoke compliance short of coercion." This ability can be called legitimacy.[29] In categorizing authority Max Weber's classification into the traditional, charismatic, and bureaucratic types is still useful. Since we are dealing with a revolutionary regime, in the short run we may ignore traditional authority.

A. Charismatic Authority and the Politics of Charisma

The concept of charismatic authority has played a large role in both popular and scholarly writings about the politics of the developing areas. Weber defines the term as follows:

> The term "charisma" will be applied to a certain quality of an individual personality of virtue of which he is set apart from ordinary men and treated as endowed with supernatural, superhuman, or at least specifically exceptional powers or qualities.[30]

The crucial phrase here would seem to be "treated as endowed," for "It is recognition on the part of those subject to authority which is decisive for the validity of charisma."[31] Thus, the leader's "superhuman" qualities may be nothing more than an illusion produced by deft press agentry or a propaganda machine. Even considering this, it is still difficult to measure charisma under Weber's definition. For our purposes it may be more useful to see charismatic authority as non-institutionalized personal rule.[32]

This authority type often gives rise to a distinctive pattern of political action. In his analysis of the Nazi Party, Joseph Nyomarkay finds that party to have been a coalition of factions holding widely different opinions. The party could, in spite of this, remain cohesive because the leaders of all the factions were personally loyal to Hitler.[33] Ch'ien Tuan-sheng, in a rather hostile analysis, finds a similar political pattern in the Kuomintang of the 1930's and 1940's:

> The explanation for the existence of groups is to be sought in the nature of Chiang Kai-shek's leadership. He demands loyalty to his person. . . He has deep faith in himself as the guarding angel of both the party and the nation. . . As long as a man or group of men remains loyal to him and does his bidding, he will extend his protection. Two groups of his followers may differ from each other in ideas and policies, but it does not follow that therefore one of the groups must also have differences with him. . . It is, then, clear that the leader of the Kuomingtang is not only the head head of its organization but actually holds it together. Or, to state it in another way, the leader has allowed the Party to be segmented so that he alone supplied the link between the several segments.[34]

Charismatic authority may have short run utility in providing cohesion to newly formed states and organizations, where the politically relevant groups "tend to differ from each other in ideas and policies." But this provides no long run stability. The leader must be successful: "above all, if his leadership fails to benefit his followers, it is likely that his charismatic authority will disappear."[35] And even the most charismatic of men must die. When this happens, if the same group is to retain power the charisma must somehow be "routinized." An incentive to this routinization would be the desire of the leaders to stabilize their position, but this must be balanced against each leader's desire to better his own status at the expense of the others'. Also, as Ch'ien intimates, the leader during his lifetime may put obstacles in the way of routinization, and the effects of these obstacles may persist after his death or deposition.[36]

B. Institutionalized Authority

Huntington hypothesizes that over the long run the development of an institutionalized pattern of authority is required for political effectiveness and stability:

> Political community in a complex society thus depends upon the strength of the political organizations and the procedures in the society. That strength, in turn, depends upon the *scope of support* for the organizations and their level of *institutionalization*.[37]

Stability is derived from legitimate institutions, the "level of institutionalization" being measured by the adaptability, complexity, autonomy, and coherence of the organizations and procedures.[38]

"Political institutionalization" here is taken to mean the development of effective routinized authority embodied in given structures. This study is concerned with the institutionalization, or lack thereof, of the Communist Party, specifically, with the institutionalization of the role of the professional Party workers, or apparatchiks. The concern is with the development of the capacity of the apparatus to exercise effective control and leadership over other political institutions (the state and army), as prescribed in Leninist ideology and as generally practiced in the Soviet Union.

On this point, the nature of the "cohesion" of the institution must be clarified. The Soviet Union, for example, has always been at least as faction-ridden as the People's Republic of China. Nothing in the concept of institutionalization as used in this study should preclude the existence of competing groups within the institution. Given the generally Hobbesian thrust of the theoretical scheme of this study, indeed, the existence of such groups should be expected—for analytical purposes, at any rate, conflict is taken as the norm. In a highly institutionalized organization, however, groups or individuals best further their own ambitions by furthering the more general aims of the institution. Thus, the power struggles in the Soviet Union have tended over the long run to bolster the role of the apparatus. Where institutionalization is not so highly advanced, however, malcontents will have the opportunity to further their own aims by forming alliances with those outside the institution, or by undermining the routinization of the authority of their superiors. In this case, lack of cohesion will tend further to weaken institutionalization.

Huntington, unlike some other theorists of political development, stresses the conflict between institutionalization and what he calls "social mobilization.": "a change in the attitudes, values, and expectations of people from those associated with the traditional world to those common to the modern world."[39] It would also seem that other types of social change could be subsumed under this variable. Huntington argues that the political party is the best institution for controlling and channeling the growth of political participation.[40]

The political party in its Leninist form has proved to be very successful in this century in both mobilizing and controlling the population. Lenin conceived of the Party as a corps of specialists in the science of seizing power: "The organization of revolutionists must be composed first and foremost of people whose profession is that of revolutionists."[41] Total discipline must be exercised over the activities of these specialists: the Party must "control (in the literal sense of that term)...every act the person commits in the political field."[42] Lenin at first seems to have thought of this tightly knit organization merely as a machine for seizing power from a despotism,[43] but he soon learned that it could also serve as an instrument of rule.[44] Revolution is "social mobilization" *par excellence,* and the Leninist Party is an instrument for controlling the direction and force of this mobilization, especially after the Party has come to power. The Soviet Union has been one of this century's relatively few stable polities.

Leninism stresses authority deriving from an ideology manifested through the will of an organized Party, and is a form of bureaucratic authority. Schapiro and Lewis point out in a perceptive essay that all successful Leninist movements have tended to be dominated by a single individual, and that these individuals weakened the role of the Party.[45] The power struggle hypothesis presented below explains part of this paradox. It should be noted, however, that the Leninist Party is something of an "ideal type," only approximated in the real world. The CPC never approximated its model as closely as the CPSU has done. Even Stalin, who came to power through his position in the Party apparatus, never slighted the Party to the extent that Mao has been willing to do. Stalin referred to Lenin for his authority. Mao, when able, as often as not refers to himself (his "Thought"). Under Stalin the apparatus retained crucial functions, especially that of patronage. Under Khrushchev the apparatchiks regained a predominant role in Soviet politics.[46]

4. THE POWER STRUGGLE HYPOTHESIS

The "anti-thermidorian" interpretation of the Cultural Revolution, with its emphasis on the millenarian ideology and its attacks on the bureaucracy, has become almost trite.[47] Formerly, however, students had tended to think that the phenomena here called "Thermidor" were "almost inevitably a part of the process of revolution."[48] It is thus surprising that most interpretations of the Cultural Revolution fail to provide a satisfactory explanation for this unexpected development. Many analyses seem content to make statements about Mao Tse-tung's personality and political philosophy, and perhaps to assert that the Cultural Revolution is not a power struggle.[49] Of course, the Cultural Revolution or any other major change cannot be interpreted solely as a power struggle, or solely as any one thing else. But the power struggle hypothesis seems able to provide an explanation for much of what happened.[50] A general hypothesis here is that one way of explaining why certain political or social changes occur is to examine who benefits from these changes, and how the beneficiaries come to realize their desires.

Another hypothesis is provided by Joseph A. Schlesinger: "Ambition is the heart of politics... The central assumption of ambition theory is that a politician's behavior is a response to his office goals."[51] Politicians will act in a rational manner, espousing ideologies and policies which enable them to maintain or expand their power.[52] "Power," of course, is a notoriously slippery concept. Everyone has some idea of what the term means, but any attempt at rigorous definition will meet with well-founded objections. Schlesinger avoids the problem by concentrating upon "office." In the United States there is probably a fairly high relation between power and office, but this may not hold generally. Nelson Polsby defines power in terms of changes in the comparative probability of the outcome of specified events, and advocates its study through an examination of the decision-making process.[53] This is not easy to do in the case of the People's Republic, as for the most part open policy debate is discouraged. Nonetheless, much of the evidence for this study comes from an examination of the public utterances of men on the CC. The problem of determining support or opposition to policies through these speeches and articles can be done in several ways. The most obvious is simply to determine which leaders voiced support for which policies at which times. Not every leader voiced support for every policy; the study assumes in general that those who did endorse a policy were the supporters of that policy at the time they made their endorsement.

This method is not necessarily always valid. Thus, John Wilson Lewis notes:

> Official statements do not necessarily represent the views of individual leaders making the statements. Indeed, according to the doctrine of democratic centralism, the fact that an individual makes a policy statement might indicate that he opposed the particular policy prior to the decision and is symbolizing continued leadership unity by his announcement of the new policy.[54]

The problem here is not always insurmountable. The revelations of the Cultural Revolution allow a kind of independent check on the implications drawn from the public statements. Thus, judging from his public statements, Ch'en Yun would appear to have been the major supporter of "conservative" policies in the upper echelons of the elite; and, sure enough, during the Cultural Revolution he was attacked as an archconservative. In 1958, judging from his public statements, one would be led to think that Wu Chih-p'u was a major proponent of agrarian radicalism; and some remarks by Mao Tse-tung at the Lushan conference, revealed during the Cultural Revolution, indicate this judgement would be valid. It is, in fact, sometimes possible to get a fairly good idea of which statements by given leaders are made for the sake of showing unity. Thus, prior to Lushn, T'ao Chu had published several articles critical of some aspects of the Great Leap. Following Lushan he published two articles telling how much he favored the Leap. During the Cultural Revolution he was criticized for his articles critical of the Leap. It is thus a fairly safe inference that his writings immediately following Lushan were "unity" statements.

Another approach is to consider a given statement in the light of the whole body of statements by the particular leader. Thus, from 1958 until mid-1960, Tseng Hsi-sheng was a major spokesman for the most radical line. In mid-1960 he published a rather "rightist" article, and has not been heard from since. Around the same time the policy as a whole shifted to a rightist direction. It is a fairly safe inference that Tseng's last article was a kind of self-criticism.

Other types of information can be gleaned from a rather detailed study of the contents of public statements. Chinese Communist writings tend to be montonous in style, content, and wording. This makes minor variations rather significant. Some rules of thumb here are rather well known. There is, for example, the matter of the conjunction 但是 — *tan-shih*, one of the Chinese words for "but," "however." This usually serves to qualify strongly what has gone before. For example: "The great mass movement has produced excellent results, 但是 quantitative success must not lead us to neglect the problem of quality." In most contexts, this statement would be construed as criticism of the mass movement. (The example is made up; in real life the statement would usually be somewhat more verbose.) Another clue is the frequent use of citations of the mistaken opinions of "some comrades" (or, more harshly, "some people"). This helps us determine the grounds upon which the policy debate was carried out. If the identity of the mistaken comrades can be ascertained (and opinions similar to those criticized can occasionally be found in prior public utterances), we can determine part of the line-up on each side of the debate.

Clearly, the use of public statements as evidence has its pitfalls, and relies in large part upon subjective judgment. The temptation to over-interpret is sometimes hard to resist. But the alternative to using such statements is probably not to undertake such a study at all. Ultimately, the methodology must be judged by its fruits.

The "power" approach used here represents a middle road between two other popular approaches. These might be termed the "forces" and "personality" approaches. Under the "forces" approach, politics are often seen as derivative phenomena, the products of "deeper forces." Reality is often understood in terms of the behavior of abstractions, such as reified social categories.[55] This approach is often useful in predicting general evolutionary trends, provided nothing unexpected happens. It is not so useful when unexpected events intervene. We might consider a passage from a popular interpretation of recent Chinese politics: "Mao is increasingly out of touch with Chinese reality. And he is currently trying to turn the clocks of his country backward... (H)istory would seem to be on the side of those who argue for an adaption to changing realities."[56] To apply, somewhat unfairly, a pedantic literalness to this kind of reasoning, China is seen running according to some kind of "clock," that is, one assumes, along a pre-determined course. The entity which determines this course is called "history," and has at least enough consciousness to be partisan, to take sides. This sort of viewpoint ignores the consideration that the Maoists constitute an important segment of Chinese "reality," and that "history" will be in part the consequences of the actions of Mao and other powerful men (although, of course, the consequences may not be those the powerful men expect or desire).

The "personality" approach, advocated by Robert Tucker and developed by Schapiro and Lewis, stresses the personality of the leader as the decisive factor in much of totalitarian politics.[57] This approach does avoid abstract reification, but at the cost of other problems. The most obvious is that of acquiring reliable data. A trained psychoanalyst apparently finds it difficult enough to evaluate his patient over an extended face-to-face confrontation. Most of us have to work with at best second-hand information (for example, what Mao chooses to tell Edgar Snow). And some of us lack the training of an Erickson or a Lifton.

The personality approach also begs a rather important question. Lewis writes in another essay:

> Mao seems to have understood that a direct connection existed between his own dominant status and the revolutionary character of Chinese society. What this paper will attempt to show is that Mao did not similarly grasp the importance of the political commissar.[58]

This is a very perceptive statement. But even if we wish to discuss the Cultural Revolution as the product of a cognitive deficiency of Mao Tse-tung, the personality approach does not tell us why this lack of understanding made any difference—it does not tell us why Mao was able to act on his ignorance.

Another problem of the personality approach is its lack of analytic parsimony.[59] If the approach is taken seriously, we will be forced to conduct long-distance, usually amateur, psychoanalysis of every new tyrant who mounts the stage.

The stress on "power" in this study may appear to be a "single-factor" explanation, and, hence, unsatisfactory. There is some truth to such criticism, but I think the criticism is essentially irrelevant. It is not pretended here that the study of power relations is some kind of philosopher's stone, a *fa-pao* that yields answers to all questions. Power struggle is held to be a factor, not necessarily the factor, in Chinese politics, and to trace the influences of this factor would seem to be a legitimate enterprise. Somewhat more strongly, I would suggest that the power approach is justified if it 1) explains the known facts in a simpler and more complete manner than do other approaches; 2) increases our understanding of the significance of the known facts, facilitates comparison with other systems, and at least indicates what factors should be taken into account in making theoretical predictions concerning the system under study; and 3) leads to no substantive error. It should also be stressed that this emphasis on power is part of a theoretical strategy; it is assumed in this study that Chinese politicians seek to expand or maintain their "power." (To say they want to "maximize" their power would probably yield greater deductive rigor, but would be more difficult to handle empirically—thus, a kind of "satisficing," not a "maximizing" model is used.) The value of this assumption is not so much determined by its literal truth, but by its utility in explaining behavior. Classical economics assumes that men are rational and greedy. Many men are greedy but not rational, rational but not greedy, or neither rational nor greedy. Nevertheless, the classical theories elegantly explain their object, fluctuations in the price of goods.

The power approach does involve a kind of reductionism. The real world is a complex place, where everything depends upon everything else. Any useful explanation of things must involve reductionism of some sort. The theoretical plan of this study is in part a reaction against other sorts of reductionism—trends in political science which reduce politics to economic (a rather old-fashioned view), cultural, social, psychological, cybernetic, or other factors. In this study politics are treated as autonomous, with political effects explained in terms of political causes.

The emphasis on the quest for power, then, should not be misunderstood. Lifton writes of the theories of reporters who conceived of the Cultural Revolution as a power struggle:

> . . .the great shortcoming of the individual-power struggle theories was their failure to place such struggles and rivalries within a larger psychological framework. They thus contained a number of implicit but unexplained and highly dubious assumptions about "power" and "rivalry" as ultimate human motivations.[60]

The approach used here contains no assumptions at all about "ultimate human motivations." Men may be motivated by many things, but to achieve their desires by political means they require power. The power approach disregards the ulterior motivations. Similarly, the power approach studies social forces as they manifest themselves in the behavior of individual persons (whose behavior in fact makes up these forces); and it provides a general framework, which the personality approach does not, for interpreting this behavior.

Even in the most degenerate policy the power struggle rarely assumes the form of Hobbesian war of all against all. There will be limits upon the methods used in the struggle which will prevent the operation of the power hypothesis in its "pure" form. The power explanation will operate only within certain "parameters". Borrowing a term from Schlesinger, we might call these limitations the structure of "political opportunities."[61] Within a given policy there will be only a finite number of alternate strategies for advancement.

An article by John C. Harsanyi provides some insight into the general nature of the limitations on the rationality-power struggle approach. He develops a series of "postulates":

> 1)...people tend to be impartial and public spirited when it *costs* little to be impartial and public spirited.
>
> 2)...third parties whose interests are not directly affected will find it natural to assess the situation in terms of more general impartial criteria.
>
> 3)...at any given moment people's free rational choice is restricted by personal commitments undertaken at earlier periods. But undertaking such a commitment itself tends to be a matter of rational choice.[62]

Postulates 1) and 2) seem to say the same thing: a person would be a "third party" by virtue of his receiving neither loss nor gain from the decision made, whatever that decision might be. If a particular leader will neither gain nor lose power regardless of the outcome of a particular dispute, he may act from other than power considerations—his notion of the common good, ideology, friendship, caprice. The third postulate contains the notion of foregone opportunities, paths we may no longer take. The scope of this postulate can be broadened. It can include commitments made by other people which tend to limit our own freedom of action. Some aspects of the "political culture" might be thought of as restraints upon our behavior resulting from choices taken by our ancestors. In a Communist state, certain aspects of the ideology, at least in outline, limit the opportunities of the participants.[63]

The protagonists of this study are almost all "Han" Chinese, and all without exception are communists. It would be expected, then, that all of them would share a certain core of beliefs, attitudes, and orientations, although one would be hard put to specify exactly what this core consists of. Since this study focuses upon conflict among them, this more general area of agreement among them is irrelevant, as it would not be, say, when studying how they react to the "masses," to the Russians, or to the Americans. (Their common culture and ideology, of course, do have a bearing on the ways they fight among themselves.) Neither common Chinese culture nor common communist ideology dictate common stands or opinions. Communists often like to say that Marxism-Leninism is not a dogma, but a guide to action. The reverse is more nearly true. The ideology inculcates certain habits of thought, and certain biases toward various social categories, but provides at best a negative guide to action (thus, communists rarely strive for policies calculated to enhance the long term social, political, and economic status of, say, a traditional nobility). The ideology of the CPC was broad enough at one point to include the quasi-social democrat Ch'en Yun and the enthusiasts for the Leap.

Part of this area of agreement, and the part most relevant to this study, would include what might be called the "rules of the game." These rules, derived from culture, ideology, or history, can often be traced back, as Harsanyi's third postulate would indicate, to previous decisions, and, in terms of this study, to previous power struggles. Thus, since Mao's rise to power, high ranking members of the CPC do not have each other executed,[64] although they sometimes do seem to drive each other to suicide (and are much less squeamish when it comes to lower ranking members and to the "masses").

Institutionalization should be seen in the light of Harsanyi's third postulate. Strong institutions limit and channel the methods which can be used in the power struggles. Those who benefit from strong institutions will work to build them, since through these institutions they themselves gain power. Once institutionalization is achieved, the power motive provides a built-in mechanism for maintaining it.[65]

Ingenuity could probably encompass the whole structure of opportunities within the power struggle hypotheses, tracing the evolution of the political culture and rules of the game to decisions in decades or ages past. This would be neither practical, nor, probably, desirable. Once the power struggle begins to explain everything in general, it explains very little in particular. Here, then, we may sketch some aspects of the structure of opportunities not directly or adequately explained by the power struggle hypothesis. The power struggle hypothesis here does not convincingly explain, for example, why some of the CC members joined the Party in its very early years (as it would explain why their grandchildren might join today). Naturally these people wanted political power—otherwise they would not have founded or joined a political party—but to join the CPC at that time was probably not the most "rational" way to attain it. Here we must look to other factors— the history and ideals of these men, the objective conditions of China, the compelling nature of Marxist teachings, the intrigues of the Comintern, or whatever.

Another, more important matter inadequately explained by the power struggle hypothesis alone is the emotional import of such concepts as revolution and Thermidor. The initial dynamics of revolutionary movements seems to entail a push to the extremes—"no enemies to the left." Left (or "left") deviation, as the Chinese Communists often lament, appears to many to be a much less serious thing than right deviation. Attacks from the right do not usually cause Marxists in office much concern, since ideology provides many means of refuting or avoiding the import of the rightist critiques, at least to their own satisfaction. The more powerful attacks of leftist "establishments" would appear to come from the left—Michels, Trotsky, Djilas, some of the "Maoist" pronouncements. The harried administrator is not in an easy position—convenience and habit lead him to adopt "Thermidorian" policies and methods. But, if he is at all sensitive, he must have an ambivalent attitude toward the leftist critique—he is being attacked in terms of values he shares and understands, or at least in terms of values he feels he should share and understand. Once the more vocal "anti-thermidorians" have been purged, there is no special problem; but in the face of the attacks the bureaucrat must be unsure of the legitimacy of what he is doing. The power hypothesis clearly shows why some elements will attempt to use the symbols of Thermidor and revolution; it can even explain why these symbols retain their potency in the pre-Thermidor period. But it does not explain their initial potency.

In an undeveloped polity, many opportunities have not yet been foregone. In such a polity those who will be frozen out of power by the development of an institution will work to weaken that institution, and, if such is perceived to be in their interest, will work to weaken institutionalization in general.

5. POLITICAL OPPORTUNITIES IN CHINA: THE TWO ROADS

A useful simplification in discussing Chinese Communist politics is the Maoist concept of the "two roads." These are the "proletarian revolutionary road," emphasizing the charismatic leadership of Mao Tse-tung, and the "capitalist road," emphasizing the institutional authority of the Party. (These terms as used in this study follow the Maoist usages; the "capitalist road" has no necessary connection with "capitalism" as that term is usually used in the west.) Nyomarkay argues that dissensus can exist in a political movement based upon a charismatic leader without endangering the overall unity of the movement, but in an "ideological movement" "disagreements about the ideology are automatically disloyal acts, and, therefore, illegitimate."[66] The CPC during much of its history had many marks of an ideological movement, but also retained charismatic elements. The presence of these charismatic elements probably permitted the long-term coexistence of the two roads until the middle sixties.

study groups into the Communist Party of China. Given its allegiance to the Comintern, the Party was, of course, organized along Leninist lines; but "the Party during its early years was neither ideologically nor organizationally a united entity. The northern branch, under Li's leadership, remained largely independent of, although not in direct opposition to, the Central Committee at Shanghai."[73] Li Ta-chao, perhaps a major intellectual influence on Mao Tse-tung, "saw Lenin more as a revolutionary than as an organizer," and "always remained reluctant to accept the stress on discipline and organizational restraint that was the essence of Leninism."[74]

The major obstacle to the institutionalization of the CPC was its alliance with the Kuomintang. The union of the two "revolutionary" parties became a pet idea of Stalin's. Behind the doctrinal claims and controversies, it seems one of Stalin's prime motives was the construction of a stable and unified China strong enough to resist Britain and Japan and not hostile to the Soviet Union. The KMT was felt to be the alternative to the warlords, and the Communists should thus ally themselves with that Party, in the hope of eventually dominating it. The Comintern sent agents to help Sun Yat-sen organize his party along Leninist lines, something which did nothing to help make the KMT vulnerable to Communist infiltration, especially at its top level.[75] The alliance did allow Communist organizers to build grass roots support, but the "Chinese Communist Party, expanding rapidly at its base, had lost all its cohesion."[76] The CPC had become in effect a federation of local organizations, each bound up with the local KMT organization. When Chiang Kai-shek moved against the Party in 1927 there was little it could do to save itself.

In 1928 the Party's Sixth Congress was convened in Moscow and adopted the Party's first constitution.[77] This constitution, at least in its early years, was the epitome of formalism. Real power was held not by the CC, but by local leaders who, adapting themselves to the realities of Chinese politics, had begun to build base areas. The most important of these local leaders, as it later turned out, was Mao Tse-tung. The CC and the Politburo, of course, were not content to rest with their formalistic position, and did strive to gain control of the local forces. Their most severe conflict was with Mao, perhaps because of Mao's relative proximity to the Party headquarters at Shanghai.

The conflict between Mao and the CC has been studied in ideological terms, and in terms of conflicts over policy. Benjamin Schwartz has developed the thesis that Mao, basing his strength upon a peasant army

A. *Formalistic Leninism and the Rise of Mao*

Mao Tse-tung's own attitude toward the party is now seen as having been ambiguous. One of the most astute Western students of Mao has said:

> Mao...sees the Communist Party as merely one instrument among others, and not as something unique and sacred which is itself the embodiment of legitimacy...[Mao]...has constantly sought to prevent all organizations, including the Party itself, from becoming ends in themselves.[67]

Mao's attitude toward the Party can be traced to his own position within the Party, which in turn is a result of the nature of the early CPC and the methods whereby Mao attained his power within this party.[68]

Mao's generalization about power and the gun did apply almost literally to the conditions of China in the early twentieth century. China had lapsed into a fairly traditional pattern of dynastic decay: the growth of decentralized military power within the hands of regional satraps.[69] Warlordism provided the structure of political opportunities at that time. According to a recent student of the subject, the warlord required an army and control over such territory as would allow him to maintain his army.[70] These, in effect, were the rules of the game, and they applied to all players, including the KMT and the CPC. Part of the eventual superiority of the parties over the warlords was their ability to attain authority. But within both parties there was a tension—in Maoist terms, a "contradiction"—between the "gun" required to attain power and authority necessary to consolidate it. Also within each party was a "contradiction" between institutionalized and personalized authority, each of the charismatic leaders tending to emphasize the "gun."

According to the definition by Fred Riggs, the failure of organization charts of the bureaucracies of newly independent countries to reflect the realities of control and command is called "formalism."[71] This charge is most often made against those polities which pretend to western institutions, such as parliamentary democracy and a rational (Weberian) bureaucracy. But formalism is not limited to would-be democratic governments or organizations. An examination of the early CPC would indicate that while it was Leninist in "form," in reality the Party was not quite that.

Serious interest in Marxist thought in China began around the time of the May Fourth Movement. It was promoted at first by two Peking University professors, Ch'en Tu-hsiu and Li Ta-chao.[72] In 1921 these two men, with the help of Comintern agents, united several Marxist and ignoring the cities, represents a Leninist heresy. With Lenin the Party had become, if not a proletarian party, at least the "vanguard of the proletariat." Mao, however, in effect conceived of the Party as pure vanguard, with only a nominal connection with any proletarians. The leaders of the CC were orthodox Leninists subservient to the Comintern (Stalin), and for ideological reasons wanted to agitate among proletarians; they thus desired control of cities.[78] This conflict can also be seen in organizational and political terms: an argument over who should be able to set policy, regardless of the wisdom of the policy.[79] The Center's policy was certainly unwise, indicating that formalism is not always "dysfunctional." Had the CC been able to discipline Mao, the results would have been bad for the Party.

In 1927 Mao had retreated to the Chingkangshan region on the Hunan-Kiangsi border, finding refuge with bandit gangs in that area. He was later joined by forces under General Chu Te.[80] Mao began developing his experience in people's war by conducting an underground struggle against the regular CPC Hunan Committee, which thought it should control the Chingkangshan forces.[81] The Central leader, Li Li-san, wanted to use the troops in the countryside to attack cities.[82] Mao and his military supporters, like the non-ideological warlords, knew the folly of squandering men and safe territory for unsure results, and, after an unsuccessful attack on Ch'angsha, ignored similar orders.[83] Chou En-lai, then a supporter of Li Li-san, criticized Mao in the name of the Central Committee: "During a certain period...the local Political Security Bureau [a Maoist outfit] placed itself above the Party and its regular political authority."[84]

In January, 1931 control over the Center was won by a group of young Communists recently returned from Moscow, known, somewhat derisively, as the "Twenty-Eight Bolsheviks." After instigating some ham-handed acts of terrorism the CC was forced out of Shanghai in late 1931, and moved to Mao's base. For the first time there was real danger to Mao on his own turf. Mao, as Chairman of the soviet area government, was safe from direct attack, and the "Bolsheviks" first concentrated on attacking the relatively minor guerilla leaders, Lo Chung-lung and Ho Meng-hsiung.[85] These men were accused of "liberalism" (自由主義), here meaning that they are unwilling to submit themselves to the orders of the Center.[86] The struggle became vicious. Liu Shao-ch'i was expelled from the Party for supporting Mao.[87] In July 1934, Mao was placed under house arrest.[88]

Fortunately for Mao the Bolshevik military policies proved

ill-advised, and in late 1934 the Communists were forced to vacate their Kiangsi base area. In December and early January an "enlarged" meeting of the Politburo was convened at Tsunyi, in Kweichow. In traditional Communist historiography this meeting marks the final victory of Mao over his opponents.[89] Recent studies indicate things were not that simple. In one account, Liu Shao-ch'i presented a detailed critique of the Center's "leftist" line since 1928, a critique which later became the official interpretation of that period, but which was rejected at the time as too extreme. The meeting decided to criticize only the Bolshevik military line. Mao was promoted to the Politburo, and replaced Chou En-lai as head of the Military Affairs Commission.[90]

It would seem, however, that at least informally Mao was recognized by those on the Long March as the main leader. This was accepted also by certain independent Communists, such as Ho Lung,[91] but not by others, especially Chang Kuo-t'ao. Maoists later complained, "Chang Kuo-t'ao had transformed the Fourth Front Army into his own political instrument,"[92] a charge similar to those which had once been brought against Mao. Starvation forced Chang to evacuate his base in Szechuan, and he moved some 20,000 troops toward Sinkiang. Only seven or eight hundred survived. This took care of Chang's source of autonomous power, and by now tried to make peace with the new Yenan Center. Mao, to make sure, (says Chang Kuo-t'ao) murdered two of Chang's officers and arrested about 100 others. Chang thereupon left the Party.[93]

B. Liu Shao-ch'i and the Leninization of the CPC

Having achieved *de facto* leadership of the Party, Mao began to see certain advantages to organizational discipline. In 1937 he wrote a short essay (a self-criticism?) denouncing "liberalism."[94] In 1938 a CC plenum demoted most of those in the Bolshevik faction, and issued resolutions on "strengthening Party work."[95] But the organizational ideology behind the resolutions still seems to have been the work of members of the Bolshevik faction, particularly Wang Chia-hsiang.[96] Perhaps to remedy this situation Mao turned to Liu Shao-ch'i, who knew as much as the Bolsheviks about Marxism-Leninism, and by that token more than Mao. Liu has been called the leading ideologist of the CPC.[97] This is true in a limited sense: Liu is not a master theorist, but a competent ideological technician. His ideology is a rather stolid Marxism-Leninism-Stalinism, enlivened at times by an apt quotation from the Confucian canon. Liu joined the Socialist Youth Corps in 1920, and the CPC soon after its founding. During the 1920's Liu was a labor agitator in Shanghai, and at some point studied in the Soviet Union. He was apparently present at Tsunyi, but may not have completed the Long March. In 1935 he led a student strike in Peiping. He became head of the North China Bureau, directing Communist underground activities in that area. In 1939 he was called to Yenan.[98]

The Party at that time was a rather heterogenous composition. In *The Self-Cultivation of a Communist Party Member* (the literal translation of what used to be known as *How to Be a Good Communist*) Liu writes: "Those who have entered our Party not only come from different social classes, but also carry with them all types of different purposes and motives." Members include peasants who want land, patriots opposed to Japan, social misfits, vague idealists, opportunists desiring lower taxes, people who joined because their relatives did.[99] Liu's job was to mold these elements into a cohesive, disciplined group of professional revolutionaries. This would be accomplished by "self-cultivation" —a Confucian term, 修養, which, for Liu, meant in practice that "A member's interests are unconditionally subordinate to those of the Party."[100] Liu carries Leninism to its logical end: a person becomes "proletarian" by virtue of his obedience to the Party.

Liu stresses obedience to the institution, not to the leader. *Self Cultivation,* in its earlier versions, contains no reference to Mao or his thought. People like Li Li-san and Chang Kuo-t'ao, Liu says, "after taking at random certain of the Marxist-Leninist termonology, proclaimed themselves the Marx or Lenin of China...and demanded that the Party respect them and treat them as 'leaders.' " But the legitimacy of a leader derives only from the will of the organized Party.[101] Even giants like Marx, Engels, Lenin, and Stalin can do only part of the work. "The task of communism is a long term and collective task, to be done by myriads of people."[102]

By the early 1940's Mao was strong enough to extirpate the "Bolsheviks," and launched the "rectification" movement. Mao himself tended to emphasize ideological rectification; but it has been said, "The proper understanding of the Leninist concept of the Party lies at the very heart of the whole...movement."[103] This Leninism was supplied by Liu. His major work during this period is *Inner Party Struggle,* the bulk of which is a critique of improper methods of struggle.[104] Liu denounces "excessive and mechanical" struggles, especially "struggle meetings." These only humiliate and do not educate. They disrupt unity. They may be fine for use against those outside the Party, but

21

they are not for use among comrades.[105] Another bad type of struggle is "unprincipled struggle," struggles over personalities or ameneties. These are "struggles without content."[106]

What, then, is "principle"? Well, principles are "general laws governing the development of things."[107] Liu elaborates: mobilization of the masses is a principle; but the number of departments in a mass organization is a "practical" question, not a proper object of struggle. Controversy here should be resolved by vote, compromise, or reference to higher authority. Guerrilla warfare is a principle, and a commander who concentrates on attacking cities violates principle. But the fact that he has attacked a city does not in itself mean that he has violated principle, since local conditions may have warranted the move.[108] "Principle," while in some sense "objective"—Marxism has unlocked the secrets of the "development of things"—is in effect whatever the ruling group says it is. Questions of principle are either right or wrong, and not subject to vote or compromise.

Liu here has produced a minor *tour de force*. His analysis strengthens the discipline and cohesion of the Party: the question of principle becomes a weapon to be used at will by the rulers. But freedom of discussion on matters deemed "practical" helps maintain flexibility, as does the casual attitude toward principle when violations of principle prove expedient. A cadre in a minority position on a "practical" question can maintain his position without being shot, humiliated, or hounded out of the Party, provided he is willing to obey the majority. Liu provides a routinized method for solving most disputes within the Party, and for confining disputes within narrow bounds.

C. *The Mao-Liu Synthesis: Leninsim and Charisma*

While Mao and Liu did represent two different trends within the Party, it does not follow that these trends were always antagonistic to each other. In fact, all reliable evidence indicates that Liu was one of Mao's closest supporters in the early days, and during the 1940's Liu seems to have been the initiator of the "cult of Mao." The factors behind this are unclear. Mao's alleged vanity and the advantages which could accrue to Liu by playing to this vanity may have had a role. The Communists may have wished to build up their own charismatic figure to compete with Chiang Kai-shek for the favor of the general population, and, within the Party, to compete with the prestige of Stalin, which the Bolsheviks may have felt they could draw upon. Many top Party leaders may have been too old or too important to begin "self-cultivation," and it may have been expedient to supplement appeals for party discipline with appeals to personal loyalty, something within the intellectual grasp of, say, Ho Lung.

Arguing against the Bolshevik faction in 1943, Liu asserts: "It may be said...our Party has witnessed more important changes and has accumulated more experience of the revolutionary struggle...than any other Communist Party in the world,"[109] including presumably the CPSU. Liu continues:

> And especially worthy of mention is the fact that in the long, strenuous, and complicated twenty-two years of revolutionary struggle it has finally been possible for our Party, the proletariat, and the revolutionary people of our country to find their own leader in Comrade Mao Tse-tung.[110]

Mao is a "great and resolute revolutionist," whose "guidance" "must permeate every link and every department of our work."[111]

The cult reached something of an apex in 1945, when Mao's Thought was enshrined in the new Party Constitution:

> The Communist Party of China takes the theories of Marxism-Leninism and the combined principles derived from the practice of the Chinese Revolution—the Thought of Mao Tse-tung —as the guiding principles of all its work.[112]

In Liu's explanation of the new constitution, Mao becomes practically the motive force behind the revolution: Mao is "the leader and organizer of our Party and the current Chinese revolution." He "has developed our national thought to a degree never before achieved, and has shown the suffering Chinese people the only clear road to liberation— the road of Mao Tse-tung." He "organized" the revolutionary movement prior to 1927, "created" the Soviet districts and the Red Army, "created and led" the Liberated Areas, the New Fourth Army, the Eighth Route Army.[113]

It has been said that the cult of Mao "focuses not on his personality but on the correctness of his thought."[114] This is a subtle comment—in most cases (as above) a distinction without a difference. But not always. Mao is not a pure charismatic leader, but a charismatic leader of an ideological party. It was not sufficient that Mao simply exist and lead; he must also Think. As will be seen, in some situations this tended to limit Mao's own options in a way those of other charismatic leaders have not been.

However taken Liu may have been with Mao and the Thought, he did not abandon Leninism. He adds to his discussion of Mao: "Comrade

Mao Tse-tung is the leader of our Party, but he is also an ordinary member at the service of our Party. He has in all respects the most scrupulous attitude of obedience toward all Party rules."[115] For Liu, Mao always existed for the Party, not the Party for Mao.

In this same speech Liu gives his most thorough analysis of democratic centralism. The democratic aspect of this principle is best manifested in the fostering of criticism and self criticism. Leaders must admit their mistakes and allow subordinates to participate in discussion.[116] Liu's forte, however, is centralism: "Inner Party democracy must be broadened, but the resolutions of the Party must be carried out."

> Some comrades put conditions on the implementing [of Party resolutions], such as their personal agreement with the resolution, its correctness, the ability, position, or seniority of the superior, his cultural level, or whether he belongs to their group. It must be said that none of these conditions should hold.[117]

The "image" of the Party given by Liu in 1945 is that of a highly disciplined machine loyal to the "thought" of a supreme leader, who leads the Party by virtue of his superior wisdom. The picture would seem to owe something to Mencius as well as to Lenin.

D. The Consolidation of The Position of The Party

The emphasis on the cult of Mao began to wane after the Seventh Party Congress, and by 1948 there was some talk of collective leadership.[118] After the victory Mao withdrew from public view. The withdrawal of a still powerful charismatic leader, according to Lipset, tends to make the peaceful transition from the charismatic to institutional rule more probable.[119] After Liberation the CPC began to set its own house in order, purging more than 59,000 of its more dubious elements between 1950 and 1951.[120]

The most serious threat to the unity of the Party (and perhaps the country) came from a faction headed by the Politburo member Kao Kang, who controlled the Northeast Region. In February, 1954, a CC plenum charied by Liu Shao-ch'i passed a resolution urging "unity of leadership, solidarity of the Party." It criticized cadres who "exaggerated the function of the individual, stressed individual prestige, thought themselves Number One under Heaven." They turned "their districts or departments into independent kingdoms."[121] Mao was not cited as the authority for this denunciation of individualism. Rather, the formula was "the Party Center headed by Mao Tse-tung" (or, sometimes, "Comrade Mao Tse-tung") (以毛澤東為首的黨中央). This formula has Mao grammatically subordinate to the "Party Center" (the main noun, the subject or object of the sentence, is "Party Center"; "headed by Mao Tse-tung" modifies Party Center, specifying which Party Center the writer has in mind). The term "Party Center" is a vague one. It sometimes refers to the Central Committee as a whole, but more often probably does not. But in all cases it seems to refer to an organization rather than to a person. The chosen formula stresses the primacy of this organization.

The point of the 1954 denunciations became clear in 1955, when Teng Hsiao-p'ing announced a "Resolution on the Anti-Party Alliance of Kao Kang and Jao Shu-shih." (Jao was head of the CC Organization Department, and also held posts in the Shanghai area.) According to Teng:

> In Manchuria and elsewhere [Kao Kang] created and spread many rumors depreciating the Party Center and puffing himself up. He stirred up dissention among comrades, stirred up dissatisfaction toward the comrades at the Party Center, and instigated a movement to split the Party. He set up his own faction within the movement. Kao Kang...treated Manchuria as his own personal independent kingdom.[122]

Kao had been denounced at the 1954 plenum, but the villain "not only refused to bow his head and confess his crimes, but, on the contrary, killed himself as a final gesture of defiance to the Party."[123]

It is sometimes asserted that Kao Kang threatened the position of Mao, and also that Kao's defeat was a defeat for the major Russian influences in China.[124] There is little evidence for either of these propositions. Those who purged Kao do not seem to have been any less "pro-Soviet" than was Kao, nor is there much evidence that Kao himself was particularly pro-Soviet. There is no hint that Kao aspired to displace Mao. His defeat was a victory for "collective leadership."[125] He headed an "anti-Party group," not an "anti-Mao group." Kao's program, as presented by his enemies, indicates rather that Kao threatened the civilian leaders at the Party Center:

> [Kao] said our Party was divided into two parts: one is the so-called "base areas and military Party," the other is the "white areas Party." He said the Party was created by the army. He proclaimed himself the representative of the "base areas and military Party" and thought he should have important power. Therefore, the Party and central government should be reorganized according to his plan, and he himself should become the CC Secretary General or vice-chairman and also premier.[126]

Mao himself was always strongly associated with the "base areas and military Party." The obvious representative of the "white areas Party" is Liu Shao-ch'i. Kao's alleged lust for the premiership may have been stressed by Liu and Teng to win the support of the current occupant of that position, Chou En-lai. In 1955 Mao returned to active political life. This should probably not be seen as a sign of his personal triumph over Kao Kang. It is more likely to reflect a growing fear of the now supreme Party apparatus.

Kao's plan, with its stress on the military and his desire to represent other military leaders (who at that time tended to be in control of the areas they had conquered from the Nationalists[127]) contained the seeds for a revival of warlordism. Kao's defeat signaled a return to civilian government in China. With the concurrent talk of collective leadership the defeat also signaled a trend toward government by institutions, not individuals.

E. *The "Maoist" Alternative: The Ideology of the Cultural Revolution*

The fall of Kao Kang paved the way for the stress on the institutional authority of the Party at the Eighth Party Congress in 1956. This institutionalism had run its course by the time of the Cultural Revolution. It may be helpful here to sketch some "Maoist" notions of the relations between the Party and the leader as they were articulated during the Cultural Revolution. Some writers like to stress Mao's hostility to any elite.[128] He has certainly shown himself hostile to the idea of the Party apparatus as an elite. During the Cultural Revolution Mao's supporters tried to outline an alternative pattern of authority.

A somewhat simplistic view was presented by the soldier, Yang Ch'eng-wu. Yang presents Mao as a pure charismatic leader:

> The attitude toward Chairman Mao and the Thought of Mao Tse-tung [hereafter, TMTT], in our great era, has become the most efficacious touchstone and watershed between revolution and counter-revolution, between true revolution and false revolution, between Marxism-Leninism and counter-revolutionary revisionism.

Yang wants to "establish very particularly" (大樹特樹[地]) "the absolute authority of the Great Supreme Commander Mao Tse-tung," and also the "absolute authority" of his Thought. This is done mainly by learning from Lin Piao.[129]

An article by Lin Chieh (a fairly prominent radical in 1967, of obscure origin and fate) carries the attack against the institutional processes of the Party. Lin says Liu Shao-ch'i says "We emphasize organizational obedience; whoever puts conditions on his obedience is wrong;... .The rule of democratic centralism is that whatever is decided by the majority, the upper-level, or the Center must be obeyed, even if that decision is a wrong one." This, says Lin Chieh, is "out and out slavism," a demand for "blind obedience."[130] It ignores the democratic aspect of democratic centralism. "Centralism must be based upon correct opinions... To sacrifice truth (真理), give up principle, surrender to a mistaken majority—this is thoroughgoing opportunism."[131]

Thus far one might think Lin Chieh is going to argue for some kind of liberty. But Lin is more subtle than that. He is as much opposed to what he calls "anarchy" as he is to "slavism." "Anarchy stresses 'doubting everything, overthrowing everything,' making anarchy an absolute, similarly without regard to truth." No jesting Pilate need pose the obvious question, for Lin has already answered: "Chairman Mao is the greatest Marxist-Leninist of this age. Every word of every sentence he says is truth."[132]

Both Yang Ch'eng-wu and Lin Chieh were extremists, and both were purged. But no direct attack was made against the ideas they expressed,[133] and these ideas, in a somewhat muted form, remained the basis of legitimacy following the Ninth Congress. As the Red Guards were to learn, this new line is as authoritarian as the old one, but also more arbitrary. "Blind obedience" is no longer owed to the Party, but to something called "truth" which is what the Leader and especially his spokesmen say it is.

6. SUMMARY HYPOTHESES

Politicians act in such a way as to expand or maintain their power. Institutionalization occurs when those whose power position will be benefitted by institutionalization are able to overcome their rivals. Similarly, those who will be harmed by institutionalization will resist the process. The institution most feared by those outside of it is the Party bureaucracy, or apparatus. This is either because of the inherent potential power of this instituion, or because the Soviet experience leads others to think it has great potential power. The institutionalization of the Party will be resisted by those in the state bureaucracy and the military. The charismatic leader will look askance upon any kind of institutionalization, but, because the Party apparatus is seen as the greatest threat, will tend to unite with the state and the army against the Party.

Men act to fulfill their own ambitions, not those of the institution to which they belong, although normally the two may not always be in any necessary opposition. But in times of severe conflict, members of the Party apparatus who are not in control of that institution will tend to unite with the enemies of that institution against their bosses. If these men thereby come to occupy the top posts in the apparatus, they also will try to institutionalize their positions (and thus strengthen the institution), and will become vulnerable to the same pressures as their former bosses.[134]

Thermidorian tendencies are concomitant with institutionalization, and thus accusations of thermidorian inclinations will be a potent weapon against the apparatus. Men who have worked and sacrificed all their lives for the revolution will be sensitive to implications that they have betrayed the revolution, and such accusations will tend to make them lose confidence in the legitimacy of their own rule.[135] However, the anti-thermidorian ideology of the enemies of the apparatus tends to undermine the legitimacy of all types of institutional legitimacy, making the restoration of stable authority difficult.

II

THE CENTRAL COMMITTEE AS A POLITICAL INSTITUTION

The Eighth Congress of the Communist Party of China, held in September, 1956, in Peking, elected the members and alternate members of the Eighth Central Committee. The Second Session of this Congress, held in May, 1958, elected additional members (that is, promoted two alternate members) and additional alternate members. A total of 195 persons at one time or another belonged to the Eighth Central Committee. The statistical analyses in this study use the 180 persons still alive in the fall of 1965, on the eve of the Cultural Revolution.

This is not an "elite study."[1] The focus of this study is not so much the characteristics of the CC membership, but a study of the politics of the CC with a view to evaluating it as a political institution. While it is probably true that the membership composition of an institution has some bearing upon the performance of that institution, one may not make a theoretical jump from knowledge of the characteristics of the members to statements about the characteristics of the institution.[2] In the Chinese case, to put the matter most cautiously, there would seem to be no *a priori* grounds for assuming that the personal characteristics of the members would hinder institutionalization. To generalize from other studies of the composition of this Central Committee: at the time of their election the membership in general was neither excessively old nor excessively young; the higher ranking members tended to be well educated, especially relative to the general population of China; the lower ranking members had less formal education, but these people could look back upon an entire career in the Party in the pursuit of their chosen profession as revolutionary; the membership in general tended to come from the old Communist heartland, especially from Hunan; but the newer members show a somewhat greater diversity of geographical background. This is a subjective impression, but it seems that the members of the CC tended to be men and women of proven ability, with several decades of experience in war, subversion, and Party in-fighting. They seem to be people of fairly high caliber—higher, one gets the

29

impression, than that of their colleagues in the Soviet Union since the Great Purge.

This chapter examines the "framework" of the political struggle at the peak of the CPC, concentrating upon an evaluation of the CC as an instrument of potential Party control. This involves a study of 1) the recruitment pattern into the CC, with attention to the role of Party work in bringing about advancement; 2) the structure of the CC, to determine whether the structure should tend to guarantee the supremacy of the higher organs over the lower organs; 3) the role of the CC *per se* in the decision-making process; and 4) the "job structure" of the Central Committee, to determine whether the Party workers were able to exercise control over their co-workers in the state and army.

1. CAREER PATTERNS OF CENTRAL COMMITTEE MEMBERS

Table I outlines the way in which the members spent their time up until the year 1955.[3] In discussing the CPC, the term "Party" can be used in at least two different ways. It may refer to the totality of the members, or it may refer to an organizational structure and those holding posts within that structure. It is this latter meaning which is more important in attempting to evaluate the degree of institutionalization of the Party. For example, Mao says that the "Party" must control the gun, not the gun the Party. Of course, the major military leaders were all Party members. Mao meant in effect that the activities of the Party members engaged in military activities must be controlled by the Party members on the leading bodies of the Party, and, implicitly, by the members of the staffs of these bodies. The Party in this sense will be referred to as the "apparatus," and the professional Party workers as "apparatchiks."

It is reasonable to assume that a man will come to acquire a viewpoint biased in favor of the organization he has worked for for most of his life. Thus, we might hypothesize that the strength of the Party as an institution is a function of the number of those within the ruling council of the Party who have had their career in the apparatus. Table I indicates that only a minority of the members of the Eighth CC held such posts at any given time, although this proportion tended to increase over time.

Table II gives the jobs of members just prior to their election to the Eighth CC, breaking the membership down according to rank and time of election. Among the full members the plurality are drawn from the government center. The 1956 alternates are drawn primarily from the army, but with the local Party men close behind. Only among the lowest ranking groups, the 1958 alternate members, do apparatchiks form a

Table I

Career Patterns of CC Members[a]

	1925	1930	1935	1940	1945	1950	1955
Non-Party	52%	14%	2%	(1)[e,f]	(1)[e,f]	—	—
Underground[b]	17%	26%	18%	11%	11%	—	—
Party Center	2%	5%	14%	21%	17%	12%	16%
Party Local	(1)[e]	6%	7%	14%	17%	17%	18%
Govt. Center	—	—	—	—	—	16%	34%
Govt. Local[c]	—	2%	2%	5%	6%	30%	14%
Soldier	—	15%	21%	25%	30%	17%	13%
Commissar[d]	2%	8%	13%	12%	13%	5%	2%

N for each column = 180

a. The table tells what each member was doing in the particular year heading the column. If a member held two or more posts, he is listed under what seemed to be his more important post. The following categories are omitted: those whose position is not known; those in school in the USSR or working for the Comintern; those in jail; those who had joined the Party but do not seem to have been working in any Party capacity; those otherwise inactive.

b. This means: 1) those engaged in secret activities in KMT areas; 2) low level Party workers in white areas; 3) guerrillas not integrated into one of the main Communist armies.

c. This includes work in the governments of the soviet and liberated areas.

d. In this table, and in this study generally, "commissar" means one engaged in political work in the army. The 1925 "commissars" were working in the KMT army.

e. Numbers in parentheses are absolute numbers.

f. This gentleman is Saifudin, until 1949 a member of the CPSU.

Table II

Job Prior to Election

	Old Membs.	Promoted Alts.	New Membs.*	1956 Alts.	1958 Alts.	Total
Party Center	21%	25%	19%	9%	14%	17%
Party Local	5%	13%	16%	25%	45%	21%
Govt. Center	53%	37%	36%	21%	23%	32%
Govt. Local	5%	17%	10%	21%	—	13%
Soldier	13%	13%	9%	31%	19%	17%
N	38	24	31	65	22	180

*Those promoted to full membership from alternates in 1958 are simply counted as full members.

majority; but if the Center and local apparatchik categories are added together, Party workers would also form a plurality among the promoted alternates and the new 1956 alternates.

Table III summarizes the results of a study of 85 transfers of position among CC members between 1957 and 1965. These data show a slight tendency for CC members to move into the apparatus. But most movement is within the same category. This supports Klein's finding of increasing specialization within the CPC,[4] and is probably evidence of growing institutionalization.

Table III

Transfers, 1957-1965

Party into Party	29%	Movement within same category—	70%
Party into Govt.	5%	Net gain for Party:	12%
Party into Army	—	Net gain for Govt.:	−11%
Govt. into Party	16%	Net gain for Army:	− 1%
Govt. into Govt.	35%		
Govt. into Army	4%		
Army into Party	1%		
Army into Govt.	4%		
Army into Army	6%		
N=85			

Generalizing from data similar to those presented in Tables II and III, Klein has hypothesized that the Party will be "the most frequently used path to power of future leaders."[5] This is a logical projection, but like all projections it holds only if nothing unexpected happens. "As is well known," the unexpected did happen. The tables, in addition to indicating the probable growing influence of the apparatus, also provide some clues about the weakness of the apparatus. Thus, while the newer, and thus lower ranking, members of the Central Committee tended to come in large part from the apparatus, the higher ranking members did not. There might have been a certain lack of commitment to the idea of the institutionalization of the Party at the very apex of the Party.

2. THE STRUCTURE OF THE PARTY CENTER

A. The Leading Organs

In the 1945 Constitution the structure of the Party was nearly as personalized as its ideology. The highest policy making body was the

Politburo, and the "routine functions" of the Party were carried out by the Secretariat. The leadership of both of these bodies (which strongly overlapped) was vested in the Chairman of the Central Committee,[6] that is, in Mao Tse-tung. The structure of the Party described in the 1956 Constitution is more complex. The control over the supposedly "routine" functions performed by the Secretariat is no longer under the direct command of the Chairman of the Politburo, thus breaking up the concentration of power in the hands of the chairman. Similarly, the new set-up may have inhibited the prominent tendency of the CPSU for the men discharging the "routine" functions to come to dominate policy. The 1956 structure would seem to help to assure the coincidence between formal authority and real power; perhaps it also reinforced the tendency noted above — a lack of commitment to an institutionalized Party by the men at the top.

Table IV

Structure of the Central Committee, 1965

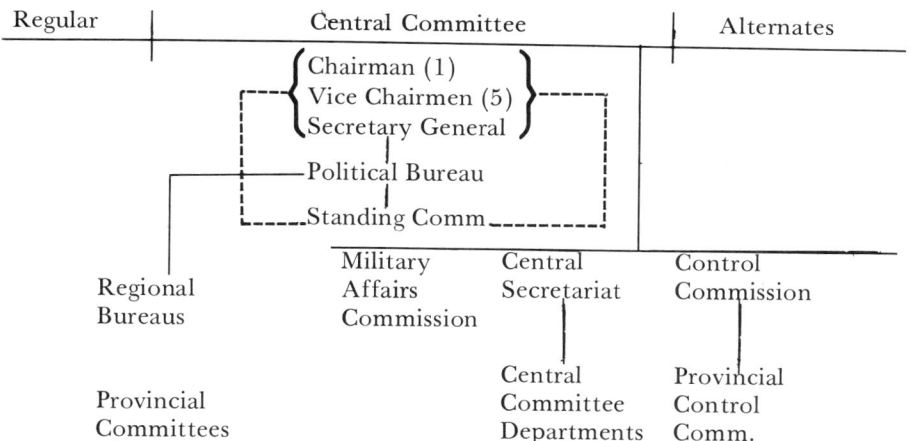

SOURCES: Adapted from Intelligence Section, Min. Defense (ROC), 匪偽人事資料彙編組織表 (Organization Charts on Bandit-Puppet Personnel), Vol. 9 (Taiwan, 1968) Section 1, p. 1. Hereafter cited as "Organization Charts." Pao Ching-an, 匪情手冊 (Handbook of Bandit Affairs.) (Taipei, 1968) 2, 2, 16, 494 pp., pp. 37-38. Organization Charts has the MAC appointed by the Politburo, while Pao has it elected by the whole CC. This latter interpretation seems more likely.

1. THE POLITBURO

The Politburo elected by the Central Committee, was the policy-making organ of the Party when the CC was not in session.[7] The Politburo itself was not in constant session, and day-to-day control over policy was formally vested in the Politburo Standing Committee. This body, composed of the Chairman, vice-chairmen, and secretary of the Central Committee, exercised the policy functions which the old Secretariat, somewhat improperly, used to exercise.[8] Even the Politburo Standing Committee (PBSC) cannot be regarded as a ruling organ: thus, Chu Te seems to have been so much deadwood since prior to Liberation; and Ch'en Yun fell from grace around the time of the Great Leap (both men, however, were reelected to the CC in 1969).

Table V lists the members of the Politburo, along with the other posts they hold. The PBSC, in addition to the Great Man, had the two top apparatchiks, Liu Shao-ch'i and Teng Hsiao-p'ing; the top bureaucrat, Chou En-lai; and the top soldier, Lin Piao. On the Politburo, Tung Pi-wu and Liu Po-ch'eng were extremely old, as was Chu Te, and their places were probably more honorary than anything else. P'eng Chen, Lu Ting-i, Ch'en Po-ta, and K'ang Sheng should all be considered primarily members of the Central Apparatus. Ch'en Yi, Po I-po, Li Fu-ch'un, Li Hsien-nien, and T'an Chen-lin, despite the presence of the latter three on the Secretariat, were primarily central bureaucrats. In opposition to Soviet practice, the Chinese Politburo contained a number of soldiers: Lin Piao, Chu Te, Liu Po-ch'eng, Ho Lung, P'eng Te-huai, and (stretching the point) Ch'en Yi and Ulanfu. But, with the somewhat exceptional case of Ulanfu, only one member held an active purely military post at any one time: P'eng Te-huai prior to 1959 and Lin Piao after that.

The Politburo was mainly a club of Central leaders. P'eng Chen, although he exploited his position in Peking for all it was worth, was most active as a member of the Secretariat. The only other local leader elected in 1956 was Ulanfu. His election was probably a tribute to his unique position in China: he monopolized the top Party, state, and military positions in Inner Mongolia; no other leader held such a personal stronghold over a province.[9] In 1958 two other local leaders, K'o Ch'ing-shih (1st Secretary, Shanghai; died May, 1965) and Li Ching-ch'üan were elected.

2. THE CENTRAL SECRETARIAT

The Central Secretariat, elected by the Central Committee, undertook the "routine work" of day to day party administration "under the

Table V

Members of the Politburo, 1965

Politburo Standing Committee

Mao Tse-tung	Chairman, CC; Chairman, MAC.
Liu Shao-ch'i	V. Chairman, CC; Chairman, People's Republic of China.
Chou En-lai	V. Chairman, CC; Premier, State Council.
Chu Te	V. Chairman, CC.
Ch'en Yun	V. Chairman, CC; V. Premier, State Council; Chairman, CC Economic and Finance Committee.
Lin Piao	V. Chairman, CC; V. Chairman, MAC; V. Premier, State Council; Minister of National Defense.
Teng Hsiao-p'ing	Secretary General, CC; V. Premier, State Council.

Other Full Members

Tung Pi-wu	1st Secretary, Control Commission.
P'eng Chen	Secretariat; 1st Secretary, Peking; Mayor, Peking.
Ch'en Yi	V. Premier, State Council; Minister of Foreign Affairs.
Li Fu-ch'un	Secretariat; V. Chairman, CC Economic and Finance Committee; Vice Premier, State Council; Chairman, State Planning Commission.
P'eng Te-huai	formerly V. Chairman, MAC; Minister of National Defense; purged 1959.
Liu Po-ch'eng	V. Chairman, MAC.
Ho Lung	V. Premier, State Council; V. Chairman, MAC; Chairman, State Council Physical Culture and Sports Committee.
Li Hsien-nien	Secretariat; V. Chairman, CC Economic and Finance Committee; Vice Premier, State Council; Minister of Finance; V. Chairman, State Planning Commission.
Li Ching-ch'üan	1st Secretary, Southwest Regional Bureau; 1st Commissar, Chengtu.
T'an Chen-lin	Secretariat; V. Premier, State Council; Director, State Council Agricultural and Forestry Department; V. Chairman, State Planning Commission.

Alternate Members

Ulanfu	2nd Secretary, North China Regional Bureau; 1st Secretary, Inner Mongolia; V. Premier, State Council; Secretary, CC Minorities Work Commission; Chairman, State Council Nationality Affairs Commission; Governor, Inner Mongolia; Commander, Inner Mongolia.
Chang Wen-t'ien	formerly V. Minister of Foreign Affairs; purged 1959.
Lu Ting-i	Secretariat; Director, CC Propaganda Department; Chairman, CC Cultural Work Committee; V. Premier, State Council; Minister of Culture.
Ch'en Po-ta	Deputy Director, CC Propaganda Department; Editor, *Red Flag*; 1st Secretary, Party Newspaper Work Committee; member, CC Rural Work Committee.
K'ang Sheng	Secretariat.
Po I-po	V. Pres., State Council; Dir., State Council Industry. Communications Staff Office, Chmn, State Ex. Comm.; V. Chmn., State Planning Comm.

supervision of the Politburo."[10] This body, then, was the apex of the central Party apparatus. Seven of the thirteen members and alternates in 1965 were also members of the Politburo. The members elected in 1956 at the time of their election all worked in the civilian or military Central apparatus, with the exception of P'eng Chen (a local apparatchik) and T'an Chen-lin (a state worker). In 1958 the bureaucrats Li Fu-ch'un and Li Hsien-nien were elected. In 1962 the Party soldiers Huang K'o-cheng and T'an Cheng, followers of P'eng Te-huai, were removed, and Lu Ting-i, K'ang Sheng, and Lo Jui-ch'ing were elected. In the early 1960's Li Hsueh-feng and Liu Lan-t'ao became regional first secretaries. It is not clear whether they continued to function as members of the Central Secretariat.

The individual secretaries seem to have had areas of specialization. Table VI lists these probable areas. Some of these listings are open to question. Thus, Li Hsueh-feng, formerly head of the CC Industry and Communications Department, and Liu Lan-t'ao, formerly alternate secretary to the Control Commission, at one time probably did perform the functions ascribed to them, but probably did not after they had been moved to their regional posts. K'ang Sheng's identification with "special work" 特務工作, that is, secret police work and espionage, is generally accepted, but seems based upon no publicly available evidence. Prior to his election K'ang seems to have acted primarily as an ideologue in the foreign affairs field.[11] This is speculation, but in addition to any espionage work, K'ang may have taken over Wang Chia-hsiang's area of foreign affairs work. Wang had sided with P'eng Te-huai in 1959, and, while he was not publicly removed from the Secretariat, was inactive from that time on.

The secretary with his area of specialization may have provided the focal point for the various "systems" through which China was governed during the period under discussion, supposedly providing Party control.[12] A generalized, and somewhat simplified and idealized diagram of a system is presented in Table VII. This chart omits the "political offices" because of some uncertainty as to their exact function. This particular pattern of control does not seem to have held within the army. In other cases the various links in the system would seem somewhat redundant. Thus, Li Hsien-nien, the secretary in charge of Finance and Trade, was also a member of the Politburo, a Vice Premier of the State Council, Vice Chairman of the CC Economic and Finance Department, and Minister of Finance. It is a safe bet that he was also head of the Party cell in the finance ministry. Table VII diagrams a pattern of Party control. In the case of the Finance and Trade System, the term "Li Hsien-nien control" might be more meaningful than "Party control."

Table VI
The Secretaries and Their Specializations

Teng Hsiao-p'ing	General Supervision
P'eng Chen	Supervision of Party and Govt. Work
Wang Chia-hsiang	Foreign Affairs
T'an Chen-lin	Agriculture
Li Hsueh-feng	Industry and Communication
Li Fu-ch'un	Economic Planning
Li Hsien-nien	Finance and Trade
Lu Ting-i	Theoretical Work
K'ang Sheng	Special Work
Lo Jui-ch'ing	Military Work
Liu Lan-t'ao (A)	Control Work
Yang Shang-k'un (A)	Party Administration
Hu Ch'iao-mu (A)	Literature, Education

SOURCE: Seminar for Research in Bandit-Puppet Materials, 共匪黨政軍組織機構演變, *(Changes in the Bandit Party, State and Army Organizational Structure)* Vol. 1 (Taiwan, 1965) 2, 78 pp., plus charts; pp. 1-2 in second part.

Table VII
A Functional System

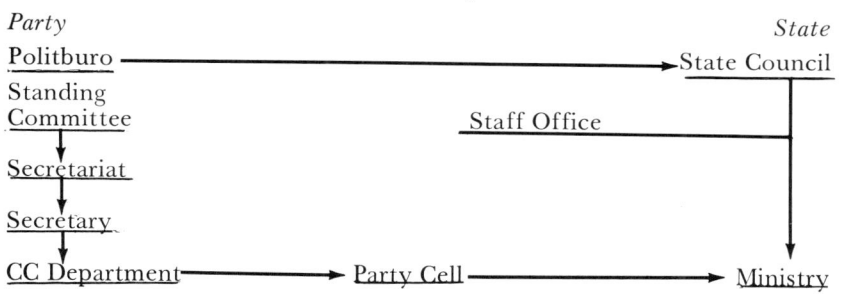

Arrows indicate who gives orders to whom.
Adapted from: Institute for Research on Mainland China Problems, 匪黨控制方式與工作方法 *(Bandit Party Control and Work Methods)* (Taiwan, 1966) 172 pp., p. 76.

3. THE CONTROL COMMISSION

In 1949 the Party established Disciplinary Supervision (檢查) Committees. After the pruge of Kao Kang it was announced that these had played a "positive function," but apparently not positive enough. "Not a few cadres in Party organizations, because they are busy with economic and other technical work, have become careless about political thought work. Thus, bad elements within the Party have taken advantage of the situation to become active." The Supervision Committees were replaced by Control (監察) Commissions. The Central Control Commission was elected by the National Conference of the CPC (a less formal body than the Party Congress) and approved by the CC. Subsequently personnel changes were made by the CC alone. The Control Commission was supposed to handle violations of the Party Constitution and Party and state laws and orders, in close coordination with the state supervisory organs. Its purpose was "to strengthen Party discipline, strengthen the struggle against all kinds of lawlessness within the Party, especially to prevent a re-occurrence of the kind of danger presented to the Party in the Kao Kang-Jao Shu-shih incident."[13]

The targets of the Control Commission include the "arrogant," those who demand special privileges, those who turn their areas or offices into independent kingdoms, those who "wheel and deal" (拉拉扯扯), those who "form factions to disrupt Party unity,"[14] in short, anyone who might challenge or disregard Central authority.

The establishment of the Control Commission marks a step in the institutionalization of the Party Center. The Commission provides a routinized channel for implementing discipline, with some attention to due process; the Commission could go after bad men only when they had violated specific laws or orders. The appointment of Tung Pi-wu, the Party's foremost advocate of "socialist legality" as Secretary of the Commission symbolizes this commitment to routinized, rather than arbitrary, control.[15] Tung, however, even then was a very old man, and the actual leadership of the Commission, before his transfer to the Northwest Regional Bureau, was probably held by Liu Lan-t'ao.

Despite connotations of socialist legality at the time of its founding, the Control Commission in general did not function as an autonomous judicial branch within the Party. Liu Lan-t'ao said that "The inspectors must also be controlled";[16] and the work of the Control Commission is "carried out under the direction of the Center and the Party Committees at all levels."[17] In practice, the targets of the Control Commission were determined by the current preoccupations of the policy leadership.

The Commission, although the hierarchical equal to the Secretariat, was a much less influential body. Only one member, Tung Pi-wu, had Politburo status. The bulk of its membership was not even on the Central Committee. The Control Commission membership included several members of the state judicial organs. Hsiao Hua, the head of the army's General Political Department (GPD), was also a member. Hsiao, prior to his promotion, may have been the army's chief thought policeman. By 1965 the Control Commission also included some members of the provincial secretariats, a new development since 1958.[18] The Commission was set up, in part, to prevent the growth of local "independent kingdoms," and originally its members all worked at the Center. The local members may have been watchdogs of the Center in their localities; or they may have been the clients of local bosses, in which case their membership in the Commission would serve to defeat one of the major purposes of the Commission.

B. The Central Party Apparatus

Table VIII lists the subordinate departments and committees functioning under the Central Secretariat in 1965. This list is taken from a Nationalist source (the Communists themselves publish no such charts) and is longer than the lists found in other sources; by the same token, this list may be less reliable. In this section the various "political offices" will not be discussed, as they seem to constitute a special case. The remaining departments and committees may be discussed under the following headings: 1) Party administration, propaganda, and internal security; 2) Foreign affairs; 3) Economic affairs; 4) Control of non-Party groups and organizations. As will be apparent, the functions of certain departments and committees tend to overlap more than one category.

1. PARTY ADMINISTRATION, PROPAGANDA, AND INTERNAL SECURITY

The General Office seems to have served as a kind of staff office to the Central Secretariat.[19] It was charged with the care of Party archives[20] and served as a clearing house for letters addressed to the CC.[21] The Organization Department was responsible for routine "cadres work" — recruitment, assignment, training, "struggle," inspection, and "policy."[22] Through liaison with government departments the organization department also kept tabs on state workers, reaching everywhere except into the military.[23] Potentially, the Organization Department would seem to have been a very influential organ. Stalin used the counterpart in the Soviet Union, the Orgburo, to ease his own way into the dictatorship.

However, the Orgburo was a body co-equal with the Secretariat, which Stalin also headed, while the Organization Department was subordinate to the Secretariat. Its head, An Tzu-wen, was a fairly low ranking CC member, with no position on either the Politburo or Secretariat.

Table VIII
Central Departments and Committees, and Their Members Who Were on the CC, 1965

General Office —
  Yang Shang-k'un, Director;
  Li Chieh-po, Vice Director.
Organization Department —
  An Tzu-wen, Director;
  Shuai Meng-ch'i, Chang Ch'i-lung, Vice Directors.
Social, or Inspection, Department —
  personnel unknown;
  Director possibly K'ang Sheng, Hsieh Fu-chih, or Lin Feng.
Propaganda Department —
  Lu Ting-i, Director;
  Ch'en Po-ta, Chou Yang, Hu Ch'iao-mu, Chang Chi-ch'un, Hsu T'e-li, Vice Directors.
United Front Work Department —
  Hsu Ping, Director;
  Liao Ch'eng-chih, Chang Ching-wu, Vice Directors.
Political Committee
  personnel unknown.
Political Work Department —
  Lin Feng, Director
International Liaison Department —
  Wu Hsiu-ch'üan, Director.
Foreign Affairs Political Department —
  Ch'en Yi, Director. (?)
Economics and Finance Committee —
  Ch'en Yun, 1st Secretary;
  Li Fu-ch'un, Li Hsien-nien, Secretaries.
Rural Work Department —
  Teng Tzu-hui, Director;
  Liao Lu-yen, Ch'en Po-ta, Ch'en Cheng-jen, Vice Directors.
Forestry Political Department —
  no CC membership.
Finance and Trade Political Department—
  Yao I-lin, Director;
  Yeh Chi-chuang, Vice Director.
Industry and Communications Political Department —
  T'ao Lu-chia, Director.
Basic Construction Political Department —
  no CC membership.
Education Political Department —
  no CC membership.
Defense Industry Political Department —
  Chao Erh-lu, Director.
Cultural Work Committee —
  Lu Ting-i, 1st Secretary.
Party Newspaper Committee —
  Ch'en Po-ta, 1st Secretary.
Women's Work Committee —
  Ts'ai Ch'ang, 1st Secretary,
  Teng Ying-ch'ao, 2nd Secretary;
  Chang Yun, Secretary.
Youth Work Committee —
  Hu Yao-pang, 1st Secretary.
Employees' Work Committee —
  Liu Ning-i, 1st Secretary.
Overseas Work Committee —
  Liao Ch'eng-chih, 1st Secretary.
Minorities Work Committee —
  1st Secretary vacant;
  Wu Lan-fu (Ulanfu), Secretary.
Bureau for the Translation of the Works of Marx, Engels, and Lenin —
  no CC membership.
Higher Party School —
  Lin Feng, President.
Political Studies Office —
  no CC membership.
Committee on Organizations Under the Direct Control of the Center —
  Yang Shang-k'un, 1st Secretary.
Red Flag Editorial Department —
  Ch'en Po-ta, Editor in Chief.
General Political Department —
  Hsiao Hua, Director.

SOURCE:
Organization Charts, Sect. 1, p. 2.

The Propaganda Department and its various off-shoots were broad in scope. The department included sections dealing with science, art and literature, newspapers, news agencies, education, health, and political propaganda.[24] Propaganda was thought of as the handmaiden of organization, and the two departments were supposed to maintain close liaison.[25] The Propaganda Department handled the theoretical education of low ranking cadres, and supervised the system of Party schools. High level cadres were taught in the Higher Party School.[26] In addition to working within the apparatus, the department spread the Party line among the "masses," and supervised the output of artists and writers.[27]

It will be noted from Table VIII that a good many departments and committees seem to deal with different aspects of propaganda. This proliferation may have been a result of the antagonism between the director of the Propaganda Department, Lu Ting-i, and his ranking vice director, Ch'en Po-ta. In 1958 *Red Flag* magazine was founded as the theoretical organ of the CC, with Ch'en as its editor. At some point the editorial board seems to have become a CC department. Ch'en was apparently also head of a "Party Newspaper Committee." The older newspaper section of the Propaganda Department seems to have been staffed by men loyal to Lu. Lu himself at some point acquired for himself the Cultural Work Committee, perhaps in 1965 when he also became Minister of Culture.

The Party's secret police and other "special work" activities at one time were the province of the "Social Department" (社會部). The work of the Social Department consisted of espionage, "inspection and research" (defined largely in terms of routine police work) and "intelligence" (情報) — collating and systematizing information received from espionage and inspection and research.[28] In its early days the Social Department was a very free wheeling organization. Liu Shao-ch'i once told special work trainees, "Another special characteristic [of your work] is that you have no one to supervise you."[29] The unsatisfactory nature of this kind of arrangement soon became apparent, and by 1946 (apparently after K'ang Sheng had been removed as Social Department head) its cadres were warned that they enjoyed no special privileges, and that they were not to make a fetish of secrecy. The agents had apparently been keeping secrets from their superiors,[30] something other employers of spies have sometimes been troubled with. The controls over the secret police in China have been more successful than those in Soviet Russia, perhaps because the Chinese learned from the Russian experience.[31] Indicative of this control is the fate of K'ang Sheng. He was removed as head of the Social Department probably in 1945, and, in 1949, rustificated to Shantung. In 1956 he was demoted from full to alternate member of the Politburo, making a full come-back only in the Cultural Revolution.³² In 1956 the Social Department seems to have undergone reorganization, with supervision of local police work being taken over by a Political Work Department. The name of the Social Department, either at that time or later, was changed to the "Inspection Department."

2. FOREIGN AFFAIRS WORK

The International Liaison Department was responsible for relations with other Communist parties. The Overseas Work Committee handled matters pertaining to the overseas Chinese. Its first secretary, Liao Ch'eng-chih, also handled overseas Chinese work for the State Council. The Employees' Work Committee, in addition to supervising the trade unions, also maintained liaison with foreign Communist-dominated union organizations. Its head, Liu Ning-i, was also deputy director of the State Council Foreign Affairs Staff Office.

3. ECONOMIC WORK

Originally the CC departments and committees were to provide policy guidance and supervision for government ministries, acting at each level as a link between the state organization or firm and the Party committee. In 1958 Ma Ming-fang, then director of the CC Finance and Trade Department, explained his department's functions. The description would also apply to the other departments dealing with economic affairs:

> The Party committee's finance and trade department can help the Party committee do the following work: study and discuss the work of [state] finance and trade departments; decide long and short term plans for finance and trade; unify the implementation of all work; organize auxilliary work; carry out inspection of the implementation. The Finance and Trade Department, under the leadership of the Party committee, should give more attention to political thought work and economic work. If political work is separated from economic work, it lacks content and strength. If political and economic work are coordinated, economic work can perform a limitless function. This point has been proven by experience.³³

The scope of the economic departments was greatly enlarged during the

Great Leap, apparently at the expense of the state agencies. Ma's department had acquired direct operational responsibilities by 1960—he claimed that year that the department is "also in control of quite a number of...enterprises."[34] Perhaps in recognition of, or reaction to, the increased scope of the Party, the Economics and Finance Committee seems to have been set up around 1962. This organ, headed by the three best economic thinkers on the Central Committee—Ch'en Yun, Li Fu-ch'un, Li Hsien-nien—seems to have been the Party analogue for such agencies as the State Planning Commission. It is unclear what role the economic departments continued to play after the establishment of the "political offices" in 1964.

4. CONTROL OF NON-PARTY CATEGORIES

The Communists found it expedient to keep liaison with various "mass," or non-Party groupings in society. This liaison was handled at the Center by specific CC departments and committees. The major committee here was the United Front Work Committee, headed by Li Wei-han until he was purged in 1964, and then by his deputy, Hsu Ping. Its purpose was to "unite with" the "non-laboring people to supplement the great strength of the worker-peasant alliance."[35] "Non-laboring," in Chinese Communist jargon, means those who do not work with their hands; and "people" (人民) is a flexible term, meaning mainly what the currently dominant group wants it to mean, but including at its broadest those not opposed to Communist rule. The United Front Work Department dealt mainly with the "national bourgeoisie" and "their" intellectuals; the "democratic parties"; the elite (上層人士) of the minority groups; and the religious groups.[36]

Other departments and committees dealt with specific categoric groupings of the population. The structure of control was rather simple: the "masses" were herded into the appropriate mass organizations, which were headed by the leading functionaries of the relevant CC committee (Table IX).

In addition to their control functions, these committees were also charged with cadre recruitment and cultivation among the categories in their charge, and at times even acted as a kind of lobby for these cadres.[37] This recruitment-cultivation-lobbying function was performed by the Minorities' Work Committee for cadres from the non-Han nationalities.[38]

Table IX

The CC Mass Control Apparatus (1965)

Women's Work Committee
    1st Sect.—Ts'ai Ch'ang—Chmn., All China Federation of Women
    2nd Sect.—Teng Ying-ch'ao—V. Chmn., All China Federation of Women
    Sect.—Chang Yun—V. Chmn., All China Federation of Women

Employees' Work Committee
    1st Sect.—Liu Ning-i—Chmn., All China Federation of Trade Unions

Youth Work Committee
    1st Sect.—Hu Yao-pang—1st Sect., Communist Youth League

C. The Military Party

Table I shows that a good many members of the Eighth Central Committee at one time or another served in the army. The proportion was especially large during the war years from 1930 to 1949. The special position of the military in the CPC was reflected in the Party structure. The Eighth CC had two organs specializing in military affairs: the Military Affairs Committee (MAC) and the General Political Department (GPD). The MAC was the top policy-making body in the field of national security, but not much is known of its composition below the top level.[39] Its known membership is listed in Table X:

Table X

The CC MAC, 1965

Chairman:
    Mao Tse-tung—Chmn., CC; PBSC.

Vice Chairman
    Lin Piao—V. Chmn., CC; PBSC; V. Premier, State Council; Minister of National Defense.
    Ho Lung—PB; V. Premier, State Council; Chmn., State Council Physical Culture and Sports Commission.
    Nieh Jung-chen—V. Premier, State Council; Chmn., State Council Science and Technology Commission.
    Hsu Hsiang-ch'ien—a marshal, prior to abolition of ranks.
    Yeh Chien-ying—a marshal, prior to abolition of ranks.
    Lo Jui-ch'ing—Secretariat; V. Premier, State Council; V. Minister Defense; Chief of Staff, PLA.
    Yang Ch'eng-wu—Deputy Chief of Staff, PLA.

Secretary General:
    Vacant

Deputy Secretary General:
    Hsiao Hua—Control Commission; Director, GPD.

During the Cultural Revolution it was revealed that Mao himself was the chairman of the MAC, and he has probably held this post ever since the Tsunyi Conference. But the effective head of the committee has been the minister of defense, whether P'eng Te-huai[40] or Lin Piao. The other vice-chairmen in 1965 included only two active duty soldiers; the remainder were all marshals (until the military ranks were abolished). Hsu Hsiang-ch'ien and Yeh Chien-ying were probably retired. Nieh Jung-chen was in charge of military research. Ho Lung's post as head of the Physical Culture and Sports Commission would not seem to be much of a power base, but the old bandit seems to have had a more generalized kind of influence. As Lin Piao once said, "Ho Lung had a long reach, reaching not only into the army but also everywhere into the localities... Many military services had his men."[41]

The General Political Department was responsible for political work in the army. It was the apex of the system of political commissars.[42] Although technically subordinate to the Secretariat, the GPD in reality seems to have been more responsive to the wishes of the *de facto* head of the MAC.[43] The two bodies were linked institutionally: Hsiao Hua, the Director of the GPD, was also in effective charge of the MAC secretariat. T'an Cheng, the previous director of the GPD, was purged with P'eng Te-huai, indicating this link between the GPD and the MAC was not merely a fluke produced by the machinations of Lin Piao.

The structure of the GPD somewhat parallels that of the civilian apparatus. Under the GPD were an organization department, a propaganda and culture department, a youth work department, and a mass work department.[44] The military Party thus ran its own household, including purges,[45] independently from the civilian Party below the Politburo level. For good measure, the secretary of the Central Secretariat in charge of military affairs was an active duty soldier during the bulk of the tenure of the Eighth CC. Were the army united (which it was not) the civilian apparatus would have no hold over it. As things were, the relations between the civilian and military Party were determined by the political by-play rather than by administrative routine.

D. *The Political Offices*

In the spring of 1964 "political offices" were set up in the economic ministries, with the announced function of furthering "political thought work" in these ministries.[46] Franz Schurmann has argued that the purpose of these committees was to bring greater central control over the activities of the ministries, supplanting to some degree the functions of the local party committees.[47] In view of the nature of the political situation at that time (a general all-round weakening of the institutional Party) this explanation is convincing. It may also be supplemented: one purpose of the establishment of the political departments would seem to be, somewhat paradoxically, to decrease Party control in general over the state bureaucracy.

At first glance the political departments would seem to be superfluous: the CC already had organs dealing with economic matters. But by 1964 the attack on the apparatus which culminated in the Cultural Revolution had already begun. The political offices were explicitly patterned upon the system prevailing in the army: they "apply the experiences of the PLA" to the "particular characteristics of each ministry."[48] This could easily mean that the political offices were to function like the GPD, taking over the role of the Party Center in the ministry, and cutting the ministry off from the apparatchiks.

The men most closely associated with the founding of the political departments were Chou En-lai, Po I-po,[49] and Li Hsien-nien.[50] All were primarily state bureaucrats, although Li also held posts in the apparatus. Chou and Li belonged to the group within the CC based mainly upon the central bureaucracy. Po I-po was associated with P'eng Chen's group, based mainly upon the central apparatus.

E. *The Regional Bureaus*

The Ninth Plenum of January, 1961, took steps to rationalize the local Party structure. The highly centralized Party structure built up prior to the Leap had apparently been eroded in the course of the enlargement of the scope of the Party. The plenum set up six regional bureaus "to represent the strengthened leadership of the Center over the several provincial, municipal, and autonomous region Party committees."[51]

The leadership of these regional bureaus was not announced (or perhaps even decided) at the time of the plenum; Table XI lists the regional first secretaries who were eventually appointed, along with their prior or concurrent positions. Two of the first secretaries came from the Party Center, and one from the central bureaucracy. The remaining three were powerful local bosses. In the latter cases it is not clear that the formation of regional bureaus did in fact bring about strengthened Central control. Thus, T'ao Chu and Li Ching-ch'üan seem to have used the regional bureau to build up a factional following. (Alternatively, their appointments as first secretary may have been a recognition by the Center of their already strong local following.) Whether the appointment of K'o

Ch'ing-shih followed the same pattern is unclear, since he died prior to the Cultural Revolution

Table XI

Regional First Secretaries

Bureau	First Secretary	Former or Concurrent Post
North China	Li Hsueh-feng	Chmn., CC Ec. and Comm. Dept.
Northeast China	Sung Jen-ch'iung	Min., 2nd Min. Mach. Building
Northwest China	Liu Lan-t'ao	Alt. Sect., Control Commission
Southwest China	Li Ching-ch'üan	1st Sect., Szechuan
Central South China	T'ao Chu	1st Sect., Kwangtung
East China	K'o Ch'ing-shih	1st Sect., Shanghai

The subordinate members on the regional bureau committees were for the most part provincial or military leaders within the area encompassed by the bureau, but Wu Chih-p'u and Tseng Hsi-sheng were removed from their provincial posts when they were made regional secretaries.

In 1965 the Party took further steps to rationalize its local structure, when it was decreed that the first secretaries of regional bureaus could not at the same time hold office as provincial or municipal first secretaries.[52] This had the effect of tidying up the chain of command, at least on paper. If the move were intended to weaken the factional control of T'ao Chu and Li Ching-ch'üan, it seems to have failed.

3. THE CC AS A POLICY-MAKING BODY

The Party Constitution treated the CC as a kind of parliament of the Party. Indications are, however, that the CC *per se* only rarely acted as a body for collective decision-making. One major fuction of a plenum seems to have been to ratify decisions made elsewhere. Franz Schurmann cautiously concludes, "One thing is certain: if a plenum has been announced, this means that a major policy decision has been made."[53] The true situation may have been somewhat more complex. Thus, it will be argued later that the third plenum perhaps endorsed two contradictory lines of economic policy. In a few cases decisions were made at the plenum. The decision to launch the Cultural Revolution was made by the 11th plenum. This, however, was an enlarged plenum, with non-CC members speaking and voting.

None of this need imply that major decisions were made by a small group at the top, say the Politburo.[54] There is evidence that this was not the case. Parris H. Chang has attempted to compile a list of all major Party meetings since 1949, both plenums and meetings of other types, and has noted a correlation between the times of many of these meetings and major policy changes. During the 1950's decisions appear to have been made at "informal and *ad hoc*" meetings but in the 1960's these were replaced by Central Work Conferences. Those attending the Central Work Conferences would usually include the Politburo members, members of the Secretariat, vice premiers, heads of the CC departments and some of their deputies, heads of the regional bureaus, high ranking army officers, and provincial first secretaries.[55] This would include the bulk of the CC, although some members would be excluded. The Conferences would also be attended by some not on the CC: not all provincial first secretaries were CC members (though the vast majority of them were), nor were all high ranking officers. Chang concludes from his data:

> The policy making process was relatively open—"open" in the sense that the process was not monopolized by a few top leaders who largely agreed on their objectives and made the major decisions alone. Rather, the process was accessible to a significant number of Party officials below the top level of the leadership hierarchy (the Politburo), many of them from the provinces; and these officers participated, in a real sense, in the deliberations and formulations of the regime's policies.[56]

This description is plausible, whether or not one wishes to characterize the process as "open." Chang's description tends to support some major assumptions of this study—that policy making in China was a political process characterized by give and take and by efforts to reach consensus or compromise, that the high ranking Party members were more than mere puppets of those still higher.

4. PARTY, STATE, ARMY: THE PROBLEM OF PARTY AUTONOMY AND CONTROL

Many observers of the Chinese Political system prior to the Cultural Revolution were impressed by the extent of what they took to be Party control. A Doak Barnett has said, "The Party constitutes the elite of the elite, and monopolizes ultimate policy and decision-making power."[57] Powell finds Party control of the army resulting from what he calls the "multiple hat policy":

> The Military Affairs Committee provides an excellent example of the Party's multiple hat policy, or the practice of dominating other major institutions of the State by placing Party leaders in controlling

positions. In addition to their high Party positions, the known members of the MAC occupy most of the key military and military-related posts in Communist China.[58]

Despite this high degree of "Party control," however, the "Party" proved to be very weak in the onslaughts against it in 1966. It may be that scholars like Barnett and Powell failed to make a necessary distinction between "Party control" and "control by Party members." Suppose, for example, that someone interested in the politics of the Catholic Church were told that organization is run by priests. He would then know something about the Church, but not enough. He would also want to know about the relative influence of priests working within the various institutions of the Church, such as the Papacy, the College of Cardinals, the religious orders, the local sees. In somewhat the same way, the studies such as those by Barnett and Powell have made it very clear that Communist China was run by Communists.

This in itself is significant, and tells us much about the polity—more, for example, than would a statement to the effect that Alabama is run by Democrats, or even that Taiwan is run by the KMT. Thus, for most purposes, any study of Chinese politics can safely ignore any role played by "non-Party personages" or members of the "democratic parties." The only meaningful exception to this, perhaps, is the role played by some of the "mass organizations" in the Cultural Revolution. But once we know this we must examine the nature of the relations among the Communists.

The distinction was made earlier between the Party as the sum of its members, and the Party as a structure of offices. "Institutionalized Party control" will here mean control over non-Party organizations by the Party bureaucracy, or apparatus. This concept of Party control is close to that held by the men of the Party Center. In 1959 Liu Lan-t'ao said:

> It is necessary for all revolutionary organizations, whether in the government, the military, or the popular organizations; the public security, courts, or state control organs and other political organs; in finance, in economics, in culture and education, in science and hygene, *etc.*, to work under the direction of the Party committees at the Center and the locality.[59]

But Liu's vision of this totalitarian ideal did not seem to include the fusion of Party and non-Party functions in the same person. Some people say, said Liu, this view really makes no distinction between Party and government (黨政不分). They are wrong. All organizations should

49

be completely subordinated to the Party, but

> Naturally this is absolutely not to say that the Party can take over the work (代替辦工) of the state organizations, the popular organizations, and other non-Party bodies, muddying the principled distinction between the Communist Party and non-Party organizations...Thus, if there is ever any "union of Party and society" or "union of Party and state" this will be wrong.[60]

The multiple hat policy, in fact, was seen as threatening the autonomy of the Party, working to the benefit of the non-Party organization. Teng Hsiao-p'ing held that a Party member who works in a non-Party organization tends to respond according to the requisites of that organization rather than to those of the Party:

> Some comrades working in state organizations falsely claim the special nature of their work does not require that they obey Party leadership. They try to turn their own sections into independent countries (獨立國家). This is a dangerous deviation which must be overcome.[61]

Even under conditions of almost pure control the guardians sometimes tended to act as the spokesmen for those they were supposed to control. It has been noted that CC members in mass control work acted as a lobby for cadres drawn from the category under their jurisdiction. At certain times, as in the relaxed atmosphere of the 1956 Party Congress, these people also acted as a kind of lobby for the "masses" they controlled. Thus, Li Wei-han urged respect for the "lawful rights" of the capitalists, and asked the comrades to hear the opinions of the "non-laboring masses."

> They represent one aspect of social opinion and demands, and also have a certain experience in politics and expertise in work, and are often able to give us cogent opinions and criticism. Sometimes the opinions and criticism are not cogent or correct, but this allows us to analyze and manage the problem, retaining a clear head.[62]

Teng Ying-ch'ao was sensitive to the problems of women under the new order, especially those arising from the demands that they "participate in labor." She urged that women be given equal pay for equal work, and that the value and dignity of housework (she called it "household labor,"— 家務勞動 —, perhaps to make it sound like something a real proletarian would enjoy) be recognized.[63] The head of the science section of the Propaganda Department delivered a speech called "Go a Step Forward in Strengthening the Party's Leadership of Science Work," the thrust of which was that the cadres on the whole were not qualified to lead scientific work. "In leading scientific work, the Party must depend entirely upon the scientists." The comrades should not meddle in the genetics dispute—it is a young science and the question is a specialized one. More money should be allocated to basic research. Organizational work among scientists should be strengthened, but it should not interfere with the work of specialists.[64]

This lobbying function was no danger to the rulers. The mass organizations were in no sense a power base, and their leaders in general were rather low ranking CC members. The lobbying function would bring outside opinion to the attention of th leaders, allowing them to handle it as they saw fit—by concession, repression, or any combination they might like, "retaining a clear head." But we have the testimony of Teng Hsiao-p'ing that Party members in state organizations also tended to see things from the point of view of their own area of responsibility. This might mean that a man as important as Chou En-lai could be relatively indifferent to the desires of the apparatchiks. The Party men in the army would also be subject to the same pressures, perhaps to a greater degree because of the rather isolated nature of military life, and the isolation of the military from the civilian apparatus. In the army there was a Party organization independent from the civilian Party, headed by a member of the Politburo Standing Committee. In this case, "Party control" must take on a rather special meaning.[65]

By examining the job structure of the CC in 1965 we may be able to draw some hypotheses about the CC as an instrument of "potential Party control" on the eve of the Cultural Revolution. Members may be divided into three groups the "apparatchiks," or members of the Party bureaucracy; the "bureaucrats," or those working in the state bureaucracy and a "mixed" category composed of those occupying posts in both hierarchies. The terms "bureaucrat," "bureaucracy," "apparatchik," "apparatus," refer here only to the distinction between those working in the Party or state machines, and not to any other characteristics they might have. The apparatus itself was a rather complex bureaucracy; it is called "apparatus" here to distinguish it from the organization technically charged with administering the state. Similarly, Chou En-lai was not a "bureaucrat" in the sense of a dull fellow sitting in an office carrying out routine functions. He was, rather, a generalist and a policy-maker. This, in fact, is true of almost all the CC members who served on the State Council. The name "bureaucrat" here implies only that they worked in (in Chou's case, headed) the state machine. For present purposes, soldiers are subsumed into the "bureaucrat-apparatchik" categories—those working only in the "state" chain of command, under the Ministry of Defense and the General Staff, are considered bureaucrats; "commissars" and those holding posts in Party organs (the MAC and the GPD) are considered apparatchiks. Those working in both belong to the "mixed" category.

Table XII presents the job structure of the CC divided along these lines, at the Central level. The members are classified according to their functional positions, that is, according to the nature of their actual jobs. Men in the most generalized leadership positions, such as the Chairman and Vice-Chairmen of the CC or the Republic, are not listed unless they also occupy some kind of functional role. Vice Premiers of the State Council who hold no other post in the government are not counted as bureaucrats (for example, Teng Hsiao-p'ing). But the post of Premier of the State Council is considered a bureaucratic post.

Counting local party men, "pure" apparatchiks made up 35.5% of the membership and alternate membership of the CC in 1965, a larger proportion than any other category. But in the Soviet Union, a country where institutionalized Party control seems to have been generally maintained since the death of Stalin, apparatchiks constitute between 50.4%-65.1% of the CC membership (apparently depending upon the definition of the term "apparatchik").[66] In striking contrast with the CC CPC, bureaucrats and soldiers constitute only 7.2% of the membership of the Soviet Central Committee.[67]

But numbers, of course, are not the only factor, or even the most important factor in determining relative influence. Other factors listed in Table XII include the highest ranking person in each category, along with his rank; the number and proportion of each category on the Politburo; and the average rank of the members in each category. These various measures of relative potential influence are combined into a kind of crude index in Table XIII. In this index, the category enjoying the highest rank according to each measurement is given two "points"; the next highest is given one point; while the lowest ranking gets nothing. Tie scores are averaged. The points for each category are then summed. The index can vary between zero and eight. (Number and proportion on the Politburo are counted as one item.) Thus, for the "general" category (that is, for the CC workers at the Central level taken as a whole) the apparatchiks are given two points for having the highest ranking member, and one point for each of the other measures. This gives them five points for that category.[68]

Reading across each row, we can rank each category according to its

Table XII

Job Structure of the Central Committee—Central Level 1965

	Apparatchik	Mixed	Bureaucrat
1. General			
Number	37	24	41
Highest Ranking member	Teng Hsiao-p'ing 003	Lin Piao 008	Chou En-lai 005
No. on PB	5	8	3
% on PB	14%	33%	8%
mean rank	68.5	66.9	104.8
2. Internal Control, Propaganda, Police			
Number	25	7	8
Highest Ranking member	Tung Pi-wu 006	Ch'en Po-ta 010	Yank Hsiu-feng 050
No. on PB	1	3	0
% on PB	4%	43%	0%
mean rank	86.7	39.7	118.0
3. Foreign Affairs, Intelligence			
Number	1	7	6
Highest Ranking member	Wu Hsiu-ch'üan 056	Liao Ch'eng-chih 021	Chen I 019
No. on PB	0	0	1
% on PB	0	0	17%
mean rank	56.0	81.3	96.0
4. Economic Work			
Number	3	12	14
Highest Ranking member	Ch'en Yun 007	Ch'en Po-ta 010	Yeh Chi-chuang 045
No. on PB	1	4	1
% on PB	33%	33%	8%
mean rank	82.3	77.9	100.0
5. Military Affairs			
Number	4	7	13
Highest Ranking member	Liu Po-ch'eng 018	Lin Piao 008	Hsiao Ching-kuang 030
No. on PB	1	2	0
% on PB	25%	29%	0
mean rank	62.0	51.8	102.8

SOURCE: See Appendix for list of offices of CC members in 1965.

Table XIII

Index of Potential Control

	Apparatchik	Mixed	Bureaucrat
General	5	6	1
Internal Control	5	7	0
Foreign Affairs	3	2	6
Economic Work	5	6.5	.5
Military	4	8	2

relative "control potential" in each issue area. According to the index, the "mixed" category (the wearers of multiple hats) rank highest in every area except foreign affairs, the only area where bureaucrats predominate. (This is probably deceiving; foreign policy was probably not set by the functionaries of the foreign ministry, but by the Politburo Standing Committee and high ranking ideologues such as Ch'en Po-ta and P'eng Chen.)

It would seem that the CPC did not in fact conform to the traditional Leninist pattern of Party control, but rather followed a pattern that has been noted in the new African polities:

> The role of the national party in the post-independence era was not the same as that of the nationalist movement in the pre-independence era. The revolutionary conquest of power required different emphases and different programs from those involved in the building of a nation. As the leaders of the movement moved into positions of governmental authority, they became enmeshed in an ongoing machinery which had its own requirements and constraints different from those of a political party.[69]

Under these conditions, "if an individual has a key position in both the Party and government he tends to operate in terms of the priorities, exigencies, and pressures of the government structure" — the same conclusion reached by Teng Hsiao-p'ing. As a result, "the one-party state in Africa has become in places the non-party state."[70]

After Liberation high ranking Party members (CC members and those soon to become CC members) tended to move into the Central Bureaucracy; the higher ranking members on the CC have tended to hold posts in both Party and state. By 1965, despite the better judgment of some members, there was almost a fusion of Party and state in China.[71] In William Riker's terms, the CPC had come to be a "coalition of the whole," in that all of the politically relevant groups were represented in the top councils of the Party. This kind of coalition is inherently unstable.[72] The Central Committee was not an organ for institutionalized Party control, the apex of a single hierarchy; rather, it was more a congress of the bosses of several segmentary hierarchical systems. In Huntington's terms, the Communist Party in China lacked autonomy.

At the start of the Cultural Revolution Mao Tse-tung complained of "independent kingdoms" in the Party Center.[73] He meant that the apparatchiks obeyed Liu Shao-ch'i, Teng Hsiao-p'ing, and P'eng Chen, rather than himself and his friends. In fact, the CC can in part be looked upon as a confederation of independent kingdoms. It was somewhat churlish for Mao to complain about this. Other elements may not have had much control over the apparatchiks, but neither did the apparatchiks have much control over the other elements, who were thus able to develop power bases independent of the Party apparatus. Trotsky or Malenkov would probably have appreciated such a set-up.

III

POLITICAL GROUPINGS ON THE CENTRAL COMMITTEE AND THE NATURE OF THE PURGE

Studies of Communist Chinese politics since the Cultural Revolution sometimes speak rather loosely of "Maoists" and "Liuists." When the actual events are analyzed, however, it becomes clear that this is something of a simplification. Based upon their behavior during the Cultural Revolution, or the accusations made against them, it is possible to separate the members of the Eighth Central Committee into at least seven political groupings at the time of the Cultural Revolution. Six of these are associated with individuals: P'eng Chen (PC); Ho Lung (HL); Liu Shao-ch'i and Teng Hsiao-p'ing (LT); T'ao Chu (TC); Chou En-lai (CEL); and Lin Piao (LP); and one less "personalized" group, here called the "Cultural Revolution Group" (CR). Even this is an oversimplification, since the boundaries of the groups were rather fluid, and some of these more general groups in fact seem to have been federations of smaller groups.

The discussion here only deals with members of the Central Committee, whereas group membership was, of course, not limited to CC members. It seems the lower one goes into the hierarchy, in fact, the more complex the situation becomes. Because of the limitations of the topic here, the role of such important persons as Yao Wen-yuan, Chang Ch'un-ch'iao, and even to a lesser extent Chiang Ch'ing will not be treated in any detail.

It is not in all cases justifiable to call these groups "factions," since not all had a well articulated factional structure. The extent to which the groups had a factional nature is, of course, a matter for empirical determination. In addition to this problem, the present chapter will attempt to evaluate the characteristics of the several groups. Finally, the influence of group membership as opposed to certain other factors on whether a member of the CC was purged will be studied.

1. DETERMINING GROUP MEMBERSHIP

Group membership is assigned according to a variety of criteria of differing reliability.[1] The classification is made in a series of "elimination" steps, most of which are based upon the member's behavior or the accusations made against him during the Cultural Revolution, and not upon his background, position, or other *a priori* considerations. In certain cases, however, it was necessary to use such *a priori* considerations. The classification does not in general include those who were purged prior to the Cultural Revolution and who played no important role in that series of events. (An exception is Li Wei-han, who had been purged, but later came in for heavy attacks as a member of P'eng Chen's group.) Nor does it include the Chairman, who was a focal point for several of the groups, but not a member of any particular group. Each group includes the man or men it is named for. The CR Group was led at the CC level by Ch'en Po-ta and K'ang Sheng; but its most dynamic leader, Chiang Ch'ing, the wife of Mao Tse-tung, had no Party rank at all until 1966.

The series of classification steps are listed and explained below:

1. A member associated with the "leaders" of a group or with a known member of a certain group is classified as a member of that group. Thus, when Ou Meng-chueh is called "the mistress of the T'ao Chu black inn,"[2] she is classified as a member of the T'ao Chu group. If a person under attack is "protected" by someone, he is classified in the same group as his protector; protection here takes precedence over attack. Also, at this point, accusations of affiliation with Liu Shao-ch'i are ignored; this is because once anyone came under attack it was virtually certain that sooner or later someone would say he was associated with Liu. Persons associated with the "February Adverse Current" are classified with Chou En-lai.[3] Those civilians identified with the "May 16 Corps" are classified with the Cultural Revolution Group.[4] This perhaps begs an important question, but a rule of "transivity" is applied. Thus, if A is associated with B and B with C, A is held also to have been associated with C. If a member is identified with persons in more than one group, he is classified in that group in which, according to the attacks upon him, he seems to have been most active.

2. Those accused of being "anti-revolutionary revisionists" prior to February, 1967, are classified with P'eng Chen.[5] P'eng was held to be the leader of the anti-revolutionary revisionist line.[6] The reason for the cut-off date is that after January, 1967, the power struggle became mainly a fight over the spoils among the victors, and words came to be used much

more loosely. Consequently, those accused of anti-revolutionary revisionism after that time are not counted here.

3. Those now remaining who were accused of affiliations with Liu Shao-ch'i are classified in the Liu-Teng group.

4. Liu Shao-ch'i was "the greatest person in power within the Party walking the capitalist road." Teng Hsiao-p'ing was "another person in power within the Party walking the capitalist road." This similarity, plus the coincidence of their political falls, justifies their being classified together. Any person not yet classified who was called a "power holder on the capitalist road," or some variant, is put in the Liu-Teng group.

5. At this point it is necessary to make certain *a priori* classifications:

a. Chang Ai-p'ing was a deputy chief-of-staff of the PLA. In the late summer of 1965, when Lin Piao's authority was under attack, he had written an article praising Comrade Shao-ch'i.[7] He is placed in the Liu-Teng group.

b. I found no detailed accusations against K'uei Pi. But he was a life-time associate of Ulanfu, so he is classified with Ulanfu in the Liu-Teng group. Ch'ien Ying had a long history of association with both Chou En-lai and Tung Pi-wu; she is placed in the Chou En-lai group. Using the normal criterion in these cases (here, apparent time of purge) lacks the right "feel." Once criteria are decided upon they should not be tampered with, but in these two cases at least following the normal criterion would almost certainly yield wrong results.

c. Teng Ying-ch'ao is the wife of Chou En-lai, and Ts'ai Ch'ang is the wife of Li Fu-ch'un. They are classified with their husbands in the Chou En-lai group.

d. All attacks on Lin Piao were indirect, and no one was criticized for belonging to any "Lin Piao faction." It is assumed that Lin Piao had his support in the army. Hence, soldiers who have not already been placed are classified with Lin Piao. As noted below, these soldiers tend to break into two fairly distinct factions. But each of these factions seems to have accepted the overall leadership of Lin.

6. Some members are hard to classify mechanically according to the above criteria. Their classification is based upon the indirect evidence of what they said themselves, and what others said about them.

a. Hsieh Fu-chih is a difficult case. Chiang Ch'ing once said, "Hsieh Fu-chih is a good comrade. He used to serve Teng Hsiao-p'ing, but he was the first to expose Teng Hsiao-p'ing."[8] This would seem to be enough to place him with the CR group. However, when he took over Peking, he said of his two deputies: "Among the broad mass of cadres in

Peking, the majority are relatively good. Many among them, like Comrades Wu Te, Liu Chien-hsun, and others, have already begun to stand on the side of the proletarian revolutionary faction."[9] This is a rather blatant example of how to damn with faint praise. There is reason to believe that Wu and Liu were both associated with the CR group. Hsieh came under attack from the May 16 Corps, and, with the regional soldiers, was the prime enemy of Yang Ch'eng-wu.[10] These factors, and the generally moderate tone of Hsieh's pronouncements, suggest affiliation with Chou En-lai, and he is so classified. But Hsieh seems to have been acceptable to all of the victorious groups. Or, alternatively, he was too strong to do anything about. By the end of the Ninth Congress he was a member of the Politburo and in charge of the city of Peking, the national police, and probably some of the army. This great potential power, however, could easily make him an obvious target, but by the spring of 1970 he was a very sick man.

b. Liu Chien-hsun, to whom Hsieh Fu-chih had so patronizingly referred, had a difficult time. He was accused of having said that the Great Leap was like a "blind [or mad] man on a blind horse," and of having opposed Mao's analysis of the contradictions in society in 1962. He was said to have praised Wang Kuang-mei (the wife of Liu Shao-ch'i).[11] But by May, 1968, he was attacking the "February adverse current," complaining that attacks on the "extreme left" were really part of a plot against him. He urged the strengthening of the "factional nature" (派性) of the revolutionary faction.[12] This suggests he had managed to cast his lot with the CR group.

c. P'an Fu-sheng had been purged in 1958 for rightism and localism, but he made a comeback during the Cultural Revolution. In July, 1968, he defended "proletarian factionalism"[13] at a time when the "moderates" who wanted to restore unity took a dim view of any kind of factionalism. P'an's rhetoric suggests affiliation with the Cultural Revolution Group.

d. Liu Ko-p'ing had been purged in 1960 for "plotting rebellion," "crimes against the Party," and localism. The story goes that Liu Shao-ch'i had had him confined to a mental institution.[14] But he was later made vice-governor of Shansi (under the Eighth Central Committee the vice-governorships were in some cases a kind of political boneyard— purged CC members, after periods of obscurity, would often be made vice-governors). During the power seizure in Shansi Liu played an active role. In April, 1968, Lin Piao said: "The Shansi alliance has not formed. You troops in Shansi have done a bad job. You have opposed Liu

Ko-p'ing."[15] During most of China at that time the local soldiers were struggling against the "leftists." Their opposition to Liu Ko-p'ing suggests Liu was a follower of the CR Group.

3. Wei Kuo-ch'ing, first secretary of Kwangsi, took on military functions at the outset of the Cultural Revolution. He was attacked in the same terms used against the regional soldiers in the Lin Piao group.[16] He is thus classified with Lin Piao.

7. The Cultural Revolution tended to wax and wane, sometimes with the "moderates" in control, sometimes with the radicals. Some members about whom no other information is known may be classified according to the time they disappeared. The attack on P'eng Chen was carried on during the spring and summer of 1966; the attack on Liu and Teng began in full force in mid October, 1966 (although Liu had been demoted in August). Those purged prior to mid-October, and who have not yet been classified, are placed with P'eng Chen.

From October, 1966, through January, 1967, matters were fairly chaotic. But by the end of January the non-Maoists had suffered a decisive defeat. The remainder of the term of the Eighth Central Committee was mostly taken up by infighting among the victors. During the spring and summer of 1967 the radicals generally held sway, making repeated attacks on members of Chou En-lai's group. After the "Wuhan Incident" in July, 1967, the influence of the regional commanders, a conservative factor, increased. In September the stress began to be placed upon unity.[17] Ch'en Po-ta's organ, *Red Flag,* ceased publication in November, 1967, and there are indications this closure was intended to be permanent: subscribers for 1968 living in Peking had their money returned.[18] But in late spring and summer, 1968, another attack on Chou En-lai's men began, this time the target of choice being Nieh Jung-chen.[19] *Red Flag* resumed publication in July. But the leftists were growing feeble. The regional soldiers were packing the radicals' shock troops, the Red Guards, off to the farm, gunning down the less cooperative.[20] From the 12th Plenum in October, 1968, until the convening of the Ninth Congress in April, 1969, the conservatives were pretty much on top.

With this rough chronology in mind, we may make the following divisions:

Purged between February through September, 1967: Chou En-lai Group.
Purged between October, 1967, through April, 1968: CR Group.[21]
Purged between May through September, 1968: Chou En-lai Group.
Purged between October, 1968, through April, 1969: CR Group.

In general, the cut-off dates here are May 1 and October 1. These dates are useful, since on these days the leadership was accustomed to putting itself on display, and the observer could then see who was still in favor. But, of course, the dates are arbitrary. It is fortunate that the actual turning points in the struggle did tend to occur around the times listed above.

This criterion is probably the least reliable of all the criteria. While general trends in the power struggle can be traced, they do not form neat, self-contained packages. During some periods, one expects, leftists were purging rightists and rightists were simultaneously purging leftists. Some of those already classified were purged at an "inappropriate" time. Thus, Ulanfu was removed in the spring of 1966,[22] but what little evidence there is connects him with Liu Shao-ch'i rather than with P'eng Chen. (It is likely, however, that his relations with Liu were not particularly close.) While each individual case of those classified according to time of purge may be open to doubt, it is felt that the classifications in general are fairly accurate.

8. Some survivors remain to be classified. Of the non-condemned groups Chou En-lai's came under the most severe attack. Members subjected to long sustained attack in general terms are classified with Chou En-lai. Those who suffered only minor attacks, or who were cleared soon after attacks on them began, are classified with the Cultural Revolution Group. This has the effect of putting a few semi-retired members into the CR Group camp. These men may have been mostly inactive. However, since certain of the Grand Old Men did come in for vicious assaults, the classification of this spared residue may not be entirely incorrect.

Table I gives the results of the classification, along with a tentative sketch of the internal structure of each group, with some comments on the degree of cohesion and internation of each group.

2. NATURE OF THE GROUPINGS: AN OVERVIEW

As noted above, these groups do not necessarily constitute "factions, if by "faction" we mean a self-conscious group bound together for a common purpose. The organization of these groups was on the whole rather diffuse. In the case of the Liu-Teng group there may have been, by 1966, no organization at all, but merely a kind of vaguely felt affinity. In this section the nature of the structure and inter-relations among the groups will be discussed. Again it should be repeated that only the relations among CC members are discussed.

Broadly speaking, the groups may be divided into the "condemned"

Table I

Groups on Central Committee

(Solid lines indicate personal relations revealed during the Cultural Revolution or, in a few cases, **imputed** for purposes of this study (as with husbands and wives). Boxes delineate what seem to be active subgroups within each group, characterized by a high degree of cohesion and interaction. Dotted lines show ties of individual members with those outside the group with which they are classified. Numbers in parentheses indicate according to which criterion the member is classified.)

A. P'eng Chen Group (PC) (27 members)

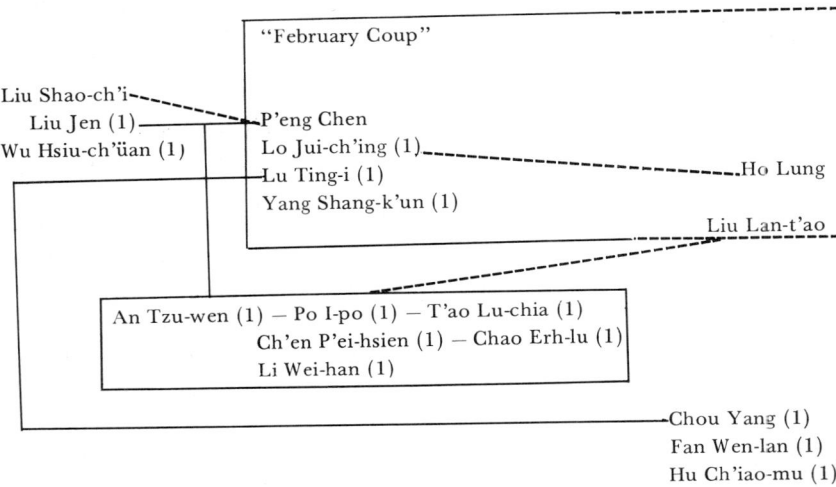

Chang Su (2)	Chang Yun (7)
Chiang Nan-hsiang (2)	Chu Te-hai (7)
Hsu Ping (2)	Ch'eng Tzu-hua (7)
Li Ta-chang (2)	Huang Huo-ch'ing (7)
Lin Feng (2)	Huang Ou-tung (7)
Yang Hsien-chen (2)	Ma Ming-fang (7)

This in general seems to have been a cohesive faction, characterized, at least among those classified by (1), by a high degree of interaction. Members in "Coup" box cooperated closely with Ho Lung; those outside probably did not.

B. Ho Lung (HL) (17 members)

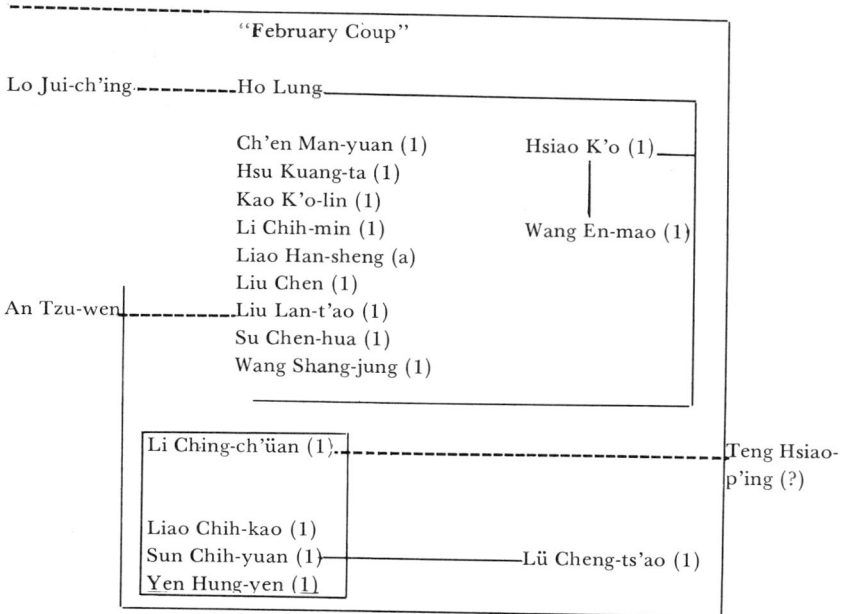

High degree of cohesion and interaction.

C. Liu-Teng (LT) (21 members)

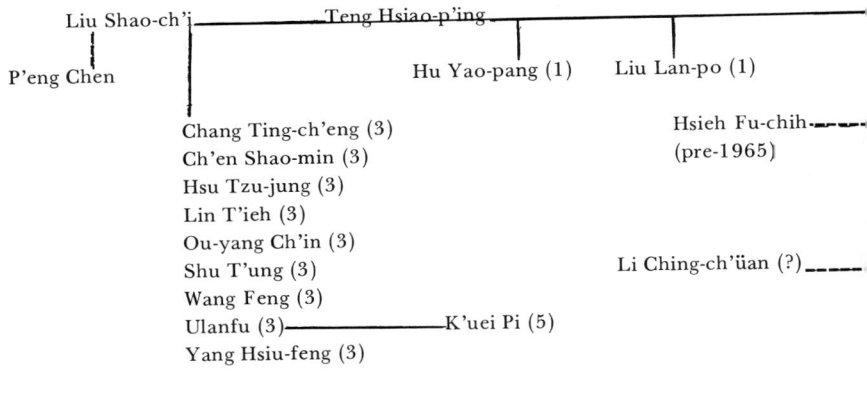

Chang Ting-ch'eng (3)
Ch'en Shao-min (3)
Hsu Tzu-jung (3)
Lin T'ieh (3)
Ou-yang Ch'in (3)
Shu T'ung (3)
Wang Feng (3)
Ulanfu (3)——————————K'uei Pi (5)
Yang Hsiu-feng (3)

Chang Ching-fu (4)
Chiang Wei-ching (4)
Chou Huan (4)
Liu Tzu-hou (4)
Wang Shih-t'ai (4)
Yeh Fei (4)

Chang Ai-p'ing (5)

Little evidence of interaction during Cultural Revolution. Mao said Liu and Teng did not "band together." The group may have consisted of those who opposed Maoist policies, and who resisted Liu's demotion at the Eleventh Plenum. Group may in part also be the remains of a disintegrated Teng Hsiao-p'ing faction.

D. T'ao Chu Group (TC) (10 members)

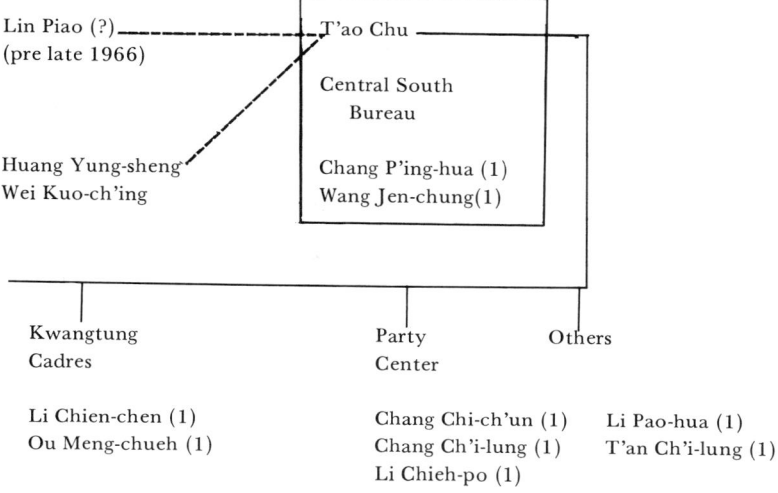

Lin Piao (?) ──────── T'ao Chu
(pre late 1966)
                        Central South
                          Bureau

Huang Yung-sheng   Chang P'ing-hua (1)
Wei Kuo-ch'ing   Wang Jen-chung (1)

Kwangtung Cadres	Party Center	Others
Li Chien-chen (1)	Chang Chi-ch'un (1)	Li Pao-hua (1)
Ou Meng-chueh (1)	Chang Ch'i-lung (1)	T'an Ch'i-lung (1)
	Li Chieh-po (1)	

Probably high degree of cohesion and interaction, with possible exception of "others." Those in box took charge of propaganda department after purge of Lu Ting-i. A Maoist group until late December, 1966.

E. Chou En-lai Group (CEL) (36 members)

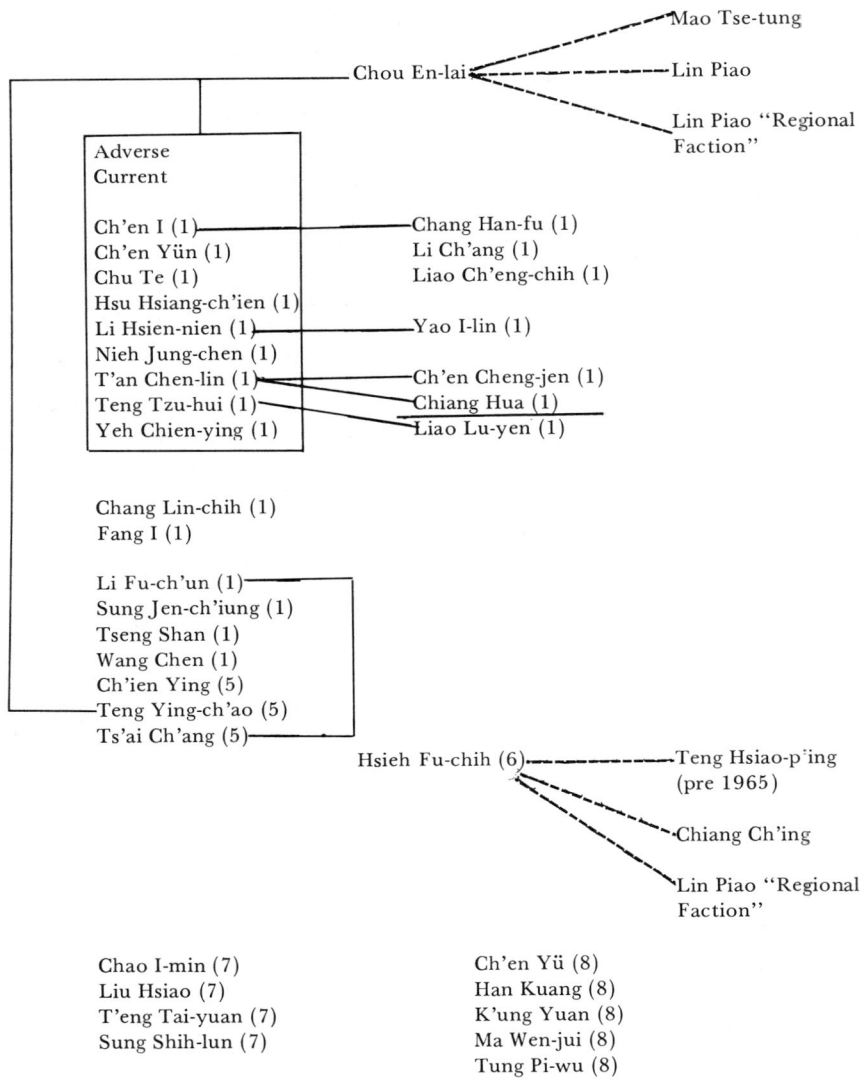

High degree of interaction, especially among higher ranking members. Somewhat less cohesion (these men had minds of their own). On the whole, group more concerned with preserving its position than with acquiring a new one.

F. Lin Piao Group (LP) (18 members)

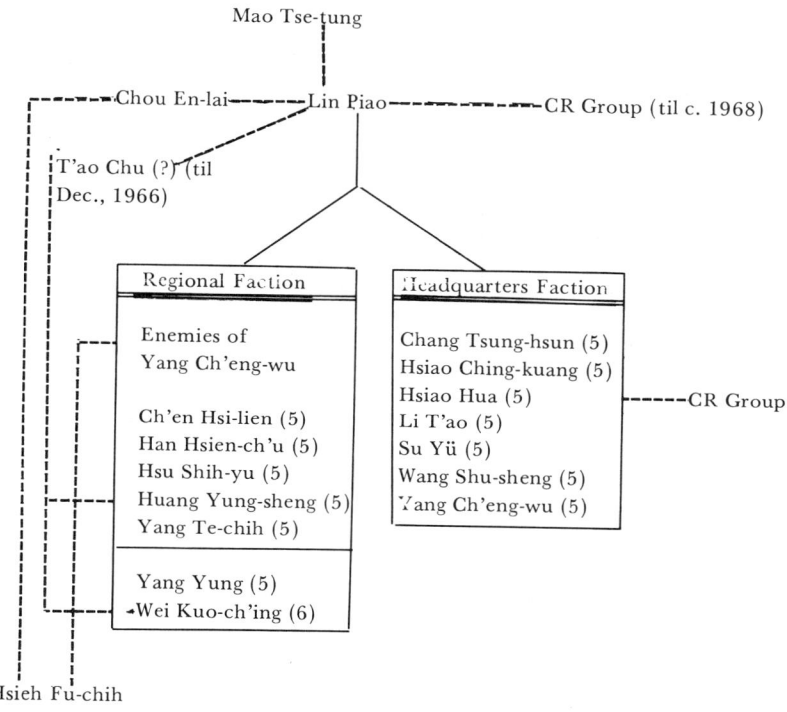

Others

Chang Ta-chih (5)
Chung Ch'i-kuang (5)
T'ang Liang (5)

Each of two major subgroups characterized by high degree of interaction and cohesion. Each hostile to the other, loyal to Lin Piao.

G. Cultural Revolution Group (CR) (23 members)

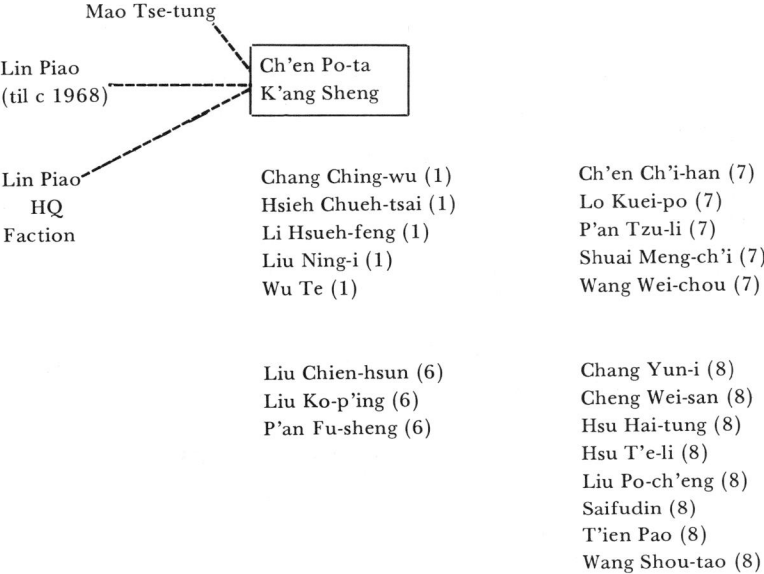

At highest level, much interaction and cohesion; elsewhere hard to judge. The active members of this group represent at the least a tendency, characterized by support deriving from mass organizations, hostility to adverse current, support for "proletarian revolutionary factionalism." The group acquired the form given here during course of Cultural Revolution, and was probably not ready-formed at beginning of that struggle.

H. Others

1) P'eng Te-huai's followers inactive in Cultural Revolution:

    Chang Chung-liang
    Chang Wen-t'ien
    Chia T'o-fu
    Chou Hsiao-chou
    Hsi Chung-hsun
    Huang K'o-ch'eng
    Hung Hsueh-chih
    P'eng Te-huai
    T'an Cheng
    Teng Hua*
    Wan I
    Wang Chia-hsiang

2) Not classified

    Chao Chien-min
    Chao Po-p'ing
    Ch'en Shao-yü
    Ch'ien Chün-jui
    Feng Pai-chü
    Ku Ta-ts'un
    Li Li-san
    Liu Ch'ang-sheng
    Mao Tse-tung*
    Tseng Hsi-sheng
    Wang Ho-shou
    Wang Ts'ung-wu
    Wu Chih-p'u
    Yeh Chi-chuang

*Elected to 9th CC.

---

and the "saved." The P'eng Chen, Liu-Teng, and Ho Lung groups were condemned. Tao Chu's group was originally "Maoist," but later was also condemned. The rest, although taking heavy casualties, were not condemned as a whole, and in fact were given some kind of recognition in the "triple alliance" that emerged from the chaos.

A. The Condemned

The struggle against P'eng Chen began in the fall of 1965, and P'eng had been decisively defeated by early summer, 1966. The core of his group consisted of himself; Lu Ting-i, director of the CC propaganda department; Yang Shang-k'un, director of the CC General Office; and Lo Jui-ch'ing, chief of staff of the PLA[23] (but on Lo, see below). These men were all members of the Secretariat. With their lower ranking for apanages (e.g., Liu Jen under P'eng Chen; Chou Yang under Lu Ting-i) they seem to have constituted a genuine faction at least by late 1965.

Attached to the P'eng Chen group is a smaller group centered around An Tzu-wen and Po I-po. These men, like P'eng Chen, were accused of plotting against Lin Piao,[24] but they do not appear to have been part of the inner circle planning the "February coup." P'eng and Po hail from Shansi, and An from Shensi, in distinction from the bulk of the elite, who come from the Yangtze valley, particularly Hunan.

The Ho Lung group is composed of soldiers opposed to Lin Piao, supplemented with local apparatchiks affiliated with Li Ching-ch'üan.[25] This, with at least the inner core of P'eng Chen's group, was accused of plotting a *coup d'etat*.[26] (A more detailed consideration of the adventures of the various groups is deferred until later.) Lo Jui-ch'ing provided the link between the P'eng Chen and Ho Lung groups, and may have been the "brains" of the Ho Lung group, with Ho Lung merely a figurehead. In that case, it is somewhat arbitrary to classify Lo with P'eng Chen. He is so classified because they come under attack at roughly the same time. The bulk of the Ho Lung group was not purged until January, 1967.

The above two groups both appear to be fairly well articulated factions, and seem to have constituted the active opposition to the ambitions of Lin Piao. By contrast, the much reviled "Liu-Teng" group appear as rather passive victims of the Cultural Revolution. As the Cultural Revolution rolled on, Liu Shao-ch'i, the only man with enough prestige to rival Mao Tse-tung, came to be execrated as the font of all evils and the backstage manipulator of every challenge to the Chairman's authority from the 1920's on. The Red Guards liked to stress the close connections between P'eng and Liu. P'eng was Liu's deputy, and later his successor, in the Northern Bureau prior to Liberation. The Maoists also came to lump all of their enemies into the same camp. But the early primary evidence indicates that Liu and P'eng were not working together in 1966. P'eng was purged in May, 1966; Liu was demoted in August, and purged in October. At that time Mao Tse-tung said: "Even though their mistake was the same, the P'eng Chen group banded together secretly, whereas the Liu-Teng group committed their mistakes openly."[27]

To some degree, the pattern of charismatic politics seems to have extended even into the apparatus, with Liu Shao-ch'i as a kind of surrogate Mao.[28] Teng Hsiao-p'ing and P'eng Chen were "natural" enemies, but both seem to have accepted for the time being the primary of Liu. If the Liu-Teng group did not in fact "band together," this may explain why the group is perhaps the most amorphous of the various groups identified. Teng Hsiao-p'ing was a powerful man in 1956. But it will be argued later that Teng lost much of his influence with the adoption of the "capitalist road" in 1961. Teng seems to have had a hard time holding his followers together. We have already seen how he was doublecrossed by Hsieh Fu-chih. According to Peking gossip picked up by Japanese correspondents, Li Ching-ch'üan was "known" as the "right-hand man" of Teng Hsiao-p'ing.[29] But in the Cultural Revolution Li was with Ho Lung. (It is possible this gossip was based purely on Li's past service under Teng in the Southwest Bureau in the early 1950's; at the same time, however, Ho Lung was the military boss of this region.)[30] After the purge of P'eng Chen, when Liu and Teng took charge of the Cultural Revolution, Li Hsueh-feng, first secretary of the North China Bureau, was made first secretary of Peking; Li came under heavy attack in the fall of 1966, and it is probable that he too was close to Teng. But Li Hsueh-feng managed to make peace with the Cultural Revolution group.[31] The Liu-Teng group may be in part a vestigial Teng Hsiao-p'ing faction; and other members of this group may have been simply certain members who were not anxious to disrupt the 1965 *status quo*.

T'ao Chu, judging from his public pronouncements, was among the most able and literate of the apparatchiks. There is vague evidence that for a long period he was at odds with the Party Center. After the purge of Lu Ting-i he was made director of the propaganda department. In the late 1940's he had been a commissar under Lin Piao, and he was probably one of Lin's main supporters in 1966. His group, probably a fairly well articulated one, was composed of three main strains: cadres of the Central South Bureau, Kwangtung cadres, and some people at the Party Center. It seems to represent a split in the apparatus, an opposition to the Central Establishment under Liu, Teng, and P'eng. The group was purged in December, 1966.

B. The "Saved"

The group which formed around Chou En-lai is perhaps the most impressive for the quality of its personnel. It includes such men as Ch'en Yun, Li Hsien-nien, Li Fu-ch'un, Teng Tzu-hui, Nieh Jung-chen, and Ch'en I—easily among the most able in the CPC hierarchy. Chu Te is not noted for any particular intelligence or ability, but was a good leader of men and enjoyed great prestige and respect. This group seems to have shared certain policy orientations over a long time, but, while protected by Chou, did not act uniformly as a group subordinate to every wish of Chou En-lai. In February of 1967 certain members of the group led a minor rebellion against the way things were going in the Cultural Revolution. Chou En-lai scolded the members of this "adverse current," but later publicly protected them.[32] The members of this group tended to display more courage and character than most CC members under attack. Ch'en I told a struggle meeting:

> Now it is my turn to speak. I am a Politburo member, Director of the State Council Foreign Affairs Staff Office, minister of

Foreign Affairs, and also a vice-premier. So I am a big shot (頭頭), a big shot in the foreign affairs system. Until I am fired I will retain my leading authority. I say you can break my head and spill my blood, but I cannot give up my leadership authority.[33]

This statement is typical of the assertions by many of the major figures of this group, including Chou himself, of the legitimacy of the established structures of authority, and this perhaps marks the major ideological difference between the Chou En-lai group and the other "Maoist" groups. Of course, such statements by his allies did little to help Chou in his attempt to preserve the state structure; but craven subservience might have been even more disastrous.

The early attacks against the group concentrated upon Chou's allies. But by, at the latest, the spring of 1968 the "Provincial Proletarian Alliance" (省無聯), a Red Guard group composed of proverbially hot-blooded Hunanese, began calling Chou En-lai "the general representative of China's Red Capitalist class."[34] By this time, however, Chou had formed an alliance with the regional commanders, and his personal position was safe. Of the higher ranking members of his group only T'an Chen-lin failed to be elected to the Ninth CC (while others such as Ch'en Yun and Teng Tzu-hui, who had been in disfavor for years, were reelected). But the group as a whole seems to have been demoralized and discredited. Aside from Chou, only Li Hsien-nien and Yeh Chien-ying remained active by the spring of 1970.

The Lin Piao group was split between the men at the headquarters and the regional commanders. Lin came to power partly through an alliance between himself and his military ideologues, particularly Hsiao Hua, and the radicals around Chiang Ch'ing. Once Liu Shao-ch'i had been defeated, there would be a tendency for this alliance to break up. The early evidence for this also reveals the headquarters-region tension. In January, 1967, Chiang Ch'ing said that "to criticize Hsiao is to love the PLA." Ch'en Po-ta said Hsiao "tried to change the army led by Chairman Mao into a bourgeois force."[35] (This illustrates the farcical aspect of the power struggle at that time—Hsiao seems to have been one of the few soldiers who did not want to turn the PLA into a "bourgeois force.") Ch'en and Miss Chiang soon found they had been hoodwinked, when the source for the rumors against Hsiao was traced back to Yang Yung, commander of Peking. Yang was purged.[36]

The conflict between the local soldiers and the radicals grew more acute after the period of military takeovers—roughly, February 1967 on. The Red Guard groups and, to a lesser degree, their high ranking backers were no more willing to accept the new authority than the old; while the soldiers, attaining power, found they had had enough of struggle. The situation in Fukien is typical. Han Hsien-ch'u, a deputy chief of staff of the PLA, had been sent down from Peking to take over from the old first secretary of the Province and commander of the Fukien Front, Yeh Fei, a Liu-Teng man. The Red Guards addressed Han:

> The first time the peasants came into the town they had been instigated by Yeh Fei to drive out the students coming south [i.e., the roving Red Guard groups] and suppress the mass movement. Han Hsien-ch'u was struggling against Yeh Fei. Why didn't you cut even a single fart about this problem?(連一個屁都沒放) [37]

Once Han had taken over, he had no more use than had Yeh Fei for the "mass movement."

During the period of radical ascendency in Peking, the regional soldiers did not receive support from headquarters in their attempts to restore law and order.[38] Matters came to a head with the "Wuhan Incident" in July 1967. In Wuhan certain mass organizations backed by the regional commander had launched a full scale attack against the leftist factions. Hsieh Fu-chih and Wang Li were arrested (or "kidnapped") when they came from Peking to investigate. The dispute was mediated by Chou En-lai, and paratroops and gun boats were sent in to restore order and central control.[39]

The immediate response in Peking was to attack a "handful in the army." The handful was warned:

> In our time, no matter who you are, how high your position, how mature your qualifications, how strong your backstage supporter, if you oppose the TMTT, oppose Chairman Mao's proletarian revolutionary line, you will be ground to pieces by the wheels of history, you will become piles of dog shit despised by humanity.[40]

Cooler heads, however, had realized that clubs now were trumps, and more support was forthcoming for the soldiers. Hsiao Hua disappeared soon after the Wuhan Incident, and the timing suggests this was a sacrifice offered to the regional men. The major backing for the regional soldiers came not from Lin Piao, but from Chou En-lai.[41] In the spring of 1968 Yang Ch'eng-wu, acting chief of staff of the PLA, was purged, and accused of affiliations with the ultra-left, particularly with those who had been most vehement in attacking the "handful in the army." Yang was identified also as an enemy of the regional commanders Ch'en Hsi-lien, Han Hsien-ch'u, Hsu Shih-yu, Huang Yung-sheng, and Yang

Te-chih.[42] Huang Yung-sheng, commander of the Canton region, became the new chief of staff.

To term what is called by that name in this study the Cultural Revolution Group is technically inaccurate. The original group of this name seems to have been a kind of joint sub-committee of the Secretariat and the Propaganda Department headed by P'eng Chen. This group was purged and a new Cultural Revolution Group formed, headed by Ch'en Po-ta, with Chiang Ch'ing as vice-chairman in 1966. K'ang Sheng was a member of the first group, an "advisor" to the second.[43] The reorganized CR Group included some followers of T'ao Chu, then director of the Propaganda Department; but these men were soon purged. The core of the new group was composed of relatively young intellectuals who had been members of a kind of discussion group organized by Chiang Ch'ing in the early 1960's. Many of these also worked for *Red Flag*.[44] These include such men as Yao Wen-yuan and Chang Ch'un-ch'iao (who survived); and Ch'i Pen-yü, Wang Li, and possibly Lin Chieh (who were purged).

Aside from Ch'en and K'ang, the CC members classified with the CR Group were not members of the group itself. Rather, they seem to have been persons who came under the protection of the group. The most active of them seem to share the same power base as the CR Group, the "mass" (radical Red Guard) organizations. This group of people seems to be fairly heterogeneous in origin and possibly even in political opinion: Li Hsueh-feng and Liu Chien-hsun were condemned as inveterate conservatives at one time, while P'an Fu-sheng had once been purged for rightism. But on the whole the CR Group represents the most radical line in recent Chinese politics.

3. CHARACTERISTICS OF THE GROUPS

Presented below is a statistical analysis of the various groupings revealed within the CC. The main tool of analysis is the "Kendall's Q" coefficient of correlation. This is an easy to calculate measure of association for two nominal scale variables, giving not only the strength but the direction of the correlation.[45] A disadvantage of Q is that the variables associated must be dichotomous. Most of the variables studied here are "naturally" dichotomous—one is either a member of T'ao Chu's group or one is not (according to the way the groups have been defined here); one has either studied in Russia or one has not. But other variables, such as age, are "continuous." Here the need to dichotomize leads to some loss of information.[46]

A. Background and History

Table II gives the correlations for each group with age and education.

Table II

Age and Education

	P'eng Chen (PC)	Ho Lung (HL)	Liu-Teng (LT)	T'ao Chu (TC)
Born pre 1906	.033	−.289	−.135	.043
More than HS Ed.	.571	−.356	−.187	−.600
Study in W. Eur.	.329	−1.000	−.020	−1.000
Study in USSR	.174	−.047	−.201	−1.000
Any Forn. Study	.430	−.704	−.091	−1.000

	Chou En-lai (CEL)	Lin Piao (LP)	Cultural Revolution (CR)	Total
Born pre 1906	.404	−.691	.357	150
More than HS Ed.	.091	−.733	.701	126
Study in W. Eur.	.490	−1.000	.088	152
Study in USSR	.122	−.636	.458	152
Any Forn. Study	.421	−.757	.220	152

The "oldest" groups (members tending to have been born prior to 1906) are Chou En-lai's and the CR Group. Lin Piao's group, and, to a lesser extent, Ho Lung's, tend to be young. The best educated groups are the CR Group and PC, while LP, TC, and HL tend to be relatively less well educated than the general run of the CC. Sixty-one of the 82 members in the sample who received more than a high school education belong to PC, CR, or CEL. These three groups are also the most "cosmopolitan," in the sense that their members have studied abroad. CEL tends to have studied in Western Europe, and the CR Group in the Soviet Union. PC occupies an intermediate position, resembling CEL more than the CR Group.

Chinese often put great stress upon provincial origins. Table III evaluates the role of provincial origin in the formation of the political groups identified on the CC, for those members for whom reliable information on this point could be found. Perhaps the most striking fact is that in no group are natives of Hunan outnumbered by those of any other province. Moreover, as the correlations show, nowhere are the Hunanese really spectacularly over or under represented. The table also presents the results of the correlation of birth in the province most heavily represented after Hunan, or tied with Hunan, for each group. For LT there are as many members each from Shensi and Szechuan as from

Hunan; all three correlations are presented. If for any group a province adjacent to that providing its second highest number of members is also heavily represented, the correlation is calculated for both provinces together.

P'eng Chen had a following from his native area of Shansi-Shensi, although the correlations with birth in Shensi are higher both for HL and LT. Chou En-lai also had a strong following from his native area, as did Lin Piao. Natives of Hopei are heavily over-represented in TC. The general impression, however, is that provincial origins are not very important in determining group affiliations. Thus, Shensi is over-represented in PC, HL, and LT; and Hopei in both TC and CR. Common provincial origin may have been a factor in determining certain specific alliances among the members, but on the whole the split at the time of the Cultural Revolution seems to have been one among the Hunanese who had risen in the Party along with Mao Tse-tung.

Table III
Provincial Origins

PC		HL		LT		TC	
Hunan	.386	Hunan	.316	Hunan	−.325	Hunan	.433
Shensi,		Shensi	.422	Shensi	.343	Hopei	.766
Shansi	.297			Szechuan	.334		
CEL		LP		CR			
Hunan	−.090	Hunan	.267	Hunan	−.069		
Kiangsi,		Hupei	.468	Hopei	.390	N=138	
Kiangsu	.615						

Table IV traces some factors in the personal histories of the groups' members. The "relations" measure tells the extent to which the members of a given group were associated prior to 1949 with other members of

Table IV
Personal Histories

	PC	HL	LT	TC	CEL	LP	CR	Total
"Relations"*	.730	.876	−.333	−1.000	.328	.553	−.405	161
Chingkangshan	−.481	.404	.404	−.352	.343	.538	−.713	135
Kiangsi Soviet	−.131	−.290	.163	−.757	.435	.613	−.369	121
Long March	−.215	.449	.033	−.141	.030	.361	−.161	133

*Includes double counting.

that group, relative to the extent to which they were associated with members of other groups.[47] Because of the nature of the relationship between Liu Shao-ch'i and P'eng Chen prior to 1949, and the importance attached to this by their enemies in the Cultural Revolution, Liu is counted here (and here only) as a "member" of the PC group as well as his own. The reverse, of course, is not true (P'eng is not counted a member of LT). The groups most clearly based in part on past associations turn out to be PC, HL, LP and CEL. The PC group includes most of the members who once worked in the old Northern Bureau, first under Liu Sho-ch'i and later under P'eng Chen (but not all—e.g., Liu Ning-i). Ho Lung's and Lin Piao's old army subordinates also tend, by and large, to cohere.

The remaining factors measure the extent to which the members of each group tended to share in the historical experience of what might be called the "Maoist mainstream.": presence at Chingkangshan, in the Kiangsi Soviet, and on the Long March. The mainstream groups include LP, and, to a lesser extent, HL and CEL. Ho Lung's men are not well represented in the Kiangsi Soviet, as Ho at that time was carrying on far-flung guerrilla operations on the periphery of the Soviet. Chou En-lai was not at Chingkangshan, but many of his allies were. Many members of this group, such as Ch'en I, went underground and remained behind at the time of the Long March. The PC group tends to have engaged in white areas underground work prior to Liberation. The historical experiences of LT, TC, and CR are varied.

B. Current Work, 1965

Table V gives the extent to which the members of each group tended to work in the central apparatus, the bureaucracy, or the army. Correlations of membership against work in the apparatus and bureaucracy

Table V

Work at Center

	PC	HL	LT	TC	CEL	LP	CR
Apparatus	.421	−.263	−.302	−.003	.193	−.443	.073
Bureaucrat	−.182	.022	−.072	−.690	.603	−.367	−.279
Pure Apparat.	.710	−.005	−.225	.193	−.062	−.462	.076
Pure Bur.	−.184	.625	.003	−1.000	.397	−.042	−.456
Mixed	−.044	−.533	−.302	−.216	.471	−.222	.038
Army	−.240	.485	−.281	−1.000	−.455	.964	−.756

are made in two ways. The top two lines in the table measure group membership against work in the apparatus or bureaucracy regardless of any other jobs the member may hold. The following three lines revert to the categories used in the second chapter: pure apparatchiks, pure bureaucrats, and mixed. Full time soldiers who held jobs in the Ministry of Defense are classified as bureaucrats as well as soldiers. But here those holding only military posts (for example, deputy chiefs of staff who were not concurrently vice ministers of defense) are considered simply soldiers.

Table V shows that the PC group was the domain of the central apparatus, particularly for members of the "pure" apparatus. The bureaucrats tended to ally with Chou En-lai, although the "pure" bureaucrats are more strongly over-represented in Ho Lung's group. Most impressive is Chou En-lai's following among those with "multiple hats." The men holding both Party and state posts seem to have perceived their interests in a similar fashion as the pure bureaucrats, rather than as the pure apparatchiks. This tends to support the reasoning in the second chapter, where it was hypothesized that men holding Party and state posts would tend to emphasize their position in the state. "Multiple-hatism" redounded to the benefit of the top bureaucrat, Chou En-lai, rather than to the group in which the apparatchiks are most over-represented.

The relationship between group membership and current service in the army is what one would expect. Given the way in which the groups were defined, Lin Piao's following in the army is not surprising. But Ho Lung also had a heavy military following. While all other groups except TC included some professional soldiers, the LP-HL split reflects the major cleavage in the PLA in the mid-1960's. As noted above, there was another cleavage among those soldiers who followed Lin Piao.

Table VI measures the extent to which the members of the different groups held positions on the leading policy making bodies. All groups

Table VI

Positions on Leading Organs

	PC	HL	LT	TC	CEL	LP	CR
PB	−.115	−.071	.056	−1.000	.444	−.450	−.006
Secretariat	.587	.173	−.272	−1.000	.052	−1.000	.063
MAC	−.245	−.078	−1.000	−1.000	.151	.702	−.242
Prem., V. Prem., SC	.036	−.333	.064	−.031	.680	−.364	−1.000

aside from T'ao Chu's were represented on the Politburo, Chou En-lai's rather heavily and Lin Piao's rather lightly. The other groups all have a rather "equitable" representation on the Politburo, that is, each is represented to about the same extent as the CC membership as a whole is. PC, the group favored by the central apparatus, has strong representation on the Secretariat. Lin Piao's group is strongly represented on the MAC, evidence Lin exercised policy control over this body. The vice-premiers are scattered among all groups except the CR Group; but the impressionistic observations of many others are confirmed: they were most heavily represented in CEL. It is interesting to note, however, that in 1965 Ho Lung, Teng Hsiao-p'ing, T'ao Chu, and Lin Piao were all vice-premiers of the State Council.

In Table VII group membership is correlated with work in the various "systems".[48] The P'eng Chen group is particularly strong in the propaganda system, as is the CR Group—a reflection of the Lu Ting-i-Ch'en Po-ta split. PC also has strength in general Party administration, as

Table VII
Groups and "Systems"

	PC	HL	LT	TC	CEL	LP	CR
Internal	.240	− .365	− .102	− .067	− .005	− .004	.140
Propaganda	.745	− .123	−1.000	.189	−1.000	−1.000	.388
Agriculture	−1.000	.483	−1.000	−1.000	.717	−1.000	− .115
Industry	.333	.154	.045	−1.000	.346	−1.000	−1.000
Finance	−1.000	−1.000	−1.000	−1.000	.898	−1.000	.119
United Front†	.247	−1.000	.546	− .004	− .163	−1.000	.124
Foreign††	− .188	− .131	− .262	−1.000	.348	− .179	.208
Military†††	− .403	.451	− .097	.380	− .493	.976	− .701
Party Admin.	.403	− .585	− .178	.343	− .171	− .578	.149

† Including women's work, youth work, and minorities work.
†† Including members of various "friendship" societies.
††† Including provincial secretaries who also served as provincial or regional commissars; otherwise, the correlations would be the same as in Table V.

---

do, to a lesser degree, T'ao Chu and CR. Ho Lung had support in the agricultural system, the army, and, to a slight degree, in the industry and communications bureaucracy. The members of the economic systems, however, tended to line up behind Chou En-lai. Chou derived support from both apparatchiks (e.g., Teng Tzu-hui) and bureaucrats in the economic sphere. Chou was also strong in the foreign affairs system, with some rivalry from the CR group. Lin Piao, of course, is strongest in the military system. T'ao Chu, because of his support from provincial commissars, also shows strongly in the military system. T'ao's group found its major strength in the provinces, but after he moved to Peking he seems to have picked up support in the Party administration system and the propaganda system. LT, also strong in the provinces, shows strongly at the Center only in the United Front system.

Table VIII examines the regional base of the various groups. The first row considers the degree to which the different groups were based upon the local Party apparatus. Not included in the computation are regional soldiers who did not hold local Party posts. Also local notables such as T'ien Pao and Saifudin, who seem to have held no important Party posts, are excluded. The first row indicates that TC, LT, and HL were based fairly substantially in the regions. CEL is the most "centralized" group.

The following rows, calculated only from among those CC members serving in the regions (but not necessarily members of the regional secretariats) may help us visualize a kind of "political map" of China in 1965. Ho Lung's men, insofar as they served at the localities, were concentrated in the west of China. The LT group is concentrated in North China, the Northwest, and, to a slight degree, in the East. T'ao Chu was of course strong in his own Central South region, and also in the neighboring East China region. Lin Piao's support in the Central South (Huang Yung-sheng and Wei Kuo-ch'ing) is probably a reflection of an

Table VIII

Local Party

	PC	HL	LT	TC	CEL	LP	CR
Local	−.063	.244	.570	.712	−.741	−.080	.261
NE	.603	−1.000	−.061	−1.000	.412	.111	.111
N	.231	−.200	.649	−1.000	−1.000	−1.000	.063
E	−.120	−1.000	.091	.710	.424	.200	−1.000
CS	−1.000	−1.000	−1.000	.837	−.328	.429	.429
SW	.488	.805	−1.000	−1.000	−1.000	−1.000	.294
NW	−1.000	.710	.442	−1.000	−1.000	.200	−1.000

earlier alliance between Lin and T'ao. P'eng Chen had some support in Manchuria, but this was not a major factor in the composition of his group.

We may now sum up briefly what we have learned so far about the nature of the groups. PC, HL, and CEL seem to have been the best "articulated" factions, based both upon personal and institutional ties. The personal relations in PC were rather complex, but its institutional base was simple: in large part, the PC group was the central apparatus. Ho Lung's group was complex in term of both personal and institutional relations. Its core was the army, but it enjoyed support from the state bureaucracy and from some of the regions. Chou En-lai's group was based upon the state bureaucracy, particularly its upper-levels; the bureaucrat-apparatchiks; and the men in the economic systems. T'ao Chu's group was drawn from the Central South and East China regions, with some support at the Party Center. The members do not seem to have had important personal relations prior to 1949, and the group may have been of fairly recent formation. The Liu-Teng group was of miscellaneous composition. It may have been in part merely a kind of "opinion group," consisting of members out of sympathy with Mao but who did not join P'eng Chen or Ho Lung; in part it may have been the remains of a disintegrating regionally-based Teng Hsiao-p'ing faction. The CR group is also quite miscellaneous, including apparatchiks not affiliated with P'eng Chen; old, semi-retired members; members previously purged making a comeback; and some regional apparatchiks. It was probably formed through a series of *ad hoc* alliances during the course of the severe 1966-1969 power struggle.

C. Lin Piao's Group

Because of the method of selection, there has not been much we could say about Lin Piao's group except that its members were soldiers, and, more significantly, that they tended to have had "relations" with Lin prior to 1949. Here we will see whether the members of Lin Piao's group differ in any important respects from the other military men on the Central Committee. Lin Piao's group, as far as the method of classification is concerned, is a residual category: it is composed of soldiers not included in other groups. If it is found that this residual group of soldiers differs from soldiers not in the group, we will have more confidence in the validity of the classification.

Table IX correlates membership in Lin Piao's group with certain selected characteristics, the total "universe" being all of the soldiers on the CC, including soldiers "purged" prior to the Cultural Revolution and the more important ex-soldiers (e.g., Chu Te, Ch'en I). Wei Kuo-ch'ing is not included in these calculations.

It was seen in Table II that Lin Piao's was the "youngest" of the groups. This relationship also holds when his group is compared with the other soldiers.

William Whitson has hypothesized that the old field army systems continue to structure both military and political loyalties among the Chinese Communist elite.[49] Lin Piao would seem to have found some support among all of the old "factions," at least at the CC level. But there is a very high correlation between membership in the LP group and past service in Lin's old outfit, the Fourth Field Army. Among the field armies, Lin is weakest in the First Field Army, formerly under P'eng Te-huai and Ho Lung. Col. Whitson found that only the First Field Army "suffered a significant loss of representation among the total elite," and that "the average power distribution at all levels which existed in 1966 has not changed radically over the tumultous two-year period."[50] This would tend to cast doubts upon the explanatory power of the field army hypothesis. But the present test, concentrating upon actual group membership, rather than upon the incidence of the purge, is perhaps a more direct and valid test of Col. Whitson's hypothesis than the test he himself chose; and at least as far as the LP group is concerned, the hypothesis is supported.

Table IX

Lin Piao's Group and the Other Soldiers

Born pre 1906	−.764	at Whampoa	.082
4th Field Army†	.864	Nanchang Rebellion	−.789
3rd Field Army†	.011	Chingkangshan	−.218
2nd Field Army†	.219	Long March	−.220
1st Field Army†	−.584	Headquarters work††	−.500
"Russian" Faction†	−.655	Regular Army††	.273
"Volunteer Army" Faction†	−.021		

N = 43

† Information on field army groups and "factions" from Huang Chen-hsia, *op. cit.*, pp. 760-762.

†† Soldiers purged prior to the Cultural Revolution are classified according to the job they last held. "Headquarters" is opposed to "local." The term "regular" army is used to distinguish those engaged in conventional military work rather than political work.

Other items measure the extent to which the careers of members of the LP group paralleled that of Lin Piao. The correlations here are all either low or negative. Relative to the other soldiers, the LP group is not outstanding for having attended the Whampoa Academy, participated in the Nanchang rebellion, been at Chingkangshan, and made the Long March. (Relative to the full CC membership, of course, the group is over-represented on all of these.) The relative youth of Lin Piao's group is probably a factor here. Relative to the other soldiers the Lin Piao men tend to have worked away from headquarters and to have engaged in orthodox military work, rather than in military-political work.

In sum, the Lin Piao group would seem to be, like the PC, HL, and CEL groups, a relatively well articulated one, based upon both personal and institutional ties. This seems true despite its divided nature.

4. THE INCIDENCE OF THE PURGE

For the purposes of the following tables, a "purged" member is one who was not re-elected to the Central Committee at the Ninth Congress, plus members who committed suicide. This Congress did not mark the end of the power struggle, and one's position at the Congress is not always a good indicator of one's position in the elite. Lo Kuei-po was not re-elected to the CC, but he continued to be active in the Ministry of Foreign Affairs. Hsiao K'o was not re-elected either, but for some unexplained reason he reappeared in public on October 1, 1969. Both of these men are considered "purged." Wang En-mao, after having been relieved of his Sinkiang positions, was made an alternate member of the 9th CC; T'an Ch'i-lung of Shantung was also re-elected; but neither have been heard from since. They are considered survivors.

Failure to be elected to the Ninth CC, then, is the "operational" definition of the purge. Elsewhere in this study the term is used more loosely, and perhaps more meaningfully, to refer to a member's removal from active public life. Unlike Soviet practice, the Chinese were not in the habit of removing disgraced members from the Central Committee. The only exception would seem to be Liu Shao-ch'i, who was relieved of "all" his posts by the 12th Plenum in October, 1968. It is difficult to generalize about the "mechanism" of the purge at the CC level. The Control Commission, the Party watchdog agency, does not seem to have been active against such high ranking cadres. The 1957-1958 localists were removed by the provincial committees to which they belonged, probably at the initiative of the Central Secretariat. Prior to 1967, other purges on the whole seem to have been decided by Central meetings: P'eng Te-huai was removed by a CC plenum; Lo Jui-ch'ing by a Central work conference; P'eng Chen by an enlarged Politburo meeting; Liu Shao-ch'i was demoted by a plenum, and removed from active politics by a work conference. By 1967 Party procedures had been disrupted; members would be attacked in wall posters or Red Guard papers. If the attacks were successful, the member would disappear. Some were arrested by the army or the public security agencies. By mid-1968, unofficial sources of information had mostly dried up. A member's status could then be judged only by whether he appeared on those occasions when he might have been expected to appear.

Group affiliation explains a great deal, but not all, of the incidence of the purge (Table X). The Q correlation between belonging to a condemned group and being purged is .874. However, a few members of the condemned groups were re-elected to the CC, and a good many more members of the saved groups were purged.

Table X

Purge by Groups

	PC	HL	LT	TC	CEL	LP	CR	Total
Purged	24	14	19	9	17	6	8	97
Not Purged	2	1	2	1	19	12	14	51
Q (Purged)	.836	.755	.762	.762	.607	−.471	−.617	

Note: Those who died of natural causes, January, 1966-April, 1969, are excluded. Suicides are considered to have been purged. No executions of CC members were announced.

The Cultural Revolution was a power struggle, but not an "unprincipled" struggle; it revolved in part around issues of policy. The group explanation of the purge may perhaps be supplemented with an explanation based upon the Cultural Revolution as an "abortion of Thermidor." Thus, it is hypothesized that those CC members sharing "thermidorian" characteristics tended, on the whole, to fall victim to the purge. This general hypothesis may be broken down into several specific ones:

1. Purged members will tend to be younger than those who are not purged.

The "younger" members, whose born in 1906 or later, it is hypothesized, have had a greater opportunity to work longer in the day to day work of a large, complex organization. They will tend to be less "radical" than both the older members, who entered the Party at or close after its founding, and the Red Guards, who had been indoctrinated with militant ideology but had never had the experience of carrying out actual work and thus lacked appreciation of the difficulties of attempting to bring about social change.[51]

2. Purged members will tend to have spent all of their working careers within the Party.

These people will be more likely to acquire the thermidorian concept of the organization as an end in itself than will have those who left other kinds of work to enter the Party. This latter category will think of the Party as a means to some other end.

3. The purged will tend to have a lower educational level than those not purged.

Those for whom the organization provided their opportunity for upward mobility will tend to be relatively more concerned about the fate of the organization.

4. The purged will tend to be less "cosmopolitan" than those not purged.

"Cosmopolitan," it will be recalled, means "having studied abroad." It is asserted that those whose formative experiences were entirely in China will have a more "parochial" outlook, and will be more easily satisfied with small gains than those with more experience with the wider world. (Obviously, this is hypothesized only as a general tendency—Mao would be considered "parochial" in the table.)

5. The purged will tend to be alternate members of the CC.
6. The purged regulars will tend to have been elected in 1956.

These hypotheses assert that the lower ranking and more recent members, closer to mundane realities, will tend to be more conservative in outlook than those who have been longer at the rarified atmosphere at the top.

7. The purged will tend to have been engaged in economic work.
8. The purged will tend to have worked at the localities rather than the center.

The reasoning here is essentially the same as for hypotheses 5) and 6). These people are held to be closer to the actual mechanics of ruling a country, and thus will tend to be relatively conservative.

Table XI

The Thermidor Hypothesis

	1	2	3	4	5
Born pre 1906	−.432	−.328	−.480	−.150	−.100
Career in Party	.532	.443	.481	.132	−.225
More than HS Ed.	−.093	.127	−.191	.048	−.131
Cosmopolitan	−.183	−.426	−.121	−.042	.148
Regular	−.533	.111	−.707	−.261	−.034
Elected pre 1956	−.435	.067	−.357	−.620	.215
Economic Work	.083	1.000	.246	−.374	.803
Local Work	−.027	−.412	−.454	.502	.259

The columns represent: 1) purged v. not purged; 2) purged in condemned groups v. not purged in condemned groups; 3) purged in saved groups v. not purged in saved groups; 4) condemned groups v. saved groups; 5) "conservative" groups v. "radical" groups.
N same as for Table X, but for columns 1-3 includes Mao Tse-tung and Teng Hua, considered as belonging to "saved" group.

Column 1 of Table XI indicates that these hypotheses are for the most part supported,[52] although the education and cosmopolitanism hypotheses are supported only weakly. The relationship between being purged and engaging in economic work is also weak, while the "local work" hypothesis, as it now stands, must be rejected. These latter two hypotheses, however, may perhaps be "saved" by some proper qualification. Column 4 shows a negative correlation between economic work and membership in a condemned group; but column 5) shows a strong positive correlation between economic work and "conservatism." What this means in effect is that virtually all economic workers belonged to Chou En-lai's group, and this was probably the main factor in deciding their survival. According to column 2), no economic worker who belonged to a condemned group survived. There is hardly any relationship at all between being purged and engaging in local work, and what relationship there is in the "wrong" direction. There is a positive correlation between local work and membership in a condemned group, and also between local work and membership in a conservative group. The influence of the conservative regional soldiers in Lin Piao's group, most of whom survived, is a partial explanation for the low, "wrong" relationship in column 1). Another possible factor is that some local cadres may have come with a built-in power base: some of the "power holders" may indeed have held power, enabling them to ride out the purge.

In columns 2) and 3) the Thermidor hypothesis is tested "controlling" for group membership. Column 2) computes the relationship between each factor and the purge for members of the condemned groups. Since only six members of these groups survived, the numbers in column 2) should perhaps not be taken too seriously. These six include the historian Fan Wen-lan, one of the few CC members who did not hold an important Party or state office; his harmlessness and ill health may have saved him. He died in the summer of 1969. Chang Ting-ch'eng was identified with Liu Shao-ch'i by Chiang Ch'ing, but had been rehabilitated by October, 1967. The rest, Li Ta-chang, Liu Tzu-hou, Wang En-mao, and T'an Ch'i-lung were all local workers, reinforcing the previous speculations about the "power" of local leaders.

Column 3) lists the thermidorian correlations among those in the saved groups. The findings of column 1) are not "washed out." Some are weaker, and some are stronger, the correlation between being purged and engaging in economic work very much so. Local workers in a favored group stood a good chance of survival. In general, however, those purged within the saved groups tend to be the members with thermidorian characteristics.

Column 4) calculates the degree to which thermidorian characteristics are associated with members of the condemned groups, and column 6) computes the same information for the "conservative" groups, these being the condemned groups plus Chou En-lai's group and Lin Piao's regional soldiers.[53] The relationships tend to be in the expected directions, but thermidorian factors on the whole seem more potent in predicting whether one was purged than in predicting group membership. The best general predictor of the purge remains group membership, but this is reinforced by the independent impact of thermidorian factors.[54]

IV

THE ROLE OF THE "PARTY" UNDER THE EIGHTH CENTRAL COMMITTEE

The second chapter presented a kind of static analysis of the potential for Party control, as revealed in the structure of the Central Committee. This chapter is concerned with giving a more dynamic analysis, in order to determine the actual role played by the institutionalized Party during the earlier part of the tenure of the Eighth Central Committee—that is, up until the outbreak of the Cultural Revolution. This will be done primarily by examining the position of the institutionalized Party in the ideological pronouncements of the Communists during this period.

The political struggle *per se* will be discussed in greater detail later on. But a discussion of ideological shifts cannot be entirely divorced from considerations of relative power. In fact, in this connection the Marxist concept of ideology as the system whereby the "ruling class" rationalizes its position is a useful tool of inquiry. This chapter will examine the role of the Party *vis-à-vis* the Leader and the other political institutions, the state and the army. The relative position of these actors in the ideological pronouncements should provide clues to the then current power relations within China.

1. THE EIGHTH CONGRESS:
INSTITUTIONALIZED PARTY CONTROL AND THERMIDOR

The Eighth National Congress of the CPC was convened in Peking in September, 1956, after a long preparation. This Congress in retrospect appears to be the highpoint of the institutionalization of the Party. This institutionalization is reflected in the constitution adopted at the Congress. Relative to the 1945 constitution, Party procedures had been regularized. The term of the National Congress and the Central Committee it elects was limited to five years; the Congress itself should meet in annual session. The CC may postpone a session or call it in advance, but if one-third of all of the members of the Congress want a session, one must be held. As before, the CC was supposed to meet in plenary session twice a year, but in 1956, unlike in 1945, there was no provision for allowing the Politburo to postpone a session or call it in advance.[1] Such provisions were ignored in practice, especially in later years. However, their inclusion in the 1956 constitution indicates a reaction among the Party bosses against the rather arbitrary procedures of the 1945 constitution. Central Committee members themselves were granted more security of tenure. Under the 1945 constitution a member could be removed by a two-thirds vote of the CC.[2] In 1956 a member of any Party committee could be removed only by the body which elected him, which, in the case of the CC, meant the Party Congress. "If there is an urgent need," two thirds of the CC may expel a member, but the decision must be ratified at the next session of the Congress.[3]

The most dramatic change in 1956 was the absence of any mention of Comrade Mao Tse-tung or his Thought. According to the new preamble:

> The Communist Party of China takes Marxism-Leninism as its guide to action. Only Marxism-Leninism clearly demonstrates the laws of socialist development, and correctly points to the road toward communism.

The Party did not abandon the more useful tenets of "Maoism." Marxism-Leninism was still not a "dogma," but a "guide to action"; and "The Party in its own actions upholds the principle of uniting the general principles of Marxism-Leninism with the concrete practice of the struggle of the Chinese revolution."[4] But previously Comrade Mao Tse-tung had done the concrete applying; now it was the Party as a whole. Within the body of the constitution, "collective leadership" was made an explicit part of democratic centralism.[5]

Teng Hsiao-p'ing, the most vigorous opponent of the "cult of Mao,"[6] explained the new constitution. Teng noted that some changes had been made in the preamble of the constitution, but tactfully refrained from spelling them out. He said merely, "There has been a basic change in the political guide for the present period."[7] It seems the old guide, the Thought of Mao Tse-tung, was out of date. Teng blandly asserted that the CPC had never been cursed with any "cult of the individual," that "within our Party it has been a tradition that we have collective, not individual leadership." But there are still many defects in the actual practice of collective leadership. Teng softens the implications of his analysis with: "Marxism has never denied the role of leading personages in the governing of the Party."[8]

Liu Shao-ch'i also discussed Mao's relative fall from grace, but in more subtle terms than Teng:

> Everyone knows that the reason our Party's leader, Comrade Mao Tse-tung, could act as the great helmsman in the work of our revolution and merit the highest confidence of the whole Party and people is not only that he is skilled at coordinating the universal truths of Marxism-Leninism with the concrete practice of the Chinese revolution, but also because he firmly trusts in the strength and wisdom of the masses, leads the work of the Party according to the mass line, and firmly upholds the principle of Party democracy and collective leadership.[9]

Mao's own wisdom is no longer stressed; rather, he is great because he listens to other people; he is also great because he does not impose his own opinions on others. He leads because he "enjoys the highest confidence of the whole Party and people." Liu had in effect returned to his *Self-Cultivation* position. The drafters of the 1956 constitution were looking forward to Mao's political demise: "When necessary, the Central Committee may appoint an honorary chairman."[10]

The de-emphasis of the role of the leader was accompanied by an emphasis on the role of the Party itself. Liu Shao-ch'i criticized "a very small number of comrades who expect to weaken the leadership function of the Party in the work of socialist construction."[11] This small number of comrades probably worked in the state economic planning and administering bureaucracy. The then approved system of Party control over factories (and, by extension, all state offices) was one of "collective leadership and individual responsibility."[12] This had replaced "one man management," a system supposedly favored by Kao Kang. This system had allowed the factory manager (or the state bureaucrat) to ignore the Party, and resulted in the subordination of the Party to the manager.[13] Under the new system, policy direction and supervision were to come from the Party committee, and this direction and supervision would extend to all aspects of the work. But the responsibility for the outcome rested with the manager.[14] Liu Shao-ch'i admitted that the comrades were not all particularly qualified to lead much of the work in the economic sector. His solution was for the members to study technology.[15]

This system of Party control did not imply that the Party should do everything itself. Rather, while guaranteeing the supremacy of the Party, the Party during the Eighth Congress seemed self-confident enough to relax controls over society, allowing a kind of "return to normalcy." The growing institutionalization of the Party coincided with a thermidorian policy. Liu Shao-ch'i set the tone here: "Now the storm of revolution has passed, the new relations of production have been established, and the task of the struggle is now to protect the smooth development of socialism."[16] The country was seen as basically united under Communist rule. Class struggle, for example, continues, but it is a struggle against the "standpoint, concepts, and methods" of the bourgeoisie, not against specific members of that class. The struggle is to be carried out through education.[17]

The rein of terror against the enemies of the regime was to be replaced by the rule of law. Tung Pi-wu argued that the suppression campaigns and the like may have been needed in the past, but now they are obsolete.[18] He said that the past campaigns were too arbitrary, noting they had tended to feed the "petty bourgeois revolutionary fanaticism" of some comrades.[19] Lo Jui-ch'ing, then Minister of Public Security and the man responsible for the conduct of the purge campaigns, also discussed some of their defects. The campaigns were definitely a good thing, but death sentences had been passed down too casually.[20] Police should no longer use the third degree (逼供信) and "corporal punishment" (肉刑).[21] Also, we should distinguish between active counter-revolutionaries and those who merely have "bad thoughts"—things we often used to confuse in the past.[22]

2. THE MAOIST COUNTER-ATTACK ON THE PARTY

The dominant image of Chinese society presented at the Eighth Congress was of a unified, post-revolutionary country. legitimately ruled by a Communist Party now determined to carry out economic development, with an emphasis on orderly, gradual change. Mao Tse-tung played no important role at this Congress, delivering only a short opening speech. But in his speech Mao found a canker in the thermidorian rose: "Among comrades there still exist viewpoints and styles contrary to Marxism-Leninism. These are subjectivism in thought, bureaucratism in work, and sectarianism in organizations." These practices separate us from the people and hinder unity within and without the Party.[23] From Mao's point of view, Thermidor and institutionalization were beginning to bring about bureaucratism. Mao spoke only of "comrades," leaving vague the precise locus of bureaucratism. Liu Sho-ch'i found bureaucratism most rampant in the state organizations, and as a cure suggested strengthened Party leadership.[24] Later, and rather as an aside, he also admitted to some bureaucratism within the Party. The solution here is to "implement the principle of collective leadership and broaden inner-Party democracy."[25] Teng Hsiao-p'ing was more even-handed, mentioning bureaucratism in the Party and the state at the same time.²⁶ Chou En-lai, a cautious man, confined his remarks about bureaucratism to state institutions.²⁷

"Bureaucratism," as noted in the first chapter, is often concomitant with institutional development, and in 1956 this charge was aimed at a vulnerable point of the apparatus. Mao at that time certainly had reason to fear the apparatus. A charismatic leader works as a balancer of forces, but with the defeat of Kao Kang and his "clique" based apparently on the military and on certain regions, one of the major checks on the influence of the apparatus had been eliminated. By the time of the congress Mao stood in imminent danger of becoming "honorary chairman." Mao's counter-attack was directed at the apparatus's touchiest spot.²⁸

The nature of the "bureaucratism" of this period is well captured in a controversial short story published the month of the congress, "The Young Newcomer in the Organization Department."²⁹ This was an early product of the Hundred Flowers movement. A new Party member, Lin Chen, is assigned to work in the organization department of a Party Committee in Peking. He is, of course, filled with youthful enthusiasm, but soon discovers that his colleagues treat their jobs as dull and routine. Lin is assigned to organizational work among factory workers. He discovers one factory manager is given entirely to bureaucratic ways, is disgruntled with the system of "collective leadership and individual responsibility," and disregards Party leadership. The workers are apathetic. Since production is going well, Lin's superiors do nothing about the situation. Lin makes a direct appeal to the workers, and is called to task for not going through the proper channels. Word comes down from the Center that an anti-bureaucratism campaign is in order, and Lin takes this opportunity to act. He does get the bad manager dismissed; but because he criticized his superiors for not taking action, he is reprimanded for lack of discipline. As a kind of final straw, he discovers that a girl fellow worker who had sympathized with his ideas is married and has old-fashioned ideas about marriage; considers Lin naive; and thinks of him as a younger brother. At the end of the story Lin feels he has a more realistic view of himself and of Party work, but he is resolved never to give up his ideals. He will not adopt the attitude of his boss, "That is the way it goes" (就是那一回事)

The most interesting character, as it often happens, is not the protagonist, but the main antagonist, Liu Shih-wu, head of the organization department. Liu is a tired, competent, cynical man. He once tells Lin he wished he had more time to read stories, since they allow him to dream of marvelous things. Our hero, something of a young prig, is shocked: is not Party work marvelous? Liu says Party work is never the way it is presented in stories: "A story can say, As a result of energetic work, many new warriors enlisted in the vanguard of the proletariat, *wan sui!* [hurray! *banzai!*] " But in the organization department it is the never-ending routine of inspection, criticism, re-inspection, security checks. . .[30] One night while in his cups Liu talks of his life before Liberation. He had been a guerrilla behind enemy lines, and had suffered a leg wound. As a result, one of his legs is shorter than the other.

"How young I was then, how enthusiastic. . ."
"And now you are not young and enthusiastic?"
"Of course not. . .But I sure am busy."[31]

The story vividly delineates the condition of revolution in Thermidor. Superficially, everything is going well; but there is an underlying malaise. The storm of revolution indeed has passed.

Mao seems to have tried to exploit this malaise, taking advantage of the situation to create rifts. Under the 1956 conditions, non-Party intellectuals could easily come to feel the Party was just another ruling group like any other. The young intellectuals in the Party, like Lin Chen, would feel frustrated and disillusioned. The condition would also be a source of profound ambiguity for the more sensitive among the professional revolutionaries, men of the Liu Shih-wu type.

Mao launched two separate attacks upon Party bureaucratism. The first began in the summer of 1955, after the defeat of Kao Kang. At a meeting of provincial, municipal, and district Party secretaries (thus bypassing the Central Committee) Mao ordered a speed-up in agricultural cooperativization, calling also for greater activism within the Party: "Certain of our comrades are like women with small [*i.e.,* bound] feet waddling along the road from east to west grumbling to the passers-by, 'Too fast, too fast!' "[32] Mao urged greater unity with the "masses," and also a more generally radical outlook: "The problem now is not one of going too fast. It is wrong to say now that we 'exceed realistic possibilities,' or 'exceed the level of awareness of the masses.' "[33]

This led to a minor "leap forward," with the formation of many co-ops. But the agricultural situation was already infirm, and the results on production were poor. Perhaps because no political interests other than Mao's own were involved, the first leap came to a quiet end around April, 1956. In the spring of 1956 Mao circulated an inner-Party memorandum, "Ten Great Relationships," setting forth his "dialectical" view of economic development. The text of this memorandum used here (published by a Nationalist source; the Communists themselves, as far as

I know, have not released it) carries an editorial introduction: This text is based upon notes made from a speech by the Chairman. "Comrade Mao Tse-tung has recently read it over, but did not feel very satisfied. He has agreed to send it down for opinions." The Party cells should discuss the document and report back to the Center. The Center will then decide upon revisions.[34] This is exemplary inner-Party democracy, but it is not the way the Party bosses acted when they wanted something done. In effect, Mao's program had been tabled.

Stymied in one policy area, Mao moved to another—this time, the relations between the Party and the non-Party intellectuals. Mao now actively encouraged some of the emerging thermidorian trends—adopting, perhaps, in Solomon's apt phrase, a policy "right in form but left in essense."[35] Here again was another call for "unity with the masses," another assault on the entrenched autonomy of the apparatus. Lu Ting-i, speaking for Mao, announced in the spring of 1956 that a hundred flowers should bloom, a hundred schools contend. No one was exempt from criticism, Lu said; the Party in particular could be criticized. Some people are afraid this will breed disunity. They want mechanical obedience; we need "self-conscious and willing unity."[36] "Some Party members try to monopolize philosophic and scientific thought, and think they know everything（自以為是）..., acting just like idealists or bourgeois scholars. This is extremely dangerous."[37] Mao was launching an appeal to the articulate non-Party public, going over the head of the Party to invite criticism of the Party.

The apparatus as a whole was not particularly eager for this, and there was in fact no immediate upsurge of political criticism. But by the fall of 1956 the apparatus did make a few gestures toward criticism of the Party work style. On October 9 the *People's Daily* published a rather churlish editorial, which seems to reflect the views of Teng Hsiao-p'ing. Lu Ting-i's views of the perniciousness of mechanical obedience are repeated. Then the editorial goes on to say: no one person is always right. "In fact, there has never been a single person whose ideas are always correct." This platitude is not as innocent as one might think—good Maoists now recognize at least one exception. The editorial quotes "Comrade Teng Hsiao-p'ing" to the effect that we can even learn from mistaken opinions. But "to hold a liberalistic attitude toward mistaken opinions is incorrect, as need not be further explained."[38] "Some leaders" do not like cadres who have an independent view. They think only yes-men （唯唯諾諾） have organizational discipline.[39] The purpose of this editorial, which stresses a freer exchange of views *within* the Party, would seem to be to stiffen the backbones of the apparatchiks against Mao's attempts to open the Party to outside criticism, rather than to arouse this criticism.

The CC held its second plenum in November, 1956. Here Mao again warned against "subjectivist, sectarian, and bureaucratic deviations." "He emphasized: only if we uphold the Marxist-Leninist principle of depending on the masses, avoiding any form of the work style of becoming separated from the masses, will we and the Soviet Union and all the People's Democracies and the socialist strength of the whole world be able to overcome the difficulties of the road ahead and arrive at a great victory." Mao urged a "rectification" of the Party,[40] that is, a purge. But still nothing happened.

On February 27, 1957, Mao delivered his speech, "On the Correct Handling of Contradictions Among the People." Mao argued that there are two types of "contradictions." Some are between the "enemy and us," and they are "antagonistic" contradictions; others are "among the people," and they are non-antagonistic. The definition of the "people," it turns out, varies with the "historical conditions,"[41] or, in other words, the convenience of the rulers. But in any case, under present historical conditions, some disagreements with the Party are legitimate.

On March 5 Lu Ting-i announced a new rectification:

> The experience of the past few years proves. . .our Party cadres can be infected with the dust of bureaucratism. Some of our old Party members have become arrogant or have forgotten their Party experience, and a serious defect in style of becoming separated from the masses and from reality has arisen. These conditions demand that we arrange a new rectification movement encompassing the whole Party.[42]

On May 1 the Central Committee published a directive ordering a new rectification;[43] and the blooming and contending broke forth in a mounting crescendo of criticism of the Party and its policies, even its most basic ones.[44]

The nature of the criticism seems to have been more severe than Mao had expected. As early as the middle of May he told the Youth League:

> The CPC is the nucleus of the people of the whole country. Without this kind of nucleus the work of socialism will not overcome. . . Comrades, get united, firmly and bravely struggle for the victory of socialism. All words and actions which depart from socialism are entirely mistaken.[45]

On June 8, some low ranking apparatchiks announced that they "also want to contend a bit."[46] On June 9 the *People's Daily* declared in an editorial, "We need active criticism, and also correct counter-criticism."[47] The time for criticism, in fact, was over. By June 11 "unity under socialism" had become the dominant theme.[48] On June 19 Mao's contradictions speech was finally published, having been "revised and strengthened by the author, and also supplemented, according to the needs of the current situation."[49] In the official version of the speech, the people still have freedom.

> But this freedom is a directed freedom, this democracy is democracy guided from the center; it is not anarchy. Anarchy is not in accord with the interests or will of the people.[50]

The "people" were also told:

> There is in this world only concrete freedom, concrete democracy, and no abstract freedom or abstract democracy. In a society with class struggle, if there is freedom for the exploiting class to exploit the working class, the working class has no freedom from exploitation.[51]

The policy of the rectification of the Party by the masses came to an end, as the Party took up the much more congenial task of rectifying the masses.

3. THE TRIUMPH OF THE PARTY

On June 22, 1957, the apparatchiks gave their interpretation of the events of the past few months. "The spring of 1957," said a *People's Daily* editorial, "was an unusual time for the political and intellectual circles of our country." All of the usual events stem from Chairman Mao's February speech on contradictions within the people—a remark with possibly snide connotations. The popular masses brought out many correct criticisms. "On the other hand, certain bourgeois rightist elements whose hearts nourish dissatisfaction with socialism used the Party's slogan to broaden their own influence."[52] They distorted the true meaning of the attack on bureaucratism, subjectivism, and sectarianism, and tried to overthrow us. The editorial tries to give the impression that all of this had been anticipated:

> The Party, working on the principle that the awareness of the masses must be cultivated in the wind and the rain and not in a hothouse...decided temporarily not to respond, allowing the masses to recognize [the rightists'] faces...Thus, the brains [of the rightists] became ever more heated. As far as they could see, opposition to

the Party was everywhere: It was simply the eve of the Hungarian incident.[53]

This passage has given rise to a "conspiracy theory" of the Hundred Flowers movement: it is argued that the Party lured its opponents into showing their hand. This explanation is, on the whole, not very convincing, but it may be true in part. The crackdown did not come until the end of the first week in June, but Mao seems to have taken a harder position by mid-May. At that time, a fairly united Party may indeed have decided to give free reign for a while to its critics, allowing them to give vent to the rather extreme ("Kill the Communists") statements that flourished during the latter half of that month.[54]

The 1955 purge campaign, in somewhat bad odor during the 1956 congress, was now rehabilitated. Mao's contradictions speech was quoted: "In our country there are still counter-revolutionaries, but not many."[55] (In the original, of course, the stress was upon the "not many.") Some people, it was said, do not much like the "theory of hard to avoid" (難免論). (This is a reference to a piece of Party jargon used to justify the excesses of any campaign: in any complex struggle, the reasoning always goes, mistakes and defects are hard to avoid; fortunately, the mistakes and defects always turn out to be minor, localized, and already being corrected.[56]) The *People's Daily* found this an excellent theory:

> Naturally, if avoidable mistakes are not avoided, one may not escape responsibility by using the "hard to avoid" theory. But if a struggle like the purge is not implemented, counter-revolutionaries will remain; and if it is implemented, then some mistakes will definitely be hard to avoid.[57]

The 1956 emphasis on socialist legality was over. Bad elements were not to be coddled. And determinations of violations of the law were to be made by the Party, not by the courts: "We know that the Party is the nucleus of the strength of the proletariat, and that without the Party leadership there is no proletarian dictatorship and no socialist system." Hence, legal organs are to obey the appropriate Party committee.[58]

Lo Jui-ch'ing, the regime's top policeman, greeted the new year in a nasty mood. He discussed the 1955 purge movement with none of the defensiveness he had shown at the 1956 congress. Lo says the very victims of the purge had expressed their gratitude. They said: "This is the political equivalent of being washed clean." The thoroughness of the purge enabled us to avoid an Hungarian incident[59] —a statement tantamount to a confession the rulers felt their rule could be maintained only by terror. Lo also voiced approval for "mass participation" in the purge—a highly arbitrary procedure, at the extreme a form of officially manipulated lynching:

> The mass line is the line of a thorough purge. The rightists fear a thorough purge, so with all their strength they attack the mass line. They still stubbornly maintain that a mass purge is unlawful. From their point of view, legality means the masses endure destruction by the counter-revolutionaries and do not rise up and struggle against them.[60]

The rightists thought the storm of revolution had passed. This says Lo, distorts the true meaning of the Eighth Congress.[61]

The increased scope of the authority of the Party was accompanied by a new militancy and toughness. The grip of the Party over the common man was tightened in a "socialist education campaign."[62] The position of the more hard-line apparatchiks was represented by Teng Hsiao-p'ing. He was particularly uncompromising toward the intellectuals. Even those who are not rightists reek with other undesirable traits: individualism, liberalism, anarchism, equalitarianism, and nationalism. They need an education in revolutionary spirit, which they will get by working in factories and on farms.[63] In November, 1957, they were joined by Party cadres, a renewal of the attack on bureaucratism which had been more or less shelved in June.[64] This aspect of the "sending down" (下放) may have represented a concession to Mao's views on Party building; but the major purpose of the sending down at this time, in contrast to those of the 1960's, seems to have been to strengthen Party control in the rural areas.

The Party also set its own house in order, attacking members who had sympathized with the rightists during the blooming and contending period. These people—apparently Lin Chen-type young idealists—turn out to have been "bourgeois individualists."[65] In December, 1957, this inner-Party purge was expanded into an "anti-localism" campaign. A student of this campaign has noted that many issues were involved, but "the Party itself chose to regard the various mistakes of the purge victims as the result of bourgeois individualism," and that "the key. . .would appear to be organizational discipline."[66] An additional result (and probable motive) of this campaign was the radicalization of the local apparatus, pushing them into support for the Great Leap Forward.

The Leap began in 1958, growing out of the rectification and anti-localism campaigns. The Party of the Great Leap was one built in the Liuist, not Maoist, image. On July 31, 1958, the *People's Daily* reproduced a *Peking Daily* article, "What Kind of Ambition Should a Party Member Have?" The article criticized the views of one Chang Chia-jen (張家仁). The issues of the *Peking Daily* which carry Chang's original argument are not available outside mainland China, so the argument must be reconstructed from the obviously distorted version of it given in the critique. Chang, it seems, was an "idealist and bourgeois individualist." He

> takes the standpoint of the bourgeois class and examines the question [of ambition] from an idealist view. Under the pretext of "liberating thought" and promoting the "Communist style" [NB: These are both Maoist catchphrases—PM] he talks up (誇大) individual ambition, "independence,". . ."putting individual liberty above organizational discipline". . .He is against Party members being tools of the Party.
>
> Chang Chia-jen and others think that members who serve the Party and cheerfully obey all Party orders are "brainless' and "barren"(沒有出息) tools; moreover, they arrogantly say they can have no respect for that kind of member. We say, we are tools above all.⁶⁷

Chang, it would seem, expressed a "Maoist," Lin Chen-Lin Chieh type view of the nature of the Party, with a stress on individual spontaneity and initiative over blind obedience to the dictates of the organization. (It might be noted that the notion of people as "docile tools of the Party" was one of the views most strongly criticized by the Red Guards.) These "Maoist" views of the nature of the Party were rejected in 1958. Mao had failed in the short run in his effort to undermine the organizational cohesion of the Party, although he had succeeded in radicalizing that organization.

Thus far, the tightened discipline within the Party and the increased control of the Party over the daily lives of the "masses" have been stressed. The people, of course, were always at the mercy of the whims of the powers that be. More significant, perhaps, was the reallocation of power within the ruling stratum itself, as the Party organizations took over many functions of the state.

The encroachment by the Party on the courts has already been discussed. By July, 1957, the rectification had spread to the other state organs.⁶⁸ The major assault on the position of the state came during the Great Leap. During the Leap, "politics," that is, the Party, took command. Chiang Wei-ch'ing, first secretary of Kiangsu, explained that "the rectification movement is a communist thought liberation movement."

This thought liberation propelled the Great Leap, which was a liberation from the conventional bourgeois views of economic development.[69] This is in part a reflection of the distrust felt toward all educated people following the Hundred Flowers. But it also implied a rejection of the role of the experts and technicians employed by the State Council.

The most dramatic encroachment upon what had been the sphere of the state was the people's commune policy, in which the lowest level state organs in the country-side were in effect displaced by Party organs, and the national planning machinery was partially dismantled.[70] A summary of a meeting of the cadres of Sputnik (衛星) Commune in Honan, the model for all other communes, says the commune should take over all functions of the village (鄉), the lowest state administrative unit. The commune, in turn, was to be led by the Party. A Party organization should be set up at the commune level which would "absorb" all administrative personnel, although technically the Party remained distinct. New cadres should be recruited, and those with right opportunist thought purged.[71]

Although apparently originating with Mao Tse-tung rather than with the apparatchiks, the then popular idea of the withering away of the state also supported the current pretentions of the Party. The communes, it was argued, eliminate the vestiges of private ownership, and thus all of the inequities of capitalism. As this trend goes on, "The only duty of the state will be to oppose external aggressions."[72] "Domestically it is beginning to lose its functions."[72] The civilian bureaucrats were being given notice; but there was no hint that the Party also would wither away. This particular theme, however, was soon abandoned.

This vast expansion of the scope of authority of the Party does not mean that the Party was strengthened as an institution. At the 1956 congress the Party had been the leading control organization, but did not directly manage everything. Now the Party had also become an all-embracing manager, in danger of becoming a "coalition of the whole," or at least the politically relevant whole. As a result of short-term political greed, the apparatchiks appear to have undermined their overall position.

This seems to have been noticed by one of the more astute bureaucrats, Li Hsien-nien. "Some comrades have doubts," Li said. "After the cadres are sent down and government personnel become commune personnel, has their position been lowered?" Not at all. State organizations merged with the communes will also remain the basic level state organizations, and will still hold a "leading position." "The people's communes are under the leadership of the Party," but this means the leadership of

Party members in the communes, including the state personnel.[73] This is a counter-infiltration by the state into a bloated Party organization, undercutting the autonomy of the Party.

The Party had also created other problems for itself. At the Lushan conference in the summer of 1959, P'eng Te-huai said: "It is difficult for our Party to correct leftist errors but very easy to correct rightist errors. When adopting the left line none of us desires to express his opinions, because that line is very powerful."[74] This was certainly not true in late 1956, but had become true during the course of the rectification and the Leap. The Party had boxed itself in. The Party adopted an extreme "left" line to counter the right line of its opponents and to justify its expansion of its influence. But by expanding its influence so that it became the prime manager, the Party exposed itself to the forces making for Thermidor. Economic circumstances soon forced the Party to abandon the "left line" policies, but political circumstances did not allow a systematic repudiation of this line. The Party men who were forced to take the "capitalist road" became politically vulnerable.[75]

4. THE CULT OF MAO PRIOR TO THE RISE OF LIN PIAO[76]

As noted earlier, the 1956 congress represented a low ebb in the cult of Mao. The Hundred Flowers movement represents an attempt by Mao to regain his influence, although it was not marked by a revival of the "cult." The attempt was moderately successful, although, perhaps, not exactly in the way Mao might have hoped. The movement did not result in any immediate weakening of the apparatus, but, rather, in an expansion in its scope.

However, during the thermidorian phase the Party had operated upon the premise that its rule was accepted as legitimate by at least the articulate segments of the public. The Hundred Flowers demonstrated that this was not completely so. By the fall of 1957 some in the Party seemed to have felt the need to supplement the new tough line with any charisma Mao might have. In November, 1957, K'ang Sheng, a long time Mao supporter who had been demoted at the Eighth Congress, made a reappearance, explicating the master's thought on the October Revolution.[77] During the early stages of the Leap there was a systematic effort to build up Mao's charisma. Mao made a series of well publicized tours of China in the early part of 1958. During these tours he was hailed in such terms as "our beloved and respected leader," language which had not been heard for some time. The masses not only loved and respected him, but were also familiar with his every word: "Hearing Chairman Mao's words, everyone could not help but think of the words he had uttered as early as 1934: 'The fate of the victory of agricultural production lies in water control.' " This was still a human Mao, teasing and making little jokes with the masses. But he was beginning to acquire divine attributes: "Chairman Mao left. An incomprehensible warmth and happiness remained in the people's hearts."[78]

Shortly after the reports on Mao's trips began the press also began carrying reports of tours by other leaders, especially by Liu Shao-ch'i. One of the numerous chronicles of Liu's crimes published during the Cultural Revolution puts the following remark in Liu's mouth: "In the past I was for the cult of Chairman Mao, but now I am for the cult of Teng Hsiao-p'ing."[79] If Liu in fact said this, it does not imply he wished to raise high the red flag of the Thought of Secretary-General Teng. Rather, it means Liu had rejected the cult of the individual completely, in favor of Teng's emphasis on institutional authority. Liu's statement is dated from 1959, but he would seem to have held this view (if not consistently) since at least 1956. By juxtaposing his own visits with those of Mao, Liu was perhaps diluting Mao's impact, stressing that there was more than one great man in China. Liu did not challenge Mao's pre-eminence—he generally chose to appear in the humble guise of "Comrade Shao-ch'i." (No one *ever* refers to "Comrade Tse-tung.") But like Mao, Liu left an aura behind him:

> Comrade Shao-ch'i left. The spirit that he directed was quickly transmitted to every hamlet in the county. The resolve of the peasants to implement mechanization within three years was made even firmer, and the will to work was total.[80]

In any case, the cult of Mao was back in fashion. In the public report of the second session of the Eighth National Congress, held in May, 1958, the one who coordinates the universal principles of Marxism-Leninism with the concrete practice of the Chinese revolution was once again Chairman Mao.[81] The phrase the "Thought of Mao Tse-tung" was revived by Ch'en Po-ta, reportedly Mao's private secretary, in connection with the idea of the transition to communism:

> Very obviously, under the guidance of the TMTT, under the banner of Mao Tse-tung, in this time when "one day is like twenty years," during the universal high tide in economics and culture, our people are able to see that the time when we will make the transition from socialism to communism is not far off.[82]

A climax of sorts was reached on October 1, National Day:

> Today we have everywhere entered an era like the mythological

(神話) age. The old Greek myths were nothing but "myths." Today, the myth of heaven on earth (人間的天堂) has already appeared, in the era of Mao Tse-tung.[83]

This sort of hyperbole came to a temporary end after Mao's forthcoming retirement as state chairman was announced in December. During early 1959 the discussion of Mao's role seems to have been carried on in esoteric terms. In March, Kuo Mo-jo, Mao's court sycophant, urged the rehabilitation of Ts'ao Ts'ao as portrayed on the stage. Ts'ao Ts'ao, a general of the Three Kingdoms period and a noted poet, had come to acquire over the centuries an apparently mostly undeserved reputation as the blackest of villains in the popular mind. Kuo said that Chairman Mao admires Ts'ao Ts'ao. Ts'ao killed a lot of people, but not as many as is generally supposed. Ts'ao came from a landlord family, but he opposed the landlords of his time. He made mistakes, but learned from them. He was an objectively progressive leader.[84] This is a somewhat defensive plea for the recognition of the role of the great man in history, and for "Ts'ao Ts'ao" we should probably read "Mao Tse-tung." This is more obvious when we read a rebuttal to Kuo. This writer addresses himself to "Comrade Kuo Mo-jo," implying this is an official Party matter. He teaches us that Chairman Mao teaches us: "The people, only the people, are the motive force of history." We should write about the people, and not concern ourselves with the likes of Ts'ao Ts'ao "and other feudal rulers."[85]

The cult of Mao regained strength after the Lushan Plenum held in the late summer of 1959. This was the result of the rather complex political struggle at that meeting, and the possible causes will be discussed later. After the plenum Liu Lan-t'ao, in a speech attacking the rightists (those who agreed with P'eng Te-huai at Lushan), once more revived the phrase the "Thought of Mao Tse-tung." When we have followed the Thought, he said, we have succeeded; when we have departed from it we have failed. Mao's leadership is indispensable. We depend upon and benefit from his example, wisdom, experience, and his coordination of the universal truths of Marxism-Leninism with the concrete practice of the Chinese revolution.[86]

Mao's heyday perhaps began on January 1, 1960. On that day, Wu Chih-p'u, the arch-radical first secretary of Honan, announced that everyone in his province was studying the works of Mao. Mao advocates the "communist style." He is the "great helmsman of the revolution." He can teach us all about the dictatorship of the proletariat, the united front, peasants, economics, art and literature, imperialism, and the international communist movement. We must systematically study all he has said about all of these questions.[87] From 1960 onwards ritual citations of the TMTT became a part of many writings. The ground was being laid for Lin Piao's ploy.

5. THE PARTY ON THE CAPITALIST ROAD

Liu Lan-t'ao's speech in September, 1959, marks the revival of the cult of Mao. But the main thrust of this speech, which has been discussed earlier, was a reassertion of the leading role of the Party, coupled with an implicit critique of the over-expansion of the Party. This theme was taken up later in 1959 by An Tzu-wen, head of the Organization Department, in a discussion of Party organization on the communes. An too was beginning to see that the expansion of the scope of the Party was not an unmixed blessing, and that it was undermining routine control: "In certain communes, some people use all kinds of excuses, one-sidedly exaggerating the 'independent' activities of their system, and the special function performed by their department." But An was not yet willing to go to the root of the problem: he reasserted the direct management function of the Party on the commune.[88] Basic reforms, in fact, were postponed for more than a year, until the Ninth Plenum held in January, 1961.

This plenum initiated what the Maoists now call the "capitalist road," a stand-down from the radical policies of the Leap. During this new thermidorian period, as during the previous one, there was an emphasis on the institutionalization of the Party. The plenum announced a new rectification movement, but its targets were not clear. They included "bad elements who have sneaked into the Party," and also "good intentioned cadres" who lack awareness of the "distinction proclaimed by the Party between socialism and communism..."[89] These latter, at least, would include some of the more radical Party members. This rectification was not accompanied by any large scale purge, although two of the more prominent radicals, Wu Chih-p'u and Tseng Hsi-sheng, were later quietly demoted.

The period following the Ninth Plenum saw a general retrenchment of the Party. An important *Red Flag* article in October, 1961, argued:

> The Party is the vanguard of the working class, the highest form of class organization of the working class, the leader and commander of all other organizations. But it cannot take the place of all other organizations. The development of the functions of all other organizations under the united leadership of the Party does not weaken the nuclear leadership function of the party, but strengthens

it. We must not mix together the Party organization and all kinds of other organizations.
The Party should supervise the management organizations, not replace them.[90] The work load of basic level cadres was also reduced, following the plenum, supposedly to give them more time to study Marxism-Leninism and the Thought. They were told they must not engage in "blind busyness."[91]

The Party also seems to have tried to broaden its base. Cadres from minority groups once again were actively to be recruited.[92] As a category these had been somewhat in disfavor since the anti-localism campaign. There was a renewed emphasis upon the Party constitution,[93] and also upon broadening "inner-Party democracy." Ou-yang Ch'in said in July, 1961: "In order completely to develop democracy, it is necessary to hear all of the differing opinions of the cadres and the masses."[94] It is customary to blame the enthusiasm of the low ranking cadres for the excesses of the Leap.[95] But in fact the low ranking cadres had been under heavy pressure not to stress the difficulties they were encountering. The new stress on "democracy" seems intended to remove this pressure, encouraging low ranking Party members to be frank about unsuccessful policies, and thus avoiding a repetition of the mistakes of the Leap. This pressure against the low ranking cadres was openly admitted: "There is one way of speaking: Honest men are glorious, but they always come to grief. This way of speaking is not entirely correct (Sic: 不完全對)." In fact, under some circumstances, honest men will meet with troubles. "Although this condition exists, it is not good."[96] The new line was that "Party organizations must teach members to use the democratic prerogatives of Party members stipulated in the constitution," particularly free debate at Party meetings.[97]

But "democracy" was to remain subordinate to organizational discipline. The Maoist notion of service to "truth" was rejected:

> Some comrades still contrast support for truth with working according to the constitution: they contrast principle and organization. For example, a Party organization has passed a resolution. Some comrades feel this resolution is not in the spirit of the directives of the Party Center and of the higher levels. But because they obey the organization, they do not pass their own opinions up to the leadership. Opposed to this, some comrades support truth, pass their opinions on to the upper levels, and refuse to implement the resolution of the Party organization.

Both of these methods are held to be wrong.[98]

In sum, the period of the capitalist road saw a retrenchment of the "Liuist" version of Party building, although those who walked that road continued in general to quote Mao. This line was abandoned after the tenth plenum, held in September, 1962.

6. THE EVOLUTION OF THE ROLE OF THE ARMY

In 1959 the defense minister, P'eng Te-huai, was purged and replaced by Lin Piao. While differences in military doctrine were not the occasion of the purge, they did exist. The official Maoist version of this conflict had been formulated as early as 1961:

> But during the period when Comrades XXX and XXX [P'eng Te-huai and Huang K'o-ch'eng] were in charge of the work of the MAC, they violated Chairman Mao's military-building principles, promoted dogmatism with all their might, and followed the bourgeois military road of an unadulterated military outlook and of warlordism...Since Chief Lin [林總 —Lin Piao did not approve of formal military titles] took charge of the work of the MAC he has instituted a systematic management which follows the military-building principles of the Thought of Chairman Mao.[99]

Western students of Chinese Communist military politics tend, on the whole, to share this interpretation.[100] But the true situation does not seem to have been as simple as the Maoists have made it out to be. Thus, Alice Langley Hsieh, basing herself solely on the public record, pronounces P'eng a "spokesman for the Party."[101] This does accurately describe some of P'eng's behavior, if not his intentions.

In his speech to the Eighth Congress P'eng stressed the modernization and "regularization" of the army, "regularization" being the process whereby the PLA would become more like other armies, particularly the Soviet army. The stress here was on the military, not the Party, chain of command.[102] The Party committee, apparently, was not to have any operational responsibilities, but would help the army avoid "deviations of a purely military viewpoint or individualism."[103] P'eng said that "aside from strengthening our study of Marxism-Leninism and the works of Mao Tse-tung, we must also increase our study of modern military technology and modern command...systems."[104] He said that modernization and regularization of the PLA would not interfere with what he called "democracy."[105] He accepted absolute civilian policy control: "Leaders of troops thoroughly carry out the political line of the Party Center and the laws and orders of the government."[106] P'eng, in short, with his stress on autonomy within the army under a generalized civilian policy control, seems to have embraced what has been called the "professional" military ethic.[107]

Perhaps because of this rather passive professionalism on the part of the defense minister, the civilian apparatus exercised much more influence over the internal affairs of the army under P'eng Te-huai that it was able to do under the supposedly more "political" Lin Piao. In May, 1957, T'an Cheng, then head of the GPD, announced that the rectification would also apply to the army.[108] In September Teng Hsiao-p'ing reiterated this, attacking "rightists" in the army and noting the occasional poor relations between army officers and the Party.[109] By the summer of 1958 the rhetoric later made famous by Lin Piao had already become commonplace:

> Among some personnel, a simple military outlook, warlordism, and dogmatism have again stuck out their heads. These personnel falsely say that the leadership of the Party committee is not fitted to the needs of modernization and regularization. They one-sidedly stress the suddenness and complexity of modern war, and claim the Party committee system hinders the decision-making ability and centralization of the chain of command. They even want to eliminate the system of leadership by the Party committee.[110]

During the fall of 1958 the "sending down" of officers to serve a while in the ranks was stepped up.[111] This, perhaps the most obnoxious aspect of civilian Party interference for the officers, was quietly brought to an end by Lin Piao.[112]

It is perhaps not wise to overstress the differences between P'eng and Lin. Both men were in the same position, and would thus share many of the same political interests. Both men wished to control the army themselves, and both probably wished to keep the army free from interference from the civilian apparatus. Lin Piao certainly, and P'eng Te-huai probably, held ambitions beyond the military sphere, although Lin was much more systematically aggressive in this respect. The main difference between the men, perhaps, was one of strategy. P'eng pursued the passive strategy of professionalism until the summer of 1959, when he may have made a very clumsy and half-hearted attempt at direct military intimidation of the Party. Lin chose a more subtle and elegant strategy of advancement: he maximized his own personal influence within and without the army by stressing the role of the military Party,[113] using the Thought of Mao Tse-tung as his ideological base.

Part of Lin's strategy can be seen in his first major pronouncement after becoming Minister of Defense, published on October 1, 1959.

Lin wrote:

> Some comrades think: war now is not like in the past. In the past our army's weapons were of low quality; in order to win we needed to stress reliance on man, the courage and wisdom of man. Now war is fought with technical means, with steel, with machinery. In the face of these things the role of man is secondary. What they emphasize is machinery, and they want to turn the revolutionary soldiers and officers into mechanical men without revolutionary originality or spirit. We are just the opposite from them. We feel: weapons and techniques are important of course, but the factor of man is even more important.[114]

The professional attitude was abandoned. At that time Lin had not fully developed his strategy, or at least kept it concealed. The title of his essay raises high the "red flag of the military TMTT," a rare phrase at that time, and the text contains numerous citations to Mao. But the Thought *per se* is not exalted in the text. The article is a pledge of allegiance to the Party and the policies of the Leap as well as to Mao; and the main thrust is toward Party leadership in the army. Lin says: "Party spirit is no abstract thing...There must be absolute obedience to the Party, and no individual ambition..."[115] This was prudent: P'eng Te-huai had fallen because he did not display "absolute obedience," and because the comrades felt he displayed "individual ambition."

The politicization of the PLA served several functions for Lin. By seemingly giving in to the wishes of the civilian apparatus, he may for a time have lulled them into feeling there was indeed Party control of the army. The politicization of the PLA also put those who favored professionalism within the PLA, and were thus inclined to support P'eng Te-huai, in an untenable position. At the same time it would allow Lin to use the Party to legitimize his own ambitions. On this point, Lin's rhetoric must to some extent be differentiated from his practice. He was never as primitive and impractical as he liked to pretend. At the same time that he was stressing such slogans as "grasp Thought," Lin was also introducing the first large scale, systematic military training program for the PLA, with actual training time biased heavily in favor of pure military training. Lin Paio favored a 60/40 or even 70/30 rating of military to political training.[116]

The attack on the professional attitude was accompanied by what the *Work Bulletins* called an "internal purge (purification) movement." The attack on professionalism culminated in the elimination of military ranks in 1965.[118] This move seems to have been contemplated as early as

1961. In the *Work Bulletins* Lin Piao is almost always called "comrade" or "chief"—the approved nomenclature in 1965—and rarely by his formal title of "Marshal." The significance of the 1965 abolition of ranks was also made clear in 1961, when NCO ranks were abolished on the obviously specious grounds that such ranks were not appropriate to a conscript army. Appointment to the functions performed by NCO's would be decided by the Party committee, and approved by the camp commander.[119] By 1965, it would seem, all military appointments were in the hands of the military Party.

Lin did not confine his work to the army. He also attempted to place demobilized soldiers, no doubt those who had taken well to the indoctrination, in key positions in the local Party branches: "Historically, our army has been the school of our Party cadres...In fact, the army is able to train cadres for the localities...Our Party has grown out of the barrel of the gun."[120]

In his indoctrination Lin did not stress "Marxism-Leninism," a monopoly of the Party Center, but, rather, the Thought of Mao Tse-tung. This was not original with Lin. In the first chapter it was hypothesized that those outside the central apparatus would tend to look to the charismatic leader for protection against the apparatus. At the 1956 congress, the kindest words about Mao and his Thought were those spoken by P'eng Te-huai:

> Comrade Mao Tse-tung, according to the scientific principles of Marxism-Leninism and the actual practice of the Chinese revolution...has made a detailed and clear explanation [of military matters], and these works are the guide to action for our army in revolutionary war. History proves that whenever the Party has implemented the general line of the Center and of Comrade Mao Tse-tung the revolutionary war has succeeded; and when it has been disregarded, it has failed.[121]

Lin Piao raised the Thought to an at least equal level with Marxism-Leninism. Lo Jung-huan, a military apparatchik member of the Politburo, once eased out of active office by P'eng Te-huai, explained in 1961:

> Some people call the classic works of Marx, Engels, Lenin, and Stalin "theory," while the rest are not theory. This viewpoint is improper...We do not want to look upon truth as a dead, unchanging thing...If you refuse to study Comrade Mao Tse-tung's things (*sic:* 東西) then you do not have a proper Marxist-Leninist attitude, but are opposed to Marxism-Leninism, and, at the lowest limit, see the things of Marxism-Leninism as dead and absolute.[122]

The audience of the *Work Bulletins* were told, in fact, that for the most part, if they mastered the living study living use of the TMTT they need not bother about Marx, Engels, or Lenin.[123]

By 1964 Lin's strategy had paid off handsomely. In February the "whole country" was told to "learn from the Liberation Army," particularly in regard to studying the TMTT. The words of Comrade Lin Piao, it was said, were intended primarily for the army; but they apply equally well to all other organizations.[124] From that date, as far as the formal ideology was concerned, the source of legitimacy was not the organized Party but the Thought; and the Thought was best embodied by the army, not the Party; and, it was re-iterated time and again, the achievement of the army was the work of Comrade Lin Piao.

7. THE HUMILIATION OF THE PARTY

In 1961 and early 1962 the Party had taken steps to strengthen itself, but many factors were working against it: Lin Piao's independent "Party-building" line; the attitude of Mao Tse-tung; the unsettled power situation; the illegitimacy of the capitalist road policies. Other obstacles to stability seem to have been built into the composition of the Party. One of the "capitalist road" articles discussing Party building noted that 80 *per cent* of the Party members had joined since Liberation, 70 *per cent* since 1953, and 40 *per cent* since 1956.[125] The leadership, however (with the merely technical exception of Saifudin) was drawn entirely from the minority which had joined prior to 1949, and, indeed, virtually all of the CC members had joined by 1935. The Party leadership was increasingly becoming a gerontocracy. The statistics would indicate a lack of opportunities for upward mobility for the bulk of the Party members. This probably resulted in much discontent within the Party for ambitious men to exploit. At the same time, the performance of the Party during the Leap is not likely to have enhanced the legitimacy of that organization in the eyes of the "masses." The "Maoists" were able to take advantage of all of this potential for discontent.

The Maoist counter-attack began in earnest at the 10th Plenum in September, 1962. Toward the end of 1962 a "sending down" movement was announced. This would later develop into a new socialist education movement, but its beginnings were moderate. The emphasis in the beginning was on conducting "investigation and research."[126] The new line does not seem to have been settled upon until mid-1963. In March, 1963, Chao Han, one of the major spokesmen for the capitalist road policies in Party building, published an essay arguing against the Great Leap concept of the Party as manager; this also implied criticism of physical labor for cadres. Chao was concerned with preserving the autonomy of the Party, or, as he put it, maintaining the distinction between the Party and the masses:

> Some comrades mistakenly think that because Party cells should lead administrative organs and mass organizations this means that they can monopolize their work (包辦) . In fact, leadership and monopolization are two entirely different things. In leadership you must place yourself in a position of command, but in monopolization you drown yourself in concrete work. Leadership should develop the function of the led, but monopolization weakens the function of the led, leaving them nothing to do.[127]

In May what seems to have been the voice of Teng Hsiao-p'ing was again heard in the land. The *People's Daily* again instructed its readers that any single leader

> ...no matter how rich his experience, how deep his knowledge, how astute his powers of perception, cannot possibly grasp all aspects, all linkages, and the "core" of every single thing.[128]

The following month, however, the pronouncements began to take on a more Maoist tone. The *People's Daily* published what seems to be a rebuttal to the argument developed by Chao Han in March. Cadres must participate directly in physical labor. "To consider yourself a cadre, a leader of the masses and not the same as the masses, to consider yourself something special (特殊化) in fact means putting yourself above the laboring masses. This is a dangerous position." It means you are separated from the masses and in danger of undergoing metamorphosis (蛻化 —shedding the skin) and "changing your nature."[129]

The cadres, however, were not very eager to participate in labor. A production brigade secretary from Hopei, Wang Chih-hsiang, provides a vivid account of "How I Decided to Participate in Labor." "Last year," Wang wrote, "I only labored for two days. When I did not participate in labor I did not see very much, nor did I hear very much, and there were quite a few errors in my work." Some "old poor peasants" came to ask him to join in labor, but Wang just muttered things like, "We are working on these statistics." A "friend" came to visit him once, and said,

> Chih-hsiang, you cannot forget our bitter burden under the landlords. The landlords sat around and ate and drank and played music, and we called them stinking vermin that ate our flesh and drank our blood. We then made an oath that on the day of our triumph we would not only settle accounts with the landlords, but would also work alongside our poor big brothers...

Touched, Wang decided to go to work. "On the first day I...hoed a little, and also hauled some manure. I thought to myself, I'll haul a little manure and some firewood and let the members see me." The "commune members" (i.e., regular peasants), however, were not impressed. "The lazy dragon has come out of his lair," they laughed. "This will be a good year." Wang worked for two days, then decided to take a six days' rest. After all, he did not want to "monopolize the work."

Later some more "masses" came to see him, a rougher bunch this time. "Do you eat or not?" they asked—a reference to the socialist maxim that he who does not work neither shall he eat. "Even if I were vomiting blood," Wang decided, "I could not abandon labor."[130]

The implications of this article are interesting. We see here a break within the Party—Comrade Wang and his "friend." We also have a good view of the working of a "contradiction" between the Party and the masses. The contempt and hostility of the peasants for the cadre were probably genuine, but their manifestation was certainly not spontaneous. They would not have dared to show their feelings unless they knew they could get away with it. And we know that during this time the "poor and lower-middle peasants" were being organized to help rectify the Party. Even as early as 1963, then, one segment of the Party was using popular discontent to improve its own position *vis-à-vis* another segment of the Party, using the strategy of disgracing certain local "power holders" in the eyes of those they administered. The climax of this process was the Red Guard movement. In the early 1960's the autonomy of the Party was being eroded, and the foundation of the Cultural Revolution was being laid.[131]

APPENDIX: THE APPARATCHIK-COMMISSARS

During the 1950's most of the political commissars in the localities were career military men or career commissars. During the late 1950's and early 1960's increasing numbers of provincial secretaries began to be appointed commissar (and a few soldiers also became regional secretaries). By 1965 at least 23 CC members holding provincial or regional Party posts were serving as commissars for the troops in their areas. The bulk of these men were purged during the Cultural Revolution. (The exceptions here are Liu Chien-hsun, T'an Ch'i-lung, Wei Kuo-ch'ing, and Wu Te.) Lin Piao's strategy in the 1960's was a kind of ideological infiltration into the Party. The heavy casualty rate among the apparatchik-commissars suggests the hypothesis that the Party was attempting a kind of organizational counter-infiltration into the army.

This hypothesis may be tested by determining whether the local apparatchiks who were made commissars tended to belong to groups hostile or favorable to Lin Piao. The "hostile" groups include those associated with: P'eng Chen; Ho Lung; Liu Shao-ch'i and Teng Hsiao-p'ing. Groups friendly to Lin at the outset of the Cultural Revolution include those of: T'ao Chu; Chou En-lai; Lin Piao; and the Cultural Revolution Group. The results of tabulating the apparatchik-commissars according to group membership is given in Table II:

Table II

Political Relations of the Apparatchik-Commissars

	Hostile	*Friendly*
Appointed Commissar	13 (36%)	10 (56%)
Not Appointed	23 (64%)	8 (44%)

Kendall's "Q" for "hostile": $-.377$

These data suggest that the hypothesis must be rejected. The apparatchik-commissars are drawn disproportionately from groups favorable to Lin, at least at the beginning of the Cultural Revolution. This suggests a counter-hypothesis that Lin Piao had not only succeeded in stealing the ideological thunder of the apparatus, but had also managed to give his supporters within the apparatus some access to military power.

V

POLITICAL RELATIONS WITHIN THE CC PRIOR TO THE CULTURAL REVOLUTION

This chapter traces, in rough outline, the course and development of the various power and policy struggles among the Party elite from 1956 to 1965. It draws both upon the analysis of the evolving Party line delineated in the last chapter and the group analysis of the third chapter. The line was, of course, a product of these power struggles, but also, once decided upon, became a factor in further struggles. Here we concentrate upon the mechanics of how the various lines were determined, and thus trace the changing nature of political oppotunities. We also concentrate upon the role played by the various groups, or at least their leaders, in the struggle.

The evidence used is mostly the contemporary speeches of the members and what was said about the members during the Cultural Revolution. The speeches for the most part are those reproduced in the central press, since collections of local papers outside mainland China, except for the Canton papers, tend to be incomplete. There are suggestions that a more systematic study of the provincial press would add subtleties to, but not change the general outline of, our knowledge of politics at the Center.[1] Studies of Chinese politics after the Cultural Revolution will probably not be able to treat the provinces in so cavalier a manner. Mainly for purposes of simplicity, arguments over foreign policy will not be treated at all.

1. POLITICS OF THE EIGHTH CONGRESS

Table I gives the correlations between the members' status at the Eighth Congress in 1956 and their group affiliations revealed in the Cultural Revolution. The table also includes a P'eng Te-huai (PTH) group, consisting of members who seem to have joined with P'eng in 1959 and who were not later associated with any other group. In this table a person is considered to have the "same" status if his rank on the Eighth CC falls within five points of his rank on the Seventh CC. If he ranks more than five points higher he is considered to have been "promoted." If he ranks more than five points lower he is considered to have been "demoted."

Table I

Groups and 1956 Status

	PC	HL	LT	TC	CEL	LP	CR	PTH
Promoted	-.210	-.126	-.020	-1.000	.192	-.199	.252	.255
New Members	.370	.133	.290	-.217	-.594	-.213	.064	-.019
Alternates	.143	-.011	-.121	.293	-.295	.408	.121	-.577
Same	-.067	-1.000	-.377	.053	.692	-.287	-.416	-.102
Demoted	-.452	-.182	-.333	.052	.500	-1.000	.019	.133

N=165

This table does not give strong evidence that factional activity played much of a role at the Congress. The groups may, of course, have not had the same form in 1956 that they had in 1966, and in some cases this is almost certainly true. In any case, the table gives no straightforward picture of factional activity. The Chou En-lai group is over-represented among those whose positions were static and among those who were demoted, but also, to a lesser degree, among those who were promoted. Likewise, P'eng Te-huai is over-represented both among the promoted and the demoted. Lin Piao's group is strongly over-represented among the alternates, but Lin himself seems to have been inactive at that time, and there is nothing to indicate that he had anything to do with bringing this elevation of his future followers about. The PC, LT, and HL groups are over-represented among the new members, but not to a strong degree.

This need not indicate that "politicking" played no role at the Eighth Congress, but it does probably indicate that the results did not yield any clear-cut factional victory. Some changes at that Congress give hints of inner-Party struggles. Thus, both P'eng Chen and K'ang Sheng were demoted in Party rank, with K'ang falling farther, becoming a mere alternate member of the Politburo. The two men may have been long-term rivals. There is a story that in 1945 Mao wanted K'ang Sheng to be secretary of the Northeast region, but Liu Shao-ch'i wanted P'eng Chen, and Liu had his way.[2] Now, in 1956, a decision may have been made to cut both men down to size.[3] The atmosphere at the Eighth Congress was conservative and conciliatory, and probably more likely to have been produced by and to be conducive to bargaining and compromise than a simple factional victory.

Table II

Speeches and Group Membership

PC	.120	CEL	.391
HL	-.377	LP	-1.000
LT	.351	CR	-.300
TC	-.057	PTH	.146

N=165

Table II correlates having delivered a speech or written report at the Congress with group membership. Here again the relationships are weak. The groups containing the most military men, except for PTH, were particularly silent. The over-represented groups are CEL, LT, PTH, and PC. This tends to emphasize the conservative tenor of the Congress.

2. A HUNDRED FLOWERS BLOOM

The Hundred Flowers policy has been analyzed as a counter-attack by Mao on the position of the Party. Here we shall analyze, insofar as it is possible, the actual course of that struggle. In 1955 a vigorous campaign had been carried out against those intellectuals who were independent of the apparatus in their thinking, and, to some extent, organizationally. The campaign was conducted in the same terms as that against Kao Kang, with attacks on "independent kingdoms,"[4] suggesting a similar source.

In January, 1956, Chou En-lai urged a change in this policy. Intellectuals were called "our country's most precious resource." Only about ten percent of them are anti-revolutionary. Within proper limits, we should trust intellectuals. There is lack of understanding between the Party and the intellectuals, and the fault is on both sides.[5] Chou also said, "The Party Center has decided to make opposition to rightist conservative thought the central question of the Eighth Party Congress and demands that the whole Party take up this struggle."[6] From all other indications, the "Party Center" had decided no such thing. Rather, Chou would seem to have been launching his own counter-attack on the Party in roughly the same terms used by Mao in the cooperative movement, and appealing for support from educated public opinion. The Party's 1955 attack on the intellectuals was itself an indirect attack on Chou:

the intellectuals with scientific skills were indeed a "precious resource" of the State Council. Chou was now turning the tables, urging leniency toward intellectuals and accusing the Party of rightism. In May Lu Ting-i, speaking for Mao, urged the blooming of a hundred flowers, the contending of a hundred schools. Here seems to be an instance of the hypothesized alliance of the bureaucracy and the leader against the apparatus (with, obviously, some support from elements of the apparatus).

There was a lag of nearly a year between the call for blooming and contending and open criticism of the Party. The lag was a result both of the caution of the intellectuals and of opposition within the Party. At the Eighth Congress the arch-philistine Chou Yang, the man in charge of supervising literary output, gave a general endorsement of the hundred flowers line. He said socialist realism was not the only style, just the best ("most progressive"); he put in a pitch for his own favorite style, "revolutionary romanticism." But on matters of content, he preferred to quote Lenin:

> Just as Lenin pointed out, socialist literature is really the freest literature. In our country a writer in his own works can openly expose the evils of imperialism, capitalism, and peace with the enemy; sing the praises of national independence and the greatness of the people's revolution; sing the praises of friendship of the peoples of all countries; spread the ideals of exalted communism; bravely criticize all backward phenomena in the new society; and say what he wants to say.[7]

In the following months the opponents of the policy became bolder. In January, 1957, some functionaries of the GPD published an open criticism of the hundred flowers policy.[8]

Mao's contradictions speech seems to have been a turning point. Table III lists CC members who declared themselves in favor of the hundred flowers and Party rectification prior to June, 1957, in the *People's Daily*. To this list should probably be added T'ao Chu, who was an outspoken supporter of the policy in Canton.[9] K'o Ch'ing-shih, "Chairman Mao's good pupil,"[10] seems to have acted fairly consistently as a spokesman for Mao. Hsieh Fu-chih, although grouped with Chou En-lai, was then probably still with Teng Hsiao-p'ing. The remaining supporters of Mao's policies were all either P'eng Chen's or Chou En-lai's men.

Richard Solomon believes that P'eng Chen and Liu Shao-ch'i were the main opponents of Mao's policy.[11] The problem with this hypothesis is that P'eng, aside from his close associate Lu Ting-i, was the main public supporter of Mao within the Party apparatus. It is true P'eng thought rectification should be like a "gentle breeze and light rain,"[12] and that this mild interpretation of the rectification may have been the product of a compromise between Mao and P'eng in late April, 1957, as Solomon argues.[13] But it still seems useful to distinguish those who wanted a light rectification from those who would have been content with none at all.

Table III
Support for Rectification, 1957

Name	Source	Group
Lu Ting-i	PD, March 5	PC
P'eng Chen	PD, April 22	PC
Chou En-lai	PD, April 26	CEL
Huang Huo-ch'ing	PD, April 28	PC
K'o Ch'ing-shih	PD, April 28	unclassified
Teng Tzu-hui	PD, May 7	CEL
Liu Jen	PD, May 10	PC
Hsieh Fu-chih	PD, May 10	CEL
Po I-po	PD, May 11	PC

Full sources, where relevant, in bibliography. No citation there indicates mention in a news story.

P'eng actions make sense in terms of his political position at the time. The concurrent demotion of P'eng Chen and K'ang Sheng has been noted. The main beneficiary of P'eng's fall, however, was his boss in 1957, Teng Hsiao-p'ing, who had been promoted over P'eng's head. If Teng were then in charge of the central apparatus, P'eng would have an incentive to rectify the apparatus. But since he could expect to take it over himself, he would not want too severe a rectification. Mao would then seem to have headed a coalition of the state bureaucracy and certain "outs" in the apparatus: P'eng Chen and Lu Ting-i at the Center, and T'ao Chu, K'o Ch'ing-shih, and, perhaps, Hsieh Fu-chih in the localities.

Liu Shao-ch'i's position on the policy is obscure. His enemies, of course, are in something of a bind: had he favored the hundred flowers he would have been in agreement with Mao, and this could not be allowed (but, as in the case of T'ao Chu, could possibly be distorted or ignored); had he opposed the movement, he would have been right and Mao wrong, and this too could not be allowed. At the Eighth Congress Liu had mentioned the hundred flowers in connection with scientific research, and also said the Party should use persuasion with artists and writers, not force. But he was also afraid of "workers" being damaged by the "bourgeois or petty bourgeois thought of the intellectuals."[14]

Liu seems to have been silent about rectification in the national press, but delivered a speech in favor of it in Canton.[15] At the Youth League Congress in 1957 Liu made a speech which was not published at the time, but was later heavily criticized:

> In his speech the top Party person in power openly made these blatant remarks: With the disappearance of landlords, capitalists, and small producers, only the workers, peasants, and intellectuals will remain. I am afraid all you can see in the future are workers and peasants; you will not be able to come into contact with landlords and capitalists.[16]

These blatant remarks were later held to have been an open contradiction of Mao's thesis that contradictions continue to exist under socialism. But Mao's contradictions speech had not yet been "revised...by the author," and the stress was still on the benign nature of the contradictions. The positions of Mao and Liu may have been substantially the same.

But there is vague, inconclusive contemporary evidence that the rectification was not reflecting well on Liu's position in the Party. In his call for a new rectification Lu Ting-i mentioned only Mao's contributions to the previous one, and omitted those of Liu.[17] In April Tung Pi-wu quoted a letter someone had written to him referring to "our leaders... Chairman Mao, Comrades Chou En-lai, Liu Shao-ch'i, and others." The official order, of course, was Mao-Liu-Chou. Here Chou En-lai, a known Mao supporter, is raised above Liu. But later, in his own voice, Tung reverts to the normal order.[18] It is possible that rectification was directed in part against Liu, but for reasons of expediency or conviction he favored some aspects of it. Liu's exact position on this matter remains unclear.

The discussion of P'eng Chen's position implied that Teng Hsiao-p'ing would have been opposed to rectification. There is negative evidence that this was so. Teng was silent about rectification during the "unusual spring," but he delivered the report on the rectification at the Third Plenum.[19] By this time the leading role of the Party had been reasserted. The stress was on Party discipline and on not coddling the intellectuals and their petty bourgeois ways. During the spring Teng had an opportunity to declare himself in favor of rectification, but he chose not to do so. He delivered a speech at the youth congress, but did not talk about rectification or the hundred flowers, contenting himself merely with trite statements against sectarianism, dogmatism, and bureaucratism. He alluded to some statements by "Comrade Mao Tse-tung" in his text, but omitted Mao from his list of "long lives" at the end.[20] In contrast, Hu Yao-pang concluded his address to that Congress with a rousing "Long live our great leader, Chairman Mao Tse-tung."[21]

The short-term political effect of the failure of the hundred flowers seems to have been the further strengthening of the position of Teng Hsiao-p'ing, although Teng's own efforts had little to do with this. Proabably to consolidate more firmly his position, Teng began to promote an anti-localism campaign in the fall.

3. THE POLITICS OF ANTI-LOCALISM

Five local apparatchiks on the CC were criticized during 1957 and 1958: Ch'en Man-yuan of Kwangsi, P'an Fu-sheng of Honan, Feng Pai-chü and Ku Ta-ts'un of Kwangtung, and Chao Chien-min of Shantung.[22] The earliest purge, that of Ch'en Man-yuan, would seem to be a special case. He was removed from office immediately after the crackdown on the hundred flowers, but his sins seem to have been that he had the style and attitudes which had been a target of that movement. He "developed to a serious degree an arrogant and self-satisfied attitude and a bureaucratic work style." The occasion for his purge was a famine in Kwangsi, for which he and the provincial governor were held responsible.[23]

The anti-localism campaign began in December, 1957.[24] As early as September, however, Teng Hsiao-p'ing was hinting at such a campaign. He discussed the "localization of cadres," the idea that cadres should be natives of the places where they worked. There is nothing wrong with this in itself, said Teng, but it is not the "main problem." The main problem is the "communization" (共產化), not the "localization" of cadres. Some local cadres even try to cause trouble for cadres sent from outside.[25]

By the time of the second session of the Eighth Congress in May, 1958, the purge had extended to Chekiang, Kansu, Anhwei, Yunnan, Kwangsi, Tsinghai, Hopei, Kwangtung, Sinkiang, Honan, and Shantung.[26] The purge can be discussed in three parts: the purge in general, the campaign against local nationalism, and the Kwangtung purge.

A. The Anti-Localist Purges

The anti-localism purges were ratified at provincial Party congresses carried out in preparation for the second session of the Eighth National Congress. The "model" purge was that of Chekiang. The major speech was delivered by Chekiang First Secretary Chiang Hua and was carried by the *People's Daily*. Readers were advised that "Although this is long, it is worth reading patiently in its entirety."[27] Chiang Hua has been classified in the Chou En-lai group because the Red Guards belabored him for his past associations with T'an Chen-lin (a working of the "transivity" rule). But in December, 1957, he does not seem to have been speaking for Chou. He is liberal with quotes from Teng Hsiao-p'ing.

His speech is an attack on the "localists" within the Chekiang Party. These people were infected with rightist conservatism. For example, they were concerned only that farmers had enough to eat and did not care about thought education. It is also clear that they had been in sympathy with the blooming and contending. Chiang was particularly harsh here: some people think our correct handling of the rightists has led to left deviation. This is not so. Persuasion will not work with these rightists, despite what "some comrades" think. "The bourgeois rightists and their anti-socialist elements absolutely do not die quietly." They respond only to dictatorship, oppression, suppression. "On this question, there are not a few comrades within the Party who have not studied enough the directives of the Party Center and Chairman Mao."[28]

But some of these comrades, perhaps, made their voices heard. K'o Ch'ing-shih delivered a speech at the Shanghai congress; Chou En-lai was present at the congress. Both men had been strong supporters of the hundred flowers. There was no major Party purge in Shanghai, and the tone of K'o's speech is different from Chiang's. The editorial board of the *People's Daily* did not think as highly of this speech. The speech is very long, the reader is told, and most of it concerns Shanghai alone. Those who lack the inclination to read the whole thing need read only certain parts.[29]

K'o says some comrades do indeed have rightist thought. "This black wind, while not very serious, is worthy of attention."[30] For the most part these comrades are still among the people.

> Some comrades like to use oppressive methods to handle contradictions among the people, always thinking persuasion is too slow or of too little effect. This is without foundation. These people seem to be very "left." In fact they are, on the contrary, very right. Facts prove that among the people persuasion is the most positive and effective Marxism.[31]

It can perhaps be argued that the "contradictions" in Shanghai were in fact "among the people," while the situation in Chekiang was objectively more serious, but this would not be very plausible. This would seem instead to indicate a disagreement within the Party: some, like

Teng Hsiao-p'ing and apparatchiks like Chiang Hua favored a tough line, while others like Chou En-lai and K'o Ch'ing-shih favored a milder policy. K'o was always close to Mao, and this may indicate that Mao himself was out of sympathy with the way the purge was developing.

Other evidence on this point is ambiguous. Among the CC members purged at this time, Chao Chien-min, Feng Pai-chü, and Ku Ta-ts'un for all effective purposes dropped out of politics. But P'an Fu-sheng emerged from the Cultural Revolution as boss of Heilungkiang Province, to be "re-purged" in 1971. It is possible that his relations with the "Maoist" groups date back to 1957.[32] If we consider those CC members who ruled purged provinces but who were themselves not purged as the "beneficiaries" of the purge, it is not clear that the purge advanced the status of Teng Hsiao-p'ing, the strongest advocate of the purge (Table IV). But it is notable that not a single provincial leader associated with P'eng Chen "benefitted" from the purge (or, by another interpretation, all of P'eng Chen's men were strong enough to prevent a purge in their provinces). Chou En-lai's extraordinary showing can be explained away: Chiang Hua was probably acting as a spokesman for Teng Hsiao-p'ing, and Hsieh Fu-chih was at that time supposedly also one of Teng's cronies.

Table IV
Beneficiaries of the Purge

	PC	HL	LT	TC	CEL	LP	CR	PTH
Beneficiaries	0	1	3	3	3	0	2	1
Not Beneficiaries	7	3	5	3	1	0	2	1
Kendall's Q	-1.000	-.333	.021	.318	.714	-1.000	.569	.250

It will be argued later that during the early 1960's power in the Party Center tended to shift away from Teng Hsiao-p'ing to P'eng Chen, and thus the "Liu-Teng" group is not an accurate reflection of the strength Teng may once have had. The anti-localist purge provided Teng with his main opportunity for strengthening his hold on the provinces. The total evidence is consistent with, if not supportive of, this hypothesis.

B. The Campaign Against Local Nationalism

The anomalous position of Ulanfu has been noted before. His satrapy in Inner Mongolia would be an obvious target in any campaign to strengthen the power of the Center. It was later alleged against Ulanfu that he wanted to detach Inner Mongolia from China, but this is unlikely, especially since it is hard to see what Ulanfu would have gained by such a move. But it is possible that he would have liked to run his own show in Inner Mongolia, with no meddling from the Center. During the 1956 Congress Ulanfu complained that the Party had not been active enough in recruiting cadres from minority groups, and said that often Han cadres would not let minority cadres exercise their proper functions.[33] Obviously, Ulanfu would have preferred to recruit his own Mongol cadres, a process he could control, rather than have to rule through the Han cadres the Center saw fit to assign to Mongolia.

Mao Tse-tung does not seem to have been unduly worried about Ulanfu's position, and may even have supported it as a balance to the influence of the central apparatus. At the second plenum of the Eighth CC Mao "demanded that the entire Party absolutely oppose Great Han chauvinism."[34] He did not even, as did Ulanfu, add parallel strictures against "local nationalism."

In July and August, 1957, a conference to "rectify" the minority areas was held. Mao Tse-tung and Chou En-lai attended the closing session, in this case probably implying their approval for what was going on, as there seems to have been no compelling reason for their being there. Ulanfu made the concluding speech. All nationalities in China, he said, "will develop into socialist nationalities, and must undergo the necessary social reforms."

> But when will these reforms be made, and how will they be implemented? This will be decided by the peoples of the nationalities and...the leaders who are united with the people [i.e., of the locally dominant race] and absolutely not by the force of the People's Government or by Han working personnel.[35]

In September Teng Hsiao-p'ing had other ideas. Great Han chauvinism is a very bad thing, he said, but he was more concerned at present about "nationalism," "a serious aspect of bourgeois thought."[36] In December, as the anti-localist campaign was warming up, the *People's Daily* carried a speech by Saifudin of Sinkiang, like Ulanfu a "minority cadre," unlike Ulanfu a compliant Party hack. Saifudin agreed with Teng Hsiao-p'ing: "At present local nationalism is the most dangerous deviation in thought." Some "sincere comrades" (Ulanfu?) also dislike local nationalism, but want special privileges for their own nationality. (In his August speech Ulanfu had stressed the "special characteristics" of each nationality.) Saifudin explicitly contradicts Ulanfu's main thesis: "The fate of all nationalities in Sinkiang is exactly the same as that of the Han. We must certainly move forward with [literally, 'under'] the help of Han cadres."³⁷ In January, 1958, Liu Ko-p'ing, of Moslem origin (the Communists consider the Moslems in China a separate nationality) weighed in with another attack on local nationalism. From this we learn that the nationalities conference had apparently been reconvened.³⁸ The concluding speech at this meeting, published in March, was made by Wang Feng. This speech bears the marks of a compromise. The main problems, he thinks, include "unprincipled demands for autonomy," which lead to "fragmentationalism"; conservatism; and bourgeois nationalism which disrupts the Party organization.³⁹ But there are concessions to the views of Ulanfu. Minority cadres should certainly be "cultivated," as long as they "become communized." Moreover, "Han Party members and cadres must earnestly criticize Great Han chauvinism, and are not to relax this criticism just because local nationalism has achieved a new growth."⁴⁰ There is perhaps the implication that minority cadres themselves should go easy on complaints about Great Han chauvinism.

In May Ulanfu capitulated. He recited the currently modish slogans ("The liberation in though brings about a liberation in production. . .") and denounced "dogmatism and pragmatism," "rightism," and "nationalism, especially local nationalism." There is need for "socialist relations among nationalities." Many Mongol cadres, he said, turned out to be rightists. He concluded with the assertion that Inner Mongolia would follow all of the directives of the Party Center.⁴¹

If Teng Hsiao-p'ing had intended to purge Ulanfu, he failed. The rectification did not penetrate deeply into Mongolia. But Teng did manage, temporarily, to bring Ulanfu to heel. As in the more general campaign against local nationalism, it seems likely this was not in full accord with the opinions of Mao Tse-tung.

C. *The Kwangtung Purge*

Because of a fairly strong native Communist movement (coupled, perhaps, with Kwangtung's rather special status as the main non-Mandarin speaking area) the problem of localism in Kwangtung was perhaps more serious than in the other Chinese areas, and an anti-localism purge had been carried out in the early 1950's.⁴² The 1957-1958 purge claimed the two most important localists, Feng Pai-chü, the former Communist boss of Hainan recently "promoted" to vice-governor of Kwangtung; and Ku Ta-ts'un, a provincial secretary. The charges against these men, as revealed by Ou Meng-chüeh (herself a Cantonese), were rather routine. As with the other "localists," to the outsider it seems one main fault was that they retained too much "bourgeois" common decency—*i.e.*, holding an overly humane attitude toward the "enemy." Ku had said of the social suppression movement: "For every man we kill we make nine enemies."[43] More importantly, they chafed under the rule of "outside" cadres. They said that these cadres "do not understand the historical conditions of Kwangtung," they are "subjectivist," they "screw up the work" (把工作搞壞了.).Feng Pai-chü had a "theory" (Miss Ou's quotes): "Command by cadres sent south violates Marxist principles."[44]

All this is very much in line with the general anti-localist rhetoric. Miss Ou calls the purge a "victory for the Party Center."[45] But was it? Elsewhere Miss Ou writes that the decision to purge was made in August, 1957.[46] If true, this would be in advance of the Center's decision to fight localism. Ku and Feng had been relatively inhibited since the first anti-localist campaign, but in August, 1957, Feng at least was in good enough favor to have a speech of his published.[47] That month the ruler of Kwangtung, T'ao Chu, had problems other than localism on his mind. He told reporters that because of the anti-rightist movement "some people think the Party rectification is a fake." We must not slacken our opposition to bureaucratism, sectarianism, and subjectivism.[48]

All this together indicates that by August T'ao Chu was at least mildly dissatisfied with the trends at the Center, and that he was planning a purge. The decision to make this an anti-localist purge may have been a way of staging the purge in such a way that Teng Hsiao-p'ing could not object to it. This too had its utility for T'ao, by eliminating once and for all any potential opposition from the native apparat. But the decision itself seems to have been made independently of and prior to that of the Center. This may help explain T'ao's position in the Cultural Revolution, when he was able to lead a bloc of local apparatchiks in opposition to the men in control of the Center. Kwangtung seems to have been an instance of what might be called "neo-localism": a high degree of autonomy for the "cadres sent south."

4. ECONOMIC RADICALISM

The September, 1956 Congress had been thermidorian in economic policy, as in most else. Chou En-lai set the tone with an attack on "blind adventures" (盲目冒進) which he felt had sometimes characterized previous economic projects.[49] Arch-moderate Ch'en Yun, then Minister of Heavy Industry, the "patron saint of counter-revolutionary economism" (反革命經濟主義祖師爺)[50] criticized the 1955 "high tide of socialism." He spoke of the need for the Party to rely on the "skills and experience" of the "national capitalists."[51] He opposed the extension of the "unified selling and purchase" system on the grounds that even as it was it tended to hold up production.[52] The other members of the future Chou En-lai group who spoke on economic management did not push moderation to the extremes of Ch'en Yun, but their statements tended to stress "reasonableness," "balance," caution, and a limited reliance on the free market.[53]

Beginnings of a change were in evidence at the Third Plenum of September, 1957. The economic pronouncements of that Plenum are rather murky. For this plenum, Schurmann's generalization that plenums coincided with major policy decisions may not hold.[54] It is hard to determine exactly what the third plenum accomplished, at least in economic policy. According to the public pronouncement of the plenum, Ch'en Yun had delivered a report on increasing agricultural production, and this report had been "approved."[55] Ch'en's speech was not published, but its contents are probably reflected in a series of three directives dated a week prior to the convening of the plenum.[56] These directives advocate a system of material incentives for farmers, the "three packages [i.e., contracts] and one reward" (三包一奖), involving bonuses for farmers who over-fulfilled their quotas.[57] An easy-going approach to class struggle was also urged. We must "depend" upon the poor and middle farmers (the more Maoist formula would read "lower middle"). As for the "rich":

> We certainly want to strengthen ideological leadership, criticizing the capitalist thought of these people...But economically we should have proper regard for their reasonable interests, sincerely implement mutual benefit policies, and do nothing to damage their interests. If we do not act in this way we will commit the mistake of "left" deviation.[58]

All this is probably what the plenum "approved." But the plenum also "passed the 1956-1967 Program for Agricultural Production (Revised)."[59] This was a revival of Mao's program of development which had been shelved in 1956.[60] The "passing" of this program was not unequivocal: "The revised draft will be propagated among the villages of the country for discussion, and will be discussed at the National Party Congress and the People's National Congress..."[61] The public report of the plenum probably reflected a deadlock within the highest councils of the Party, a deadlock this grossly "enlarged" meeting (more than 500 participants) was in no position to resolve.

At the plenum, in some aspects of this policy arena if not elsewhere, Mao seems to have had the support of the central apparatus. Teng

Hsiao-p'ing said:

> Within the Party in the most recent period there has appeared serious right deviationist thought: it is the thought that the struggle between the two roads in the countryside has already been concluded, and that the class line may be relaxed.[62]

The proposals of the three pre-plenum directives were exactly to "relax" the "class line."

During the fall of 1957 the radicals picked up strength. On December 28 Chu Te announced that in 1958 China could make a "huge leap forward" (巨大躍進) in agriculture,[63] although it is likely that no specific plans had yet been made. In February the reports of provincial secretaries began coming in. The main support for the Leap seems to have come from the provincial apparatus, although the decision to make the Leap, if there ever was anything clear cut enough to be called a decision, clearly came from the Center. If those who unequivocally pronounced themselves in favor of the Leap in the central press prior to October, 1958, are counted as "radicals" (a measure involving some oversimplification, as will be noted) there is a .610 Q-correlation between being a provincial secretary and radicalism. Table V lists the most vocal supporters of the radical policies, along with the general nature of their jobs and their later group affiliations.

The Table indicates that the support for the Leap came primarily from the Party, particularly the local Party. The central bureaucracy is represented by the probably reluctant Nieh Jung-chen, the agricultural bureaucrats T'an Chen-lin and Liao Lu-yen, the minister of education Chiang Nan-hsiang (who did not have responsibility for economic affairs), and by Po I-po, whose relations with the central apparatus were closer than those with the bulk of the bureaucrats under Chou En-lai. It should be noted that P'eng Chen's local following is represented only by T'ao Lu-chia, then in Shansi.

Schurmann argues that many of the specific leap policies were first devised locally.[64] Mao Tse-tung said at Lushan of the probable inventor of the commune system in its early form: "Whenever the name of Wu XX (Chih-p'u) is mentioned, everybody gets nervous."[65] The local apparatchiks were responding to two forces: the threat of rectification and the promise of absorbing the local state machinery.

The Communists were quite explicit about the link between rectification and the Leap. As a slogan of the time had it: "Ride the wind of rectification, propel a great leap forward in production."[66] Wu Chih-p'u said of his former boss, P'an Fu-sheng, "Comrade P'an Fu-sheng is a

Table V

The 1958 Radicals

Name	Source	Job	Group
K'o Ch'ing-shih	PHB, 1958	LA	Unclassified
Wang Jen-chung	PD, Feb. 15, 1958 RF, June 1, 1958	LA	TC
K'ang Sheng	PD, Feb. 15, 1958	CA	CR
Tseng Hsi-sheng	PD, March 15, 1958	LA	Unclassified
Nieh Jung-chen	PD, March 15, 1958 PD, Aug. 2, 1958	CG	CEL
Liu Lan-t'ao	PD, March 18, 1958	CA	HL
Wang Ts'ung-wu	PD, March 18, 1958	CA	Unclassified
Chou Yang	PD, March 31, 1958 RF, June 1, 1958	CA	PC
Ch'en Po-ta	PD, May 5, 1958 RF, July 1, 1958 RF, July 15, 1958	CA	CR
Chiang Wei-ch'ing	PD, May 14, 1958	LA	LT
T'ao Lu-chia	PD, May 16, 1958	LA	PC
Lin T'ieh	PD, May 16, 1958	LA	LT
Ulanfu (?)	PD, May 21, 1958	LA	LT
Yeh Fei	PD, May 22, 1958	LA	LT
Chou Hsiao-chou (?)	PD, May 23, 1958	LA	PTH
Liu Shao-ch'i	PD, May 27, 1958	–	LT
T'an Chen-lin	PD, May 28, 1958	CG	CEL
Chang P'ing-hua	PD, May 28, 1958	LA	TC
Mao Tse-tung	RF, June 1, 1958	–	Unclassified
Liao Lu-yen	PD, June 3, 1958	CG	CEL
Chao Chien-min (?)	PD, June 7, 1958	LA	Unclassified
Fan Wen-lan	RF, June 16, 1958	–	PC
Ma Ming-fang	PD, June 23, 1958	CA	PC
Po I-po	RF, July 15, 1958	CG	PC
T'ao Chu	RF, August 1, 1958	LA	TC
Li Hsueh-feng	RF, August 1, 1958	CA	CR
Lu Ting-i	PD, September 2, 1958	CA	PC
Wu Chih-p'u	RF, September 16, 1958	LA	Unclassified
Chiang Nan-hsiang	RF, September 16, 1958	CG	PC
T'an Ch'i-lung	RF, October 1, 1958	LA	TC

? – indicates doubts about sincerity of commitment.

CG–Central Government; LA–Local Apparatus; CA–Central Apparatus. For full citations, see bibliography. No item there indicates support expressed in news story.

through pessimist, the opposite of communist optimism *(sic).*" He wants to walk the capitalist road, covering this up (美其名) with the Leninist slogan, "Two steps forward, one step back." "When he could not walk the capitalist road he felt the road ahead too vast, and fell into pessimistic despair."[67]

The provinces did not, however, have general policy initiative. At the Center the critical factor in inducing the leap seems to have been rivalry between Liu Shao-ch'i and Chou En-lai (a pair of natural rivals), or, in institutional terms, the state bureaucracy which had been running the economy and the Party apparatus which wanted to run it. With the benefit of hindsight some Western observers now find traces of moderation in Liu's pronouncements of 1958.[68] But the accusations against Liu during the Cultural Revolution, which are quick to seize upon any sentence of Liu's which could be given a "moderate" interpretation, for the most part skip demurely over any crimes he may have committed in 1958. One source does not:

> In 1958 Liu took the lead of whipping up the wind of extravagant things. He called for "fields that give a higher and higher yield," "reaping a bigger harvest through less planting," and "free meals," thus bringing about the subsequent difficulties that lasted over a period of time.[69]

In other words, Liu had been a supporter of the Leap.

In his speech to the second session of the Eighth National Congress in May 1958, Liu closed in on Chou En-lai. Some comrades think "right is better than left," "slow is better than fast." Rectification took care of this kind of thinking. We made a leap in early 1956, but "some comrades" said this was a "reckless advance" (Chou En-lai and Ch'en Yun had said this). A great and quick effort is needed to lift China out of poverty, but "some comrades" (the planning bureaucrats Li Fu-ch'un and Li Hsien-nien probably) fear imbalance. This is wrong. We must advance on all fronts at once. "Some people" say this will impose great hardships on the people; the alternative is continued poverty, which imposes greater hardships.[70]

Chou En-lai had much to lose in the Leap, but he kept his own position ambiguous. In February, 1958, he pronounced himself in favor of the "general line," but in a rather curious way: "We want much fast good cheap (多快好省)," he said, "not little slow inferior expensive." This, of course, was hardly the point. No one had argued that "little slow inferior expensive" were desirable in the abstract. By posing the problem in these terms Chou was perhaps trying to trivialize the general line, turning it into a self-evident platitude. Chou even confined his remarks to the "educational front," and his actual position was moderate. There is a struggle between the "socialist and capitalist roads" in education, he said, but socialism has won a "basic victory." "But among some intellectuals there still exists not a little bourgeois thought and style."[71]

During the Leap Chou and his friends would have liked to do away with the "bourgeois thought and style" of the intellectuals. The radicals, however, would have preferred to do away with the intellectuals as a "class." After the crackdown on the Hundred Flowers the tougher Nieh Jung-chen had replaced the genial Ch'en Yi as the man in charge of coordinating scientific work.[72] Both men were later part of Chou's group. In 1958 Nieh engaged in a sort of debate with the radicals. In March Nieh made a few of the appropriate noises: "The big leap forward in production demands a change in production techniques." But he did not accept the entire "red and expert" line then being touted. Scientists sometimes have "bourgeois thought," Nieh says, but nevertheless "Old scientists are a precious resource of the state." We should also train young scientists. Nieh says scientists should work on matters of immediate concern to the state, and not on whatever strikes their fancy, but this was nothing new. The "mass line" means that scientists should "listen to" (Nieh does not say accept) the opinions of ordinary people (in practice probably Party cadres) and not look down upon them.[73]

Wu Te wrote on the same subject in May, with a somewhat different focus. "On the question of science and technology," Wu said, "the attitude of 'slavish spirit' among cadres is greater than in other areas." Cadres who do not understand science often "deify specialists...and have a superstitious fear of 'specialists.'" We must depend upon the masses, not "specialists." Some fear the masses will "make chaos." "This is without foundation." There is nothing wrong with expertise in itself, as long as it is "red and expert." This means "the liberation of the spirit under the leadership of the Party."[74]

The opponents of the Leap and the other policies that went with it seem to have put up a stubborn resistance. Thus, the communes were not approved by the Party Congress, or even a CC Plenum, but by an "enlarged" meeting of the Politburo—enlarged by the addition of the provincial secretaries and the heads of the Party cells of the "state ministries concerned."[75] These latter were probably the ministry of agriculture, which, unlike most of Chou En-lai's domain, was taking a radical line in 1958.[76] Even while the Politburo meeting was in session the *People's Daily* published two articles lauding the communes, perhaps forcing the issue.[77] The initial formal announcement of the communes seems to contain a sop for the economic bureaucrats. When these men were running things in the early 1950's the country followed the Soviet model, giving priority to the construction of heavy industry.[78] Mao, however, always seems to have favored emphasis on agriculture (and was probably right on this point—but the crux, as in many things, is in the execution). Now it was said that the communes have solved the agricultural problem; in 1959 attention should be devoted mainly to industry, especially steel.[79]

It would seem that the bulk of the opposition of the Leap came from the economic bureaucrats on the State Council, especially those affiliated with Chou En-lai, except for the bureaucrats concerned with agriculture.[80] But the opposition was not limited to this.[81] Only one of P'eng Chen's local apparatchiks, for instance, seems to have given a whole-hearted endorsement of the Leap. And even some of the local secretaries who did endorse the Leap may have had reservations. Ulanfu's statement, for instance, is mainly a pledge of allegiance to the Party Center and its policies, and Inner Mongolia was among the first provinces to abandon the more extreme aspects of the Leap. Chou Hsiao-chou of Hunan, a "conservative" in 1956[82] and one of the main members of P'eng Te-huai's group in 1959, did endorse the Leap in 1958. But his statement presents problems. In Hunan, he says, some feel "arable land is small and the population large." But this does not worry those of us whose thought has been liberated. All we have to do is to work on the mountains to increase the area of arable land. Chou then lists a series of seemingly perfectly rational objections to this scheme—mainly that it would damage embankments, cause erosion, and drain resources away from the already productive land. These problems can be overcome, Chou says, but he does not say how.[83] In view of Chou's overall record it seems possible that his overt support for the Leap masked covert reservations.[84] At Lushan Mao identified Szechuan, along with Honan and Hupeh, as "leftist" provinces in the spring of 1959.[85] But the first secretary of Szechuan, Li Ching-ch'üan, seems to have made no detailed endorsement of the Leap in 1958. His rather surprising promotion to the Politburo in 1958 may have been a kind of bribe, buying his acquiescence in the policies of the Leap.

In 1959 T'ao Chu was the most vocal provincial doubter of the efficacy of the Leap policies, but he supported the policy in 1958. That year the comrades not only knew more about technology than the technicians, but also knew more about farming than the farmers. T'ao Chu was one who expressed this idea. He argued against the idea that "food production is limited by natural conditions." There is, said T'ao, no limit. If we want to increase food production, all we need do, for example, is plant our rows closer together.[86] But T'ao had a strong qualification: "We of the Communist Party believe that the laws of nature cannot be changed by man's will, but that if man today correctly grasps the laws of nature he can overcome and change nature."[87] In fact, at that time the Party was on the whole tending to follow Mao, who had argued that China was so "poor and blank" that the ordinary "laws of nature" to a large extent did not apply, and that there was little that could not be done by human will.[88]

At the second session of the Eighth National Congress in May, 1958, Lin Piao was made a member of the PBSC. K'o Ch'ing-shih, Li Ching-ch'üan, and T'an Chen-lin were made members of the Politburo, apparently as rewards for (or inducements to) radicalism. Wang En-mao and Yang Hsien-chen were promoted from alternate to full CC members, apparently as a matter of routine, as prescribed in the Party Constitution. Twenty-some alternate members were elected, with only minor indications of factional advantage (the main beneficiaries being Ho Lung and

Table VI
Q-Correlations, Group Membership of 1958 Alternates

PC	-.328	CEL	-.278
HL	.440	LP	-.081
LT	.271	CR	-.567
TC	.251	PTH	.378

N=21

P'eng Te-huai; the main "losers" were the CR Group, and the PC group). Ch'en Po-ta, Mao's private secretary, became editor of the newly founded theoretical magazine, *Red Flag*. This session was held prior to the adoption of the communes, perhaps the greatest defeat for the state bureaucrats. But the fate of Chou En-lai's men at this session is interesting. Only Ch'en Yun seems to have suffered for his moderate views (although he had delivered a speech (unpublished) to the session—perhaps a self-criticism). Li Fu-ch'un and Li Hsien-hien, hardly members of the radical group, were appointed to the Secretariat. The infiltration of the apparatus by the bureaucracy had begun.

A photograph of the head table at the session is also interesting. Seated from the audience's left to right are: Li Ching-ch'üan; Ulanfu; Lin Piao; Liu Shao-ch'i; Teng Hsiao-p'ing; Mao Tse-tung; Chou En-lai; Chu Te; P'eng Chen; K'o Ch'ing-shih.[89] If normal order is followed, the precedence here is Mao-Teng-Chou; if the traditional Chinese order is followed (it usually is not) the precedence is Mao-Chou-Teng. In any case, Teng is unusually high, and Liu is unusually low. Perhaps this may be a possible interpretation: Teng's high position signifies the triumph of the apparatus (the "Party"); Chou's position indicates his policy defeat does not mean his personal position is affected; Liu's low position may be a rebuke for going too strongly after Chou En-lai. Ch'en Yun is absent.

The period of 1956-1958 was perhaps the decisive one in the career of the Eighth CC. Ignoring the complexity of the issues and the role of peripheral players such as P'eng Chen, the political struggle of that time may be thought of as a three-handed game among the Leader (Mao), the Party (perhaps Teng here more than Liu) and the state (Chou). Alliances could form along two dimensions: the role of the Party and the rate of economic growth. In late 1956 the Party and the State, while disagreeing over the extent of the role of the Party, were allied against Mao on economic issues. During the Hundred Flowers the Leader and the state ganged up against the Party in an attempt to limit the scope of its powers. After this failure, Mao and the Party drifted toward the same position—Mao accepting a greater role for the Party, the Party pushing for rapid economic growth; in the process the bureaucracy was isolated. This alliance between the then strong Party apparatus and the charismatic leader was somewhat unnatural, and soon broke down.

5. THE RETIREMENT OF MAO AND THE FIRST MODERATION OF THE LEAP

The 1958 harvest was the best one in the regime's history, although it was not as good as Peking claimed at the time. Even this apparent success of the radical policies, however, did not convince all of the doubters. They thought the results were due to good weather. T'an Chen-lin told them this was not so: "The decisive factor in the large summer harvest is primarily Party leadership, politics takes command."[90] In the People's Republic usually only poor showings are attributed to the weather. But even in the good year of 1958 problems with the "three red flags" began to crop up.

The first cautious criticism of the communes was voiced by Li Hsien-nien in October. He found the communes generally good, but with reservations. "For example, chickens and eggs no longer remain in private ownership. . .; cooking is no longer done at home; and there is little leisure." So some overall plan must be made at an early stage to find a way to raise chickens. Most of Li's complaints relate to his own bureaucratic interests. He did not like the merger of the commune with the village, but "this is a creative experiment and we can try to make it work and gain more experience." He was dissatisfied with the distribution system on the communes: "What are state workers [who do not farm land] in the rural areas to do? . . .I think the form overawes people (逼人); this problem needs timely study." Li also says each commune plan must be balanced with the national plan—a justification for retaining local financial units.[91]

On November 9 the *People's Daily* announced the need to "guarantee rest for the peasants," but in somewhat bad grace: the rest must be "planned," and over-work is a good thing.[92] In late November there were the first indications of a major policy change: Hu Yao-pang told the Youth League about "building socialism," not, as previously during the Leap, "communism."[93] On December 18 the decisions of the Sixth Plenum were announced.

The meeting was held in Wuhan, the third of a series of meetings. Mao had convened a meeting of "some" Central and local leaders in Cheng-chow on November 2. He may have been attempting some new kind of spectacular play, again by-passing the CC. If so, he did not succeed. Immediately afterwards another meeting "was convened" (not necessarily by Mao) in Wuchang. This seems to have been a larger meeting, consisting of "Central leaders" and the first secretaries of the provinces. The major decisions announced after the plenum seem to have been made at this meeting.

The decisions were not announced for a week after the plenum. The interval had apparently been used to prepare Party opinion for the announcement of Mao's retirement (effective April, 1959) as state chairman. This seems to have aroused relatively little interest in the west, with few doubts voiced about its voluntary nature. Those in China were not so credulous. The *People's Daily* spoke of "rumors" circulated by the "enemy," and noted that a "minority" did not accept the official explanation.[94] The truth of the matter is still hard to ascertain.

Mao's own statements about this during the Cultural Revolution are confusing. They all come from unofficial sources, and when speaking extemporaneously Mao tends to ramble. At one point he says of this series of meetings: "I was dissatisfied, but I could not do anything."[95]

Elsewhere he spoke of setting up the PBSC and the Secretariat. "I retired to the second line and placed Liu Shao-ch'i and Teng Hsiao-p'ing in the front line. . .When I retired to the second line I did not supervise daily operations. . .This stemmed from the consideration of fostering these people's authority so that no great changes would arise in the country when the time came for me to meet the king of heaven." Mao says this was a mistake, but it was he who had first made the proposal.[96] But the PBSC and Secretariat were set up in 1956, and during 1957 and 1958 Mao was very much in the "front line," supervising daily operations. After 1958, until 1966, in domestic policy Mao was either inactive (at some times) or exerting his influence behind the scenes (at others). Mao may have proposed to set up the two lines in 1956, under pressure from the apparatus, and then reneged on his promise; in late 1958 he may have been forced to honor the deal.

The official announcement of Mao's retirement, in retrospect at least, seems permeated with gentle sarcasm: "This will allow him to collect his energy to manage the direction, policy, and line of the Party and state, and will also give him time to undertake work in Marxist-Leninist theory. . .In this way there will be even greater benefit to the Party and to the people of the whole country."[97] In other words, it could be better for the country if Mao would not directly attempt to run it.

The notion that Mao's retirement from the ceremonial post of state chairman would allow him to "collect his energy" is also odd: one would not have thought the post would be such a strain. When Liu Shao-ch'i took over the job, he found his work-load increased:

> Wang Kuang-mei even said shamelessly to her children, "Papa is so very busy that he can spare no time for rest. Chairman Mao does not attend to the concrete major affairs of state now and has assigned them to Papa. You must not disturb him."[98]

Perhaps the best conclusion is that Mao had, for all practical purposes, become "honorary chairman" of the CC, with Liu as the effective chairman. Mao's retirement as state chairman may have been a face-saving device Mao accepted "voluntarily," rather than have the matter of the Party chairmanship come to a head.

The plenum provided Mao with some Marxist-Leninist theory to study:

> The change from rural cooperatives to people's communes is. . . not equivalent ot the change from socialism to communism. . .We cannot stand still in the state of socialism, but neither can we sink into empty thoughts about transcending socialism and entering communism by a leap.

Minor concessions were made. Thus, for the meantime, there would no longer be attempts to build urban communes;[99] the attacks on the family system were blunted: the Chinese people, said their spokesman, only want to eliminate the "feudal" family system which no longer exists even under capitalism; the conjugal family may await the advent of communism.[100] The status of the state bureaucracy was restored somewhat, with a re-emphasis on imagery of a more balanced growth—"walking on two legs."[101] But no basic reforms of the Leap system or the communes were then introduced. The apparatchiks, or, at any rate, the victorious coalition whatever its composition, seemed to wish to retain as much of the system as possible, while making Mao the scapegoat for the more obvious excesses.

After the plenum, at least at the central level there was a more moderate atmosphere, and the Chou En-lai bureaucrats began to reassert their functions. In late December Li Hsien-nien advocated the retention of some private ownership on the communes, as long as it did not interfere with collective production.[102] The following month he advocated cost accounting (經濟核算) (nothing like "capitalist cost accounting," he explained) to rationalize commune management. Despite what some comrades seem to think, Li said, " 'Free food' [i.e., in the mess halls] does not mean you do not have to figure out how much the food costs."[103] Such accounting, of course, would be done by those in Li's employ.

In January Ch'en Yun re-emerged after a long absence from the public press with a plea for more Soviet aid.[104] Khrushchev's penchant for hare-brained schemes did not cross international boundaries, and the resurection of Ch'en Yun may have been intended to signal the Russians that the wild men were no longer in complete control of the Chinese economy. In March Ch'en published a critique of the mass movement. In 1958, he said, we paid too much attention to "unadulterated speed" (圖快). This created confusion. Better results come from safe working conditions and quality engineering; quality requires technical skills as well as political awareness.[105] This was Ch'en's last public statement. Another "conservative," Teng Tzu-hui, re-emerged as a major spokesman for agricultural policy. In June Teng announced a major concession: Henceforth participation in the mess halls would be voluntary. "Do not make a commune member's willingness to join the mess hall the criterion of whether he is progressive or not."[106] While the conservatives were becoming more outspoken, some 1958 "radicals" seem to have had a change of heart. Po I-po, a 1958 radical and something of a weathervane in economic and other matters, said in early 1959 that while "man" was certainly the decisive factor in production, this must not lead us to neglect the importance of "matter."[107] K'o Ch'ing-shih and T'ao Lu-chia announced in the spring of 1959 that the "whole country is a single chessboard,"[108] marking a renewed interest in rational central planning.

Chou En-lai was more politically cautious than his subordinates, saying even more mass mobilization would be desirable. He spoke both of the "subjective capacities of the people" (a 1958 catch-phrase) and "objective material capacities" (stressed by Li Hsien-nien). But Chou strongly asserted the interests of the Central bureaucracy: "The most important problem at present is to strengthen centralized leadership, overall planning, firmly grasp all kinds of organizational work and concrete methods. . . ."[109]

In early 1959 there was also a more tolerant attitude toward certain cultural activities. In 1958 Ch'en Po-ta had said the proper attitude was to "stress the present, slight the past." He criticized those who wanted to waste their time on ancient history or archaeology.[110] In 1959 he made a partial recantation. He said that he had not intended to take "a boorish attitude toward our natural heritage." "This absolutely does not accord with our original intention." There is, however, still some merit in my original idea, in that some scholars do tend to be overly preoccupied with the past.[111] This atmosphere was conducive to the Ts'ao Ts'ao debate and the writings about Hai Jui.

The extent to which this new prominence of the State Council bureaucrats in the economic field and the correlated moderate tone were reflected in the provinces is problematical. Kwangtung seems to have been one of the first provinces to feel the full impact of the Leap policies,[112] and T'ao Chu seems to have been the provincial leader most eager to break with these policies (with perhaps the more successful exception of Ulanfu). In February T'ao argued for the retention of some private ownership, especially of chickens.[113] Later he became more outspoken. But radical sentiments were still strong in many provinces. In March Tseng Hsi-sheng of Anhwei railed against those who thought the country unable to make a simultaneous leap on all fronts.[114] At Lushan Mao spoke of a "wind of communism" (共產風 —here probably a literal translation, "common property wind", is better), which had continued to blow after the sixth plenum, apparently most strongly in Honan, Hupei, and Szechuan. This resulted in sporadic rioting "for two or three months around the spring festival"—which would be January through March. This wind was supposedly "suppressed" by a series of Central meetings, culminating in the short seventh plenum, held in early April in Shanghai.[115]

During this series of meetings one major change in commune organization was decided upon. The "production brigade" (生產大隊) rather than the commune as a whole would become the "basic accounting unit" in rural areas. The smaller the accounting unit, the more incentive there is for the individual farmer. But the impact of this reform was no doubt vitiated by its not being promulgated until 1961,[116] by which time it was already obsolete (in late 1960 for all practical purposes the "production team" (生產隊) of about 30 or so families had become the accounting unit; this became official in 1962). The public report of the plenum also seems to contradict Mao's optimistic assessment of its results. The report speaks of the need for continuing rectification of the communes,[117] indicating the problems remained serious. Mao also gives evidence that these meetings failed to grapple with some problems. He says the excessively high production targets had become "Buddhist idols," that proposals had been made to revise them, but "the majority did not agree."[118]

The plenum may not have been entirely without effect. Wang Jenchung, of "leftist" Hupei and a future crony of T'ao Chu's, published an article after the plenum condemning the tendency to falsify statistics. "When speaking of the communist style, we must dare to speak the truth, bring out facts, and not just follow the wind."[119] In early June T'ao Chu published his famous essay, "The Brilliance of the Sun." The leadership of the Communist Party is indeed brilliant, said T'ao. It is no exaggeration to compare it to the sun. But even the sun has black spots. "Some comrades do not want to hear about defects and mistakes," but these may not be ignored. He also uses another metaphor: If we have nine healthy fingers and one injured one, we might say our hands are in pretty good shape; but this does not mean we need not worry about the injured finger.[120]

But T'ao and Wang seem to have remained exceptions. In May Li Ta-chang of Szechuan voiced some "rightist" slogans ("Seek truth from facts"), but stressed obedience to the Party as the best way to increase production. He was full of advice on farming methods, such as close cropping and deep ploughing.[121] The political interests of the provincial secretaries were still bound up with the Leap policies, and they were on the whole unwilling to yield. Meanwhile, the economy continued to deteriorate. Around the first of July the rulers of China began gathering in Lushan for a converence.

6. P'ENG TE-HUAI IS DISMISSED FROM OFFICE[122]

The defense minister, P'eng Te-huai, was an instance of that modern folk hero, the alienated man. An apparently thoroughly honorable man, he prided himself on his soldierly bluntness, which often approached simple bad manners. As this tended to make enemies for him, it was impolitic as well as impolite. He felt left out of things. According to his wife, "After 1953 I often heard him voice his discontent, saying, 'I am old, the Chairman does not like me, neither does he hold me in esteem. The young men have come up. . ."[123] A Red Guard before his time, he objected to the soft life enjoyed by the leading cadres, including the Chairman.[124] He may have had a personal grudge against the apparatus. It is said that the writer Ting Ling had been P'eng's mistress in Yenan; when P'eng objected to her purge after the Hundred Flowers he was accused of "sentimentalism"[125] — for a man of P'eng's temperament, a classic case of adding insult to injury. He was also out of sympathy with the growing split with the Soviet Union. The Red Guards have a vivid description of the great friendship between "big-bellied P'eng Te-huai" and "baldheaded Khrushchev."[126] As noted earlier, P'eng also seems to have wanted to build a professional army, something increasingly unfashionable since 1958. P'eng's discontent came to a head, however, with his dissatisfaction with the Leap policies. They were damaging the defense industries and also underminging the morale in the PLA.[127] But it would probably not be wrong to hold that P'eng's main motives were humanitarian.

On July 14, after the Lushan meeting had convened, P'eng addressed a "letter of opinion" to the "Chairman," summing up some complaints he had been voicing for several days. He spoke of carelessness, exaggeration, and poor planning. He concluded: "Petty bourgeois fanaticism renders us liable to commit 'left' mistakes. . .In the view of some comrades, putting politics in command could be a substitute for everything."[128]

The exact nature of P'eng's behavior at Lushan is, like other matters in the internal political struggles of the CC, still unclear. Charles, in an early but in some respects remarkably accurate article, speaks of P'eng's "intrigues."[129] In a kind of "revisionist" article, J.P. Simmonds argues that in the absence of compelling evidence to the contrary it is safer to speak of opposition rather than a plot.[130] The victors at least pretended to see a plot. P'eng was said to have headed an "anti-Party clique";[131] he is a "big plotter, a big ambitionist, a big warlord."[132] This is as close to hard evidence as we are apt to get, at least until the next great shift in the politics of the regime. P'eng himself is ambiguous on the matter of a plot. In a confession made after the conclusion of the plenum he purports to set out to explain how he colluded with Huang K'o-ch'eng, Chang Wen-t'ien, and Chou Hsiao-chou. In fact he says only that he had held conversations with Huang and Chang, and that he and these two men found they shared certain opinions. He does not again mention Chou.[133] Indirect evidence indicates there was probably some kind of rather loosely organized attempt by P'eng to challenge the political *status-quo.*

One striking factor is the mildness of P'eng's critique (in the "Letter of Opinion"—his oral presentation was somewhat rougher) relative to the severity of his treatment. Schurmann hypothesizes that the Communists tolerate differences of opinion among the leadership, but not factionalism[134]—or attempting to do anything about one's opinion. This seems generally true. Around the time of Lushan others had voiced dissent—T'ao Chu and Ch'en Yun are obvious examples. T'ao seems to have capitulated to the victorious group; but Ch'en Yun seems to have maintained dissenting positions to the end. T'ao suffered no ill consequences; Ch'en was removed from public life, but subject to no disgrace. Neither was treated as harshly as P'eng.

By examining which CC members were purged or demoted around the time of the Lushan plenum, we can derive a list of the probable members of P'eng's group. In general the members fall into three categories—former subordinates of P'eng Te-huai; former subordinates of Kao Kang[135] (these two groups sometimes overlap); and two former members of the "Bolshevik" faction. (Table VII).

The treatment received by these men differs—some were purged, others merely demoted or transferred; and the punishment of some was delayed. This might indicate that while the group was perceptible, it was not tightly organized.[136] It is drawn from the army, some provincial secretariats, and those in charge of economic affairs on the State Council (the two "Bolsheviks" in the Foreign Ministry presumably wanted to avert the coming split with the Soviet Union).

Other evidence indicates that P'eng may have been shoring up his own position for a time prior to Lushan. He was opposed to the moves against Quemoy and Matsu in 1958; but the scapegoat for the failure was the conservative, professionally-minded Chief of Staff, Su Yü. Su was replaced by P'eng's long-time crony, Huang K'o-ch'eng. After Lushan Su became a vice-minister of defense. During the Cultural Revolution he faithfully served Lin Piao.

Table VII
P'eng Te-huai's Anti-Party Clique

Party

Chou Hsiao-chou — removed as 1st Sect., Hunan; old subordinate of Huang K'o-ch'eng.

Chang Chung-liang — 1961, removed as 1st Sect.; Kansu, on charges of rightism; old associate of Kao Kang.

Shu T'ung (?) — 1960, removed as 1st Sect., Shantung, for rightism; old subordinate of P'eng Te-huai; later made Sect., Shensi; Liu-Teng group in Cultural Revolution.

State

Chang Wen-t'ien — removed as V. Min., Foreign Affairs; "Bolshevik" faction.

Chia T'o-fu — removed as Director, 4th Office, State Council; associate of Kao Kang.

Hsi Chung-hsun (?) — c. 1962, removed as head of State Council Secretariat, on charges of rightism. Former associate of Kao Kang, P'eng Te-huai.

T'eng Tai-yuan — inactive since 1959; in 1965 removed as Min. Railroads; former associate of P'eng Te-huai; classified with Chou En-lai in Cultural Revolution.

Wang Chia-hsiang — removed as V. Min., Foreign Affairs; "Bolshevik" faction.

Wang Shih-t'ai (?) — removed as V. Chmn, State Construction Commission; made Sect., Kansu; former subordinate of P'eng Te-huai; Liu-Teng group in Cultural Revolution.

Yang I-chen — removed as Minister, 2nd Ministry Commerce. Later V. Gov., Hopei.

Army

Chou Huan (?) — removed as Commissar, Mukden; made Sect., Liaoning; probably former associate of P'eng Te-huai; Liu-Teng group in Cultural Revolution.

Hsiao K'o — removed as head of military training; made V. Min., Min. State farms and Land Reclamation; old subordinate of P'eng Te-huai (also of Ho Lung); Ho Lung group in Cultural Revolution.

Huang K'o-ch'eng — removed as Chief of Staff, PLA; P'eng Te-huai associate.

Hung Hsueh-chih — removed as director, PLA Rear Services Department (old subordinate of Lin Piao).

T'an Cheng — removed as Dir., PLA GPD; P'eng Te-huai associate.

Teng Hua — removed as Commander, Mukden; P'eng Te-huai associate.

Wan I — removed as head, PLA Logistics Department; P'eng Te-huai associate.

If we grant that there was in some sense a plot at Lushan, it remains to be determined against whom the plot was directed. The Maoists, of course, maintain that P'eng was opposed to Mao, and that he "acted with the support of the greatest person in power within the Party walking the capitalist road."[137] This is unlikely, at least as far as 1959 is concerned. There was certainly no love lost between P'eng and Mao. At one point in the debate P'eng called Mao a liar: "I asked the Chairman for his impression. He said he did not know anything about it; but I think he did." Elsewhere P'eng directly criticized Mao: "Last year the wrongly issued directives of Chairman Mao caused a lot of trouble."[138] But these seem to be merely P'eng's usual lack of tact, not a challenge to Mao's authority. The only statement Liu is known to have uttered at Lushan is hostile to P'eng. In 1967 P'eng said: "I adhere to the views I expressed at the Lushan meeting. My memorandum to Chairman Mao was against Liu Shao-ch'i."[139] Since P'eng adheres to discredited views, his statement cannot be dismissed as entirely self-serving. With some qualification it seems fairly close to the truth.

In the official documents, P'eng like Kao Kang, was accused of leading an "anti-Party" group. In 1967 he was openly identified with Kao Kang.[140] He (and the other soldiers) may indeed have sympathized with Kao in 1953. Kao was the first high ranking Communist to have been purged since Liberation, and the Party may have been simply going through the hoary and revered Stalinist rituals: many of Stalin's opponents found themselves sooner or later associated with Trotsky; those disgraced during the Cultural Revolution mostly turned out to be the running dogs of Liu Shao-ch'i. In 1959 the leadership had to do with Kao, as he was all they had. Also, as noted above, many of the people who had apparently joined with P'eng had once worked for Kao. However, on these counts, P'eng could have as easily have been identified with Wang Ming (except, perhaps, for the fact that Wang in 1959 was not in official disgrace). This suggests the hypothesis that P'eng's plot was similar to Kao Kang's—that he was challenging the influence of the apparatus, wishing perhaps to increase the relative influence of the institution he himself controlled, the army. P'eng did hint at times that he would use the army to attain his goals. He said: "Were the Chinese people, not so good, we would have to ask the Soviet Union to send troops."[141] This statement, even more than his remarks about "petty bourgeois fanaticism," was a gift to P'eng's enemies. It could be construed as welcoming Soviet military intervention. But P'eng's meaning was perhaps different: were the Chinese people to rise in rebellion against the policies of the Leap, "we"—the rulers—would have to ask the Soviet Union to intervene, because the PLA (like the Hungarian army) would not fight the people. Mao voiced doubts about the army at Lushan: "If you of the Liberation Army don't follow me, I'll go find a Red Army. I think the Liberation Army will follow me."[142]

A challenge to the apparatus was not a direct challenge to Mao, and there are indications P'eng did not at all intend to question Mao's ultimate authority (although he did question Mao's judgment). It was mentioned earlier that the one remark at Lushan attributed to Liu Shao-ch'i is hostile to P'eng. This remark is also bizarre in the extreme. Liu is supposed to have said: "I would rather usurp the Party myself than have you usurp it." The Red Guard editors add: "This single remark disclosed the whole secret"[143] —apparently that Liu wanted to usurp the Party. Perhaps so, but the Red Guard explanation does not tell why Liu would be making gratuitous remarks about usurpation. It is the kind of thing that would be said in anger—very probably as a retort to a contention by P'eng that Liu had *already* usurped the Party.

What might be called the "Hai Jui" evidence, for what it is worth, also points this way. From 1959, Wu Han, a historian and vice-mayor of Peking, began writing a series of works on the Ming statesman Hai Jui.[144] During the Cultural Revolution the Maoists held that Hai Jui was a symbol for P'eng Te-huai. Wu Han's major work on Hai Jui, *Hai Jui Is Dismissed From Office,* a play in Peking opera form, was written in 1960. In this play the villains are the evil local gentry and corrupt local officials, who steal the peasants' land and perpetrate other atrocities on them.[145] Their equivalent in the 1950's would be the radical local apparatus. Wu Han's major critique of Mao, "Hai Jui Scolds the Emperor," however, was published prior to the Lushan plenum. This still may reflect P'eng's views, since P'eng claimed that he had criticized Mao in the meetings held in the spring of 1959.[146] Simmonds argues that maneuvers against P'eng had begun in May or June,[147] so it is likely that his views were known in June, when the article was published. It is equally likely, however, that the first Hai Jui article served to inspire P'eng. He was quoted in a Red Guard publication: "I could no longer keep quiet. I must act like Hai Jui."[148] The criticism of the "emperor," who may safely be taken to represent Mao, is very harsh in this article; some of it can be construed as rather nastily personal: "All you want to do is live long and never grow old." But it is quite loyal opposition for all that. Hai Jui scolds the emperor for "cultivating the Way" (玄 修 —the traditional analogue, perhaps, to studying Marxist-Leninist theory) and not attending to affairs of state. Hai Jui urges the emperor: "You must realize there is nothing good about cultivating the Way. You must wake up now, go to court every day, study the nation and plan for the people's welfare, amend your decades of error, plan for the well-being of the people."[149] In the last analysis, the article criticizes Mao for his 1958 abdication. Some of P'eng's statements are in this Hai Jui vein: "Under the circumstances few people can be in a position to reflect the true situation to Chairman Mao."[150]

It is concluded tentatively at least, then, that P'eng did not intend to challenge the authority of Mao. His policy goal was to reform the policies of the Leap. His institutional goal was to reduce the influence of the Party apparatus, to the gain of the army.[151]

Granting this, it still remains that Mao was P'eng's most vocal opponent at Lushan. The Cultural Revolution would seem to demonstrate that Mao had no particular objection to the power arrangement envisaged by P'eng. But Lin Piao had prepared the ground with years of affirmation of the master and all his works. P'eng included in his attacks insults to the leader, and concentrated upon policies with which Mao was closely identified, and, in fact, for which Mao had already been scapegoated. An ordinary charismatic leader could possibly have risen above this. But Mao was a charismatic leader of an ideological Party. His position depended not only upon his personal qualities, but upon the correctness of his Thought. Since 1955 his Thought had tended to the "left line." Were he to have admitted the correctness of P'eng's critique, he would in effect have to deny the validity of his Thought over the past four years, thus undermining his own authority. By 1959 Mao had become a prisoner of his Thought.

Mao then chose to use P'eng's challenge to reassert his own authority. At this point a complication must be introduced. In his speech against the critics of the Leap, Mao criticized "wavering comrades." The most obvious target would be T'ao Chu. T'ao's "fingers" metaphor was cited in the public report of the plenum, and the opposite moral was drawn.[152] Shortly after the plenum T'ao published an article on "revolutionary resolution"; this was certainly a self criticism.[153] But Mao also said: "Comrade XX (En-lai) is very enthusiastic. He learned a lesson from last time. I believe XX also stands firm. Those very persons who criticized XX at that time have now replaced him."[154] The final XX is probably Ch'en Yun, but could also be En-lai again. "Last time" was at the time of the adoption of the policies of the Leap. "Those very persons" must include Liu Shao-ch'i. Liu could not endorse P'eng's institutional aims, but in terms of policy P'eng may have been preaching to the converted. (Everyone admitted the economy was in bad shape: as Mao said, "We have made a mess of things."[155]) P'eng's rebellion allowed Mao to pose as the savior of the Party, a more effective champion of the Party than its effective head. After Lushan Mao did not return to the "front line," but thereafter he was a potent symbol of authority.

Comrade En-lai, meanwhile, had "learned a lesson from last time." At Lushan he seems to have adopted the strategy he had generally used since the Tsunyi Conference, and was to use thereafter: he took whichever side Mao took. At Lushan this may have allowed him to score points on his rival, Liu Shao-ch'i.

The most important personnel change at Lushan was the appointment of Lin Piao to replace P'eng Te-huai. Lin had been inactive during most of the 1950's. His health was known to be poor,[156] and some think he had been wounded in Korea.[157] Mrs. Hsieh thinks Lin was acceptable to all groups in 1959 because his inactivity had prevented him from making enemies.[158] But Chou Ching-wen claims that it was an "open secret" that factional jealousies had kept Lin down.[159] Despite his inactivity, Lin had continued to rise in Party rank; in 1958 he became a member of the PBSC, outranking Teng Hsiao-p'ing. At Lushan, the police chief, Lo Jui-ch'ing, became chief of staff. He later joined with P'eng Chen, but his policy pronouncements prior to 1959 would seem to show that at that time he was in closer agreement with the hard-liners like Teng Hsiao-p'ing. His appointment may have owed more to his zest and skill in conducting purges than to factional considerations. Hsieh Fu-chih, then apparently with Teng Hsiao-p'ing, was transferred from Yunnan to take Lo's place as Minister of Public Security.[160] T'ao Chu's friend, Chang P'ing-hua, replaced Chou Hsiao-chou as First Secretary of Hunan.

The more general consequences of the meeting were perhaps more important to the Chinese people. Prior to the plenum there seems to have been a definite willingness by many to undertake radical reforms in the Leap policies. This was no longer true after the meeting, although minor reforms continued to be made. T'ao Chu said in 1961:

> The Lushan conference originally had the purpose of summing up experience and lessons and of rectifying shortcomings and mistakes. But in the course of the conference there appeared an anti-Party clique headed by P'eng Te-huai...This could not but call for opposition to rightist opportunism. However, at that time the comrades in our province were not clear about it. They did not confine the opposition to rightist opportunism within certain limits of the Party; instead, they continued to implement the spirit of the Chengchow conference [There were two such conferences, in November 1958 and February-March, 1959; the reference is unclear] throughout the whole country. As a result an anti-rightist movement was set in motion and the past shortcomings and mistakes, instead of being corrected, were aggravated.[161]

In effect, Lushan nailed home the "left line." It was a victory for "Party leadership," but over the long run this was a hollow victory. Those who favored reform now ran the danger of being associated with an anti-Party group. By continuing the policies of the Leap the Party was destroying the economy and undermining the basis of communist rule. By reforming the policies it would undermine its ideological authority; and because of the charismatic leader firmly committed to the policies, there was a place for other ambitious men to grab hold to take up the ideological slack.

7. MOVING TOWARD THE CAPITALIST ROAD: 1959-1960

Those at Lushan did realize that things were not going as well as they might; the plenum itself corrected some of the grossly exaggerated 1958 figures.[162] After the plenum the Party Center and the State Council authorized a limited free market in rural areas.[163] National development priorities were definitely shifted to agriculture.[164] Some voices of moderation continued to be heard,[165] and there were a few attempts to contain the emerging anti-rightist struggle. In a National Day article Liu Shao-ch'i took pains to emphasize that the Party had always been as vigilant against left deviation as against right.[166]

Nonetheless, the general pressure was from the left. A symptom of this, perhaps, was the emergence of one of the most radical local bosses, Tseng Hsi-sheng, as a main trend setter in late 1959 and early 1960.[167] There are some indications that national policies were not being implemented in the provinces. Immediately after the plenum, for example, Chou En-lai reiterated that the mess halls were now voluntary.[168] But both Li Ching-ch'üan and Tseng Hsi-sheng published articles rhapsodizing on the love of the masses for the mess halls.[169] We may assume that people in Szechuan and Anhwei were still under considerable pressure to eat in the mess halls. In industry there was a return to the 1958 rhetoric, as Po I-po, K'o Ch'ing-shih, and Sung Jen-ch'iung ridiculed those who thought the mass movement in this sector had resulted in chaos.[170]

Those who had previously been somewhat "right" were under pressure to assume a more leftist stance. At Lushan Mao had treated Li Fu-ch'un, head of the State Planning Commission, to a great deal of mostly unwarranted sarcasm ("I'm not trying to make excuses. The reason is that I am not the Chairman of the State Planning Commission."[171]) Mao said Li lacked "anxiety," meaning enthusiasm for the Leap.[172] In October, 1959, Li did his best to show enthusiasm.[173] That same month Teng Tzu-hui told how much he liked the people's communes, the "bridge to communism."[174] Li Hsien-nien was silent after Lushan, and he may have been in trouble. In early 1960 the major statements concerning finance work were made by Ma Ming-fang, the apparatchik in charge of that area.[175] In November, 1959, Ou-yang Ch'in of Heilungkiang talked about the growth of bourgeois habits among finance workers, and stressed the need for Party leadership of this kind of work.[176] In April, 1960, Li Ta-chang of Szechuan wrote that finance and trade work is supposed to be a job for the state, but the state comrades have not been doing very well. They need better leadership.[177] Li Hsien-nien may have saved himself in mid-1960 by adopting strongly leftist rhetoric, complete with ostentatious appeals to the Thought.[178] T'ao Chu also seems to have been in trouble. After Lushan, in addition to publishing a piece on "revolutionary resolution,"[179] he also "sang the praises of the people's communes." He explained that the rather poor showing in Kwangtung in 1959 was due to natural disasters, not to the commune system. Had it not been for natural disasters, he said, there would have been an enormous harvest. In an apparent reference to his earlier sun metaphor, he said, "The dazzling brilliance which shoots from our people's communes cannot be covered by the black shadows of a small handful of men."[180]

Leftism after Lushan was not confined to economic policy. In October, 1959, Lu Ting-i announced a "cultural revolution." The term then meant the "enlightenment (知識化 —literally, "intellectualization") of the working and farming masses and the laborizing of intellectuals." In essence (aside from the drive to promote general literacy) this was a renewal of the policy to discredit educated men outside the Party. Lu thought the Party committees should take over all cultural work.[181] On cultural matters, however, it seems to have been safer to argue with the Leftists. T'ao Chu had apparently learned to hold his tongue about economic doubts; but he and Chang P'ing-hua were the most important spokesmen for moderation in cultural policy at that time. In January, 1960, Chang urged the rather bourgeois idea of publishing ghost stories. These not only teach people not to fear ghosts (literal and figurative), but also, Chang implied, are fun to read. Chang also said he would like to see more stories about the "true, left-wing Hai Jui."[182] This is curious. Wu Han, the champion of Hai Jui, was closely associated with the men around P'eng Chen; but P'eng's followers on the CC were then taking the "leftist" line on cultural matters (although, as indicated earlier, P'eng Chen probably favored the rightist line at Lushan). Perhaps his people, working right in the Party Center, had to adhere closely to the prevailing line, but were in fact in covert collusion with T'ao Chu, also a non-P'eng Te-huai rightist at Lushan. Or, T'ao Chu's men may have been taking up Wu Han's theme on their own.

Also in January, 1960, T'ao himself wrote an article on newspaper work. He said that "a revolutionary mass movement will always find it hard to avoid mistakes and defects." There is a struggle between the old and the new. This struggle should be reflected in the newspapers, as Chairman Mao has pointed out. This would seem to be an argument for less rigid control (relatively) over the substance of news items. Also, said T'ao, our newspapers are dull. Maybe we should include more features, such as sports and chess columns. Party control of newspapers is indeed a wonderful thing, but we also need beter writing. We shoiuld cultivate specialists in journalism.[183]

T'ao's views did not prevail. In June Tseng Hsi-sheng, now an authority on journalism, published what seems to be a rebuttal to T'ao. Tseng felt there was no need for more specialists in this kind of work. What is really needed is closer Party control. In fact, this kind of work should not even be entrusted too closely with the propaganda departments of the Party committees, since these people too often come to see things from the reporters' point of view. This becomes a system "where everybody does his own thing, with no coordination, and the specialists look down on the non-specialists." The entire Party committee should take a hand in running newspapers.[184] In cultural affairs there was a greater latitude for discussion, but the pressure was still to the left.

It was noted in the last chapter that there was a revival of the "cult of Mao" after Lushan.[185] Now we can say this was probably a result of Mao's reassertion of authority at that meeting. But there is no evidence that Mao resumed an active role in day-to-day administration. In 1960 Maoism followed the charismatic politics pattern, meaning different things to different people. The 1960 Maoists fall into several categories.

The first Maoists in 1960 were the more radical provincial leaders, whose policies had been "vindicated" at Lushan.[186] Another category, which said almost the same things as the first category, seems to be the provincial leaders who sided with P'eng Te-huai; their writings would seem to be "unity" articles. Thus, in 1960, before he was accused of rightism and demoted, Shu T'ung took an extremely leftist stance. In February he wrote an article reviving Mao's 1958 idea of "uninterrupted revolution," (不断革命) meaning things are always in a process of change.[187] This is in contrast with the idea of "revolution by stages," a more conservative theory which allows the population time to catch its breath. It is this stage view which, in effect, had been reaffirmed by the Sixth Plenum. (Or, rather, the theories were combined.) Shu later published a second article, a paean to the Thought.[188] Other repentant heretics would include Chang Chung-liang, and, possibly, Ch'en Yü.[189] Ulanfu would be a special case. In 1958 he was virtually coerced into supporting the Leap, and be soon thought better of it. After Lushan, he may again have felt himself vulnerable. He thus uttered some radical noises, with an appeal to the Leader designed perhaps as a hedge against any tendency by the Party Center to clamp down once again on Inner Mongolia.[190]

The Thought also found advocates among P'eng Chen's men at the Party Center.[191] This may have been in the nature of an end-play around Teng Hsiao-p'ing; or, these people may also have been vulnerable because of conservative views expressed at Lushan. Another major group was composed of the followers of Chou En-lai.[192] This seems to have been in part a continuation of the Mao-Chou Lushan alliance. In the early part of 1960 the economic managers were taking an unusually leftist track. In March Li Fu-ch'un reiterated the primacy of political over material incentives, and also revived the idea of urban communes.[193] This may, however, have been making a virtue of necessity. In 1960 there were not many material incentives around; and it has been hypothesized that the urban communes were something of a desperation measure to control urban consumption and encourage savings. This policy (dropped in late 1960) was not accompanied by the ideological posturing that went with the rural communes.[194]

In 1960, however, Maoism could also be put to pragmatic use. A change of some sort seems to have come about in June. On June 14 the *People's Daily* cited Mao as favoring a "plan," a "reasonable ratio between savings and expenditures," and a "balance."[195] Later that month Chang P'ing-hua discovered that Mao had once uttered the proverb, "Seek truth from facts" (實事求是). Chang discussed a magazine Mao had edited in his younger years. First, Mao is put in his place: At that time there was no CPC, so naturally these are not as good as Comrade Mao Tse-tung's later works. But even at that time he advocated seeking truth from facts.[196] A few days later Ou-yang Ch'in took up the phrase, urging the Party to realize, as Comrade Mao Tse-tung does, the nature of objective laws.[197] Two days later this theme was taken up by, of all people, Tseng Hsi-sheng. Tseng had alwasy been a "subjective factors" man. Now he said:

> Some people think that if we seek truth from facts we cannot drum up work enthusiasm. This viewpoint is completely mistaken... The problems is obvious: If we do not begin from reality, but just act blindly, mass enthusiasm cannot be drummed up.[198]

This was out of phase with Tseng's pronouncements over the past two years, and particularly with those of the past six months or so. It was almost certainly a self-criticism. It was his last published article.

By August it was apparently safe enough for T'ao Chu to resume talking about the communes. He published a rather curious article, purporting to give his "personal opinion" on how to go about building communism. This turns out to be nothing but a banal recapitulation of the official policies adopted since 1949. But T'ao presented his "theory" as a series of 14 *stages* conforming to the "objective laws of development."[199] Later Ou-yang Ch'in, discussing the newly published fourth volume of Mao's works, warned against "mixing up the stages of revolution."[200] The "uninterrupted revolution" boomlet had apparently collapsed.

There was yet another twist to what might be called "pragmatic Maoism." The "mass line" was re-interpreted to mean something closer to what the uninitiated might have thought it meant: the cadres should listen to the opinions of the masses. In 1958 the Party had been eager to tell the farmers how to do their jobs. But in July, 1960, Lin T'ieh warned against talking about the "backward masses." He said, "Some comrades take a completey bureaucratic attitude toward new and fresh things," meaning they had been too diligent in carrying out impractical and unpopular policies.[201] Li Wei-han criticized comrades with a "revolutionary will" but who had become "separated from the masses" and "fallen into adventurism."[202] Li Fu-ch'un scolded comrades who grew smug when things went well(!) but refused to listen to the masses when things went wrong. "These comrades do not understand that the mass line should be implemented both in times of hardship and in times of victory." They "squander the position and prestige of the Party."[203] Chang Te-sheng of Shensi (who died prior to the Cultural Revolution) argued that change should depend on "the self-awareness of the masses," and that the Party should not "take over all the work,"[204] presaging one of the major "Party-building" lines of the capitalist road period. Even the radical Wu Te came to accept the new interpretation of the mass line, with some reservations: "No matter what opinions the masses have, they must be heard patiently and sincerely, after which [the opinions] may be analyzed and treated distinctly."[205]

Policy changes which perhaps should have been made more than a year earlier began to come about in late 1960. In the fall of 1960 stress was put upon the production teams on the communes.[206] Chang Te-sheng admitted the link between this emphasis (which included a return to the "three packages one reward" system) and the "two years' series of natural disasters."²⁰⁷ It was not until 1962, however, that the production team was made the "basic accounting unit" on the communes.²⁰⁸

In 1960, then, some members of the CC attempted to use the TMTT to justify the adoption of generally rightist policies. Under the usual conditions of charismatic politics they might have succeeded. One can even speculate that P'eng Te-huai might have fared better had he adopted this tactic at Lushan. But by 1960 Mao was irrevocably committed, if he had not been before, to the "left line." Pragmatic Maoism may have helped to set the atmosphere for the necessary reforms; but it was doomed to long term failure.

Even as late as November, 1960, some still seemed to want to use the old methods. Hu Yao-pang, later identified as a follower of Teng Hsiao-p'ing, announced the sending down of "myriads" (千百萬) of educated youths to the countryside. "The present overall situation is excellent," he said.²⁰⁹ The policy makers of the capitalist road period also recognized the labor shortage in rural areas, but they preferred to attack the problem by economic means. To be sure, some of the "incentives" used were rather harsh—they included shutting down unproductive factories, forcing the workers to return to their hometowns—but they probably resulted in a more rational resource allocation than the deceptively "cheap" forced drafts of educated youths favored by the more hard-line apparatchiks.²¹⁰

By now, however, the time for delaying was past. On December 29 the *People's Daily* announced: "This year agricultural production in our country has suffered especially severe natural disasters. . ."²¹¹ The Leap was over.

8. A WALK ON THE CAPITALIST ROAD

After the Ninth Plenum in January, 1961, the rulers embarked upon a course they now call the "capitalist road." This experiment is as interesting, in its own way, as the Great Leap Forward, and, in developmental terms, was certainly more successful. There have not yet appeared any full-scale studies of this two year period,²¹² and here, of course, is not the place to attempt one. We can, however, gain something of the flavor of the period by examining the speeches delivered by CC members.²¹³ It must be said at the outset that there are not many of these. Previously, the *People's Daily* would sometimes publish articles by CC members several times a month. The policy changes of 1960 are easy to trace. This helpful editorial policy was discontinued after 1961, and articles by CC members became conspicious by their rarity. This in

Table VIII

The Men on the Capitalist Road — Major Pronouncements

Wang Jen-chung (TC) — RF, Jan. 1, 1961: Agricultural development has not been balanced. We should listen to what the "old farmers" have to say, even if they might be conservative in their politics.

Po I-po (PC) — RF, February 1, 1961: Factory workers will be laid off. More stress will be placed on light industry and agriculture.

Liao Lu-yen (CEL) — RF, February 1, 1961: The basic accounting unit on the communes is the production brigade. Some rich peasants and former landlords "have changed very much for the better." Rural Party organizations should be "purified"—in the context, this probably means they should rid themselves of zealots.

Ma Wen-jui (CEL) — RF, March 1, 1961: There must be overall planning. Agriculture is the most important sector. Labor must be shifted from city to the country.

Chang Te-sheng (unclassified) — WB, 19 (May 13, 1961) pp. 13-14: Attack on "equalitarianism" as applied to agriculture; repeats ideas on private plots and incentives he advocated in 1960.

Wang Shou-tao (CR) — PD, May 26, 1961: There is a need for better management for transportation (it apparently was good transportation which was able to temper the effects of the famine).

Li Wei-han (PC) — PD, June 16, 17, 1961: The bourgeoisie must undergo "peaceful reform." He stresses the unity of the country.

Liu Shao-ch'i (LT) — PD, July 1, 1961: The Leap was marred by "defects in our work." But there is nothing wrong with the "three red flags" in principle, the errors were all those of application. Cadres should acquire humility, learn from the masses. The socialist revolution is over, socialist construction begins—a reassertion of his 1956 view.

K'o Ch'ing-shih (unclassified) — PD, July 21, 1961: It will take a long time to consolidate the communes. Meanwhile, we must assure a gradual rise in the living standards of farmers.

Ou-yang Ch'in (LT) — PD, July 21, 1961: He attacks "subjectivism." Cadres must carry out investigation and research.

Ch'en I (CEL) — KMD, September 3, 1961: He talked about "red and expert." Political schools should concentrate on political training, professional (專業) schools should concentrate on professional training. He regaled the audience with stories of the "feudal" and bourgeois elements that remain in his own thought (e.g., he honors his father and his mother).

Po I-po (PC) — Peking *Daily Worker*, December 31, 1961: Subjective awareness must keep in step with objective reality. The whole country is a chessboard.

Chang Ching-wu (CR) — PD, May 25, 1962: Amnesty will be granted to Tibetans who participated in the rebellion. There will be long-term coexistence with those elements of the Tibetan elite who accept Chinese rule.

Nieh Jung-chen (CEL) — CY, June 1, 1962: The youth today have no reason for envying my generation; they have a great future building communism. They should study hard and not be afraid of difficulties. They should cultivate the virtues of earnestness, responsibility, modesty, and solidarity. This last means that while "liberalism" should be opposed, at the same time young Party members should not take a harsh attitude toward mistaken schoolmates.

Teng Tzu-hui (CEL) — CY, July 1, 1962: A discussion of pragmatic factors in the policy of sending "educated youths" to the countryside. The youths can learn effective farming methods that have proven themselves over thousands of years from the old farmers; they can evaluate the local application of the general policies of the Party and State; and they can help in agricultural mechanization. The factor of ideological tempering is also mentioned—the sending down will help overcome the "still fairly popular" idea that education brings special privileges, and will teach the young intellectuals to listen to the "masses." The young people will be exposed to no physical danger in the countryside, and, while the facilities are not as good as in the city, they will have the opportunity to continue their studies.

For full citations, see bibliography.

---

itself is probably a significant indicator of the illegitimate nature of the policies pursued. Table VIII lists the major public pronouncements by CC members at this time, and their affiliations in the Cultural Revolution.

On the CC the capitalist road policies were enunciated by men in the PC, CEL, LT, and CR groups, a fairly broad spectrum. These policies may indeed have had general support in 1961, as a panic reaction. Thus, K'o Ch'ing-shih, usually a spokesman for policies favored by Mao, argued the communes could be consolidated only gradually.[214] But the Maoists thought, or later tried to claim that they thought, of these policies as a strategic retreat.[215] Others wanted the new direction to become permanent.

The prime mover here would seem to have been P'eng Chen. There is a certain consistency in P'eng's career since 1956: he favored the Hundred Flowers, was not a major supporter of the Leap, and probably wished to abandon the Leap in 1959. While there is no really hard evidence for this contention, it seems that the adoption of the capitalist road policies in 1961 marked a shift of the balance of power within the Party Center from Teng-Hsiao-p'ing to P'eng Chen. The strong, institutionally based support for P'eng in 1966 contrasts strikingly with the weak, scattered nature of Teng's alleged group of supporters. In a discussion of the 1962 debates P'eng was later called a "big Party lord" (大黨閥),[216] implying that he had control of the Party in 1962. In 1966 (before his fall) Japanese reporters, not always the most astute observers, contended that Teng had been discredited by the failure of the Leap.[217] Teng Hsiao-p'ing, in his self-examination of October, 1966, supports this view somewhat. He talks mainly about his failure to "hold high the great red banner of the TMTT" (and this in very general terms) and the errors he and "Comrade Shao-ch'i" committed in the "50 days" prior to the 11th Plenum. In 1962, he says, he joined the right opportunists. But he also says that prior to 1962 he was a bureaucrat, a mandarin. He was "subjectivist," divorced from reality: he did not learn from the masses.[218] These last are all criticisms levied in the 1961-1962 period against the supporters of the Leap.[219] Teng also said: "In the 1964 business of 'left in form but right in essence', I had different opinions, but I still did not hold high the great red banner of the TMTT."[220] This implies that in the early 1960's Teng did not have much control over what was going on in the Party Center. It is, of course, almost beyond doubt that Liu Shao-ch'i was the highest ranking supporter of the capitalist road policies; but P'eng Chen seems to have done most of the work. It is concluded tentatively that in 1961 the Party Center passed from the control of a Liu-Teng coalition to a Liu-P'eng coalition.

The August 7, 1967 *Peking Daily* carried an interesting story about P'eng Chen's 1961 activities. In October of that year P'eng had ordered the Secretariat to undertake an investigation of past policies, including a critical examination of all of Mao's speeches to the Party Center. Liu, we are told, approved of this, but it is clear that the routine work was handled by P'eng Chen and his subordinates Liu Jen and Teng T'o.[221] The article in question asserts that these men were gathering material for a "secret speech" on Chairman Mao.[222] Taken literally, this is unconvincing: the article in fact indicates that the attack was launched on the whole policy line since 1958, and not so much on Mao personally. Thus, the Maoists are reduced to saying such things as that Teng T'o criticized resolutions "personally approved" by Chairman Mao.[223] P'eng Chen's inspection revealed: "Much good fast cheap has a fundamental contradiction: much and fast cannot be good and cheap...The Great Leap Forward exceeded the level of awareness of the peasants...The people's communes were too early; they did not go through a trial period; there was no regular system.[224] Most of these criticisms were already rather trite—CC members and especially cadres of lower rank had been saying more or less the same thing publicly (but with more discretion) since late 1960. But P'eng's activities seem to have brought matters to a head, and precipitated the behind-the-scenes policy debate which lasted through 1962.

P'eng and his friends in the Propaganda Department, Lu Ting-i and Chou Yang, also promoted a new "blooming and contending" movement. In part this stemmed from a genuinely felt need to make use of trained talent.[225] But there were other motives as well. In 1962 men associated with Chou Yang encouraged writers to tell about the misery of peasants during the Leap.[226] Teng T'o, a former editor of the *People's*

Daily and a member of the Peking Municipal Committee, began publishing satirical essays against the policies of the Leap, in collaboration with his friends Wu Han and Liao Mo-sha (the "Three Family Village").[227]

P'eng Chen would perhaps have liked to develop his own influence without encroaching upon that of Mao.[228] But the logic of the structure of political opportunities would not permit this. P'eng Chen, to consolidate his own power, had to rebuild the Party, and a strong Party is a threat to the charismatic leader. And Mao, as noted above, was stuck with the Leap policies. But, P'eng Chen, to consolidate his own hold over the Party machinery, had to discredit the Leap, and to do this would be tantamount to discrediting Mao's leadership.

Perhaps Mao alone could not have stood against the Party machine. But Mao was not alone. Throughout 1961 Lin Piao had been promoting in the army a political line at odds with that being proposed for the civilians, with a special stress upon loyalty to the leader and his Thought. The general prestige of the army was rather high in 1962: Lin may have taken advantage of stepped-up Nationalist commando raids on the Fukien coast to build up a war scare,[229] and later, of course, there was the fighting with India. Probably as a move to counter the growing influence of Lin Piao, P'eng Chen and Liu Shao-ch'i pushed for the rehabilitation of P'eng Te-huai, helping him write a long essay defending his 1959 stand.[230] This, of course, could only push Mao and Lin closer together.

The position of Chou En-lai was somewhat ambiguous—something which can usually be said about his position. Some of his future allies were spokesmen for the capitalist road policies. In his 1966 self-examination, Liu Shao-ch'i maintained that one reason for his 1961-1962 mistakes was that he put too much faith in the opinions of men like Ch'en Yun, Liao Lu-yen, and Teng Tzu-hui.[231] These three men were followers of Chou En-lai. Liu no doubt had a malicious purpose in bringing up their names, but there is no reason to think he misrepresented their policies. Ch'en Yun, for example, had been in the background since the Leap, except for a brief period in 1959; but he seems to have kept up some kind of behind the scenes work. In 1961 he made an investigation of conditions in rural areas, and in his report quoted farmers saying such things as: "Those who suffered at the hands of Chiang K'ai-shek had cooked rice for their meals. Those who live in the blessed days of Chairman Mao have only congee."[232] If anything, Ch'en himself benefitted from this, becoming chairman of the CC Finance and Trade Department.[233] The May 1 *People's Daily* published without comment a photograph of what appears to be an emaciated Ch'en Yun (he may have been given a rather hard time) wedged between an obese Mao and a grinning Chou En-lai. Liu Shao-ch'i, his back to the camera, looks on.

The role of Chou En-lai's followers, and by extension that of Chou himself, since there has never been any hint he disapproved of their policies, shows the limitations of an approach to Chinese politics which concentrates solely upon the policy preferences of the participants. The policies favored by the evil cadres during the capitalist road period became the main pretext for their later purges; but in these purges Chou En-lai's group fared relatively well. Chou En-lai himself had been careful not to commit himself publicly to any controversial policy line since the Hundred Flowers; and many of his followers were purged superficially because of the policies they favored during the capitalist road period. But this must be supplemented with a more political explanation: Chou's base was the State Council. The bureaucrats, unlike the apparatchiks, presented no threat to Mao's supremacy, and, in the charismatic politics fashion, seem to have been able to hold views differing somewhat from those of Mao.

The capitalist road policies were hashed over in a series of "work meetings" held throughout 1962. During the course of these meetings Liu Shao-ch'i and those agreeing with him are supposed to have tried to put pressure upon Mao to get him to step down. Liu Shao-ch'i said (we are told): "To oppose Chairman Mao is just to oppose an individual... We need an opposition faction (反對派) both within the people and within the Party." Lu Ting-i joined in with: "In ancient times the emperors permitted opposition. T'ang T'ai Tsung had a Wei Cheng, whose special job was to oppose him."[234] The alleged enthusiasm of Liu and Lu for an "opposition faction" should probably be taken with the same grain of salt as Lu's interpretation of imperial politics. Nevertheless, had some kind of open "opposition" been allowed, this would probably have been to the benefit of the apparatus, which then favored more popular policies and also controlled the organs of mass mobilization and communication.

Around July the conflict was beginning to come to a head. Li Li, governor of Kweichow and a Maoist in the early days of the Cultural Revolution, later a member of the Ninth CC, wrote an article saying "class contradictions" existed "within the Party," and there was a need for "thought struggle" to overcome them.[235] That same month the Three Family Village published a vicious personal satire against Mao, their famous "Curing Amnesia." "There are many sick people in the world," the article began. Some of them have amnesia. The implication here, of course, is that Mao had forgotten what had happened the last time he had his way. Amnesia often develops into madness or idiocy. "If these two grave changes come about, the patient must have immediate and complete rest, with no speaking at all, and no work at all. If he is forced to speak or work chaos will result." There is no positive cure for this disease. In the Ming dynasty one recommended treatment was to pour a tub of dog's blood on the patient's head and pack him in ice. This may clear his mind somewhat. "Modern western medicine sometimes treats this disease by bashing the patient's head with a special club, puts him in shock (休克), and afterwards revives him."[236] In a more subtle vein, Liu Shao-ch'i republished his *Self-Cultivation* on August 1. As noted in the first chapter, this work tends to play down the role of the individual leader. In the new edition Liu removed his references to the greatness of Stalin, added an attack on "dogmatism," and criticized the "lack of regularity in Party life."[237] In September the Tenth Plenum was convened. This put an end to the trend toward liberalization, but neither side had the upper hand. The main outcome was a deadlock lasting some three years.

10. DEADLOCK

By September, 1962, the power struggle had become quite bitter, and it was not resolved by the Tenth Plenum.[238] Some personnel changes took place at the Plenum. P'eng Te-huai's men, Huang K'o-ch'eng and T'an Cheng, were removed from the Secretariat. This created two "military" vacancies, but only one was filled, that by Lo Jui-ch'ing. The other logical choice was Hsiao Hua, in those days Lin Piao's right hand man; but Hsiao did not become a secretary. In the *Work Bulletins* there is no sign of any trouble between Lo and Lin; Lo seems to have been enjoying himself doing the job he knew best, conducting purges.[239] But it was later said that in the early 1960's he developed into the major spokesman for the professional ("bourgeois") outlook in military affairs.[240] If true, this is a dramatic example of how routine professional work comes to take precedence over political work. His 1962 appointment to the Secretariat was said to have been arranged by Liu Shao-ch'i, Teng Hsiao-p'ing (who, like Lo, was a hard man) and (less likely), Ch'en Yun.[241] Lu Ting-i was also appointed to the Secretariat at this time. In an apparent victory for the Maoists, so was K'ang Sheng.

The deadlock is reflected in the public report of the plenum as well as in the personnel changes. The meeting "points with satisfaction" to the results of the economic reforms since the ninth plenum. This year was better than last, last year better than the year before. The people are "united under the Party Center and Comrade Mao Tse-tung." Having thus affirmed the results of the capitalist road (but without mentioning the liberalized policies), the report moves to more "Maoist" language. The transition from capitalism to communism will "take several decades or even longer" (Mao had changed his mind on this point since 1958). All during this period class struggles will continue. The remnants of the exploiting class look for a restoration, "and there exist autonomous capitalist inclinations among some small producers...Their numbers are not large—less than ten percent of the population—but given the opportunity they expect to leave the socialist road and walk the capitalist road." This indicates only that about 65 million people ("less than ten percent of the population") are going to have a somewhat harder life. But the statement then goes on to hint at the power struggle: "This class struggle is unavoidably reflected within the Party." The report concludes with rather pragmatic specific proposals: stress agriculture over industry; modernize agriculture; raise the standard of living of farmers.[242]

In the most simple terms, the nature of the struggle during the early 1960's can be seen as a conflict between two points of view, one stressing the unity of the country, the other seeing "class struggle" within and without the Party. Those who stressed unity, naturally enough, were those in control of the organized Party, whose position was supported by the *status quo*. Those dissatisfied with the arrangement wished further "struggle." In those early years the debate was carried out in rather esoteric terms. Yang Hsien-chen, former head of the Higher Party School, had once said that dialectical materialism could be thought of in terms of the old saying, "Two combine into one" (合二而一). Not so, said the Maoists; it should be thought of in terms of another old saying, "One splits into two" (一分為二).[243] Yang, speaking for the "establishment," stressed the combination of different viewpoints or classes or whatever into a kind of harmonious whole. The Maoists wanted to break that establishment, and hence liked to stress that any seeming unity was only superficial and transitory, and bound to give rise to ever new "contradictions." After the 10th Plenum the ideological initiative had passed to the Maoists, but the thermidorian elements still held the organization. The following years saw Maoist forays into the territory of their enemies, with the result that, for the most part, the Maoist policies were coopted by the Party establishment. Here three of the major struggles will be outlined: the socialist education campaign; the campaign for revolutionary successors; and opera reform.

A. Socialist Education

The 10th Plenum had professed concern over "spontaneous capitalist tendencies" developing in the countryside, and the Center later decided to initiate a "socialist education movement" to deal with them. Prior to the Leap, it will be recalled, there had also been a rural socialist education movement, and the Maoists, or at least Mao, may have been thinking of preparing for another leap. But a more immediate purpose seems to have been to contribute to the demoralization of the Party described in the last chapter. In any case, this movement is one of the more obscure and confused in the regime's history, and the analysis here is tentative.[244]

The first Center decision on the socialist education movement was a ten-point resolution dated May, 1963. This document is said to have been the work of Mao Tse-tung.[245] It does indeed have a Maoist ring: Man's knowledge does not come from the sky or from his own brain, but from the relations of production. It thus follows that if man's thinking can be changed, so can the relations of production.[246] This curious bit of logic is later modified: thought and matter are inter-related, and changes in one produce changes in the other—apparently a rather common-sense, if not profound, proposition. This theoretical section is on the whole closer in spirit to philosophical pragmatism than to Marxism: "Generally speaking, what succeeds is correct, what fails is mistaken." But (no doubt with 1958-1960 in mind), temporary failure brings about long-term success. We can have a flying leap, greater than the last.[247]

The document continues: There is an erroneous way of thinking. "Since cooperativization the means of production have become public property," some reason, "so everybody is alike and works for a living."[248] This is not true. We must depend upon the poor and lower middle peasants until we achieve communism. This thesis leads into a discussion of the implications of the movement for the position of the Party. The poor and lower middle peasants must be organized into mass (non-Party) groups.[249] Some cadres have become lax. They enjoy life too much. Hence, there must be a "four cleans" movement (四清) to attack graft in the Party: to clean up accounts, warehouses, finance, and workpoints. [The four things to be cleaned tend to vary in different documents.] The masses must be mobilized for this.[250] In the meantime, cadres must participate in labor.[251]

In September a second edition of the ten articles was issued.[252] This document, more detailed than the first one, was supposedly the work of Liu Shao-ch'i and his friends. It puts greater stress upon the existing institutions, and, in general, tries to tone the movement down. "Struggle meetings are not permitted, nor is the random (乱) forcing of people to wear [dunce] caps [or: giving a bad name]. Beatings are expressly forbidden. In some places there have been random arrests, chaotic struggles, and unlawful, undisciplined punishment incidents. This, while exceptional, must arouse our serious concern."[253] The role of Party leadership was reasserted: "Depend upon the basic level organizations and the basic level cadres"; "If we do not pay attention to leadership, chaos can result."[254] The movement is a Party rectification movement; but problems should first of all be discussed within the Party cell, and only after that should the masses be called in.[255]

A year later a third document was issued.[256] This time the stress was no longer upon the local level cadres; it was, rather, upon the work teams sent from the Center. They should "mobilize the masses, carry out the policy, be responsible for the completion of every aspect of the work of the socialist education movement."[257] The basic level cadres were to be rectified.[258] Baum and Teiwes say, "Throughout the late fall of 1964 the cadres...were attacked from all directions, and their modest efforts at self-defense were summarily dismissed as attempts to 'hoodwink the masses.'"[259] But the September, 1964, document is also attributed to Liu Shao-ch'i. It later turned out that Liu's 1964 sin was that he was "left in form, right in substance." Apparently Liu and his supporters controlled the work teams sent from the Center, and were using them for their own purposes.

The horrible example here was the rectification of the Peach Garden brigade in Hopei. Liu "directed his old lady, Wang XX [Kuang-mei]" to head the work team to that place.[260] "When Wang XX came to Peach Garden, the only thing she talked about was XXX (Liu Shao-ch'i)... who is not our great leader, Chairman Mao." She wanted everyone to read *Self-Cultivation*. More to the point, perhaps, she "locked tight against the outside, strengthened control inside." She attacked good cadres before inspectors of the county control commission: "These men eat and drink and do no work. They want to rehabilitate the four uncleans." She "cultivated trustworthy claws and teeth" [爪牙 —a traditional term for the proverbially corrupt and oppressive yamen runners].[261] This account, of course, is somewhat one-sided, but at the least Liu's enemies claimed that he was using the movement to put his own men in power in the local Party branches. The formula "left in form, right in substance" is a way of getting around the embarrassing fact that Liu had co-opted the Maoist position. The wrong ox was being gored.

In January, 1965, Mao issued a new directive on socialist education, the "Twenty-three Articles."[262] This, Baum and Teiwes find, "actually tended to ameliorate, rather than intensify, existing patterns of conflict in the countryside."[263] Mao had regained control of the movement, but at the cost of temporarily toning down its militancy.

B. Revolutionary Successors

It was noted earlier that the Central Party organizations dealing with non-Party categories sometimes acted as a kind of lobby for these categories. An exception here is the machinery for dealing with "youth," headed by Hu Yao-pang. The common view was put with more than usual crassness in 1960: Young people should be the "docile tools of the Party" (黨的馴服工具). "With no talk of any conditions, you must unconditionally obey the needs of the Party..."[264] The results of this, of course, were probably not what were hoped for. In the mid-1960's Mao confided to Edgar Show his purported serious doubts about the younger generation.[265]

The campaign to cultivate worthy revolutionary successors was pushed with great vigor in 1964, but it had actually begun in 1963, clearly as part of Lin Piao's program for his own revolutionary succession. On January 22 of that year the *China Youth Daily* brought up the subject of revolutionary successors, saying they should study the Thought and take the PLA as their model.[266] In March Lo Jui-ch'ing, to all appearances still in agreement with Lin Piao, announced the discovery of a young hero, then dead, Lei Feng, the first in a never-ending series of PLA models, a paragon in the study of the TMTT. Lo said, "The emergence of Lei Feng is not an isolated, accidental phenomenon." The army can produce many others just like him, for during the past few years our army "has firmly implemented the directives of Marshal Lin Piao."

> There are many things we can learn from Comrade Lei Feng. However, what I think is most worthy of our learning from...is his always reading Chairman Mao's books, sincerely listening to Chairman Mao's words, at all times behaving in accord with Chairman Mao's directives: with his whole heart and mind being Chairman Mao's good warrior.

If the young people of our country would learn from Lei Feng, this would be a "limitlessly powerful spiritual atomic bomb."[267] The point in Lo's statement of most interest to this study is that the army, thanks to Lin Piao, was doing a better job of character molding than, say, the Communist Party.

In May a *People's Daily* editorial expressed concern about the generation that had grown up since Liberation. It seems this generation is vulnerable to the poison of bourgeois thought. "The malodorously infamous former U.S. Secretary of State Dulles" put his faith in our third generation. His hopes must not come to pass. Our young people must learn our revolutionary traditions, study the Thought, emulate Lei Feng.[268]

Later that month K'o Ch'ing-shih, perhaps one of the major ringleaders of the Maoist faction before his death, pronounced himself a believer in the character molding prowess of the PLA. A local Shanghai unit, the Nanking Road Good Eighth Company, K'o said, had been singled out for honor by the "Minister of Defense." The boys in this company are not seduced by city lights. People often say, "Shanghai is a big dyeing vat—in goes the red of the Communist Party, out comes black." This is certainly not true of the Nanking Road Good Eighth Company; they firmly resist the candy-coated bullets. "What the enemy will never be able to understand is that the PLA, armed with the TMTT, can never be corrupted or softened."[269]

In the 1964 campaigns the apparatchiks responded. In 1964 Li Hsueh-feng, first secretary of the North China Regional Bureau and at that time probably a disciple of Liu Shao-ch'i or Teng Hsiao-p'ing, announced that he had found an excellent model for the youth to emulate, a young apparatchik, Chou Ming-shan. He was still alive, a disadvantage not shared by Lin Piao's paragons. Li Hsueh-feng used some Lin Piao-type terminology in his talk about Comrade Chou: "In his daily work Chou Ming-shan always pays attention to the living use of the works of Chairman Mao." But there is a slightly different flavor—Chou Ming-shan attributes his success above all to the "leadership of the Party and government,"[270] the established institutions.

In late 1964 the talk of cultivating revolutionary successors shifted away from the army and back to the Party. An Tzu-wen discussed the problem in September. He too spoke of the dangers of "peaceful evolution," but did not stress the PLA as a solution for this. He did stress the thermidorian theme of unity, albeit a "principled unity." He emphasized Party leadership: we must promote cadres "tempered in the organization and in labor." Harkening back to the party-building line of the capitalist road, he spoke of the need to "develop democracy within and without the Party."[271]

The bulk of the work of reorganizing the Communist Youth League to fit the current line fell to its leader, Hu Yao-pang. That organization held a congress in July, 1964. Teng Hsiao-p'ing, as was his custom, made the opening speech. Perhaps significantly, Lin Piao, K'o Ch'ing-shih, and Ch'en Po-ta did not attend the meeting.[272] Hu Yao-pang's speech was in substance similar to the article by An Tzu-wen, although he did say that young people should emulate PLA heroes.[273] But he concluded with some surprisingly rightist rhetoric: "To seek truth from facts means to be an honest man, speak honest words, do honest deeds,"[274] neatly combining two of the more prominent slogans of the capitalist road period. The YCL adopted a new constitution at the Congress. The Congress removed references to the wonderfulness of the Soviet Union which had been in the old constitution, and added the "Thought of Mao Tse-tung as its guiding thought."[275] These were the only major changes. The revolutionary successors campaign would seem to be more "left in form, right in substance." The Party organization took cognizance of the challenge, made the necessary verbal adjustments, and continued on its way.

In December, 1964, the Peking *Ta Kung News* published an interesting essay, the "self-criticism" of a girl in her mid-twenties. She had had several problems. She enjoyed frivolous movies and liked to read love stories and similar bourgeois trash. Also, she felt that the was not suited for her job as an elementary school teacher, assigned to her by the Party. She felt she was condemned to menial tasks. She had ambitions and wanted to make great contributions. But the comrades straightened her out, and made her realize how bourgeois and selfish she was. Now "I want earnestly to reform my thought and move ahead with my comrades."[276] This was always the Party's way: any bit of youthful idealism that did not fit with the whim of the organization was peremptorily dismissed as bourgeois selfishness, to be dealt with by the comrades. Of course, it would not do to over-stress the differences between Mao and the Party in this regard. Maoism in practice also likes docile tools (Lin Piao's heroes lack even the dignity of tools—they are "cogs"), except the motivating force is supposed to be the internalized Thought, not the dictates of the organization. And if anything, the organization was rather more tolerant than the Maoists of such things as a fondness for escapist literature. But "Maoism" also contains some libertarian elements—elements stressing spontaneity and service to Truth. When the matter was posed in these terms in 1966 many young people in China probably saw Maoism as a most appealing alternative to the Party. When given the opportunity, many of them turned violently against the organization that had oppressed them for so long.

C. Opera Reform

The socialist education movement, and to some degree the revolutionary successors campaign, dealt with questions of control of different organizations. The "struggle" over opera reform perhaps had more symbolic than immediate practical significance, but its symbolic significance was enormous. The overt occasion for the initiation of the Cultural Revolution grew out of this movement.

Chiang Ch'ing once told a group of Red Guards that in the early 1960's she had not been feeling well. Her doctor told her she should have a hobby—perhaps she should take an interest in cultural pursuits. She did, and grew distrubed about the prevalence of plays about ghosts and historical characters, with hardly any socialist plays ever shown. She tried to change this, but got no cooperation from the Propaganda Department or the Ministry of Culture. But in July, 1966, (she says) she learned that Ch'en Po-ta and K'ang Sheng felt the same way she did.[277] Elsewhere it is claimed that Miss Chiang won the support of Lin Piao for her crusade in February, 1966.[278]

These little stories do trace the origins of the core alliance in the CR group and the alliance between that group and Lin Piao. The dates, however, are much too recent. Miss Chiang was not working single-handed against the full forces of the Party establishment. And the interest of the PLA in "proletarian" literature dates at least to the waning days of the capitalist road period in 1962.[279] Lin Tou-tou claims her papa was enthusiastic about the modern operas prior to 1965.[280] Understandably, the Maoists in general and Lin in particular would have little liking for operas featuring historical characters such as Hai Jui.

Opera reform was featured in the press in 1964, but Chiang Ch'ing's contributions were not mentioned, allegedly because of hostility to her from Lu Ting-i's and Chou Yang's "black gang."[281] Her view, however, was publicly represented by K'o Ch'ing-shih. K'o said that the movement for reform had begun toward the end of 1963, and in the East China Bureau, his jurisdiction.[282] He published an article on the reform on December 29, 1963. He said there was a need for modern plays which reflect the socialist era. This does not mean that all plays about "dead men" are beyond the pale; but such plays must demonstrate the evils of imperialism, feudalism, and the bourgeoisie. "Some people, including members of the Communist Party," "lack interest and enthusiasm" for plays reflecting current socialism. This shows that a "you die and I live" contradiction still exists and will continue to exist until the attainment of communism. Some people do not realize that in the new stage a "new morality" has arisen. Plays now must serve the economic base of socialism.

> At some times and places there are feudalist propaganda and bourgeois things on the stage which work to destroy the socialist economic base. Some people, especially some Communist Party members, are not concerned about this, do not interfere, prevent, and oppose, and even think up reasons to defend them. What a strange situation![283]

To belabor the obvious, this article shows that esthetic considerations were not central to the reform. K'o's article is a strong assertion of the Maoist ideological line, and would be seen by members of the inner circles of the regime as an attack on P'eng Chen, who in past years had encouraged literature which, in the Maoist view, works "to destroy the socialist economic base."

But in the pattern of politics in the early 1960's, P'eng moved to co-opt and moderate the new line. He too became a supporter of opera reform. Yes, said P'eng, we need new plays, and the Peking opera is in need of reform. We should no longer have plays about kings and emperors. But "we are historical materialists, and do not oppose historical plays *in toto.*"[284] We only oppose those which glorify the exploiting class. This, conceivably, could clear the way for more works like *Hai Jui Is Dismissed From Office*. P'eng also implies that the new works lack a certain artistic value: "The revolutionary content must be united with the special artistic style of the Peking opera. This is where the difficulty of reform lies."[285]

P'eng Chen also said: "In the process of reform, it is impossible that there will not be different opinions, it is impossible there will not be arguments." This requires discussion, research, and mutual help.[286] P'eng may have been feeling harassed. At the same meeting Chiang Ch'ing had brought up this problem: "I hear there are different view points on this, and it can be argued about. We must determine which side we are on. Are we on the side of positive characters or on the side of negative characters?"[287] Miss Chiang was not worried about mutual help. She seemed to want to make disagreements matters of principle, of stand, of "which side are we on?"

P'eng inserted a curious, rather irrelevant statement into his argument:

> The People's Republic of China has nearly 700 million people under the leadership of the Communist Party Center and Comrade Mao Tse-tung. Isn't it a good thing that everyone forms a big unity?

> Some people are not satisfied with this big unity—only their small group satisfies them.[288]

This is an assertion of the thermidorian values of unity, of "two combine into one," and is probably a direct attack on the factional activities of the Maoists.

During 1964, the Maoist position seems to have been coopted by its enemies. Thus, Po I-po made an appearance as a literary critic that year, praising "socialist literature." Of course, the interpretation of this as cooption may be mistaken. Po was put in the P'eng Chen group; but he was attacked more for his background than for his policy positions. His policy positions, in fact, are hard to determine, since he pronounced himself on every side of every economic controversy since 1956. In 1964 his support for the new literature may have been an attempt to throw off the incubus of his past associations with P'eng Chen and join up with the Maoists. But in his article on literature Po seems to be at odds with the Maoist class line in its crude form. He says: "This complex and uninterrupted struggle is just as Comrade Liu Shao-ch'i says, 'It is like the ebb and flow of the waves, sometimes high, sometimes low; somestimes turbulent, sometimes mild.'"[289]

Late in the year, there was perhaps a kind of ideological counterattack, with Lu Ting-i making moves to re-habilitate writing about "dead men." "If we do not think of the bitterness of yesteryear," he wondered, "how can we know the sweetness of today?"[290] In the "struggle over literature," as in other arenas, the year 1964 ended in a deadlock.

VI

THE CENTER DOES NOT HOLD:
THE DESTRUCTION OF THE PARTY CENTER

Scott Boorman has compared Chinese Communist revolutionary strategy with the game of *wei-ch'i,* or *go.*[1] While perhaps ultimately unconvincing as a strict "model" of the Maoist revolutionary "game," this is certainly a suggestive metaphor, and it can be applied to the circumstances preceding the Cultural Revolution. In 1962 Mao's enemies occupied large portions of the board. The Maoists in effect put stones down in several places in enemy territory. These initially formed "dead" groups, well contained by the non-Maoists; but by 1965 the Maoist walls began to converge and encircle the opposition.

While the non-Maoists seem to have had little trouble meeting specific challenges, during the early 1960's there was a continuing erosion of the authority of the Party to the benefit of the army and at least the symbolic position of the leader. After the formation of the political offices in 1964 the cult of Mao reached a new peak. The non-Maoists reacted to this in different ways. Ou-yang Ch'in of Heilungkiang, classified in this study with the Liu-Teng group, for some reason seems to have acquired the duty of delivering the major speeches on the occasions of new releases of the works of Mao. In July, 1964, he discussed the Thought as the "coordination of Marxism-Leninism with the concrete practice of the Chinese revolution." This position, first enunciated by Liu Shao-ch'i back in the 1940's, was becoming increasingly obsolete. Lin Piao's notion was that Mao's Thought had universal validity. Ou-yang also said, "The study of the TMTT is a long term process of thought revolution." Here study of the Thought could conceivably be used as an excuse for policy conservatism. He also said that the study of the Thought is a way to strengthen Party leadership of the masses, not precisely the function Lin Piao had in mind when he initiated this study movement. Ou-yang says that in addition to Mao, leading cadres should also study Marx, Engels, Lenin, and Stalin.[2] For the Maoists, Mao, in general, was enough.

Liu Shao-ch'i, who personally had the most to lose from the developing trend, virtually ignored Mao in his National Day speech of 1964. The Founding of the People's Republic of China, he said, was a triumph for "Marxism-Leninism, the correct leadership of the CPC and Chairman Mao, the CPC's socialist revolution and construction." At the end of his remarks Liu failed to toast Mao.[3] In the speech Mao figured only as the leader of the Party. P'eng Chen, in late 1964 perhaps enjoying his new status as "one of Chairman Mao's closest comrades in arms," spoke on National Day of "our great leader, Chairman Mao Tse-tung," and was full of phrases such as "Comrade Mao Tse-tung often tells us. . ."[4] The only superficial indication that P'eng was not a full-blooded Maoist, perhaps, was his use of "Comrade" rather than "Chairman." But P'eng may have been involved in an attempt to ridicule Mao. The captain of the world champion Chinese ping pong team (who came under the organizational jurisdiction of Ho Lung) was given a hard time during the Cultural Revolution for making fun of the Thought. In January, 1965, he published an article which does read like a parody of Lin Piao: "If you just study technique and do not study politics, if politics do not take command, then you won't play well. . ."[5] P'eng Chen commended this article to the youth of the country for their edification.[6]

Around the time of the third session of the National People's Congress (December, 1964-January, 1965) some personnel changes were made. Some of this was old business: P'eng Te-huai was removed as a vice-premier, for example, and T'an Cheng was removed as vice-minister of defense. The "Maoists" made a few gains: Lin Piao became first vice-premier, and T'ao Chu became a vice-premier. But in general the non-Maoists held their own. The "conservatives" Ch'en Yun and Teng Tzu-hui were removed as vice-premiers, the net effect here being perhaps to weaken Chou En-lai. The Ministry of Culture, which allegedly had opposed Chiang Ch'ing's literary reforms, was purged; but the new Minister of Culture was the king of hell himself, Lu Ting-i. Yang Hsiu-feng replaced Hsieh Ch'üeh-tsai as President of the Supreme People's Court. This was later said to have been the result of dark plots by Liu Shao-ch'i,[7] but the fact remains that Hsieh was a very old man and probably quite ready for retirement. In the Party around this time Li Wei-han was removed as head of the United Front Work Department, but he was replaced by Hsu Ping, his long time deputy. Both were members of P'eng Chen's group. The non-Maoists, it seems, were not always able to prevent their friends from being purged; but they still had much say in who would replace them.

1. FACTIONAL PLAY PRIOR TO THE PURGE OF P'ENG CHEN

The Maoist coalition had been forming for a long time, but it solidified throughout 1965.[8] In his speech to the National People's Congress in December, 1964, Chou En-lai committed himself openly for the first time in years, if not to a policy position, at least to a side. He said that the Party and government organizations "can still continuously produce new bourgeois elements, new bourgeois intellectuals, and other exploiting elements. These new bourgeois and other exploiting elements are always looking for protectors and representatives in the upper levels of the leading organs."[9] References to bourgeois elements in the Party had been commonplace since late 1962; but Chou's statement "escalated" the attack: now these elements were said to be receiving protection, and even representation, at the highest levels.

In February Li Hsien-nien declared himself on the Maoist side. Politics, he said, must take command of finance work. "Workers in commerce must establish and develop a proletarianized revolutionary style." They should "grasp" the "four firsts" and the "three-eight work style"—both inventions of Lin Piao. All this must be done despite pressures of ordinary work. "The more pressed you are for time, the heavier the work, the more you should study the works of Chairman Mao."[10]

In June the pessimistic P'an Fu-sheng reappeared, now as director of the All-China Federation of Marketing and Supply Cooperatives. He published an article dealing mostly along pragmatic lines with the need to pay more attention to rural by-product production (pig bristles, *etc.*). But he too was probably Maoist at this time: "We must unite with socialist education, organize the broad masses of the workers to study the works of Chairman Mao and the directions of the Party..."[11] While the point is by no means clear, it is probable that by mid-1965 that references to organizing the masses again carried pro-Mao implications.

By the summer of 1965 at the latest the T'ao Chu group had come over to the Maoist camp, and even seemed to be in training for their eventual take-over of the propaganda department. In July Wang Jen-chung rebuked cadres who thought they were too busy to study theory. He also elevated somewhat Mao's role as a Marxist thinker: "Chairman Mao's 'On Contradictions' is a continuation of Marxism-Leninism, and is one of the best philosophical works developing Marxism-Leninism."[12] Around this time T'ao Chu pronounced himself in favor of opera reform. He does not know much about Peking opera, T'ao said, but he knows what he likes—namely, the modern ones he has seen. He says we certainly do not want any more kings or emperors on the stage. "Now there are not too many proletarian things, but too few."[13] T'ao's position, however, may have been more moderate than that of, say, Chiang Ch'ing: "Naturally, we are not going to eliminate all traditional plays in the wink of an eye, and as of now never show any more." There will still be a few "as a kind of 'sideline.'" They are good for training actors.[14]

The non-Maoist groups were not inactive in 1965. That year witnessed within the army a concerted drive against the leadership of Lin Piao. At the heat of the debate, Ho Lung published an article in the *People's Daily* discussing one of Lin's favorite subjects, military democracy. The general thrust of the article closely follows Lin's thinking, with only minor exceptions. Thus, there are vague hints that Ho did not fully approve of the abolition of ranks: he ostentatiously speaks of the good relations between "officers and men." Ho Lung also says, "Our army has no internal class antagonism; the officers and men are all class brothers."[15] Lin Piao would probably not have agreed that there was no struggle between the two roads within the army, at least as long as Ho Lung remained on the MAC. Ho Lung also includes a rather surprising statement:

> Historical proofs tell us that Party leadership of the army should consist of the united collective leadership of the Party committees at all levels, and there should never be an individual dictatorship by any Party member or head.[16]

He did not say which Party member or head he had in mind. In fact, Lin Piao is mentioned only once: the army is "under the leadership of the Party Center, Chairman Mao, the MAC, and Comrade Lin Piao"[17] —in that order. There are no references to the idea that the flourishing of democracy in the PLA in the early 1960's was the work of Chief Lin. The citations are all to Mao. Ho's article accords with Lin's ideological position, but is a challenge to Lin's leadership.

Ho Lung was probably only a figurehead for the anti-Lin forces. Some say that Ho did not compose this article; rather, it was written for him by P'eng Chen's brain trust.[18] This is quite probable. The active leader of the soldiers opposed to Lin was Lo Jui-ch'ing. The date of Lo's apostasy is unclear. In 1963 Lo was the most vocal Lei Feng fan. He need not have been dissembling: he would have no objection to an increased role for the army in the life of the country; if he could have led the army himself, he probably would have preferred it. Lin's daughter says that her papa was sick for a long time,[19] apparently in 1963 and 1964 (this coincides with an extended absence from public activities). At that time Lo Jui-ch'ing is supposed to have said: "Since Lin Piao is in bad health I will hereafter handle by myself the aspects of military units with regard to the MAC's operations. Since I will deal with various affairs boldly, I need not seek Lin Piao's instructions."[20] In 1964 Lo is said to have promoted a program of military training, neglecting political work.[21] Lo seems to have been able to keep his evil nature well-hidden.

When Lin Piao was promoted to the post of First Deputy Premier at the NPC session in January, 1965, Lo Jui-ch'ing said, "I had not thought his position would rise so high." On the other hand, Lo Jui-ch'ing, as if to try to win Lin Piao's confidence, told him, "I believe in and support the leadership of Comrade Lin Piao."[22]

In 1965 Lo presented a public challenge (as public as such things ever get in the People's Republic) to Lin Piao in the arena of foreign policy. This debate has been analyzed by Donald Zagoria and Uri Ra'anan.[23] Here it is necessary only to add a few comments on the role of the debate in the on-going power struggle, and on the institutional implications of the different policy positions. In May Lo Jui-ch'ing published an article commemorating the defeat of Nazi Germany by the Soviet Union. The article stressed the Soviet victory in conventional war, and the Soviet ability to destroy the enemy "in his nest." The United States in Vietnam was compared to Nazy Germany.[24] Zagoria argues that Lo was representing the Peking "hawks," demanding a wider role for the Chinese in Vietnam and also a reconciliation with Moscow.[25]

In September Lin Piao published his famous article on "people's war," holding that revolutionary movements must be largely self-supporting; he reasserted the efficacy of the guerilla model of revolutionary warfare. This article was also perhaps the first extended exposition of the proposition that the validity of the Thought extended beyond the borders of China since the early 1950's.[26] Zagoria argues that Lin's position represented a fairly moderate stand on Vietnam and a firm stand against the Soviet Union.[27]

Zagoria's analysis, as far as it goes, is convincing. Had Lo Jui-ch'ing managed to gain control of the PLA, he would probably have been as unwilling to feed it to American fire power as was Lin Piao. But as long as he was in opposition the advocacy of a strong stand on Vietnam was a cheap way of appearing more proletarian than thou. Lin's left in form right in substance answer was a neat response to this challenge. The debate also had institutional implications. Were China to adopt, or even threaten to adopt, a strong military stand on Vietnam, the PLA would have to prepare itself to fight a conventional war on foreign soil. This line, then, would be supported by the military "professionals" since it would tend to increase their own importance in the army. By the same token, the adoption of this policy would lead to at least a partial discrediting of Lin Piao's line.

Yeh Chien-ying also had some thoughts on general military policy at that time. In the *Work Bulletins* Yeh appears as one of the strongest supporters of Mao;[28] during the Cultural Revolution he was close to Chou En-lai. In late summer, 1965, he spoke of the defeat of the KMT. He took a position on army building intermediate between Lin and Lo, with perhaps a slight inclination toward Lin's line. The PLA, said Yeh, was able to defeat the materially superior KMT armies:

> At that time the KMT still had more troops and better weapons than the PLA. However, because of the unrighteous nature of the counter-revolutionary war waged by the KMT army and the extreme corruption of the counter-revolutionary rulers, the KMT's reactionary power had already sunk to a hopeless position.

This proves that "Just as Comrade Mao Tse-tung has pointed out, 'Weapons are an important factor in war, but not the decisive factor. Man, not matter, is the decisive factor.' " But Yeh also says that as the Communists grew stronger they did engage in conventional war, destroying and capturing cities. Yeh speaks only of Mao's contributions in this article; he does not mention Lin Piao, who commanded the armies.[29]

In September Lo Jui-ch'ing made at least a partial recantation. He praised Comrade Lin Piao's "systematic exposition" of Comrade Mao Tse-tung's military theories, and agreed that in war one must depend upon the people.[30] He did not otherwise appear very convinced. Lo was probably purged in November, and was replaced by Yang Ch'eng-wu.

P'eng Chen's views on foreign policy were not at all consistent with those of Lo Jui-ch'ing. As Zagoria points out, P'eng was one of the strongest opponents of the Khrushchev revisionists in the Party hierarchy.[31] This would indicate that on the whole views on foreign policy were not the critical factor in determining alliances (although it could also indicate that had the P'eng-Lo alliance managed to secure victory it would not have held together long).[32] In October, however, P'eng echoed Lo Jui-ch'ing, comparing the United States to Nazi Germany and Fascist Japan. P'eng also seems to have been losing his appetite for the struggle: "If there are differences of opinion, it is best to make a comparison and avoid a one-sided view."[33]

The arguments over what can be put under the general heading of "socialist education" also continued. In the Twenty-three Articles Mao wrote, "The emphasis of this movement is on ridding the Party of those men in authority who have taken the road of capitalism."[34] This was perhaps the first direct (but esoteric) attack on Liu Shao-ch'i. As noted above, however, the immediate effect of the issuing of the twenty-three articles was to tone down the militancy of the socialist education movement. P'eng Chen and those around him seem to have taken advantage of this. In January P'eng "hoped that all young people regardless of background, origin, and history, would, according to the laws of socialist development and the interests and aspirations of more than 95 percent of the popular masses...firmly walk the socialist road." "Young people of the exploiting class" could join the great enterprise of socialism as long as they "politically and in their thought draw a clear line of demarcation with their families."[35] This demand seems relatively moderate: the children are not asked utterly to renounce their families. All the socialist education documents had held that in principle the sins of the fathers should not be visited upon the children, but not in P'eng's unequivocal terms.

Chu Te-hai, a vice-governor of Kirin, is classified with P'eng Chen according to the time at which he was purged. In January, 1965, he published an article urging systematic agricultural experimentation. In this article he had great praise for results achieved in 1962, not a vintage year in the Maoist reckoning. Chu recites the appropriate leftist slogans: "Strengthen thought leadership, uphold politics takes command." Study Mao. But in substance Chu urges planned, step by step development and careful testing of results. He talks about the "three unities" (三結合): of basic level cadres, old farmers, and educated youths.[36] This is a different three unities from, and more conservative than, the three unities mentioned in the Twenty-Three Articles: cadres, masses, work teams.[37] Chu Te-hai's proposals received editorial sanction from the *People's Daily* in March,[38] at that time almost tantamount to a personal endorsement from P'eng Chen.

By late spring, however, the socialist education movement began moving leftward again, perhaps because the Maoists had managed to consolidate their control. Huang Huo-ch'ing of Liaoning, also classified with P'eng Chen according to the time of his purge, published what amounts to a critique of his past revisionist policies in cadre cultivation. He may, however, have inserted some criticism of the Maoist line. He quotes a young comrade:

> I do not like the "theories" of the revisionists, but in one respect they must be affirmed. They "change" (改) Marxism-Leninism, they "change" the revolutionary policy line of the Communist Party.[39]

This may be a harmless restatement of the Maoist teaching that Marxism-Leninism is not a static dogma; but the statement is also capable of other interpretations. In Huang's article it is not explained.

Baum and Teiwes find much confusion in the socialist education movement at that time. Some of the confusion seems merely superficial, a reflection of the articulation of different factional viewpoints. Thus, in May they find T'ao Chu urging greater mass mobilization in Canton, while on same day the *People's Daily* was urging restraint in this regard.[40] The explanation here would be that T'ao Chu was expressing the Maoist position, while the *People's Daily* had for many purposes by that time become P'eng Chen's house organ. The balance was shifting to the Maoists, and by August T'ao was urging mass mobilization in the national press.[41]

Some of the confusion, however, was genuine. As Wang Jen-chung said, "Comrades who have joined in the work of socialist education find the work exacting and the struggle very complex. Because it is complex, we must always keep clear heads."[42] This was not always easy to do. Here it may be useful to mention a couple of instances of the confusion. In November, 1964, Chang P'ing-hua, one of T'ao Chu's major lieutenants, published an article calling for mass mobilization.[43] This was at the height of Liu Shao-ch'i's left in form right in substance period. One might think that Chang had not yet decided which way to jump, but the essay has a definitely Maoist tinge: Chang recommends the emulation of the PLA heroes Lei Feng and Ou-yang Hai. Perhaps Chang had not got the word. The essay does not fit neatly into the scheme proposed in this study, and should be a warning against over-simplifying the situation in China.

Another problem area is the Tachai brigade model. During the capitalist road period peasants were rewarded exclusively according to how much they could produce. The Tachai model, in addition to stressing self-reliance, its most publicized aspect, also changed slightly the system of remuneration. In the words of one student, "Team members are being compensated now for their political activism as well as their productive capacity," a system of "giving people material incentives for putting politics in command over economics."[44] The system had been adopted by the village of Tachai in Shansi in 1963, but was not widely publicized until later.

The Maoists took the system as their own, but the comments by CC members on Tachai in 1965 and early 1966 suggest that the idea was not of Maoist origin. Some of the Maoists, T'ao Chu at least, were conservative on the matter of the distribution system on the communes. In 1964 T'ao published the first extended discussion of the communes for a Chinese audience by a CC member since 1961. In his article he looked forward to the time when the commune as a whole would become the accounting unit, but he said the time was not yet ripe. The essay as a whole amounts to a rousing affirmation of the *status quo*.[45] This was a rebuke to those who might have wanted to set quotas at the household level, but it also implies opposition to tinkering of the Tachai type.

In October, 1965, T'ao Lu-chia (P'eng Chen group), who had been first secretary of Shansi at the time the Tachai model was set up, and hence probably had a lot to do with it, praised the model, especially its self-reliance (自力更生) aspect. He urged that the model be adopted everywhere.[46] In early 1966 Chiang Wei-ch'ing (Liu-Teng group) also praised the model, implying a connection between Liu Shao-ch'i and Tachai. In 1963, he said, we in Kiangsu responded to Chairman Mao's call for class struggle, but did not respond well enough. "But after Comrade Liu Shao-ch'i personally inspected our province and issued a directive" everything went well.[47] The implication is clear and striking: Mao proposed, Liu disposed.

Around the same time Chang P'ing-hua also discussed the model. He did not say that the help of Comrade Liu Shao-ch'i had been necessary to set him straight; and he seems less enthusiastic than T'ao Lu-chia or Chiang Wei-ch'ing about self-reliance. Of course we must have self-reliance, he says. To ask always for help from the state is "departmentalism" and "individualism." These deviations are more usually associated with too much self reliance. Chang also says, "Naturally, this does not mean no aid at all from the state. . . ."[48]

In spring, 1966, the "open" debate came to an end. In early April P'eng Chen lost control of the *People's Daily*.[49] On April 7 that paper published a speech by Wang Jen-chung, originally delivered on February 12. This speech was probably intended as a summary statement of the Maoist position. Wang begins moderately enough. We must bring politics to the fore. "That is to say, many of our comrades, including myself, have not studied the works of Chairman Mao well enough. . ." This does not mean, however, that we are revisionists, compromisers, or pragmatists. But it is a warning that a Marxist-Leninist Party can become a corrupt revisionist party. This will happen if we forget class struggle, as we did in 1961 and 1962.

Wang's discussion of the relationship between "politics" and "economics," like the Maoist position on this point generally, is confused.

"Some comrades point out, if we put politics takes command in the first place, use politics to command the economy, industry, technology—they understand the reason, but what at root should they do? They feel there is no way. We cannot say this is an unreasonable question." And it gets no clear answer. "Generally speaking, politics is the superstructure in the service of the economic base. At the same time, politics is the collective expression of economics. If we simplify and say that politics serves production, politics is a means, porduction the goal, this is an error." Our purpose, in any case, is to liberate mankind. We believe in political, not material incentives. This is the main difference between us and Khrushchev. "The Khrushchev revisionists talk about material incentives, talk about money takes command, and never talk about revolution, never talk about politics." It seems that Wang wants to say that "politics" takes priority over production, but cannot bring himself to do so unequivocally. (He would not relish having to explain a poor harvest in Hupei.)

Other issues do not present such problems: "The TMTT is the peak of development of Marxism-Leninism in the present age." It is "the highest guide for all work within our country and is our compass for observing and controlling the world revolution." The role of Lin Piao is also clear: "Some comrades bring up the relationship between man and matter. This problem is understood most clearly by our comrades in the army." "How do we study the works of Chairman Mao?" The way Comrade Lin Piao teaches us.

"We must talk of class struggle every year, every month, every day. We must talk of politics takes command, studying the works of Chairman Mao every year, every month, every day. . .If I have spoken incorrectly, you all criticize and I will make corrections."[50]

2. THE PURGE OF P'ENG CHEN

In the fall of 1965, Mao criticized Wu Han's *Hai Jui Is Dismissed from Office,* saying it was a revisionist work.[51] On November 10 Yao Wen-yuan, whose previous contribution to socialist construction had been to lead the crackdown on the hundred flowers in Shanghai, published a criticism of Wu Han in the *Wen Hui News,* a Shanghai non-Party paper. Yao says: Wu Han says we should "learn from Hai Jui." What is it we are supposed to learn—"returning land"? This means "the destruction of the people's communes, the restoration of the criminal rule of the landlords and the rich farmers." Wu Han wrote this play to support the rightists. "We feel *Hai Jui Is Dismissed From Office* is no fragrant flower, but a poisonous weed."[52] The article was reprinted by the *Liberation Army Daily* on November 29, and in the *People's Daily* a day later. The *People's Daily* carried an editorial comment. This is a problem of how to treat history. Many different opinions exist. We have published several of Wu Han's works, and we also praised his opera. "Comrade Mao Tse-tung" wants a hundred flowers to bloom.

> Our direction is to permit freedom of criticism and also freedom of counter-criticism. We use methods of persuasion for incorrect opinions, seeking truth from facts so as to set men right. Just as Comrade Mao Tse-tung has pointed out, "We must master methods of debate and methods of persuasion so as to overcome mistaken thought."[53]

This was tantamount to an open flouting of Mao's authority. All high level cadres would know that the master had already uttered his Thought on this matter, and that he had not called for any freedom of counter-criticism. In the subsequent months the *People's Daily* carried defenses of Wu Han as well as attacks. On December 15 the paper said, "From an overall point of view, we should still take an affirmative attitude toward Hai Jui."[54] On December 30 the paper carried Wu Han's confession. He said: I did not intend to defend the rightists, and I was not praising the feudal system. Those who doubt this might want to take a look at the last paragraph of my September, 1959, article on Hai Jui, where I denounce rightists who misuse Hai Jui. Some readers did, unfortunately, get the wrong impression, and they think that I favor reactionary policies. This is my own fault. It reflects upon my standpoint. I must study more Marxism-Leninism and the TMTT.[55] Even after this confession, considered by the Maoists to be extremely unsatisfactory, defenses continued to appear.[56]

The problem of handling the Wu Han case had been passed to a "cultural revolution group." This group had five members: P'eng Chen, Lu Ting-i, K'ang Sheng, Wu Leng-hsi (editor of the New China News Agency),[57] and, probably, Yang Shang-k'un. While Wu Han cannot at all be considered merely P'eng Chen's stooge, he could not have published what he had without at least P'eng's tacit consent. The attack on Wu Han was a prelude to the attack on Teng T'o, in turn the prelude to the attack on P'eng Chen. It is curious, therefore, that this case should be turned over to P'eng. It seems that this cultural revolution group had been set up as early as July, 1965,[58] and the case was simply passed to this group as a matter of bureaucratic routine. The only "Maoist" member (in fact, the only member not affiliated with P'eng Chen) was K'ang Sheng. He supposedly had nothing to do with the work of the committee, although this claim is not necessarily true.[59] In February, 1966, the group promulgated a "Report Outline" on the case. Wu Han, the report says, takes a bourgeois standpoint. But "problems of academic contention are rather complicated, and some matters are not easy to define within a short time...We must insist on seeking truth from facts, and uphold the principle of everyone being equal before the truth. We must convince people with facts."[60] This sound reasonable enough, except, as the revocation of the "Report Outline" pointed out, there are various kinds of "truth," and the truth in the outline was bourgeois truth. "Everyone is equal before the truth" turns out to be a pernicious bourgeois deception. The main fault of the "Report Outline," however, was what it failed to say:

> The Report Outline does not mention what Chairman Mao has said again and again, that the main evil of Wu Han's *Hai Jui Is Dismissed From Office* is the problem of dismissal from office, thus covering up the serious political nature of this struggle.[61]

Thus far, P'eng Chen's handling of the Wu Han case follows a familiar pattern: a Maoist initiative with a partial cooption and moderation of that position by the Party establishment. This time, however, there was an added twist. Some sources allege that P'eng plotted a *coup d'etat*. In February, 1966, it is said, P'eng Chen, Lo Jui-ch'ing, Lu Ting-i, and Yang Shang-k'un held a meeting; Ho Lung and a vice-minister of defense, Liao Han-sheng, also attended. They decided that in the coming July they would hold military maneuvers, occupy Peking, and remove Lin Piao from his posts. If the coup failed they would take refuge in the Southwest, controlled by Li Ching-ch'üan.[62] Another source adds that Liao Han-sheng circulated a booklet, *Quotations From Ho Lung,* among troops in Peking, in order to prepare the atmosphere for the coup.[63] This, however, sounds like a joke.

This "coup" has not yet been discussed in the official press. In the Red Guard communications Chou En-lai was once quoted as denying there had been any such attempt, but he added to his denial: "The posted wall papers should be covered, and no additional wall posters on the February *coup d'état* should be posted because the matter concerns state secrets"[64] —hardly the most convincing of denials. Arguing against the existence of a plot is the long time lag between the times of the removals of its principals. P'eng Chen was purged in May, 1966, and Ho Lung in January, 1967.[65] However, prior to late fall, 1966, the Communist leaders liked to maintain some outward decorum, and did not allow themselves to be stampeded.

A speech by Lin Piao delivered in May, 1966, at the Politburo meeting which purged P'eng Chen, is the earliest material on this matter; it does talk about a coup. "*Coups d'état* have become a fad nowadays," Lin said. There have been many coups in Chinese history, and 61 in the world since 1960, not counting Ghana, Indonesia, and Syria. "These reactionary coups should have terrified us and heightened our vigilance." A coup is being planned against us. Lin says he will not go into details, but P'eng Chen, Lu Ting-i, Lo Jui-ch'ing, and Yang Shang-k'un are implicated. He does not mention Ho Lung. "Now Chairman Mao is still here, so we enjoy the shade of a big tree. Chairman Mao is now over 70 and very healthy and he can live to be over a hundred." But bastards (王 八 蛋) and traitors are waiting to take over.[66] This last, incidentally, implies the coup was directed more against Lin than against Mao.

The discovery of the coup attempt seems to have precipitated the Cultural Revolution. The question remains, then, why P'eng Chen would have attempted such an apparently rash move. One possible reason is a feeling that Mao's death was imminent. Exaggerated reports of Mao's death have been circulating since at least 1930, but his health has never been robust. In November, 1965, Mao dropped out of view, and he could have been sick. His reported display of vigor in July, 1966, when he supposedly swam about 10 miles in an hour and five minutes, all the time chatting with Wang Jen-chung (a man in moderate physical condition who is not a distance runner would be hard put to duplicate this on foot) must have been intended to dispel rumors about Mao's health.[67] Whether Mao was sick or not, many people even inside China seem to have believed that he was.

At the same time Lin Piao was busy consolidating his own position. Lo Jui-ch'ing had been removed as chief of staff in the fall of 1965. In January, 1966, Hsiao Hua delivered what was, to that date, the highest eulogy of Lin Piao. The PLA has "brought politics to the fore." This "is in accord with the line of the army-building thought of Chairman Mao," and the entire credit belongs to Comrade Lin Piao.[68] In February Chiang Ch'ing held a literary seminar under PLA auspices in Shanghai.[69] This seems to mark the consolidation of the alliance between Lin and the future CR group. P'eng Chen may have felt a succession struggle was on, and that he had to act fast.

In February he issued his Report Outline and plotted his coup. In March Mao summoned P'eng Chen, Chiang Ch'ing, and K'ang Sheng, criticized the Report Outline, and remarked that "the Central Propaganda Department is the home of the king of hell."[70] P'eng last appeared in public on March 28. In early April he lost control of the *People's Daily*. He was purged formally by an enlarged Politburo meeting in May, and the Report Outline was revoked. On June 4 the reorganization of the Peking Party Committee was announced. The new committee was to be headed by Li Hsueh-feng and Wu Te; they had already taken up their new positions.[71]

P'eng's supporters were purged piecemeal. The revocation of the Report Outline says,

> The Report Outline of the so-called "five-man group" was in fact the report outline of P'eng Chen alone, drawn up according to his personal opinions behind the backs of other members of the "five-man group," Comrade K'ang Sheng and other comrades.[72]

K'ang Sheng was thus officially absolved from any responsibility. The door was left open for exonerating the other members. At the May Politburo meeting Lin Piao said:

> The Lo Jui-ch'ing problem has already been solved. The problem of Lu Ting-i and Yang Shang-k'un was exposed during the investigations of underground activities, and has been fermenting for some time. Now we are going to solve it. The problems of these four are connected with each other and bear certain similarities. The worst is the P'eng Chen problem.[73]

Lin had his way in July, when the Lu Ting-i problem was solved. Lu was removed from office, and attacks began against his subordinate, that unlikely libertarian, Chou Yang.[74]

3. THE PURGE OF LIU SHAO-CH'I AND TENG HSIAO-P'ING

The fall of P'eng Chen was obviously a personal victory for Lin Piao, but others benefitted as well. Lin said that aside from himself, "Chairman Mao, Premier Chou, and other comrades" had sensed that P'eng had been engaging in factional activities.[75] Indications are that these other comrades included Teng Hsiao-p'ing and, probably, Liu Shao-ch'i. The quartet of Liu, Chou, Lin, and Teng figured prominently during the summer of 1966, not always in the most natural of contexts.

The *People's Daily* editorial commemorating the 45th anniversary of the CPC named those who had been most ardent in the praise of the TMTT: Liu Shao-ch'i, Chou En-lai, Lin Piao, and Teng Hsiao-p'ing, in that order of mention (coinciding with their formal ranks).[76] A pictorial feature on the Japanese war showed photographs of Mao, Liu, and Lin. The picture of Liu was captioned, "Comrade Liu Shao-ch'i made many reports during the War of Resistance. Comrade Liu Shao-ch'i's work,

The Self-Cultivation of a Communist Party Member, was one of the basic educational works which advanced thought education during the War of Resistance."[77] On August 2 (while the eleventh plenum was in session) Yeh Chien-ying published an article on the old Resist Japan University of Yenan. This was supposed to be a model for all schools in the country. "Chairman Mao personally held the position of head of the. . .teachers' committee."

> The Center assigned Comrade Lin Piao as commandant and commissar. He was both leader, teacher, and student—these are the three unities. He has raised the red flag of the TMTT most high, and is one of the most heroic representatives of the living study living use of the TMTT.

Between these two statements we find: Comrades Liu Shao-ch'i, Chou En-lai, and Teng Hsiao-p'ing made "important contributions."[78] In fact, Resist Japan University was for most purposes Lin Piao's own show. The contributions of the last three comrades were of a rather abstract nature, and their mention was almost certainly designed to signal the current power set-up in Peking. The most obvious beneficiary of P'eng's purge would seem to be Teng Hsiao-p'ing, especially if the hypothesis proposed earlier, that P'eng had in effect displaced Teng in 1961, is true.

At a lower level the purge of the P'eng Chen complex benefitted T'ao Chu, who became director of the Propaganda Department in July. He brought with him from the Central-South Bureau Wang Jen-chung and Chang P'ing-hua. It seems likely that T'ao was Lin Piao's prime support in the apparatus. After T'ao was purged Mao was said to have said, "Teng Hsiao-p'ing introduced T'ao Chu to the Party Center. Since the beginning I thought him dishonest, but Teng Hsiao-p'ing said he was a good man."[79] On the face of it this is unlikely, as T'ao may have, for a short period, taken over Teng's job. But, as T'ao Chu's own case shows, alliances changed rapidly in those days. A Lin-Teng-T'ao coalition could possibly have formed at some point during the summer of 1966.

There has been much written on the events of the summer of 1966. The official sources are stereotyped, but unofficial ones are sometimes contradictory. There is general agreement that Liu Shao-ch'i took formal control of the Cultural Revolution around June 1, and that he sent out "work teams." Around the time of the purge of P'eng Chen, organized groups of students in Peking began attacks on the Party committees of their schools, which were staffed by men loyal to P'eng. This was called the "mass movement." The work teams (groups led by cadres from outside the particular organization) were sent in to regularize the purge.

They ran into jurisdictional disputes with the resident students, and thereupon "suppressed the mass movement" and implemented "white terror." In addition to Liu, Teng Hsiao-p'ing, Chou En-lai,[80] and T'ao Chu[81] also sent work teams.

Liu explained his actions in terms of a fear of an anti-communist mass movement. In his self-examination of October, 1966, he said: "I feared confusion and great democracy. I feared the rising up of the masses who would rebel against us. I feared the appearance of counter-revolution upon the stage. . . ."[82] This is a pathetic picture of the old revolutionary trapped in Thermidor: Liu could not conceive of revolution not led by the Party organization; and a threat to the Party was an action against the revolution. There is no reason to doubt Liu's basic sincerity on this matter.

Beyond this, Liu's more specific motives are obscure. According to a fairly early purported statement by his daughter, Liu "took the view" that the opposition to the work teams "represented a counter-attack by the former Peking Municipal Committee." "Liu said, 'Since the bourgeoisie did not give us democracy, we would not give them democracy.' He regarded all those students opposed to the work group as bourgeois elements and gave them no freedom and democracy."[83] It seems most unlikely that Liu really thought the students were supporting the old Peking Committee.

Another story, by Mr. B. Bogunovic, a Yugoslav reporter, has Liu working in a collusion with P'eng Chen after P'eng's purge. He says that after P'eng was purged, Liu and P'eng wanted to convene a plenum and overthrow Mao. They planned to hold the plenum on July 20. Working through Li Hsueh-feng, they tried to win Teng Hsiao-p'ing over to their plan.[84] Liu and P'eng did work closely together at least in 1961-1962, and this story is, in outline at least, plausible. Against it is Mao's testimony that Liu did not engage in any plot. Mr. Bogunovic also says that in mid-July CC members began converging on Peking for the plenum, but hardly any members from the East and Central-South Bureaus had arrived, nor had any military members. He suggests that Liu and P'eng planned to pack the plenum with their supporters,[85] and the distribution of forces suggested here accords with the findings on the nature of the factions in the third chapter. On July 18, the story continues, troops loyal to Lin Piao (under Yang Yung) occupied Peking. Around July 20, refreshed from his swim, Mao returned to Peking and ordered the plenum postponed. Teng Hsiao-p'ing complied.[86] Teng may have got cold feet. But whatever his faults as a leader, Teng always did seem to have a kind of scrappy courage. Were Liu in fact in league with P'eng Chen, Teng would not be eager to pull P'eng's chestnuts out of the fire. Were Liu acting alone, Teng would not necessarily be adverse to seeing Liu fall.

When Mao returned to Peking he ordered the work teams withdrawn. On July 28 K'ang Sheng criticized the work teams: "Revolution cannot be monopolized, and the masses must be allowed to make revolution themselves."[87] Teng Hsiao-p'ing also criticized the work teams: "I am very pleased because you are going to make revolution...We have had no experience with this...The experience created by the masses is generalized by so-called leaders for general guidance."[88] With this remark about "so-called leaders" Teng was running almost too true to form.

The eleventh plenum was convened on August 1. A count of the factional affiliations determined earlier shows the Maoists with a very thin majority; but some of the later Maoists may not have been on Mao's side in August, 1966. In any case, Mao felt his position weak enough to summon help from the "masses." On August 5 he wrote a wall poster of his own, "Bombard the Headquarters." Mao criticized the behavior of "certain leading comrades from the Center down to the locality" who implemented "bourgeois dictatorship" and "white terror" and "feel very pleased with themselves about it." "This is related to the 1962 right deviation and the 1964 'left' in form but right in substance mistaken deviation—how can this not arouse people's deep awareness?"[89] This was an esoteric attack on Liu Shao-ch'i, and an open appeal to the "revolutionary students" to take revenge upon the work teams.

On August 9 the resolutions of the plenum on the "Great Proletarian Cultural Revolution" were published. It was extremely unusual to publish anything about a plenum before it had been adjourned, but it is unclear in whose interests this early publication was. The resolutions announced a "new stage in the socialist revolution," opposed by "power holders on the capitalist road who have sneaked into the Party, and by the force of the customs of the old society." There is a generalized tendency to downgrade the role of the Party in favor of pure activism: "Let the masses become educated through the movement"; "unlease the masses" (放手發動群眾); some cadres are "afraid the masses will grab them by the pigtail." Cultural Revolution units should be set up, and they should be organized "like the Paris Commune." But in spite of all this there were concessions to the "moderates." There were only a "small number" of unforgivable "anti-Party anti-socialist right-wing elements" who required struggling "until they fall, until they collapse, until they stink." In contrast to the general approach of using the masses to

183

supplant the Party, the Cultural Revolution organizations were to be "under the leadership of the Party."[90] The "four cleans" were to be carried out "if the local committee thinks it is proper." Categories with some clout in the Maoist coalition were somewhat exempt from the mercies of the masses. Scientists and technicians were to be left alone as long as they "are patriotic, active workers, are not anti-Party antisocialist, and are not in contact with foreign countries"—in effect, if they were not incompetent, openly subversive, or spies—not the most rigorous of standards. Nor were the masses to fool with the army: "The Cultural Revolution and socialist education movements among soldiers will be carried out according to the directives of the Central MAC and the GPD."[91] Conflict within the Maoist coalition is already apparent in this resolution: there will be differences of opinion among the masses; they should be handled by persuasion.[92]

This resolution, radical as it is, may still represent a compromise. The drawing up of this resolution, in fact, seems to have been the easier part of the work of the plenum. Liu Shao-ch'i said, "In the second half of the plenum the question of our [his own and Teng Hsiao-p'ing's] mistakes was discussed, and an election of the Standing Committee of the Politburo was held."[93] In other words, it was at this time that the purge of Liu began. This was the more lively part of the plenum. On August 12 the *People's Daily* reported that on the 10th Chairman Mao "received the masses who had come to the Party Center."[94] This contains a strong hint of mob pressure on the Central Committee. Mao at this point seems to have packed the plenum: the public report says "representatives of the revolutionary teachers and students from universities in the capital" also attended the meeting.[95]

The leadership lineup for the top men at the first Red Guard rally on August 18 was: Mao Tse-tung; Lin Piao; Chou En-lai; T'ao Chu; (Ch'en Po-ta); Teng Hsiao-p'ing; K'ang Sheng; Liu Shao-ch'i.[96] Lin Piao was now listed as the only vice-chairman of the CC. The demotion of Liu was obvious, as were the dramatic promotions of Ch'en Po-ta, K'ang Sheng, and, especially, T'ao Chu. Teng Hsiao-p'ing, somewhat surprisingly, seems to have held his own; but by mid-September there were rumors that T'ao Chu had replaced him as Secretary General.[97] Chiang Ch'ing appeared for the first time in Party listings, sandwiched between the new chief of staff, Yang Ch'eng-wu, and T'ao Chu's sidekick, Wang Jen-chung; her rank, by these listings, was 25th. Ch'en Yun reappeared after a long absence, now in the eleventh (rather than the fourth) place.

At the Red Guard rally Lin Piao praised Mao, called for the overthrow of "old customs and habits" and the "power holders walking the capitalist road,"[98] i.e., Liu Shao-ch'i. With the work teams withdrawn the Party organs no longer had any defense against the Red Guards, whose only check, it became clear, was the army.[99] At that time the leader of the army had no cause to restrain their mischief. While the Red Guards were carrying out their militarily-backed hooliganism, the struggle against Liu and Teng went on behind the scenes, and Lin Piao's prestige continued to grow. In October Hsiao Hua told how Lin creatively applies the thought of Mao;[100] in the old days Mao had creatively applied Marxism-Leninism.

Around the middle of October a "Central Work Conference" was convened to purge Liu and Teng. Mao seems to have made several statements at this conference. He claimed that he had not been aware of Liu and Teng's "mistakes" until the promulgation of the Twenty-Three Articles in January, 1965. This may have been when Mao decided that the two had to go (the idea had, no doubt, occurred to Lin Piao much earlier), but it is clear that Mao's hostility toward the two went back to an earlier date. At times Mao was conciliatory: "You have been severely attacked and I sympathize with you." "In regard to the mistakes made in the policy line this time [since June] we cannot blame Comrades Liu Shao-ch'i and Teng Hsiao-p'ing alone. They are partly responsible, but the Party Center is also partly responsible...however, I expect the situation to improve after this conference."[101]

Elsewhere, however, Mao displays considerable bitterness: "Liu Shao-ch'i, criticizing a certain person, reprimanded that person saying there is no one so stupid as that person. However, viewed from my position, Liu Shao-ch'i is not so very wise either...Teng Hsiao-p'ing believes himself to be a genius."[102] Mao was especially harsh toward Teng Hsiao-p'ing: "Teng Hsiao-p'ing is deaf...When a conference opens he takes a seat away from me. For six years, since 1959, he has not made any reports to me. He also had P'eng Chen take charge of the work of the Secretariat."[103] Liu, and particularly Teng, had treated Mao "as if conducting a funeral for your dead parents."[104]

At this meeting Ch'en Po-ta delivered a speech attacking the "bourgeois reactionary line" (apparently as opposed to the "anti-revolutionary revisionist line" of P'eng Chen), but named no names.[105] Lin Piao spoke, criticizing "some comrades at the Central level, including Liu Shao-ch'i and Teng Hsiao-p'ing."[106] Liu and Teng made self-criticism, which, eventually, were not accepted. At the end of the conference these men were still "comrades," and they continued to appear at the Red Guard rallies. But their political careers had come to an end.

4. THE PURGE OF T'AO CHU

Foreign observers used to look upon the Cultural Revolution as a kind of madness, but indications are that the participants, at least until late December, 1966, knew exactly what they were doing. As in 1957 one section of the Party had mobilized the "masses" as a weapon against another section of the Party. For various reasons—the weakness of the Party apparatus, the role of the army, the nature of the mass movement itself—in 1966 the "masses" were much harder to control. By early September attempts were being made to dampen the Red Guard movement. At the second Red Guard rally Chou En-lai told the crowd it was a wonderful thing that the Red Guards had come to Peking; now they should go elsewhere to "exchange revolutionary experiences" (Peking's translation of 串連 or 串聯 —which implies a "linkage"; some suggest "roving solidarity" as a good translation).[107] Even Lin Piao, who still kept the radical line, urged the Red Guards to "protect the interests of the people, cherish state property."[108] On September 5 the *People's Daily* told the children to use "civil struggle", (文鬥), not "armed struggle" (武 鬥).[109] The Red Guards were also told to keep out of factories,[110] a policy endorsed by Chou En-lai.[111] As the positions of Liu and Teng became weaker some leaders began to feel the revolutionary little generals had served their function. In early November Lin Piao told them to imitate the Long March[112] —*i.e.*, get out of town, and do it on foot (thus saving the state transportation costs). Chou En-lai also warmly endorsed this idea.[113]

Chou En-lai was the most open spokesman for moderation. But even Ch'en Po-ta took a fairly mild line after the fall of Liu. A *Red Flag* editorial of early November said:

> A distinction must be made among those who have made mistakes. Those who have originated the mistaken line (of these are only one or two—less than ten) must be distinguished from those who have carried it out; those who have self-consciously carried it out (a minority) must be distinguished from those who did it unawares (a majority)...[114]

Ch'en also criticized those Red Guards who put too much stress on their "proletarian" origin: "The founding fathers [Marx and Engels] were bourgeois intellectuals in their social position. So were Lenin, Stalin, and even Chairman Mao. Those who come from a working class background do not necessarily represent the interests of the working class."[115]

Ch'en Po-ta, however, must have had mixed feelings. As of November, 1966, he had improved his position in terms of Party rank, but he had no access to bureaucratic power. His own "power base" rested in the Red Guards and in his personal relations with Mao and Mao's wife. The Cultural Revolution had not resulted in any major structural changes. Lin Piao had replaced Liu Shao-ch'i; Chou En-lai at least had the satisfaction of having seen his long-term rival fall; T'ao Chu had apparently taken over the Party apparatus. Their social revolution, as Michels would say, had been effected. Now the Red Guard movement was being phased out, and the newly formed CR group, led by Ch'en Po-ta, Chiang Ch'ing, and K'ang Sheng, would be isolated.

The beneficiaries of the new *status quo,* however, were not yet in a position to suppress forcibly the Red Guards, who were enjoying their freedom. In late November the CR group decided to take advantage of this, and made a new move. A "writers' conference" was held in Peking on the evening of November 28. Ch'en Po-ta criticized the way in which "reactionaries and anti-revolutionary revisionists" tried to use literature to corrupt the Party. Chiang Ch'ing told how these people had frustrated her. "The old Peking Committee, the old Propaganda Department, the old Ministry of Culture colluded together and committed monstrous crimes against the Party and people. They must be thoroughly exposed and liquidated." We need to give them mass justice. Wu Te said the old Peking Committee members must be "struggled until they fall, until they stink." Chou En-lai, who gets along by going along, expressed "complete agreement with Comrade Chiang Ch'ing," and led a sing-along of "Sailing the Seas Depends Upon the Helmsman [Making Revolution Depends on the TMTT]."[116] T'ao Chu was present at this gathering, but he did not have anything to say.

Inspired by Miss Chiang's call for mass justice, in early December a group of Red Guards "grabbed" P'eng Chen and some of his followers, who had previously been under house arrest.[117] On December 12, these men were "struggled against" in a mass rally in the Peking stadium,[118] the place where, in happier times, P'eng Chen had presided over mass trials and executions. The Cultural Revolution again moved left.[119]

The most vulnerable person at this stage was T'ao Chu, the new ruler of the apparatus. He headed the potentially most powerful institution in the polity while it was in an extremely weak state. He stood to gain most from any prolonged period of stability; while the other actors would not look with unequivocal disfavor upon T'ao's fall. Chou En-lai would have liked a return to law and order, but he would not like a revived Party apparatus out of his control. Lin Piao and T'ao Chu had probably been allies, but as T'ao's position became stronger his interests and those of Lin would tend to diverge. The CR group, of course, would gain from almost any upset in the *status quo*. These general factors may have been supplemented by a personal hostility between T'ao and Ch'en Po-ta. Ch'en could reasonably have expected to take control of the propaganda machinery after Lu Ting-i's fall; but T'ao had been promoted over Ch'en's head. After T'ao had fallen, Ch'en Po-ta was his most vocal critic.[120]

T'ao had displayed some fancy footwork since the summer of 1966. In July he scolded the extreme left: "Now everyone claims he is a leftist. . .", and took cognizance of his own none too radical past: "You cannot classify one as a black gang element just because one has made one or two wrong statements. You cannot say every word you utter is in line with the TMTT. Formerly I made quite a number of wrong statements." Even then he seems to have been consolidating some kind of hold over the Party: "We must have faith in the leadership of the Party. This Great Cultural Revolution is a life and death matter, and without the leadership of the Party we cannot win the fight."[121] In late August he took a more leftist track: oppose everything and everyone, he said, except Mao Tse-tung and Lin Piao.[122] For statements of this kind T'ao was to pass into Maoist mythology as the archetypical extreme leftist. Lin Chieh's "anarchist" who opposes everything, overthrows everything was in real life T'ao Chu. This, of course, was not really what T'ao had said: what T'ao implied was that Liu Shao-ch'i and Teng Hsiao-p'ing can be criticized, and so can the CR group people (and, of course, himself); but Mao and, more to the point, Lin Piao were sacrosanct.

In October, 1966, one Wang K'uang, the propaganda boss of the Central South region and hence one of T'ao's former subordinates, was attacked in the Canton *Red Guard News* (紅衛報), (the new name for the non-party *Yang Ch'eng Evening News*). This report said that Wang had opposed T'ao Chu;[123] but the substance of the attack was quite similar to that which was to be used against T'ao. In early November wall posters were being put up in Peking attacking T'ao, but they were also being covered up with others defending him.[124] In late November T'ao was listed as first ranking advisor to the Cultural Revolution Group.[125]

T'ao's reaction to the leftward turn in December is interesting and characteristic. As in his discussion of the communes in 1964, he adopted the currently most leftist position, probably in the hopes of blocking any further leftward movement. It will be recalled that Liu and Teng had not yet been completely condemned. Even after October they were still comrades. T'ao Chu, in December, became the first ranking CC member to attack them outside the councils of the Party. "Comrades Shao-ch'i and Hsiao-p'ing," he said, did not obey Chairman Mao. But T'ao's criticism of them was mild. "They are not socialist revolutionaries. They can only become bourgeois revolutionaries...So long as they do not engage in conspiratorial activities, the matter can be disposed of as a contradiction among the people."[126] T'ao neatly demonstrated the leftism of his own heart, but he was also trying to contain and moderate the struggle. Liu and Teng should be disposed of in an orderly fashion, without unnecessary fuss. Chiang Ch'ing was not amused. She said, "I have no intention to refer to the names of that small group of hoodlums who belong to the bourgeois reactionary line. The reason is that if I refer to their names it may give the impression they are average persons."[127] By December 29 at the latest posters attacking T'ao were no longer being covered up.[128] By January 7, 1967, he had become a charter member of Liu's "clique."[129]

5. THE NEW ORDER[130]

The fall of T'ao Chu knocked the props from under the emerging stabilization. The next target on the radicals' list was Chou En-lai. Toward the end of December the "high tide of the Cultural Revolution" was to hit industry.[131] The January 1 *People's Daily, Red Flag,* and *Liberation Army Daily* joint editorial spoke of "fools" (糊塗人) who "contrasted revolution and production and think that making cultural revolution will hinder production." Red Guards should go to factories to make Cultural Revolution.[132] The fool who had opposed this policy, fairly obviously, was Chou En-lai.

But while the Cultural Revolution group set the tone for the "January Storm," they did not control all the activities. Chou En-lai was obviously vulnerable, and some wall posters openly attacked him: He was said to have "right opportunistic thought." He had said such things as, "Don't condemn others arbitrarily. I would have defended P'eng Chen if somebody had criticized him as counter-revolutionary before his downfall."[133] But attacks were also being launched against the radical faction at the same time. In early January when Liu Ning-i, the chairman of the trade union federation, who had been cooperating with Chiang Ch'ing and Ch'en Po-ta, came under attack,[134] Chou En-lai ostentatiously disassociated himself from Liu.[135] K'ang Sheng was attacked for his membership in the old Cultural Revolution Group under P'eng Chen: "When you spoke in the city of Peking you said that conspirators tried to carry out a *coup d'état* in February, but you denied it later. Are you involved in a *coup d'etat?*"[136] Another wall poster ran: "1. The Central Cultural Revolution Group took a left opportunist policy line. 2. Chiang Ch'ing is becoming fanatic. 3. The same can be said about Ch'en Po-ta..."[137]

The Cultural Revolution Group no longer had full control of the mass movement; and Peking no longer had full control of China. T'ao Chu's people were carrying out "white terror"—i.e., fighting back— in the areas they had controlled. Fighting in Nanking was especially severe.[138] Chou En-lai complained of widespread strikes and business stagnation as workers left factories for "exchange of experiences."[139] All factions by that time were eager for some kind of restoration of order, but there was a difference of opinion on how this should be done.

It has been said that the Cultural Revolution was "a movement fundamentally aimed at destroying established bureaucratic authority."[140] In fact, this seems to have been the fundamental aim of only a segment of the Maoist coalition, those with no ready access to any bureaucratic authority. Chou En-lai's main objection to the Party apparatus seems to have been that he could not control it, and he was not eager to dismantle the state bureaucracy. Lin Piao wanted to substitute the military Party for the civilian Party. In January, however, the army was not yet in a strong position to carry out takeovers. This was the time of the purge of Ho Lung. At the same time the army was becoming a target for internal squabbles among the Maoists. The attacks on Hsiao Hua, first exposing differences among the pro-Lin segments of the army, are an example of this. On January 14, attacks on PLA organs were forbidden.[141] But on the same day the *Liberation Army Daily* said, "Facts prove that the struggle between the proletarian revolutionary line represented by Chairman Mao and the bourgeois reactionary line not only exists within the army, but is sharp and complicated"[142] —which implies that even if the "rebels" were to be discouraged from beating up soldiers and stealing weapons, verbal criticism of some soldiers was still permitted.

The radical CR Group version of the new order seems to have been the "Revolutionary Great Alliance." This set up was explicated in detail on January 22. It was to seize power from the "power holders on the capitalist road."[143] The role of the army was limited: the PLA was to "support the left."[144] The soldiers eventually were able to interpret this in the way most convenient for them, but in January it had a fairly literal meaning: the PLA should back power seizures by supporting the CR Group.

The revolutionary great alliance model was most closely realized in the Shanghai seizure of power, led by Red Guard mobs under the Shanghai secretaries Chang Ch'un-ch'iao and Yao Wen-yuan, with at least the tacit backing of Ch'en Po-ta.[145] PLA influence seems to have been minimal. The Shanghai "rebels" were urged on by the then leftist organs in Peking, the *Kuang Ming Daily* (edited by supporters of Chiang Ch'ing) and by *Red Flag*. The two had somewhat different ideas of the composition of the Revolutionary Great Alliance. *Kuang Ming* spoke of the alliance between the "workers, revolutionary students, and revolutionary masses of Shanghai."[146] *Red Flag* had a mildly more conservative viewpoint: the alliance was composed of "Shanghai's working class, other revolutionary masses, and revolutionary cadres."[147]

The model for the Shanghai rebels was the Paris Commune, which had received great play in the Chinese press in 1966. The main supporter of this concept among the high ranking Party members was Ch'en Po-ta.[148] On February 5, the victors in Shanghai proclaimed the Shanghai People's Commune.[149] The idea was for a kind of plebisitary democracy at least among the "revolutionary" masses, with no bureaucratic structure. By that time, however, the February adverse current was displacing the January storm, and this latest move of the Shanghai rebels was received with stony silence in Peking. The conservatives were able to prevail upon Mao to denounce the idea:

> The People's Committee of Shanghai city demanded of the Premier that "all titles of chiefs be abolished." This is extreme anarchism and is very reactionary. . .If communes are established everywhere in the country, will the People's Republic of China have to be re-named the Chinese People's Commune?[150]

The structure of the Revolutionary Great Alliance was triune in form; this evolved into the "triple unity" or "triple alliance," in which the army and the "older" cadres had a greater role. Some implications of this model became clear in mid-February, after the hard-nosed soldier Han Hsien-ch'u had been sent to Fukien to slap that province into shape. A report from Fukien spoke of "some people" who "have anarchist thought in their brains." They are arrogant and self-satisfied. "They cannot distinguish red from green or black from white; they vaguely think of overthrowing all authority, accusing all leading cadres, opposing all dictatorship." The report noted: "The PLA is the strong pillar of the triple unity."[151]

In late February Chou En-lai gained some respite. "Cadres must be treated correctly." "The experience of this half year of fierce and fiery

Great Proletarian Cultural Revolution movement proves that the majority of the cadres are good."[152] In March an explicit definition of the triple unity was given: it "must be organized from the responsible persons of the revolutionary mass organizations who truly represent the broad masses; representatives of the PLA stationed in that area; and the revolutionary cadres."[153] The analogue of this at the Center was the coalition of the CR Group, Lin Piao, and Chou En-lai. In Heilungkiang (where the takeover had occurred earlier), at least, this was mirrored almost exactly. That province was taken over by Sung Jen-ch'iung (CEL), P'an Fu-sheng (CR), and the provincial commander, Wang Chia-tao (presumably LP). This seizure also reveals the relative status of the factions. P'an and Sung indulged in great breast-beatings about their past mistakes. Wang did not mention any of his.[154]

The political opportunities in 1967 on the whole favored the military. Nevertheless, the need for form alliances limited somewhat the scope of the soldiers' authority, and by 1969 some provinces remained under civilian rule. In Shanghai, for example, the army had always played a rather passive role. By early 1969 P'an Fu-sheng was definitely the boss in Heilungkiang (Sung Jen-ch'iung had been purged, Wang Chia-tao was inactive).[155] But in most places, even down to the most basic units, military dominance was the norm. In early 1967 the leftists still had the initiative; but after the scare caused by the Wuhan incident in July and the particularly bloody fighting throughout the country in August the soldiers came to enjoy greater latitude. In the spring of 1968, after Yang Ch'eng-wu had been replaced as chief of staff by the commander of the Canton region, Huang Yung-sheng, the local soldiers were given virtually a free hand, at least where the situation was still unstable. They proceeded to teach the radical Red Guards what their elders had known for a long time, that making revolution is not a dinner party, or sewing an embroidery, or anything so refined.

VII

CONCLUSIONS

By the fall of 1956 it appeared that the Chinese revolution was entering its themidorian phase. In 1966 and 1967 the order established in 1956 finally fell apart. At least for a time the keystone of Leninist political thought, the primacy of the organized party (or, as this usually means in practice, of the party organization), came under sharp attack. This study has attempted to determine why the Party apparatus failed to institutionalize its leading position from 1956 to 1967. The major hypothesis is that the explanation lies in the nature of political opportunities and the power struggle in China.

Students of communist affairs have perhaps tended to assume that the party apparatus should "naturally" dominate the political system, as has usually been the case in the Soviet Union. This would seem to be the basic thrust of Leninism, and also of the CPC's own "party-building" line from the late 1930's into the late 1950's. Yet, it would seem, there is nothing natural about this primacy of the party organization—even in a Leninist polity the apparatus must work to earn its position; and there will generally be ambitious men in other organizations to oppose the ambitions of the apparatus. Colonel Whitson speaks of a "multi-polar balance of power" in the Chinese military.[1] This pattern extended to other segments of the elite as well, with the apparatus becoming merely one possible power base among several.

The main reason this multi-polar balance was able to persist would seem to be the continued presence of the "charismatic leader." A charismatic leader usually works as a balancer of forces, and it is in his interests that forces remain to be balanced. Similarly, it is in the (minimax) interests of most of the leaders of the various groups in the polity to bolster the position and authority of the leader, as his presence acts as a counter to the complete predominance of any one group. This last consideration, of course, does not apply to any group which feels it has a good chance of achieving and maintaining supremacy—or, in a communist state, this consideration usually does not apply to the party apparatus.[2] The apparatus, as custodian of the ideology, is able to challenge the charismatic authority of the leader. We should expect, therefore, the development of an alliance of the leader and the other groups against the apparatus.

"Ambition" was a trait attributed, by hypothesis, to "politicians." A man may achieve his ambition in several ways. He may attempt to raise the status of the institution in which he works *vis á vis* other institutions; or he may attempt to raise his own personal standing within his institution. So, if a relatively low ranking member of the apparatus in China perceives his bosses to be in conflict with persons outside the apparatus proper, he may seek to improve his own status by allying himself with the outsiders against his bosses. A certain lack of institutionalization is perhaps a prerequisite for this kind of behavior; but, in a kind of feedback process, such behavior also undermines institutionalization.

Structural factors reinforced the presence of the leader in hindering the institutionalization of the leading position of the apparatus. One such factor was the phenomenon of "multiple-hatism," whereby a person would hold positions within the apparatus and in some other bureaucracy. Both empirical political theory and the testimony of Chinese apparatchiks indicate that such persons will tend to behave in accord with the demands of their non-party roles. "Multiple-hatism" was the exception, not the rule, on the Eighth Central Committee, but members with multiple hats tended to hold high rank in the Party. This resulted in the development of pockets of autonomy within the Party. Thus, the civilian apparatus was not guaranteed control over the Party apparatus within the army. After 1964 this same pattern may have extended to the state bureaucracy. Not because of any "multiple-hatism" as such, but because of the acquisition of multiple functions by the provincial secretariats in 1958, some provinces and regions also acquired a considerable degree of autonomy. The CC became, not an instrument for central Party control, but a federation of several fairly autonomous hierarchies, with the central apparatus as one institutional interest group among several.

It was also an interest group fairly well embodied in a faction, although in general the factional structure of the CC, at least as determined by this study, underlines the lack of institutionalization in the Party. The bulk of the members of the central apparatus appear to have adhered to P'eng Chen rather than the formal head of the apparatus, Teng Hsiao-p'ing. Still others attached themselves to the radicals of the inner court, in the Cultural Revolution Group. At the same time, there were groups of regional apparatchiks allied with leaders outside the central civilian apparatus. The state bureaucracy, by and large, was fairly cohesive under Chou En-lai. The army was split into two major factions, with the winning faction, under Lin Piao, divided within itself.[3]

Thus, there was no guaranteed supremacy of the Party apparatus during the tenure of the Eighth CC. Its roles varied at different times. The apparatus was apparently on top of the world at the time of the Eighth Congress, but Mao was already mobilizing support for a limited attack on this position, not only from outside the apparatus, but also from outside the Party itself. The unintended consequences of this move resulted in a vast expansion of the scope of the Party organization, along with a re-affirmation of the glory of the leader. This expansion of scope undermined the cohesion of the Party. The "Party," to be sure, was supreme, but for practical purposes the term "Party" almost came to refer simply to a name list.[4] Lin Piao, seizing the Party organs in the army, could both by-pass those who would have preferred a more orthodox military structure and, at the same time, achieve autonomy from the civilian apparatus. Through his ideological emphasis on the TMTT he was able to topple the leaders of the civilian apparatus, if not form a solid basis for his own authority.

This study includes a long and sometimes tedious discussion of the "political relations" among CC members. This length and tediousness, I believe, are consequences of the complexity of the subject matter. For some purposes it is possible to explain the course of Chinese politics simply by focusing upon the predilections of Mao Tse-tung (assuming that these are known). But the more closely we examine the details of what happened, the less satisfactory this kind of explanation seems to become. The major point of Chapter V, perhaps, is a reaffirmation of the truism that Chinese politics is a political process—an often sloppy process involving bargaining, decision-avoidance, compromise, and shifting interests. Unlike the Russians, the Chinese seem to have an esthetic distaste for naked power nakedly displayed, and Mao is not a Stalin. If he says to one man, Do this, it is not necessarily done. In any case, Mao perhaps avoids such bluntness. To understand Chinese politics we must not focus simply upon the leader, but also upon the whole relevant elite—in this study, perhaps arbitrarily, taken to be the membership of the Central Committee.

Within the confusion of the power plays, several trends can be discovered. There is a general (but not universal) tendency for the leader and the other groups to line up against the apparatus. This pattern seems to have been broken only for a short period in 1958, when the leaders of the apparatus were allied with Mao against the state bureaucracy. This alliance was short-lived.

It was hypothesized that the structure of political opportunities changes as a result of certain decisions. From the sound and fury of the power play, we may perhaps identify two decisive periods in the tenure of the Eighth Central Committee. The first was the time of the series of decisions leading to the Great Leap Forward, committing both the leader and the apparatus to the "left line." Through its acquisition of new functions the Party over-extended itself. Also, it found itself committed to policies which, at least as originally applied, were ruining the national economy and exhausting the popular support for the regime. The second was the defeat of the rightists at Lushan in 1959. This, of course, paved the way for Lin Piao's climb to the top. Also, at this meeting Mao and the apparatus, to meet at least a partial challenge to their positions, were forced to rally to the defense of policies of whose shortcomings all were aware. The radical reforms which had begun in early 1959 might have spared China the bitterness of the early 1960's, but after Lushan it became politically inexpedient to continue with radical reform. Eventually, of course, reform did come. But neither Mao nor the Party were able to develop a systematic ideological justification for the reforms.

At Lushan, Mao had reason to feel that the magic was gone. Every set of policies he had initiated since his return to active politics in 1955 had gone sour—the co-ops, the Hundred Flowers, the Three Red Flags. For the last, he himself had probably even been punished, losing his position as state chairman. P'eng Te-huai's challenge gave Mao an opportunity to reassert his authority. Yet he knew that P'eng's substantive critique was largely correct—"We have made a mess of things." Ordinarily, a charismatic leader has great flexibility in matters of policy; but Mao is not an ordinary charismatic leader. His position depends not only upon his personal qualities, but also on the correctness of his Thought.[5] Were Mao to disavow the left line he would have had to admit that he had been wrong; and it is difficult to imagine any future for him other than honorable retirement (or, given the ways in which the power game is played in Leninist polities, a not so honorable retirement). Eventually, in the May, 1963, document on socialist education, Mao developed an ideological explaining away of the errors of the Leap.

Mao's position depended on his continued commitment to the correctness of the Leap. Given Mao's position and attitude, the apparatus was unable to devise a "theory" to coordinate with the "practice" circumstances had forced upon it. The rest follows in an almost deterministic manner: increasing desire by the leading apparatchiks to be rid of Mao; increasing hostility of Mao toward the apparatus; increasing temptation for all but the leading apparatchiks to rally to the leader. The conflict came to a head in 1966. The current leader of the apparatus, P'eng Chen, was overthrown, as were, *seriatum*, all those who threatened to take his place. The attack on the apparatus undermined all sources of authority other than the person of the leader. The civilian party organization was smashed, and does not yet appear fully to have been rebuilt.

This study has concentrated upon the actors' policy positions. Some may feel that the "real" issue was policy preference, not power.[6] To some extent this is a false dichotomy. "Power" struggles generally involve issues of "policy," and almost any "policy" will have "power" consequences. To the degree that this is true, whether to concentrate on power or policy becomes a matter of taste and analytic convenience. At other times, however, the power-policy distinction does make a difference, and power considerations may conflict with policy preferences. The hypothesis guiding this study implies that power considerations will take priority.

This study discussed the Cultural Revolution as an "abortion of Thermidor." (A more accurate, if more grizzly metaphor would call it the eventual miscarriage resulting from a 1958 abortion.) That is, the Cultural Revolution was interpreted as a defeat for some elements in the Chinese leadership who felt it was time for the revolution to end. One section of this study discusses the impact of "thermidorian" characteristics on the purge. This is not a direct measure of policy preferences. It is held, rather, that men with thermidorian characteristics would tend, over the long haul, to be conservative; and it was found that people with these characteristics did not fare very well in the Cultural Revolution. The "bad" groups were wiped out almost to a man; but among the "good" groups those purged tended to be the thermidorian members. The relationships, however, are not strong, which implies that other factors had an important role, or, perhaps, that the measures chosen in this study were not the best ones.

But the thermidor hypothesis, coupled with a study of the policies favored by the members, shows some weaknesses in a concentration on policy preferences. The Maoist coalition included many Thermidorians: T'ao Chu at the beginning, Chou En-lai all along. Some of those apparently allied with the CR group included apparatchiks with a reputation for conservatism. T'ao Chu, P'eng Chen, and Chou En-lai rarely seem to have disagreed on policy; but their political interests were different, and their behavior was not the same. In 1965 Lo Jui-ch'ing and P'eng Chen disagreed on foreign policy, but later banded together. Liu Shao-ch'i was "moderate" in 1956, "radical" in 1958, "moderate" in 1962, and "radical" ("in form") in 1964. The popular classification of Chinese politicians into "radicals" and "moderates" is a useful simplified description of their behavior, but it does not explain their behavior. This, I think, is best done by an analysis of political interests and political opportunities.[7]

Mao, at Lushan, told a rather touching story. He was speaking of his own role in the decision to make the Leap: "In the past the responsibility was with others—En-lai, XX (Ch'en Yun?). Now, it must be said, it is with me. I have managed a whole pile of things. 'The man who first made effigies should die without posterity.' " This last sentence (始作俑者, 其無後乎   ) is attributed to Confucius, who disapproved of human sacrifice, even the surrogate sacrifice of his own day, whereby clay dolls were buried with the dead. This sentence, particularly its first four characters, is a proverbial way of referring to the first person to do anything. But Mao thought of the implications of the full sentence. "I die without posterity (我無後乎). (One son was killed in battle, the other has gone mad.)"[8] In concluding this study, it may be interesting to reflect a little on Mao's possible posterity.

Viewing from the outside in the winter of 1972, we may once again say that the storm of revolution has passed. The year following the second plenum of the Ninth CC witnessed a vigorous power struggle[9]— this time, one the outside world was not invited to sit in upon. The struggle took first Ch'en Po-ta and then Lin Piao, leaving behind a curious coalition of "moderates" and "radicals." The year 1971 saw not only the much publicized return to pragmatism in foreign policy, but also a return to pragmatism in domestic policy. The land tenure system that had evolved by 1962 was reaffirmed, a signal to the farmers that they need not worry right now about the criticisms of that system voiced in 1967. The slogans used in 1971 harken back to the 1960-1962 period: "Seek truth from facts"; "Do honest deeds. . ."; "Don't tell lies." In the earlier period the slogans had been brought out in desperation, in an attempt to forestall economic collapse. But 1971, to all indications, was a very good year. This may mean that the "policy cycle"—the flux of radical initiatives, failure, and retrenchment[11]—has finally been broken. The nihilistic trend in "culture" has been moderated, if not reversed (and this thermidor still lacks the humanistic elements of earlier ones). In other words, it is possible that China has finally entered a genuine Thermidor. The factors which previously rendered this impossible, the potential for conflict between Mao and the apparatus, no longer exists in its earlier form. With all immediate threats to the authority of the leader gone, Mao (or who ever rules in his name) can possibly revert to the policy flexibility characteristic of "charismatic politics."

Whether such a stabilization is a "good thing" may, of course, be debated.[12] The brilliant portrait of Stalin in *The First Circle,* has the old tyrant musing to himself that at some point the revolution must come to an end. This, I gather, is supposed to be a very poor attitude. But surely revolution is a means for attaining other objectives, not an end in itself; and surely it is not always the most appropriate means for attaining the other objectives. China's troubles from the last days of Ch'ien-lung do not stem from any surfeit of strong, stable government. The record would seem to indicate that in those periods in which the Chinese people enjoy political stability under a government dedicated to rational policies, they are able to handle the complex problems facing their huge, poor country with a high degree of skill.[13]

It is impossible to say, of course, what form this stabilization will take, if in fact it occurs at all. Whatever its other virtues, the Cultural Revolution did at least broaden the scope of political opportunities in China. The Chinese polity may evolve into a despotism more harsh and totalitarian than that of the Soviet Union; or it may evolve a socialism with a human face more liberal than that tried in Czechoslovakia. The "period of suspense"[14] continues, and will probably continue at least until the resolution of the problem of Mao's succession.

There are grounds for optimism; but there is nothing inevitable about this "stabilization." In studying Chinese politics one gets a strong sense of *deja vu.* We have seen all of this before, and there is no guarantee that the current moderation is any different from those which have gone before. The events of the Cultural Revolution created for China some very fundamental problems, problems the leaders have so far postponed tackling.

Democratic personages in the West used to make this kind of analysis:

> What keeps China together is no longer a traditional bureaucracy or a new administration, an "apparat," where orders and commands flow along organizationally structured chains of command. It is the living study and application of Mao Tse-tung Thought that holds China together and shapes its development.[15]

This, of course, is somewhat out of date (the "living study and application," for example, was Lin Piao's brainchild); but the basic point holds: the focus of legitimacy for the system has become the person and Thought of the leader. At the same time, the basis for institutional authority has been weakened. This does not bode well for the future of the polity once the Thinker has gone to meet the King of Heaven. The death of any dictator produces a crisis.[16] It did seem that Mao had provided better than most dictators for his own succession; this has now gone by the board.

A strong institutional structure could channel and contain the forces set loose by the succession crisis, forces which could otherwise feed upon the accumulated grievances, injustices, jealousies, and insecurity of the past few decades, producing a crisis more severe than the Cultural Revolution. It is not clear that such institutional structures can be built. The army, in the realm of ideology anyway, is less important than it used to be, but it is unclear what will replace the army. Many, obviously, would like to rebuild the civilian party, and some progress has been made in this. But most of the 1971 provincial Party committees appear to have been built up around the Party organization of the local armed forces. These soldiers, whatever they think about Lin Piao (and in their time of troubles it was Chou En-lai, not Lin Piao, who came to their aid) may be unwilling either to give up the advantages of their control over military resources or to make way for civilian superiors. The "period of suspense" continues, and we who care about what happens can only wait.

NOTES

Chapter I

[1] This would seem to be the thrust of the analysis in Samuel P. Huntington, *Political Order in Changing Societies* (Yale: University Press, 1968) xii, 488 pp. This usage is somewhat more limited than most; thus, Lucian Pye, *Aspects of Political Development* (Boston, 1966) viii, 205 pp., stresses increase in capacity as only one aspect of political development. This study, it should be noted, will treat political development as a conceptually autonomous variable, with no necessary relationship to the nature of the surrounding society (in contrast, for example, to Daniel Lerner, *The Passing of Traditional Society: Modernization in the Middle East* (Glencoe, 1958) xii, 466 pp.) or to the state of economic development (as with A.F.K. Organsky, *The Stages of Political Development* (New York, 1967) xii, 229 pp.)

[2] Huntington, *op. cit.*, p. 8. James R. Townsend, however, in *Political Participation in Communist China*, (University of California Press, 1969), a work originally completed prior to the Cultural Revolution, hypothesized that the Chinese Communist commitment to the "mass line" would hinder institutionalization. pp. 217-218.

[3] The term "syndrome" is taken from W.J.M. Mackenzie, *Politics and Social Science* (Baltimore, 1967) 424 pp., p. 328, to indicate something less than a "general theory" but more than an empirical generalization.

[4] Crane Brinton, *The Anatomy of Revolution* (New York, 1958) x, 300 pp., p. 215.

[5] *Ibid.*, pp. 218-219.

[6] *Ibid.*, p. 222.

[7] From a Tsinghua University wall poster, re-printed in *Mainichi*, April 6, 1967; in *Daily Summary of the Japanese Press* (DSJP). April 8-10, 1967, p. 36.

[8] From a letter published by Red Guards from an anti-Liu female Party member, quoted in *China News Analysis* (CNA) 661, (May 26, 1967) p. 5.

[9] CNA, *loc. cit.*, p. 5.

[10] *Tung Fang Hung*, Canton (?) Feb. 18, 1967; in *Survey of the China Mainland Press* (SCMP) 3903 (March 21, 1967) p. 2.

[11] *T'i-yü Chan Pao*, Canton, SCMP, 4061, Nov. 16, 1967, pp. 2, 10.

[12] In Teng T'o, 鄧拓詩文選 *(Selected Prose and Poetry of Teng T'o)* (Hong Kong, 1966) 151 pp., p. 134.

[13] This seems to have been a fairly probable line of development in China, had other factors not intervened, in part because in China, unlike other places, no "tyrant" was associated with the Thermidorian tendencies. See Brinton, *op. cit.*,

p. 217. One might suggest that China would have developed along the lines of Yugoslavia or Czechoslovakia. *Cf.* A. Doak Barnett, *China After Mao* (Princeton: University Press, 1967) 287 pp. The line of argument in this book is quite plausible, but fails to account for the dynamic political factors.

[14] Leon Trotsky, "The Revolution Betrayed," in Samuel Hendel, *The Soviet Crucible* (Princeton: University Press, 1963) pp. 283-296, p. 286.

[15] *Ibid.*, p. 284.

[16] Milovan Djilas, *The New Class: An Analysis of the Communist System* (New York, 1957) vii, 214 pp., p. 47.

[17] *Ibid.*, p. 38.

[18] *Ibid.*, p. 50. This study, as do Trotsky and Djilas, considers the relationship between the growth of bureaucratic authority and the development of other thermidorian characteristics in society as an empirical one, not a matter of definition. In the very short run, it might be noted, the institutionalization of the position of the Party may not lead to Thermidor. As times goes on, however, the Party bureaucracy tends to become a bureaucracy like any other, and thus is exposed to factors leading to a more general Thermidor. In China for a period, the Party apparatus took over many functions of the state machine, and this served to intensify the more general tendency.

[19] Organsky, *op. cit.*, p. 98.

[20] David Apter, *The Politics of Modernization* (University of Chicago Press, 1967) xvi, 481 pp., pp. 172-173. Joseph LaPalombara has argued that Apter's statement itself is an example of thermidorian thinking (personal communication, spring, 1968). Certainly a Maoist would disagree with Apter; but it seems to me that empirically Apter is right and the Maoists wrong on this point.

[21] Robert Michels, *Political Parties: A Sociological Study of the Oligarchical Tendencies of Modern Democracy* (New York, 1919) ix, 416 pp., p. 189.

[22] *Ibid.*, p. 305.

[23] S.N. Eisenstadt, "Bureaucracy and Political Development," in Joseph LaPalombara, *Bureaucracy and Political Development,* (Princeton: University Press, 1963) pp. 96-119, p. 109. Also Anthony Downs, *Inside Bureaucracy,* (Boston, 1967) xv, 294 pp., p. 216.

[24] Giovanni Sartori, "Politics, Ideology, and Belief Systems," *American Political Science Review,* Vol. LXIII, No. 2 (June, 1969) pp. 398-411, p. 404. The bureaucrat here is apt to have an ideology with a "closed cognitive status" and "weak emotional status."

[25] Downs, *op. cit.*, p. 154.

[26] *Hung Chi P'iao P'iao,* Canton, SCMP, February 9, 1968, p. 3.

[27] Mao Tse-tung, "Problems of War and Strategy," *Selected Works,* Vol. II (Peking, 1965) pp. 219-236, p. 224.

[28] *Ibid.*

[29] Andrew C. Janos, "Authority and Violence," in Harry Eckstein, *Internal War* (New York, 1964) pp. 130-141, p. 132.

[30] Max Weber, *The Theory of Social and Economic Organizations* (New York, 1957) x, 436 pp., pp. 358-359.

[31] *Ibid.*, p. 359.

[32] Thus "charisma," as applied to leaders today, is somewhat akin to the classical concept of "tyranny." Rule by one man who controls society by virtue of his control over one or more strong political institutions (for example, the Soviet Union under Stalin) might be called a "despotism." A polity in which the ruler is limited by other strong institutions, and whose own office is highly institutionalized (for example, the United States) is similar to the medieval European concept of kingship. Unfortunately these terms have acquired too many varying connotations to be easily used in political analysis without causing misunderstanding.

[33] Joseph Nyomarkay, *Charisma and Factionalism in the Nazi Party* (University of Minnesota Press, 1967) 161 pp., p. 145.

[34] Ch'ien Tuan-sheng, *The Government and Politics of China* (Harvard: University Press, 1961) xviii, 562 pp., pp. 128, 132. Hitler and Chiang provided cohesion for a Party; but they also provided cohesion for a nation, if less successfully. (Their similarity in this respect, of course, implies no other meaningful similarity.) This latter pattern is probably numerically more common. Thus, in Indonesia, Sukarno, with no political organization of his own, for a long time provided a balance between the army and the Communists, each disliking Sukarno less than they disliked the other. Herbert Feith, *The Decline of Constitutional Democracy in Indonesia* (Cornell: University Press, 1961) xx, 618 pp., p. 591.

[35] Weber, *op. cit.,* p. 380.

[36] The curious position of Lin Piao in the 1969 Party Constitution seems to be an attempt to transfer charisma without its becoming routinized. Later events indicate this is not an easy thing to do.

[37] Huntington, *op. cit.,* p. 12. This study will not consider in much detail the "scope of support" for the regime.

[38] *Ibid.*

[39] *Ibid.,* p. 39.

[40] *Ibid.,* p. 402.

[41] V.I. Lenin, *What Is to Be Done: Burning Questions of Our Movement* (New York, 1929) 176 pp., p. 105.

[42] *Ibid.,* p. 109.

[43] As late as 1917 Lenin still contemplated a fairly rapid "withering away of the state" and other institutionalized means of coercion. V.I. Ulianov (N. Lenin) "The State and Revolution," in *The Essential Left,* (London, 1960) pp. 147-255.

[44] V.I. Lenin, *Left-Wing Communism, An Infantile Disorder* (New York, 1940) 95 pp.

[45] Leonard Schapiro and John Wilson Lewis, "The Roles of the Monolithic Party Under the Totalitarian Leader," *China Quarterly* (CQ), 40 (October-December, 1969), pp. 49-64.

[46] On Soviet politics, see Merle Fainsod, *How Russia Is Ruled* (Revised Edition; Harvard: University Press, 1965) ix, 688 pp; Leonard Schapiro, *The Communist Party of the Soviet Union* (New York, 1960) xiv, 631 pp; Robert Conquest, *Power and Policy in the USSR: The Struggle for Stalin's Succession, 1945-1960* (New York, 1967) x, 484 pp.; Myron Rush, *Political Succession in the USSR* (Columbia: University Press, 1968) xi, 281 pp.

⁴⁷Analyses which seem to stress what I call "anti-thermidorian" factors include: A. Doak Barnett, "History's Logic Weighs Against Maoism," *Life,* Vol. 62 (January 20, 1967) p. 32; Hans Grandquist, *The Red Guard: A Report on Mao's Revolution* (New York, 1967) ix, 159 pp.; Jack Gray, "Mao's Economic Thoughts," *Far Eastern Economic Review,* Vol. LXVIII, No. 3 (January 15, 1970), pp. 16-18; John W. Lewis, "Leader, Commissar, and Bureaucrat: The Chinese Political System in the Last Days of the Revolution," in Ping-ti Ho and Tang Tsou, *China in Crisis,* Vol. I Book 2 (New York, 1968) pp. 449-461; Robert Jay Lifton, *Revolutionary Immortality: Mao Tse-tung and the Chinese Revolution* (New York, 1968) xviii, 178 pp.; Richard M. Pfeffer, "The Pursuit of Purity: Mao's Cultural Revolution," *Problems of Communism,* Vol. XVIII (Nov.-Dec., 1969) pp. 12-25, Schapiro and Lewis, *op. cit.;* Stuart Schram, "The Party in Chinese Communist Ideology," CQ, 38 (April-June, 1969), pp. 1-26; Tang Tsou, "The Cultural Revolution and the Chinese Political System," CQ, 38 (April-June, 1969) pp. 63-91; Frederick C. Teiwes, "The Evolution of Leadership Purges in Communist China," CQ, 41 (January-March, 1970) pp. 122-135.

⁴⁸Brinton, *op. cit.,* p. 25.

⁴⁹For example, Lifton, *op. cit.,* p. 5.

⁵⁰This, in fact, is the Maoist interpretation. A text for this study might be the Maoist dictum: "The basic problem of revolution is that of political power." See 無產階級革命派大聯合奪走資本主義當權派的權 (The Great Alliance of the Proletarian Factions to Seize Power from the Capitalist Power-Holder Faction." In 人民日報 *(People's Daily*=PD) Jan. 22, 1967, p. 1.

⁵¹Joseph A. Schlesinger, *Ambition and Politics* (Chicago, 1966) xv, 266 pp., pp. 1, 5.

⁵²Anthony Downs, *An Economic Theory of Democracy* (New York, 1957), x, 310 pp., p. 28. This does not, of course, mean that the policy outcome will be "rational" in any larger sense. Thus, Downs "proves" that in a democracy in which both voters and politicians are rational, financial policy will rarely work to attain a Paretan optimum. See pp. 177-182. Also, John C. Harsanyi, "Rational Choice Models of Political Behavior *vs.* Functionalist and Conformist Theories," *World Politics,* Vol. XXI, No. 4 (July, 1969) pp. 513-538, pp. 525-526.

⁵³Nelson W. Polsby, *Community Power and Political Theory* (Yale: University Press, 1963), xiv, 141 pp., pp. 3-4.

⁵⁴John Wilson Lewis, *Leadership in Communist China* (Cornell: University Press, 1966) xii, 305 pp., p. 124.

⁵⁵Trotsky and Djilas both belong to this school. Thus, we have Trotsky's curious notion that Stalin was merely the tool of a reified bureaucracy. Organsky, *op. cit.,* and Barrington Moore, *Social Origins of Dictatorship and Democracy* (Boston, 1966) xix, 559 pp., belong to this general tradition, as, in many respects, does Franz Schurmann, *Ideology and Organization in Communist China* (Berkeley, 1966) xlvi, 540 pp.

⁵⁶Barnett, "History's Logic Weighs Against Maoism," *loc. cit.*

⁵⁷Robert Tucker, "The Dictator and Totalitarianism," *World Politics,* Vol. XVII, 4 (July, 1965) pp. 555-583. Schapiro and Lewis, *op. cit.,* p. 64. Tucker

bases his argument partly upon his belief that dictators such as Hitler and Stalin did actually rule their countries (p. 560). It is not clear that this was always the case with Mao Tse-tung.

[58] "Leader, Commissar, and Bureaucrat," *loc. cit.,* p. 451.

[59] See Joseph LaPalombara, "Parsimony and Empiricism in Comparative Politics: An Anti-Scholastic View." Mimeographed, Yale University, 1967, 38, 11 pp., for a discussion of the virtues of this quality.

[60] Lifton, *op. cit.,* p. 5. My objection to the personality approach is that it fails to put psychological motivations into the larger political framework.

[61] Schlesinger, *op. cit.,* p. 6

[62] Harsanyi, *op. cit.,* pp. 521-523. He also offers a fourth postulate: "People's behavior can largely be explained in terms of two dominant interests: economic advancement and social acceptance." p. 524. This is ignored here because it seems 1) irrelevant to this study; and 2) either tautological or wrong.

[63] Seymore Martin Lipset analyzes early American politics and the development of American political culture in terms of the consequences of specific political decisions, in the first part of *The First New Nation: The United States in Historical and Comparative Perspective* (Garden City, New York, 1967) xv, 424 pp. For stimulating discussions of the role of ideology in Chinese Communist politics see Benjamin I. Schwartz, *Communism and China: Ideology in Flux* (Harvard: University Press, 1968) v. 253 pp.

[64] John E. Rue, *Mao Tse-tung in Opposition, 1927-1935* (Stanford: University Press, 1966) xvii, 326 pp., pp. 289-290.

[65] The epitome of this is the Downsian party model, in which the politician satisfies his own power cravings solely by helping to assure that his party gains office. *Economic Theory,* pp. 28-31.

[66] Nyomarkay, *op. cit.,* p. 149.

[67] Schram, *op. cit.,* p. 11.

[68] For general studies of the CPC, see Robert C. North, *Moscow and Chinese Communists* (Second edition; Stanford: University Press, 1965) viii, 310 pp.; Wan Yah-hang, *The Rise of Communism in China, 1920-1950,* (Hong Kong, 1952) 77 pp.; for Communist sources, see Hu Ch'iao-mu, *Thirty Years of the Communist Party of China* (Peking, 1952), 93 pp.; and the less blatantly propagandistic Miao Chu-huang, 中國共產黨簡要歷史 *(Short History of the Chinese Communist Party)* (Peking, 1963) 214 pp. On the 1920's see Benjamin I. Schwartz, *Chinese Communism and the Rise of Mao* (Harvard: University Press, 1966), x, 258 pp.; Conrad Brandt, *Stalin's Failure in China. 1924-1927* (New York, 1966) xiv, 226 pp.; Allen S. Whiting, *Soviet Policies in China* (Stanford: University Press, 1968) viii, 350 pp.; Maurice Meisner, *Li Ta-chao and the Origins of Chinese Marxism* (Harvard: University Press, 1967) xvii, 326 pp. For the 1928-1936 period, see Rue, *op. cit.;* and the useful documentary survey by Hsiao Tso-liang, *Power Relations Within the Chinese Communist Movement, 1930-1934: A Study of Documents* (University of Washington Press, 1964) x, 401 pp. After this there is a gap. But see Chalmers Johnson, *Peasant Nationalism and Communist China: The Emergence of Revolutionary China, 1937-1940* (Stanford: University Press, 1962) xii, 256 pp. For the early period of Communist rule, see Richard Walker,

China Under Communism: The First Five Years (Yale: University Press, 1955) xv, 403 pp.; and Peter S.H. Tang, *Communist China Today* (New York, 1957) 516 pp.; for biographical material on Mao, see his "autobiography" in Edgar Snow, *Red Star Over China* (New York, 1961) 529 pp., pp. 121 ff.; Jerome Chen, *Mao and the Chinese Revolution*, (New York, 1965) 419 pp.; and Stuart Schram, *Mao Tse-tung* (Harmondsworth, 1967) 372 pp.

[69] See Wang Gung-wu, *The Structure of Power in North China During the Five Dynasties* (Stanford: University Press, 1967) vii, 257 pp., for a study of a classic pattern of dynastic decay. On the fall of the Ch'ing and the growth of military regionalism, see Li Chien-nung, *The Political History of China, 1840-1928* (Stanford: University Press, 1967) xii, 545 pp.; Mary Wright, *The Last Stand of Chinese Conservatism—the T'ung Chih Restoration, 1862-1874* (New York, 1966) viii, 356 pp.; Stanley Spector, *Li Hung-chang and the Huai River Army* (University of Washington Press, 1964) xliii, 359 pp.

[70] James E. Sheridan, *Chinese Warlord: The Career of Feng Yü-hsiang* (Stanford: University Press, 1966) x, 386 pp., p. 18.

[71] Fred Riggs, *Administration in Developing Countries: The Theory of Prismatic Society* (Boston, 1964) xvi, 477 pp., pp. 15-18, 182.

[72] Chow Tse-tsung, *The May Fourth Movement: Intellectual Revolution in Modern China* (Stanford: University Press, 1967) xiii, 486 pp., pp. 297-299.

[73] Meisner, *op. cit.*, p. 119.

[74] *Ibid.*, pp. 204, 209.

[75] Schwartz, *Chinese Communism*, pp. 49-50

[76] Brandt, *op. cit.*, p. 127.

[77] For a text of this Constitution see News Office, Department of State Security (Republic of China) 共匪反動文件彙編 *(Collection of Communist Bandit Reactionary Documents)* (np, nd) Vol. I, pp. 89-102.

[78] Schwartz, *Chinese Communism, passim*.

[79] A rough analogy here might be the argument between President Truman and General MacArthur. See John W. Spanier, *The Truman-MacArthur Controversy and the Korean War* (Harvard: University Press, 1959) xii, 311 pp. In the then highly institutionalized American setting, the will of the President was bound to prevail.

[80] Agnes Smedley, *The Great Road: The Life and Times of Chu Teh* (New York, 1956) xviii, 461 pp., pp. 227, 250.

[81] Rue, *op. cit.*, pp. 97-98. Also Kan Yu-lan, 毛澤東及其集團 *, (Mao Tse-tung and His Clique)*, (Kowloon, 1954) 8, 250, 3 pp., p. 30.

[82] For the Li Li-san line, see Schwartz, *Chinese Communism*, Chs. 9-10.

[83] Smedley, *op. cit.*, pp. 278-279.

[84] Hsu Kai-yu, *Chou En-lai: China's Grey Eminence* (New York, 1968) xviii, 294 pp., p. 85.

[85] Institute on Mainland China Problems 匪黨的組織與策略路線 *(The Bandit Party's Organizational and Strategic Line)* (Taipei, 1952) 176 pp., p. 16.

[86] Hsiao, *op. cit.*, p. 238.

[87] *Ibid.*, p. 240.

⁸⁸ Rue, *op. cit.*, p. 263. The matter is still unclear, however, and the nature of the course of this struggle still seems open to scholarly controversy.

⁸⁹ See "Resolutions on Questions of Party History," Mao, *Selected Works*, III, pp. 177-225. This was supposedly written by Hu Ch'iao-mu under the inspiration of Liu Shao-ch'i, according to the Red Guards. It is omitted in post-Cultural Revolution editions of Mao's works.

⁹⁰ Warren Kuo, 遵義會議, Part I, in 匪情月報 (*Bandit Affairs Monthly*) (Vol. 10, No. 7) September, 1967, pp. 93-102. Kuo's account of Liu's role is supported by Chang Kuo-t'ao, in Union Research Institute, (URI) *Collected Works of Liu Shao-ch'i Before 1944*. (Kowloon, 1969) xiv, 471 pp., p. vi. A purported text of the Tsuny Resolutions has been found and translated. Jerome Chen, "Resolutions of the Tsun-yi Conference," CQ, 40 (October-December, 1969) pp. 1-38; but there are suggestions that this is not the original text.

⁹¹ Smedley, *op. cit.*, p. 332.

⁹² *Ibid.*, p. 386.

⁹³ Chang Kuo-t'ao, "Mao Tse-tung: A New Portrait by an Old Colleague." *New York Times Magazine* (August 2, 1953) pp. 5, 45-47, p. 45. Asian People's Anti-Communist League, *Factional Struggles Within the Chinese Communist Party* (Taipei, 1960) 86 pp., p. 39.

⁹⁴ Mao Tse-tung, "Combat Liberalism" *Selected Works*, Vol. II., pp. 31-34.

⁹⁵ CC CPC, 加強黨務的三種決定 (Three Resolutions on Strengthening Party Work.) News Office, *op. cit.*, pp. 129-140.

⁹⁶ Wang Chia-hsiang, 為中國共產黨的鞏固和堅強而鬥爭 (Struggle for the Consolidation and Strength of the CPC) *Ibid.*, pp. 219-235.

⁹⁷ Boyd Compton, *Mao's China: Party Reform Documents, 1942-1945* (University of Washington Press, 1952) lii, 278 pp., p. xlvi.

⁹⁸ See the biographical appendix to Liu Shao-ch'i, *How to Be a Good Communist* (Peking, 1951) 120 pp.; Howard L. Boorman, "Liu Shao-ch'i: A Political Profile," CQ, 10 (April-June, 1962), pp. 1-22; and the introduction by Chang Kuo-t'ao in URI, *op. cit.* On Liu as the CPC's major organizational theorist, see H.F. Schurmann, "Organizational Principles of the Chinese Communists," in Roderick MacFarquhar, *Mao's China: Politics Takes Command* (MIT Press, 1967) pp. 37-98.

⁹⁹ Liu Shao-ch'i, 論共產黨員修養 (*The Self Cultivation of a Communist Party Member.*) (np, 1947) 68 pp., pp. 36-37. The nature of the composition of the CPC in its period of insurgency is typical of that of other Asian communist movements. *Cf.* Robert Thompson, *Defeating Communist Insurgency* (New York, 1967) 171 pp., pp. 35-36.

¹⁰⁰ Liu, *op. cit.*, p. 9. Liu noted, however, p. 39, that the two interests need not conflict. To his enemies, this meant he advocated "joining the Party to become an official."

¹⁰¹ *Ibid.*, p. 11. Liu's enemies say this was a veiled attack on Mao. See 揭穿"修養"三次出籠的大陰謀 (Exposing the Big Plot Whereby "Self-Cultivation" Was Put on Sale Three Times), PD, April 12, 1967, p. 2. Aside from the people Liu mentions (even these names are omitted from the English translation) his most obvious target is Wang Ming, the leader of the Bolshevik faction. It is

conceivable that even at that early date, however, Liu may have seen tendencies in Mao which worried him.

[102] Liu, *op. cit.*, p. 41.

[103] Conrad Brandt, Benjamin Schwartz, and John King Fairbank, *A Documentary History of Chinese Communism* (Harvard: University Press, 1959) 522 pp., p. 354.

[104] Liu Shao-ch'i, 論黨內鬥爭 *(Inner Party Struggle)*, n. p., 1947, 49 pp.

[105] *Ibid.*, pp. 18-21.

[106] *Ibid.*, pp. 28, 3.

[107] *Ibid.*, p. 32.

[108] *Ibid.*, pp. 32-33.

[109] Liu Shao-ch'i, "Liquidate the Menshevist Ideology Within the Party" (1943). Appendix to English translation of *On Inner Party Struggle* (Peking, 1951) pp. 71-87, p. 72.

[110] *Ibid.*, p. 73.

[111] *Ibid.*, p. 77.

[112] Brandt *et. al.*, *op. cit.*, p. 422. Brandt translates 思想 as "ideas." I have changed this to the more conventional "thought."

[113] Liu Shao-ch'i, 論黨 *(On the Party)*, (Peking, 1952) 2, 154 pp., p. 12.

[114] Rue, *op. cit.*, p. 287.

[115] *On the Party*, p. 13.

[116] *Ibid.*, pp. 93-94. Liu seems to conceive of democracy as 1) a method for checking the arrogance and ambition of middle level cadres; and 2) a method for maintaining Party morale. Liu's concept of democracy is somewhat similar to that of the psychologists who used to conduct small group experiments in the United States: "As used in much of the small group literature, participatory democratic leadership refers not to a technique of decision, but to a technique of persuasion." Sidney Verba, *Small Groups and Political Behavior: A Study of Leadership.* (Princeton: University Press, 1961) 273 pp., p. 220.

[117] *On the Party*, pp. 97, 98.

[118] CNA, 743 (February 7, 1969) p. 2.

[119] Lipset, *op. cit.*, p. 24.

[120] Walker, *op. cit.*, pp. 84-85. Lewis, *Leadership*, p. 110.

[121] PD, February 18, 1954, p. 1.

[122] Teng Hsiao-p'ing, 關於高崗饒漱石反黨聯盟的決議 (Resolution on the Kao Kang-Jao Shu-shih Anti-Party Alliance) in 人民手冊 *(People's Handbook*—PHB), 1956, p. 76.

[123] *Ibid.* Suicide in the Chinese tradition represents the ultimate form of protest, and constitutes evidence that something may have gone wrong with the mandate of heaven. See Marion J. Levy, *The Family Revolution in Modern China*, (New York, 1968) xvi, 390 pp., p. 117. This may be the source for Teng's probably quite genuine indignation.

[124] See, *e.g.*, Schurmann, *Ideology*, p. 288. For views similar to those presented here, see Tang, *op. cit.*, p. 85; Teiwes, *op. cit.*, pp. 124 ff. Teiwes thinks that the Kao Kang incident was an "unprincipled struggle," involving no policy matters. But clearly it did involve at least a dispute over what the proper locus of policy-

making should be. I become ever more impressed with the anti-Mao implications of the attacks on Kao.

[125] Teng Hsiao p'ing, *op. cit.*

[126] *Ibid.* The Cultural Revolution in many ways was the fulfillment of Kao's program, although no moves have been made to rehabilitate him. Kao, like Lin Piao (and P'eng Te-huai) was a military man, and it is thus not surprising that they should see similar programs as serving their interests.

[127] Asian People's Anti-Communist League, *op. cit.*, p. 58.

[128] Grandquist, *op. cit.*, p. 106. He ignores that there is at least one obvious exception to this generalization. Mao is certainly anti-elitist to the extent that he wishes to eliminate anyone who might be able to threaten his own unique position. By the same token, Ch'in Shih-huang-ti, Julius Caesar, Peter the Great, and Richelieu might be considered "anti-elitist."

[129] Yang Ch'eng-wu, 大樹特樹偉大毛主席的絕對權威,大樹特樹偉大毛澤東思想的絕對權威 (Greatly and Very Particularly Establish the Absolute Authority of the Great Generalissimo Chairman Mao, Greatly and Very Particularly Establish the Absolute Authority of the Great Thought of Mao Tse-tung) PD, Nov. 3, 1967, pp. 2-3. Quotation from p. 3.

[130] Lin Chieh, 打倒奴隸主義,嚴格遵守無產階級革命的紀律 (Overthrow Slavism, Strictly Observe Proletarian Revolutionary Discipline) PD, June 16, 1967, p. 2. There is some irony here. Lin is quoting from *On the Party,* and his own position is not much different from Liu's in that work. Liu did say that the correctness of a decision has no bearing on whether the decision should be obeyed. But he also says "Communists should at no time promote blind obedience." 論黨. *(On the Party)* p. 96. Liu does not explain the apparent contradiction, but it seems implicit that no one should obey an order wrong in "principle." The "correctness" Liu talks about would seem to refer to the correctness of "practical" questions. Liu also seems to say that bad leaders such as Wang Ming should not be obeyed. *Ibid.*, pp. 25-26. On this point the difference between Liu Shao-ch'i in 1945 and Lin Chieh in 1967 is mainly one of emphasis.

[131] Lin Chieh, *op. cit.*

[132] *Ibid.*

[133] Unofficial sources did carry some attacks on Yang Ch'eng-wu's ideas. The deep-revolving witty Chou En-lai said Chairman Mao did not like the term "absolute authority." "Chairman Mao is very modest." *Tzu-liao Chuan-chi,* April 20, 1968, in US Consulate General, Hong Kong, *Selections from China Mainland Magazines,* 631 (October 21, 1968) p. 19.

[134] This stress upon inter- and intra-institutional conflict implies a rejection of the so-called "totalitarian model" in its pristine form. See Robert Burrows, "Totalitarianism: The Revised Standard Version," *World Politics,* Vol. XXI, No. 2 (January, 1969) pp. 272-294. However, this model still seems useful in discussing the normative vision of society of the rulers, and the nature of the relations between the rulers and the ruled.

[135] On the loss of self-confidence by the elite, see Brinton, *op. cit.*, pp. 38-43; and John R. Gillis, "Political Decay and the European Revolutions, 1789-1848." *World Politics,* Vol. XXII, No. 3 (April, 1970) pp. 344-370, pp. 346-347.

Chapter II

[1] For a pioneer study of the elite of modern China, see Robert C. North and Ithael de Sola Pool, "Kuomintang and Chinese Communist Elites," in Daniel Lerner and Harold D. Lasswell, *World Revolutionary Elites: Studies in Coercive Ideological Movements* (MIT Press, 1966) pp. 319-455. On the Eighth Central Committee, see Chao Kuo-chun, "Leadership in the Chinese Communist Party," *Annals of the American Academy of Political and Social Science,* Vol. 321 (January, 1959) pp. 40-50 (this study treats only full members); and Donald W. Klein, "The 'Next Generation' of Chinese Communist Leaders," in Roderick MacFarquhar, *China Under Mao: Politics Takes Command* (MIT Press, 1965) pp. 69-86.

[2] To do this is to commit the "fallacy of composition": "This is to assume that what holds true for each member of a class standing alone will hold true for all members of the class taken together." W. W. Fernside and W. B. Holther, *Fallacy, the Counterfeit of Argument* (Englewood Cliffs, 1959) 218 pp., pp. 27-28.

[3] For biographical material on CC members, see *inter alia,* URI, *Who's Who in Communist China* (Hongkong, 1966) v, 754 pp.; Institute of International Relations, Republic of China, 中共人名錄 *(Chinese Communist Who's Who),* (Taipei, 1967) 4, 28, 756 pp.; Huang Chen-hai, 中共軍人誌 *(Mao's Generals),* (Kowloon, 1968) 13, 790 pp.; US Department of State, Division of Biographical Information, *Directory of Chinese Communist Officials* (Washington, DC, 1966) xii, 621 pp.; K'an, *op. cit., passim;* Ting Wang, 牛鬼蛇神集 *(Anthology of Cow Devils and Snake Spirits),* (Hongkong, 1967) 8, 209 pp.; Intelligence Section, Ministry of Defense (Republic of China), "Talk About This Fellow" (談談---這個人) series, for P'eng Te-huai (1968) 3, 139 pp.; Lin Piao (1968) 2, 4, 142 pp.; Ho Lung (1968) 4, 160 pp.; Ch'en Yi (1968) 1, 2, 120 pp.; Chu Te (1969) 2, 4, 153 pp.; Nieh Jung-chen (1969) 2, 132 pp.; 匪情研究 *(Bandit Affairs),* "Important Bandit Chiefs" 重要匪酋事畧 for the following: Ch'en Yun, Vol. II, No. 6 (June 1968) pp. 123-131; Huang Yung-sheng, Vol. II, No. 11 (November, 1968) pp. 133-141; Hsiao Ching-kuang, Vol. 12, No. 2 (February, 1969) pp. 141-149; Wang En-mao, Vol. 12, No. 3 (March, 1969) pp. 135-144; Li Hsueh-feng, Vol. 12, No. 8 (August, 1969) pp. 127-136; Wei Kuo-ch'ing, Vol. 12, No. 9 (September, 1969) pp. 125-133; Liu Chien-hsün, Vol. 12, No. 11 (November, 1969) pp. 111-120; Liu Ko-p'ing, Vol. 12, No. 12 (December, 1969) pp. 137-144; Han Hsien-ch'u, Vol. 13, No. 3 (March, 1970) pp. 141-150.

[4] Klein, *op. cit.,* p. 79.

[5] *Ibid.,* pp. 79-80.

[6] 1945 Constitution, Article 39, in Brandt *et al., op. cit.,* p. 432.

[7] 中國共產黨章程 (Constitution of the Communist Party of China) (hereafter cited as "1956 Constitution"), PHB, 1957, pp. 49-55; Article 37, p. 53.

⁸ Teng Hsiao-p'ing, 中國共產黨黨章修訂的報告 (Report on the Revision of the Party Constitution) PHB, 1957, pp. 26-37, p. 36.

⁹ Frederick C. Teiwes, *Provincial Party Personnel in Mainland China, 1956-1966* (New York, 1967) vi, 114 pp., p. 23, argues that Peking put "special trust" in Ulanfu. The Peking rulers were not a notoriously trusting group, particularly in regard to non-Uncle Tom minority leaders. It will be argued later that at one time some of the Peking rulers tried to purge, or at least weaken Ulanfu. It seems more likely that, rather than trusting Ulanfu, Peking was simply recognizing local power realities.

¹⁰ 1956 Constitution, *loc. cit.*, Article 38, p. 53.

¹¹ See the following articles by K'ang Sheng: 中國革命是偉大十月革命的繼續 (The Chinese Revolution Is the Continuation of the Great October Revolution) PD, November 7, 1957, p. 7.; 南斯拉夫的修正主義恰恰適合美帝國主義的需要 (Yugoslav Revisionism Neatly Fits the Requirements of US Imperialists) PD, June 14, 1958, p. 5.; 高舉馬克思列寧主義的紅旗前進 (Raise High the Red Banner of Marxism-Leninism and Move Forward) PD, May 5, 1959, p. 3.

¹² For "systems" see A. Doak Barnett (with a contribution by Ezra Vogel), *Cadres, Bureaucracy, and Political Power in Communist China* (Columbia: University Press, 1967) xxv, 333 pp., pp. 19, 431.

¹³ National Conference of the Communist Party of China, 關於成立黨中央和地方監察委員會的決議 (Resolution on the Establishment of a Central and Local Control Commissions) PHB 1956, pp. 79-80.

¹⁴ Liu Lan-t'ao 正確地執行黨的紀律加強黨的監察工作 (Correctly Implement Party Discipline, Strengthen Party Control Work) PD, Sept. 29, 1956, p. 5.

¹⁵ See, for example, Tung's speech to the Eighth Party Congress, "Go a Step Further in Strengthening the People's Democratic Legal System," in 匪黨八全大會決議案之綜合研究 (*General Study of the Resolutions and Documents of the Bandit Party's Eighth Congress*) (Taipei, 1956) 4, 674 pp., pp. 509-516. Hereafter, this compilation will be cited as "*Bandit Congress.*"

¹⁶ Liu Lan-t'ao, September 29, 1956, *loc. cit.*

¹⁷ 為爭黨的監察工作大躍進 (For a Great Leap Forward in Party Conrol Work) PD, March 18, 1958, p. 4.

¹⁸ Teiwes, *Provincial Leadership*, p. 50.

¹⁹ Research Institute, *op. cit.*, p. 46.

²⁰ Tseng San, 讓檔案工作更好地為國家建設服務 (Let Documentary Work Serve National Construction Even Better) PD, Oct. 2, 1956, p. 2.

²¹ PD, June 3, 1957, p. 1.

²² Lewis, *Leadership*, pp. 132-133.

²³ Research Institute, *op. cit.*, pp. 41, 46.

²⁴ *Organization Charts*, Sect. 1, p. 2.

²⁵ Lewis, *Leadership,* p. 133.

²⁶ Hsu Li-ch'ün 關於黨的幹部理論教育 (Theoretical Education of Party Cadres) PD, Sept. 26, 1956, p. 3.

²⁷ For a detailed discussion of this function, guided by Chou Yang, see Merle Goldman, *Literary Dissent in Communist China* (Harvard: University Press, 1967) xvii, 343 pp., *passim.* For a general study of Chinese Communist propaganda in all its aspects (with probably an over-estimation of its effectiveness) see Frederick C. T. Yu, *Mass Persuasion in Communist China* (New York, 1964) viii, 186 pp.

²⁸ From a 1946 communique of the Social Department, reprinted in Justice Administration Bureau (ROC), 共匪特務工作 *(The Communist Bandits' Special Work)* (Taipei, 1963) 4, 206 pp., pp. 155-160.

²⁹ From a speech delivered by Liu in Yench'eng in 1941, in *ibid.,* p. 103.

³⁰ Sent in *ibid.,* pp. 153, 150.

³¹ Another factor may have been the traditional Chinese practice, whereby political control functions were incorporated into a routinized bureaucratic structure checked by the emperor and other parts of the bureaucracy. See T'ao Hsi-sheng and Shen Jen-yuan, 明清政治制度*(The Political System of the Ming and Ch'ing)* (Taipei, 1967) pp. 97-102, in first part. For the Communists the problems inherent in keeping secret agents remained, however; in 1958 the police again were warned against "fetishism" and also that they enjoyed no special privileges. See Lo Jui-ch'ing, 公安工作必須進一步貫徹群眾路線 (Public Security Work Must Go a Step Further in Carrying out the Mass Line) PD, June 3, 1958, p. 3.

³² K'ang Sheng was replaced by Li K'o-nung, who died in 1961. It is not known who replaced Li. *Organization Charts, loc. cit.,* names Lo Jui-ch'ing as head of the Social Department, but this is unlikely, since Lo was then chief of staff of the PLA. (It is doubly unconvincing since the editors of this compilation speculate that the Social Department no longer exists.) A somewhat better guess (by Research Institute, p. 47) is Hsieh Fu-chih, then Minister of Public Security. Or, K'ang Sheng may have returned to his old job—the apparent consensus of journalistic opinion.

³³ Ma Ming-fang, 財貿戰綫上的職工鼓足幹勁奮勇前進 (The Task of the Finance and Trade Front Is to Drum Up Labor Enthusiasm and Fight Forward) PD, June 23, 1958, p. 3.

³⁴ Quoted in Lewis, *Leadership,* p. 131.

³⁵ Li Wei-han, "Advance a Step in Strengthening the Party's United Front Work," *Bandit Congress,* pp. 434-438, p. 434.

³⁶ *Ibid., passim.*

³⁷ For example, at the 1956 congress, Teng Ying-ch'ao, 黨更要加強婦女工作領導團結和發揮廣大婦女羣眾的力量 (The Party Must Strengthen Its Leadership of Women's Work, United with and Make Flourish the Strength of the Broad Female Masses) PHB, 1957, pp. 94-95, discussed the "female masses," while Ts'ai Ch'ang, 積極培養和提拔更多更好的女幹部 (Actively Cultivate and

Promote Even More and Better Female Cadres) PD, September 25, 1956, p. 3, appealed for an end to discrimination against female cadres within the Party, and for free nursery care for their children. Prior to the Cultural Revolution, however, relations between the elite and the "masses" were almost entirely manipulative. For a general study, see James R. Townsend, *Political Participation in Communist China* (University of California Press, 1967) xviii, 233 pp. He argues that the women's groups were able to push the interests of their members because the Party leadership agreed with their aspirations; p. 156.

[38] Ulanfu, "The Experience and Duty of Minority Work," *Bandit Congress*, pp. 536-544.

[39] For a study of the MAC, see Ralph L. Powell, "The Military Affairs Committee and Party Control of the Military in China," *Asian Survey*, Vol. III, No. 7 (July, 1963) pp. 347-356. The work of this body is, of course, shrouded in secrecy, but some indications of its role can be found. Thus, it is probably no coincidence that the beginning of the shelling of the off-shore islands in 1958 coincided closely with a meeting of the MAC. See 中共中央軍事委員會舉行擴大會議討論了當前局勢和國防工作 (CCP Central MAC Convenes Enlarged Meeting, Discusses Present Situation and National Defense Work) PD, July 26, 1958, p. 1.

[40] Dairen *Ko-ti T'ung-hsun*, 4 (September 13, 1967) SCMP, 4081 (December 15, 1967), p. 7.

[41] *Talk About This Fellow Ho Lung*, pp. 84-85.

[42] Research Institute, p. 86.

[43] Thus, the 1961 工作通訊 (*Work Bulletins*—WB), published by the GPD, mostly transmit and explain MAC directives, heavily dosed with the thought of "Chief Lin."

[44] Research Institute, pp. 86-88.

[45] See 為貫徹執行黨中央關於發展社會鎮反內部肅反(清理)運動的指示 (Implementation of the Center's Directive on the Social Suppression-Internal Purge (Purification) Movements) (Nov. 9, 1960) WB, 1 (January 1, 1961) pp. 29-32.

[46] 工業交通部分別建立政治部 (Industrial and Communications Ministries Severally Set Up Political Offices) PD, April 4, 1964, p. 1.

[47] Schurmann, *Ideology*, p. 304.

[48] 加強財貿部門的政治工作,促進財貿隊伍更加革命化 (Strengthen the Political Work of the Finance and Trade Departments and Further Promote the Revolutionization of the Finance and Trade Ranks) PD, June 7, 1964, p. 1.

[49] PD, April 4, 1964, p. 1.

[50] PD, June 7, 1964, p. 1.

[51] Eighth CC CPC, Ninth Plenum, 公報 (Public Report), PD, January 21, 1961, p. 1.

[52] Huang T'ien-chien, 匪偽政權十八年 (*Eighteen Years of Bandit-Puppet Power*) (Taipei, 1967) 7, 11, 908 pp., p. 419.

⁵³ Schurmann, *Ideology,* p. 143.

⁵⁴ See Schurmann's argument on this point. *Ibid.* In fact, I know of nothing to indicate that the Politburo *per se* ever made important decisions during the tenure of the Eighth CC.

⁵⁵ Parris H. Chang, "Research Notes on the Changing Loci of Decision in the CPC," CQ, 44 (October-December, 1970) pp. 169-194, pp. 169-177.

⁵⁶ *Ibid.,* p. 181.

⁵⁷ A. Doak Barnett, *Cadres,* p. 429.

⁵⁸ Powell, "MAC", p. 351.

⁵⁹ Liu Lan-t'ao, 中國共產黨是中國人民建設社會主義的最高統帥 (The Communist Party of China Is the Supreme Commander of the Chinese People in Building Socialism) PD, Sept. 28, 1959, p. 2.

⁶⁰ *Ibid. Cf.* Franz Schurmann's discussion of the distinction between "management" and "control," *op. cit.,* pp. 220-364. If the same body that manages also controls, this is tantamount to no control. Liu here was reacting against the Party line of the early Leap, and perhaps also against certain notions of Khrushchev.

⁶¹ Teng Hsiao-p'ing, 1957 PHB, p. 32. Teng was speaking here only about Party members working in state organizations. He seems originally to have supported the Great Leap system, whereby Party organizations simply displaced state organizations. This was the system that disturbed Liu Lan-t'ao. What Teng does not seem to have realized in 1956 was that the crucial factor is the nature of the function the member performs, not simply the organization he belongs to.

⁶² Li Wei-han, *op. cit.,* pp. 436, 446.

⁶³ Teng Ying-chao, *op. cit.,* p. 94.

⁶⁴ Yü Kuang-yuan, 進一步加强對科學工作的領導 (Move a Step Further to Strengthen the Leadership of the Party over Scientific Work) PD, September 27, 1956, p. 5. These views, of course, soon became very unfashionable, and even in 1956 Yü had to present them as his "personal opinion" rather than as the official Party line.

⁶⁵ A recognition of the possible importance of the division of labor within the Party itself seems rather recent. See Michael Oksenberg "Occupational Groups in Chinese Society and the Cultural Revolution," Michigan Papers in Chinese Studies, No. 2, *The Cultural Revolution in China,* (Ann Arbor, 1968) pp. 91-99, pp. 23 ff. Contrast with this the "totalitarian" view of the Party in Lewis, *Leadership,* p. 144.

⁶⁶ These figures, respectively, are from Michael P. Gehlen and Michael MacBride, "The Soviet Central Committee, an Elite Analysis," *American Political Science Review,* Vol. LXII, No. 4, (December, 1968), pp. 1232-1241, p. 1234; and Herman Akimov, "On Methods of Analyzing Soviet Politics," *Bulletin* (of the Institute for the Study of the USSR) Vol. XIV, No. 10 (October, 1967) pp. 3-15, p. 11.

⁶⁷ Akimov, *op. cit.,* p. 12. This, off hand, seems rather a low estimate.

⁶⁸ This scale as it stands is purely a convenience for summarizing the more complicated data of Table XII, and lacks any theoretical significance. The scale assumes that each of the measures of potential influence is of equal value, mainly because there seemed no *a priori* reason for assigning precedence to one or another. A study of the structural characteristics of other Central Committees, and their correlated patterns of control, might lead to a refinement of the scale, and this refined scale might be useful for a comparative testing of hypotheses about Party control.

⁶⁹ Emanuel Wallerstein, "The Decline of the Party in Single Party African States," in Joseph LaPalombara and Myron Weiner, *Political Parties and Political Development* (Princeton: University Press, 1962) pp. 201-214, p. 203.

⁷⁰ *Ibid.*, p. 214. For an argument on China similar to the one presented here, see James R. Townsend, "Interparty Conflict in China: Disintegration of an Established One Party System," in S. P. Huntington and Clement Moore, *Authoritarian Politics in Modern Society* (New York, 1970) pp. 284-310, at pp. 302-304.

⁷¹ Cf. Michael Oksenberg, *op. cit.*, p. 23.

⁷² William H. Riker, *The Theory of Political Coalitions* (Yale: University Press, 1963) xii, 300 pp., *passim*.

⁷³ *Tokyo Shimbun,* May 28, 1968, *Daily Summary of the Japanese Press* (DSJP) May 28, 1967, p. 11.

Chapter III

¹ In addition to the usual Communist periodicals, information on the fate of CC members during the Cultural Revolution has been drawn from: Red Guard newspapers translated in SCMP and wall posters and newspapers translated in DSJP, particularly from the fall of 1966 into the summer of 1968; the original documents appended to the *Bandit Affairs* biographies previously cited; Ch'en Kuang, 對中共八屆中央委員候補中央委員之調查分析 (Investigation Analysis of the Members and Alternates of the Eighth Central Committee, Communist Party of China) *Bandit Affairs,* Vol. 12, No. 3 (March, 1969) pp. 11-33; Fang Chun-kuei, 從北平"五一節"集會看共匪領導集團現況 (The Current Condition of the Communist Bandit Leadership Clique as Viewed From the May Day Meetings in Peiping) *ibid.*, Vol. 11, No. 5 (May, 1968) pp. 1-11; and 從"十一"偽慶活動看共匪領導集團現況 (The Current Conditions of the Communist Bandit Leadership Clique as Seen From the Activities in the Phony National Day Celebration) *ibid.*, Vol. 11, No. 11 (November, 1968) pp. 5-12; Ch'ien Yu-shen, *China's Fading Revolution: Army Dissent and Military Division* (Hong Kong, 1969) 405 pp.; CNA, 1966-1969; Fang Ning 共匪"文化大革命"以來被整肅或受批判重要匪幹調查 (Study of the Important

Bandit Cadres Who Have Been Purged or Criticized Since the Start of the Communist Bandits' "Great Cultural Revolution") *Bandit Affairs*, Vol. 11, No. 10 (October, 1968) pp. 65-85; 匪偽人事資料彙編人物誌部份, 民國五十六年補充修正資料 *(Supplementary Revision, 56th Year of the Republic, on Collection of Materials on Personnel Rosters of the Bandit-Puppets)* (Taiwan, 1968) Vol. 1, 252 pp.; Vol. 2, pp. 253-453, 47 (hereafter cited as *Revision);* Hsuan Mo, 楊匪成武事件的幕前幕後 (The Open and the Hidden Story of the Bandit Yang Ch'eng-wu Incident) *Bandit Affairs*, Vol. 11, No. 8 (August, 1968) pp. 43-56; Wu Chin-yih, 匪軍總政治部的癱瘓與蕭匪華被整肅 (The Paralysis of the Bandit Army's General Political Department and the Purge of Bandit Hsiao Hua) *ibid.*, Vol. 11, No. 3 (March, 1968) pp. 13-18. The numerous Nationalist sources cited above are good sources for the original materials; the analyses tend toward theoretical shallowness and are rather unimaginative, but are more thorough than many others.

[2] Ch'en Kuang, *op. cit.*, p. 26.

[3] See "Chou En-lai Talks About the 'February Adverse Current,' " a translation of a Red Guard leaflet, in *Issues and Studies*, V, 12 (September, 1969) pp. 103-104. This was a group of high ranking Communists who, in February, 1967, thought the Cultural Revolution had gone far enough. Chou En-lai pacified these men and later defended them personally, but not their action. All but T'an Chen-lin, who was made the scapegoat for the whole group, survived the Ninth Congress. But only Li Hsien-nien retained anything like his original prestige.

[4] The official press maintained this group was associated (somehow; exactly how is left unclear) with T'ao Chu. See Yao Wen-yuan, 評陶鑄的兩本書 (Criticism of Two Books by T'ao Chu) PD, September 8, 1967, pp. 1-3, p. 3. At the time this article appeared extreme radicalism was going out of style; the CR Group seems to have felt it would be useful to tar the fallen T'ao Chu with the brush of "extreme leftism." It later developed, however, that the May 16 Corps, a group hostile to Chou En-lai and certain of the regional commanders, had been led by friends of Yao Wen-yuan: Ch'i Pen-yü, Wang Li, and Lin Chieh. See Canton, *Yeh-chan Pao*, 12-13, March, 1968, SCMP, 4158, April 16, 1968, pp. 1-7. These young men had worked under Ch'en Po-ta on *Red Flag*, and apparently looked to Chiang Ch'ing as their patron. The qualification "civilian" in the above condition refers to a wrinkle in the somewhat complex power struggle: some soldiers at PLA headquarters who were apparently associated with Lin Piao had at certain points allied themselves with the May 16 Corps against their colleagues in the localities.

[5] The study of the "semantics" of Chinese politics might prove interesting. H. C. Chuang, *The Great Proletarian Cultural Revolution: A Terminological Study* (Berkeley, 1967) vii, 72 pp. provides a fascinating and witty analysis of the origins and usages of many of the terms bandied about during that period, but he does not attempt to associate specific accusations with specific groupings.

⁶痛打落水狗 (Bitterly Beat the Dog Who Has Fallen into the Water) PD, July 15, 1967, p. 1.
⁷Chang Ai-p'ing, 少奇同志在淮北敵後 (Comrade Shao-ch'i Behind Enemy Lines North of the Huai) PD, August 15, 1965, p. 5.
⁸*Asahi*, January 13, 1967; DSJP, January 13, 1967, p. 10
⁹Hsieh Fu-chih, 講話 (Speech) PD, April 21, 1967, pp. 3-4, p. 3.
¹⁰Hsuan Mo, *op. cit.*, pp. 50-51, 55. The interpretation here is based upon material in this article, but differs from Hsuan's own.
¹¹An attack dated March, 1967, in his *Bandit Affairs* biography, p. 118.
¹²*Ibid.*, p. 119.
¹³Canton *Chung-hsueh Hung-wei-ping*, SCMP, 4225, (July 25, 1968) p. 9.
¹⁴*Bandit Affairs* biography of Liu Ko-p'ing, p. 141.
¹⁵*Ibid.*, p. 142.
¹⁶See Wei's *Bandit Affairs* biography, *loc. cit.*, p. 132.
¹⁷See, for example, 在毛澤東思想紅旗之下團結起來 (Get United Under the Red Flag of the TMTT.) PD, September 25, 1967, p. 1. This reports a unity meeting of "military research and military industry units stationed in Peking." Representatives from all the Maoist groups except the regional commanders attended, but Chiang Ch'ing and Ch'en Po-ta were absent. Chou En-lai seemed to be running the show. The major address was given by Nieh Jung-chen.
¹⁸Chang Man, *The People's Daily and the Red Flag Magazine During the Cultural Revolution* (URI, Kowloon, 1969) 126 pp., pp. 58-59.
¹⁹See, for example, Canton *Chung-Hsueh Hung-wei-ping*, No. 8 (July, 1968) SCMP, 4236, (August 12, 1968) pp. 1-2.
²⁰See Yingte *Pi-hsueh Hung-po*, SCMP, 4244 (August 23, 1968) pp. 1-11.
²¹T'eng Tai-yuan, probably purged with P'eng Te-huai, reappeared on October 1, 1967. He is classified with Chou En-lai.
²²See CNA, 721 (August 16, 1968) p. 3.
²³*Asahi*, December 11, 1966; DSJP, December 13, 1966, p. 11. Also Lin Piao, "Address at the Enlarged Meeting of the CCP Central Politburo," *Issues & Studies*, Vol. VI, No. 5 (February, 1970), pp. 81-92.
²⁴Peking *Chui Ch'iung K'ou*, 4 May 20, 1970; SCMP, 3790 (June 29, 1967).
²⁵*Nihon Kelzai*, February 1, 1967; DSJP, February 1, 1967, pp. 36-37.
²⁶*Ibid.*, p. 37.
²⁷*Yomiuri*, January 8, 1967; DSJP, January 7-9, 1967, p. 31.
²⁸As Liu came under heavier and heavier attack, at least in the early stages, he also became the rallying point for the anti-Maoist forces. A

group of Red Guards organized by the son of Li Ching-ch'üan coined this elegant slogan: "Whoever opposes Liu Shao-ch'i is a God damned [mother fucking] counter-revolutionary."(誰反對劉少奇,誰是他媽的反革命) *This Fellow Ho Lung,* pp. 93-94. Esteem for Liu was not limited to the anti-Maoist forces. Ch'en I was accused of having said when Liu came under attack: "Comrade Liu's instructions have my full endorsement. Comrade Shao-ch'i put it very correctly... Comrade Shao-ch'i is my teacher." Peking *Hung-wei Chan Pao,* April 13, 1967; SCMP, 4007 (August 23, 1967) p. 2.

[29] *Mainichi,* September 14, 1966; DSJP, September 16, 1966, p. 28. Also CNA, 666 (June 30, 1967) p. 6.

[30] The Japanese also seem to assume that Teng, as secretary, had the power to appoint the regional secretaries, and, thus, that these men were his supporters. In Russia one of the main resources of the Secretariat was its powers of appointment; but there is no evidence that the Chinese Secretariat enjoyed similar powers. The factional affiliations of the regional bosses would suggest the appointments were made by a process of discussion and compromise at the upper levels of the regime.

[31] Canton *Kuang-yin Hung Ch'i* 5 (March, 1968) SCMP, 4162 (April 22, 1968) p. 9.

[32] "Chou En-lai Talks About the February Adverse Current," *loc. cit.;* The members of this group had suffered hard blows to their self-respect. T'an Chen-lin said: "I should not have lived 65 years, should not have joined the revolution, should not have joined the Party, and should not have followed Chairman Mao in making revolution for 40 years." p. 104. The disgust of some members was quite profound. Chou En-lai is said to have had to have pleaded with Chu Te to participate in the 1968 May Day celebration. *This Fellow Chu Te,* p. 74.

[33] *Talk About This Fellow Ch'en I,* pp. 93-94.

[34] Canton *Kuang-ch'i,* 5 (March, 1968) SCMP, 4190 (June 4, 1968) p. 6.

[35] *Yomiuri,* January 21, 1967; DSJP, January 24, 1967, pp. 1-2.

[36] *Asahi,* January 25, 1967, DSJP, January 26, 1967, p. 14. Yang's words parallel those of Chiang Ch'ing, except Yang also mentions Hsiao's hostility to Yeh Chien-ying and Ch'en I, suggesting an early affinity between the regional commanders and Chou En-lai.

[37] *Bandit Affairs biography of Han Hsien-ch'u,* p. 147.

[38] There was, of course, growing concern about the unchecked violence. But the military house organ, reflecting the views of the GPD, warned soldiers they must support the "left" and not suppress the "masses," in this context both code words for those Red Guards affiliated with the Cultural Revolution Group. 正確對待群衆 (Treat the Masses Correctly) PD, June 28, 1967, pp. 1, 3; from LAD, June 27.

[39] For a good discussion of the Wuhan Incident, see Ch'ien Yu-shen, *op. cit.,* Chapter 1.

⁴⁰ 向人民主要敵人猛烈開火 (Open Fire on the Main Enemies of the People) PD, July 31, 1967, p. 3. The author of this piece was later identified as Lin Chieh. Use of foul language by intellectuals with "proletarian" pretentions (cf also the attack on Han Hsien-ch'u—a much more idiomatic and elegant example) seems universal.

⁴¹ Thus, Chou supported Huang Yung-sheng in his quarrels with the radicals in Kwangtung. Canton (?) *Tzu-liao Chuan-chi,* November 17, 1967, in SCMP, 4085 (December 21, 1967) p. 7. But Chou continued to criticize PLA men at headquarters (including the rather conservative Su Yü) for promoting "factionalism," a leftist error. Canton *Hsiao Ping,* 22 (February 17, 1968) SCMP, 4134 (March 8, 1968) p. 4.

⁴² Hsuan Mo, *op. cit.,* Yang's purge, it should be noted, was supported by those leaders of the CR Group who survived it. Yang and his leftist friends were accused of gathering "black materials" on Chiang Ch'ing. *Ibid.,* p. 45. This may be a frame-up, or it may indicate a split within the leftist ranks. It would not be surprising if some of Chiang Ch'ing's ideological sympathizers had become fed up with that obnoxious woman. Miss Chiang, for her part, seemed to want to turn Yang's purge to her own advantage, calling for the blood of his "back stage boss." *Ibid.,* p. 46. No one else mentioned this subject. The identity of the backstage boss has never been revealed, if indeed there ever was one. This may have been simply a warm-up for the coming attack on Nieh Jung-chen, who used to be Yang's commander. But a more likely candidate is Lin Piao himself.

⁴³ *Asahi,* November 23, 1966; DSJP, November 26-28, 1966, p. 2.

⁴⁴ Tokyo *Shimbun,* December 21, 1966; DSJP, December 28, 1966, pp. 20-21.

⁴⁵ For information about this measure, see Hubert M. Blalock, *Social Statistics,* (New York, 1960) xiv, 465 pp., pp. 231-232.

⁴⁶ Another weakness is that a zero value in any cell of the two-by-two table used to calculate Q gives a "perfect" relationship. *Ibid.* The several—1.000 values that crop up in the tables are of this nature, and are of no particular significance. The advantage of the measure is that the meaning of the results is easy to grasp, giving the strength and direction of the relationships; and it is easy to calculate manually. Since no kind of sample is used here, significance tests are not made. We are interested in "substantive" significance, not statistical significance, which is partly a reflexion of sample size, and tells only whether any particular difference is likely to occur by chance, giving little information on the extent of the difference.

⁴⁷ To "associate" with another member means to be his equal or subordinate in the same organization. For the importance of personal ties at the time of the Cultural Revolution, see Oksenberg, *op. cit.,* pp. 25-26.

⁴⁸ See Barnett, *Cadres,* pp. 8-9. I have added an additional system, "Party administration."

⁴⁹William Whitson, "The Field Army in Chinese Communist Military Politics," CQ, 37 (January-March, 1969) pp. 1-30. p. 2.

⁵⁰ *Ibid.*, p. 14.

⁵¹ For an interesting development of the hypothesis that sometimes grandparents and grandchildren will tend to share the same political orientation different from that of the middle generation, see Ronald Inglehart, "An End to European Integration?" *American Political Science Review,* Vol. 61, No. 1 (March, 1967) pp. 91-105.

⁵² Richard K. Diao, "The Impact of the Cultural Revolution on China's Economic Elite," *China Quarterly,* 42 (April-June, 1970) pp. 65-87, finds a similar incidence of the purge within the economic bureaucracy. See pp. 78 ff.

⁵³ The "regional soldiers" include the men listed as enemies of Yang Ch'eng-wu in Lin Piao's group, plus Yang Yung. Han Hsien-ch'u, who worked in Peking at the outset of the Cultural Revolution, is included among the regional soldiers. Chang Ta-chih, commander of the Lanchow Military Region, not listed as an enemy of Yang Ch'eng-wu, is not included. He does not seem to have come under the attack from the left which plagued the other regional soldiers.

⁵⁴ These factors obviously do not measure attitudes directly. Rather, it is hypothesized that those with Thermidorian characteristics will tend to be conservative, and, hence, will tend to be purged. The middle link in this chain has not been rigorously demonstrated.

Chapter IV

¹ 1956 Constitution, Article 36, *loc. cit.*, p. 63.

² 1945 Constitution, Article 65, *loc. cit.*, p. 438.

³ 1956 Constitution, Article 16, *loc. cit.*, p. 52. In fact, prior to the Cultural Revolution, purged members were not officially removed from the CC, or even from the Politburo. Liu Shao-ch'i was removed from all Party and state posts by the 12th Plenary Session of the CC in October, 1968, no doubt by a greater than two-thirds majority. Technically the CC had no direct control over state appointments, but no one was likely to quibble.

⁴ 1956 Constitution, preamble, *loc. cit.*, p. 49.

⁵ *Ibid.*, Article 19, p. 52.

⁶ See Peking *Chingkangshan,* February 15, 1967: "One Hundred Anti-Mao Tse-tung Statements of Teng Hsiao-p'ing," in *SCMP,* 3908, pp. 2ff. See also Teng's self-examination, reprinted in 中共研究 *(Studies in Chinese Communism)* Vol. 3, No. 11 (November, 1969) pp. 90-94, in which Teng emphasizes his failure to "hold high the banner of the TMTT."

⁷ Teng Hsiao-p'ing, 1957 PHB, p. 27.

⁸ *Ibid.*, pp. 31, 32.

⁹ Liu Shao-ch'i, "Political Report of the Central Committee of the CPC to the Eighth Party Congress," in 中國共產黨第八次全國代表大會 (The Eighth Congress of the Communist Party of China) (Peking, 1956) 236 pp., pp. 8-77, p. 73. (Hereafter cited as *Eighth Congress*).

¹⁰ 1956 Constitution, Article 38, *loc. cit.*, p. 53. There exists a curious document dated September, 1956, (the month of the Congress) published by a group (or person) calling itself (himself) the "Extraordinary Committee of the Anti-Mao Alliance of the Communist Party of China" (中國共產黨反毛聯盟非常委員會), asking "Who Is the Renegade to Marxism-Leninism?" (誰是馬列主義的叛徒 ?) (n.p., 1956) 63 pp. The answer is Mao. It seems unlikely, however, that Liu or Teng had anything to do with this.

¹¹ Liu Shao-ch'i, *Eighth Congress*, p. 67.

¹² Ou-yang Ch'in, 同削弱黨的領導作用的傾向作鬥爭 (Struggle Against the Deviation of Weakening the Leadership Function of the Party) PD, September 21, 1956, p. 4; Li Hsueh-feng, 加強黨對企業的領導,貫澈執行群衆路綫 (Strengthen Party Leadership Over Enterprise, Fully Carry out the Mass Line) PD, September 25, 1956, p. 5.

¹³ Ou-yang Ch'in, *op. cit.*

¹⁴ *Ibid.*; and Li Hsueh-feng, *op. cit.*

¹⁵ Liu Shao-ch'i, *Eighth Congress*, p. 67. Wu Te, however, found that once Party members learned technology they became "self-satisfied" and impatient with Party direction—another aspect of the phenomenon discussed in the second chapter. See Wu Te, 工業建設中,一個突出的矛盾 (An Emerging Contradiction in Industrial Construction), PD, September 28, 1956, p. 3. Wu seems to have been one of China's major expert-baiters, and was a prominent spokesman for the "red and expert" policy introduced in 1958, a policy designed to overcome the problem Wu discussed. See Wu Te, 解放思想,迎接技術革命 (Liberate Thought, Welcome the Technological Revolution) PD, May 24, 1958, p. 2.

¹⁶ Liu Shao-ch'i, *Eighth Congress*, p. 57.

¹⁷ Li Wei han, *op. cit.*, p. 50. Huang Huo-ch'ing, 對改造資本主義工商業和資本家的體會 (Reform of Capitalist Industry and Commerce and of the General Attitude of Capitalists) PD, September 30, 1956, p. 6.

¹⁸ Tung Pi-wu, *op. cit.*, p. 509.

¹⁹ *Ibid.*, p. 516.

²⁰ Lo Jui-ch'ing, "The Condition and Experience of the Suppression and Purge Campaign," *Bandit Congress*, pp. 520-535, p. 523.

²¹ *Ibid.*, p. 528. The first term means to "torture" (逼) the suspect until he "confesses" (供), and then "believe" (信) the confession—*i.e.*, accept it as valid.

²² *Ibid.*, p. 523. Lo in this context should not be taken too seriously. Scarcely a year later he was quite eager to return to terrorist practices.

²³ Mao Tse-tung, "Welcoming Speech," *Eighth Congress*, pp. 3-6. p. 4

²⁴ Liu Shao-ch'i, *Eighth Congress*, p. 52.

²⁵ *Ibid.*, pp. 71-72.

²⁶ Teng Hsiao-p'ing, 1957 PHB, p. 31.

[27] Chou En-lai, "Report on the Establishment of the Second Five Year Plan for the Development of the National Economy," *Eighth Congress,* pp. 189-234, p. 201. See also Ch'ien Ying, 堅決向官僚主義作鬥爭 (Resolutely Struggle Against Bureaucratism), PD, September 30, 1956, p. 5.

[28] The hypothesis developed here differs a little from that of Richard H. Solomon's excellent study, "One Party and 'One Hundred Schools': Leadership, Lethargy, or *Luan?" Current Scene,* Vol. VII, No. 19-20 (October, 1969) 49 pp. Solomon suggests that Mao's actions were motivated by a desire to "convince his colleagues that 'rightist conservatism' *was* the main danger and the Party had to be disciplined." p. 37. This assumes an inherently "radical" Mao was disturbed by what I have called the thermidorian trend, and needed to arouse his less militant comrades against it. This hypothesis seems somewhat more complicated than necessary to explain the known facts, and also seems to be a form of the conspiracy theory of the Hundred Flowers movement, which Solomon elsewhere rejects. In Solomon's view, Mao is seen as unleashing the intellectuals in order to show his comrades how conservative the intellectuals were. Solomon's hypothesis also assumes that Mao's radical millenarianism is built into his personality. This may be, but previously Mao had always been able to subordinate this aspect of his personality to political expediency, and I prefer in this study to examine hypotheses concerned with political expediency. Prior to 1955 Mao's record was one of pragmatism and good sense—he rose to power as the opponent of "left deviation." The stress on rational-power considerations in this study, of course, does not mean that they are the only relevant considerations.

[29] Wang Meng, 組織部新來的年青人 (The Young Newcomer in the Organization Department), 人民文學 (People's Literature) September, 1956, pp. 29-43. For a discussion of the controversy surrounding this story see Merle Goldman, *Literary Dissent in Communist China* (Harvard: University Press, 1967), pp. 179-180.

[30] Wang Meng, *op. cit.,* p. 39.

[31] *Ibid.,* p. 40.

[32] Mao Tse-tung, 關於農業合作化問題 (The Problem of Agricultural Cooperativization), PHB, 1956, pp. 80-86, p. 80. The particular bound-footed woman he seems to have had in mind was Teng Tzu-hui (male), head of the CC Rural Work Dept.

[33] *Ibid.,* p. 83.

[34] Mao Tse-tung, 論十個大關係 (Ten Great Relations), *Studies on Chinese Communism,* Vol. 4, No. 2 (February, 1970) pp. 116-124, p. 117. The policies advocated, however, were not particularly radical.

[35] Solomon, *op. cit.,* p. 4.

[36] Lu Ting-i, 百花齊放,百家爭鳴 (Let a Hundred Flowers Bloom, a Hundred Schools Contend) PHB, 1957, pp. 565-571, pp. 567-568.

[37] *Ibid.,* p. 569.

[38] 不要怕反對的意見 (Do Not Fear Contrary Opinions), PD, October 9, 1956, pp. 1, 4, p. 1.

[39] *Ibid.,* p. 4.

⁴⁰ 中共八屆二中全會公報 (Public Report of the Second Plenum of the Eighth CC.) PHB, 1967, pp. 147-148. By this time the Hungarian rebellion had become an additional factor in the thinking of Mao, and that of the Chinese leadership generally.

⁴¹ Mao Tse-tung, 關於正確處理人民內部矛盾問題 (On the Correct Handling of Contradictions Among the People.) PHB, 1958, pp. 9-20, pp. 10-11. Mao put forward the idea of non-antagonistic contradictions in the "Ten Great Relations." The theme was developed more fully in the Chinese reactions to Khrushchev's denunciations of Stalin. The major document here is 關於無產階級的歷史經驗 (The Historical Experience of the Dictatorship of the Proletariat) PHB, 1958, pp. 148-151, first published on April 5, 1956. This seems to be a compromise between Mao and his opponents. Following what seem to be Teng Hsiao-p'ing's thoughts, the cult of the individual is criticized as anachronistic (p. 149). But the Chinese also felt the need to pronounce on how such a thing could have come about. The solution here is Maoist: "There is a naive and frivolous way of thinking that holds that in a socialist society contradictions no longer exist." (Ibid.) Mao seems to have been biding his time, shaping and honing his ideological weapon.

⁴² Lu Ting-i, 紀念整風運動十五周年 (Commemorating the 15th Anniversary of the Rectification Movement) PD, March 4, 1957, pp. 2-3, p. 3.

⁴³ 關於整風運動的指示 (Directive on the Rectification Movement.) PHB, 1958, pp. 29-30.

⁴⁴ See Goldman, op. cit., pp. 180 ff., for the substance of many of the criticisms. Klaus Mehnert, Peking and Moscow (New York, 1964) 559 pp., pp. 209-217, gives a lively account of the atmosphere of that period. Dennis J. Doolin, Communist China: The Politics of Student Opposition (Hoover Institution, 1964) 70 pp., gives a translation of what the Party seems to have considered the most pernicious criticism. The ideas of the "student opposition" of 1957 are in many respects very similar to those of 1966. Some of the 1957 opposition might be called "Maoism without the cult of the individual."

⁴⁵ 離開社會主義完全錯誤 (To Depart From Socialism Is Completely Mistaken) Chekiang Daily, 浙江日報 , May 26, 1957, p. 1.

⁴⁶ PD, June 8, 1957, p. 2. See also Townsend, Participation, pp. 96-97.

⁴⁷ 要有積極的批評,也要有正確的反批評 (We Must Have Active Criticism, Also Correct Counter-Criticism), PD, June 9, 1957, p. 1.

⁴⁸ 全國人民在社會主義基礎上團結起來 (People of the Whole Country, Unite on the Basis of Socialism) PD, June 11, 1957, p. 1.

⁴⁹ Mao Tse-tung, 1958 PHB, p. 9.

⁵⁰ Ibid. p. 10.

⁵¹ Ibid.

⁵² 不平常的春天 (An Unusual Spring.) PHB, 1958, pp. 75-76, p. 75.

⁵³ Ibid., p. 76.

⁵⁴ For an evaluation of the "smoking out" interpretation of the Hundred Flowers, see Schwartz, Communism and China, pp. 120-123.

⁵⁵ 在肅反問題上駁斥右派 (Rebutting the Rightists on the Question of the Purge), PD, July 18, 1957, pp. 1-2, p. 1.

⁵⁶ For a good example of the use of this "theory" see Lo Jui-ch'ing, 我國肅反鬥爭的成就和今後的任務 (The Success of Our Country's Purge Struggle and the Tasks Ahead) 學習 (Study), 1 (January 3), 1958, pp. 2-9, pp. 4, 5.

⁵⁷ PD, July 18, 1957, p. 2.

⁵⁸ 克服政法工作的兩種傾向 (Overcome Two Kinds of Deviation in Legal Work.) PD, October 14, 1957, p. 1.

⁵⁹ Lo Jui-ch'ing, January, 1958, *loc. cit.*, p. 3.

⁶⁰ *Ibid.*, p. 7.

⁶¹ *Ibid.* This looks like an attack upon Liu Shao-ch'i, but the evidence on Liu's position at this time is ambiguous.

⁶² See Teng Hsiao-p'ing, 關於整風運動的報告 (Report on the Rectification Campaign) PHB, 1958, pp. 33-42, p. 33 and *passim*.

⁶³ *Ibid.*, p. 35. Teng does allow, however, that the blooming and contending did expose some defects in the work style of those eternal goats, the basic level cadres.

⁶⁴ 全國已有八十多萬幹部下放 (In the Whole Country There Are Already More Than Eight Million Cadres Who Have Been Sent Down.) 光明日報 (*Kuang Ming Daily*—KMD) (Peking) November 27, 1957, p. 1. This move had been directed in the spring, but apparently nothing had been done about it until "recently."

⁶⁵ Teng Hsiao-p'ing, 1958 PHB, p. 40.

⁶⁶ Frederick C. Teiwes, "The Purge of Provincial Leaders, 1957-1958," CQ, 27 (July-September, 1966) pp. 14-32, p. 14.

⁶⁷ 共產黨員應該有什麼樣的志願? (What Kind of Ambition Should a Communist Party Member Have?) PD, July 31, 1958, p. 7.

⁶⁸ State Council, 關於國家機關工作人員參加整風運動和對資產階級右派鬥爭的決定 (Resolution on the Participation in the Rectification Movement by Working Personnel in the State Organs and on the Struggle Against the Bourgeois Rightists.) July 26, 1957, PHB, 1958, p. 71.

⁶⁹ Chiang Wei-ch'ing, 政治掛帥以生產為中心,帶動各項工作一道前進 (Politics Takes Command; with Production as the Center, Lead Forward All Kinds of Work) PD, May 14, 1958, p. 2. Or, as An Tzu-wen had enunciated during the crackdown on the Hundred Flowers, the Party is "able to lead work in science, culture, and education." 共產黨能夠領導科學,文化,和教育工作 (The Communist Party Is Able to Lead Work in Science, Culture, and Education), 中國青年 (China Youth=CY), 13 (July 1) 1957, pp. 5-6.

⁷⁰ It is in this context that the decentralization aspect of the Leap should be understood. It seems paradoxical that decentralization should follow upon the heels of an anti-localism campaign. In fact, only state institutions were decentralized. The locus of political power now more than ever was the Party, and the Party remained centralized, although the local committees were expected to exercise initiative in economic work. On decentralization, see Schurmann, *Ideology*, p. 486; Dwight H. Perkins, *Market Control and Planning in Communist China*

(Harvard: University Press, 1966) x, 291 pp., p. 19, 214. Also *cf* Conquest, *op. cit.*, p. 304. Although rarely noted in studies of Chinese politics, the Soviet Union had gone down this road in 1957. Despite what the Chinese like to think, there is a certain affinity between "Maoism" and "Khrushchevism." A study of the two would be interesting.

[71] 怎樣辦好人民公社？ (How Can a Good Job Be Done in Running People's Communes?) PD, August 21, 1958, p. 2.

[72] 迎接人民公社化的高潮 (Welcoming the High Tide of People's Communization) RF, 7 (September 1, 1958) pp. 13-15, p. 14.

[73] Li Hsien-nien, 怎樣認識農村財貿管理體制的改進 (How to Look at the Reform of the Management System of Finance and Trade in the Rural Areas) PD, January 17, 1959, p. 2.

[74] "A Condensation of P'eng Teh-huai's Talks at the Lushan Conference in 1959," a Red Guard pamphlet translated in *Facts and Features*, Vol. II, No. 9 (February 19, 1969) pp. 27-29, p. 29.

[75] At the same time, the bureaucrats had had much of their responsibility removed from them by the apparatus, and partly for this reason, while in general they had always been skeptical about the "left line," they were not as politically vulnerable as the apparatus.

[76] For another attempt to come to grips with the cult, from a slightly different perspective, see James T. Myers, "The Political Dynamics of the Cult of Mao Tse-tung: A Preliminary Attempt at Periodization and Description of Constructs." Paper presented to the First Sino-American Conference on Mainland China, Taipei, December 14-19, 1970, 45 pp.

[77] K'ang Sheng, PD, Nov. 7, 1957, p. 7.

[78] PD, April 11, 1958, pp. 1, 2.

[79] "Down with Liu Shao-ch'i," *loc. cit.*, p. 18.

[80] 少奇同志在郫縣拖拉機站 (Comrade Shao-ch'i at the Pi County Tractor Station.) PD, May 13, 1958, p. 2. Also, K'ang Chueh 劉少奇同志在徐水 (Comrade Liu Shao-ch'i at Hsu Shui) PD, September 18, 1958, p. 2.

[81] PD, May 25, 1958, p. 1.

[82] Ch'en Po-ta, 在毛澤東同志的旗幟下 (Under the Banner of Comrade Mao Tse-tung) RF, 4 (July 16) 1958, pp. 1-12, p. 9.

[83] 神話似的現實 (The Myth-Like Current Reality) PD, October 1, 1958, p. 10. This particular piece, it should be noted, is in a rather inconspicuous place in a very much enlarged edition of the PD. The phrase "the era of Mao Tse-tung" has been used off and on since the founding of the People's Republic. It was used in passing in 1958 by Yeh Fei, the boss of Fukien. See 思想解放工作躍進 (Thought Liberation, Leap Forward in Work), PD, May 22, 1958, p. 2. The phrase was revived for a time during the Cultural Revolution, but has never really caught on. See H. C. Chuang, *The Great Proletarian Cultural Revolution: A Terminological Study* (Berkeley, 1967) vii, 72 pp., p. 15.

[84] Kuo Mo-jo, 替曹操翻案 (Reversing the Verdict on Ts'ao Ts'ao), PD, March 23, 1959, p. 7. At Lushan Mao talked about his own mistakes. Mistakes are inevitable, he said. Even Confucius and Lenin made mistakes.

⁸⁵ Yang Ping, 曹操應當被肯定嗎? (Should Ts'ao Ts'ao Be Affirmed?), PD, April 21, 1959, p. 7. The final word on this debate was had by Lu Hsueh-fu, who also presented the most reasonable argument. Lu said that artistic, historical, and political problems should not be mixed up. Artistically there is room for both the "good" and "bad" Ts'ao Ts'ao; the function of historical research should be to determine truth, not pass moral judgment; and it is wrong to try to fit historical figures into modern political categories. 試談曹操戲 (The Discussion About Ts'ao Ts'ao Plays), PD, June 9, 1959, p. 7. This rationalistic attitude was typical of the proteges of P'eng Chen. Yang Ping was probably a spokesman for Teng Hsiao-p'ing.

⁸⁶ Liu Lan-t'ao, PD, September 28, 1959, *loc. cit.*

⁸⁷ Wu Chih-p'u, 學習毛澤東同志的著作 (Study Comrade Mao Tse-tung's Works), PD, January 1, 1960, p. 7.

⁸⁸ An Tzu-wen, 進一步加強人民公社組織的領導作用 (Go a Step Further in Strengthening the Leadership Function of the Party Organization on the People's Communes), PD, December 17, 1959, p. 7.

⁸⁹ 中國共產黨第八屆中央委員會第九次全體會議 (The Ninth Plenum of the Eighth CC, CPC), PD, January 21, 1961, p. 1.

⁹⁰ Hsu P'ing-i, 更好地發揮農村基層黨組織的領導核心, (Develop Even Better the Nuclear Leading Function of Basic Level Party Organizations in the Countryside), RF, 20 (October 16) 1961, pp. 21-25, p. 24.

⁹¹ 基層幹部的學習問題 (The Problem of the Study of Basic Level Cadres), PD, January 25, 1961, p. 3.

⁹² PD, October 21, 1961, p. 1.

⁹³ Chao Han 遵守黨章, 增強黨性 (Obey the Party Constitution, Strengthen Party Nature), PD, October 17, 1961, p. 7. It will be argued later that the adoption of the capitalist road resulted from a basic shift in power relations within the apparatus. According to the party constitution a new national congress should have been convened in 1961. This new attention to the constitution may have been a subtle way of indicating the beneficiaries of the power shift wished to convene a congress to formalize their newly won position.

⁹⁴ Ou-yang Ch'in, 加強黨的建設, 不斷提高黨的水平 (Strengthen Party Construction, Continuously Raise the Level of the Party), PD, July 21, 1961, p. 7.

⁹⁵ *Eg,* Gray, *op. cit.*

⁹⁶ 說老實話, 做老實事, 做老實人 (Speak Honest Words, Do Honest Deeds, Be an Honest Man) PD, February 23, 1962, p. 5.

⁹⁷ Liu Ch'ung, 加強集中統一, 發揚黨內民主 (Strengthen the Centralized Unity of the Party, Develop Inner-Party Democracy) PD, April 3, 1962, p. 5.

⁹⁸ "Truth," it is interesting to note, here seems to mean "in the spirit of the directives of the Party Center and of the higher level." Chao Han, *op. cit.*

⁹⁹ Hsiao Hua, 關於加強管理教育工作問題 ("Problems of Strengthening Management of Education Work.") WB, 24, June 13, 1961, pp. 1-18, pp. 1-2.

¹⁰⁰ For the best general study of the People's Liberation Army, see John

Gittings, *The Role of the Chinese Army* (Oxford: University Press, 1967) xx, 331 pp.; specifically on P'eng Te-huai, see David A. Charles, "The Dismissal of Marshal P'eng Teh-huai," in MacFarquhar, *op. cit.,* pp. 20-33; J. P. Simmonds, "P'eng Teh-huai: A Chronological Re-examination," CQ, 37 (January-March, 1969) pp. 120-138.

[101] Alice Langley Hsieh, *Communist China's Strategy in the Nuclear Era,* (Englewood Cliffs, 1962) xx, 204 pp., p. 176. Cf. Charles, *op. cit.,* p. 22 n.

[102] P'eng Te-huai, "The Duty of Military Work," *Bandit Congress,* pp. 463-479, p. 468.

[103] *Ibid.,* p. 471.

[104] *Ibid.,* p. 468. Surprisingly, T'an Cheng, head of the GPD, was even more outspoken on this point. He delivered himself of this rank heresy: "It must be made clear that modernization itself is not concerned with class. . . .Many internal military systems, customs and courtesies, and command relations, if viewed superficially, are alike for communist and bourgeois armies." "Several Problems of Political Work in the New Stage of Army-Building," *Bandit Congress,* pp. 480-493, p. 482.

[105] P'eng Te-huai, *op. cit.,* pp. 474-475.

[106] *Ibid.,* p. 473.

[107] On military professionalism, see Samuel P. Huntington, *The Soldier and the State* (Cambridge, 1957), xiii, 534 pp., passim. For a discussion of other models of military politics, particularly as applied to underdeveloped countries, see Amos Perlmutter, "The Arab Military Elite," *World Politics,* Vol. XXII, No. 2 (January, 1970) pp. 269-300, pp. 270-274.

[108] T'an Cheng, 做到官兵一致，軍民團結 (Achieve Complete Unity Among Officers and Men.) in Chiang I-shan, 中共軍事文件彙編 (Collection of Chinese Communist Military Documents.) (Hong Kong, 1965) pp. 590-591.

[109] Teng Hsiao-p'ing, 1958 PHB, p. 39.

[110] 高舉黨委制的紅旗 (Raise High the Red Banner of the Party Committee) 解放軍報 (*Liberation Army Daily*—LAD) July 1, 1958, p. 2. The "party committee" seems to have had a chain of command formally independent both of the regular military chain of command and of the GPD. But in practice the GPD commissar directed the political activities within a unit through the Party committee. Alexander L. George, *The Chinese Communist Army in Action: The Korean War and Its Aftermath* (Columbia: University Press, 1967) xii, 255 pp., p. 49.

[111] GPD, 全軍各級幹部每年下年當兵一個月 (Each Year Military Cadres at All Levels Must Serve One Month in the Ranks) Chiang I-shan, *op. cit.,* pp. 617-618.

[112] Gittings, *op. cit.,* p. 227.

[113] For an overview of the politicization of the army under Lin Piao, see Ralph L. Powell, "The Increasing Power of Lin Piao and the Party Soldiers," CQ, 34 (April-June, 1968) pp. 38-65.

[114] Lin Piao, 高舉黨的路線和毛澤東軍事思想的紅旗闊步前進 (Raise High the Red Flag of the Party Line and the Military TMTT and March Forward with Big Steps) RF, 19 (October 1) 1959, pp. 16-25, p. 22.

[115] *Ibid.*, p. 24.

[116] Lin Piao, 一九六一年政治思想工作的幾點指示 (A Few Directives on Political Work in 1961), WB, January 1, 1961, pp. 7-11, p. 10. The more conservative Yeh Chien-ying favored an 80/20 ratio for troops in border areas or on islands. This ratio is not a trivial matter. A Chinese prisoner in Korea noted that political and military officers got along fairly well, except "each tried to get more time for his own type of training." George, *op. cit.*, p. 119.

[117] GPD, 為貫徹執行中央關於開展社會鎮反,內部肅反(清理)運動的指示 (Implementation of the Center's Directive on the Social Suppression-Internal Purge (Purification) Movements) WB, 1 (January 1, 1961) pp. 29-32.

[118] Ministry of National Defense (People's Republic of China) 軍人之間按照新的規定相互稱呼 (Military Forms of Address, According to the New Regulations), PD, June 7, 1965, p. 1.

[119] General Staff, PLA, 取消士兵級別制度的通知 (Announcement on the Elimination of the System of Non-Commissioned Officer Ranks), WB, 30, (August 26, 1961) pp. 20-22; the Item is classified "not for distribution."

[120] Lin Piao, 在全軍管理教育工作會議上的講話 (Speech at the All-Army Education Management Meeting), WB, 22, (May 19, 1961) pp. 1-5, p. 4. See also Hsiao Hua, 培養三八作風是我軍建設的重要任務 (Cultivation of the Three-Eight Work Style Is An Important Task in Our Military Construction), PD, May 24, 1960, p. 7.

[121] P'eng Te-huai, *Bandit Congress*, p. 464. The re-iteration of the phrase "revolutionary war" is interesting; perhaps the Thought was not so efficatious in conventional war.

[122] Lo Jung-huan, 對政治學院學習毛澤東著作的指示記彙摘要 (Summary of the Directive to the Political Academy on the Study of the Works of Mao Tse-tung), WB, 8 (February 6, 1961) pp. 11-19, p. 12, 13-14.

[123] 教學一定要區別對象聯系實際 (Education Must Distinguish the Objectives and Join with Reality), WB, 16 (April 19, 1961) pp. 7-12, p. 8. This attitude was not maintained in more open publications. As late as January, 1964, Hsiao Hua said that in addition to Mao, communist soldiers should also study Marx, Engels, Lenin, Stalin, and even (know your enemy) the revisionists old and new. 目前部隊政治工作建設的幾個問題 (A Few Current Problems in Setting Up Political Work Among the Troops), Chiang I-shan, *op. cit.*, pp. 470-484, pp. 479-480.

[124] 全國都要學習解放軍 (The Whole Country Must Study the Liberation Army), PD, February 1, 1964, pp. 1-2.

[125] Chao Huan, *op. cit.*

[126] 到農村去 (Go to the Countryside), PD, December 22, 1962, pp. 1-2.

[127] Chao Han, 做好黨的基層組織的經常工作 (Do Well the Daily Routine Work of Basic Level Party Organizations), PD, March 30, 1963, p. 5. It was discovered at the outset of the Cultural Revolution that Chao was an "ardent counter-revolutionary." He hanged himself.

[128] Chou Kuo-ch'üan 實行集體領導是實現正確領導的重要保證 (To Implement Collective Leadership Is an Important Guarantee of the

Realization of Correct Leadership), PD, May 18, 1963, p. 5. This article, like several in the previous two years, noted that the constitution stipulates Party meetings must be held at regular intervals, a not very delicate hint that it was time for another Party congress.

[129] 幹部參加勞動的偉大革命意義 (The Great Revolutionary Significance of Cadre Particiaption in Labor), PD, June 2, 1963, p. 1.

[130] Wang Chih-hsiang, 我怎樣下了決心參加勞動 (How I Decided to Participate in Collective Labor), PD, August 19, 1963, p. 2.

[131] The political struggle during this period (roughly 1963 through 1965) was, as the Communists say, complex, tortuous, and sharp; and Mao did not fully have his own way until late 1966 (and even then he probably was not in full control of events). Ten days after Wang's essay was published, for example, the *People's Daily* published an editorial saying that not all cadres should participate directly in collective labor; and that those who did not, for good reason, were nothing like "the reactionary rulers and exploiting administrators." 從經濟上看幹部參加勞動的重大意義 (The Heavy Significance of Cadre Participation in Labor, Viewed from Economics), PD, August 29, 1963, p. 1. For the demoralization of the Party, see Charles Neuhauser, "The Chinese Communist Party in the 1960's: Prelude to the Cultural Revolution," CQ, 32 (October-December, 1967) pp. 3-36.

Chapter V

[1] The longest study of provincial politics is Ezra F. Vogel, *Canton Under Communism: Programs and Politics in a Provincial Capital, 1949-1968.* (Harvard: University Press, 1969) xviii, 448 pp.

[2] Institute for International Relations, *op. cit.*, p. 501. Mao's fondness for K'ang Sheng may have something to do with the fact that K'ang comes from the same county as Mao's current wife. Chung Hua-min. Andrew C. Miller, *Madame Mao: A Profile of Chiang Ch'ing,* May 1968) v, 314 pp., p. 38.

[3] Cf. *Julius Caesar,* IV, i. The Chinese situation, of course, had hardly come to this.

[4] Goldman, *op. cit.*, p. 124.

[5] Chou En-lai, 關於知識份子問題的報告 (Report on the Question of Intellectuals) PD, January 30, 1956, pp. 1-3, p. 2.

[6] *Ibid.*, p. 1.

[7] Chou Yang, 讓文學藝術在建設社會主義偉大事業中發揮巨大的作用 (Let Literature and Art Develop a Huge Function in the Task of Building Socialism) PD, September 26, 1956, p. 4.

[8] Goldman, *op. cit.*, p. 82.

[9] Vogel, *Canton,* pp. 187-188; Yao Wen-yuan, PD, Sept. 8, 1967, p. 1.

[10] K'o Liu-liu, 懷爸爸,作堅強的革命接班人 (Remember Papa, Be a Strong Revolutionary Successor) PD, June 8, 1965, p. 6.

[11] Solomon, *op. cit.*, p. 26.

¹² 彭真同志談堅持和風細雨的方法 (Comrade P'eng Chen Talks About the Method of Gentle Breeze and Light Rain) PD, May 10, 1957, p. 1.
¹³ Solomon, *op. cit.*, p. 26.
¹⁴ Liu Shao-ch'i, *Eighth Congress*, pp. 43-44.
¹⁵ Vogel, *Canton*, p. 191.
¹⁶ KMD, April 24, 1967; SCMP, 3934 (May 8, 1967) pp. 4-7, p. 4.
¹⁷ Lu Ting-i, PD, May 5, 1957, *op. cit.*
¹⁸ Tung Pi-wu, 關於農村群眾生活問題及其他 (The Living Conditions of the Rural Masses and Other Problems.) 中國青年報 (*China Youth Daily*—CYD) April 13, 1957, p. 3. For those who like the Kremlinological approach, there is an even more esoteric piece of evidence. In his story about the organization department, Wang Meng notes that the antagonist, Liu Shih-wu, has a "strange," 古怪, name. (p. 24). Lin Mo-han, 一篇引起爭論的小說 (A Short Story That Has Aroused Controversy), PD, March 22, 1957, p. 2, gives the Party's qualified *nihil obstat* to this story, and quotes Wang's description of Liu's name. But he renders the word "strange" with the synonymous term, 奇怪. 奇 is the final character in the name of Liu Shao-ch'i. "Shao-ch'i" is itself a some what strange name, both because the character combination is unusual, and because of its literal meaning, "few strange." This is conceivably a subtle hint about the "real life" identity of Liu Shih-wu.
¹⁹ Teng Hsiao-p'ing, 1958 PHB, *loc. cit.*
²⁰ 在青年團第三次全國代表大會上, 鄧小平同志、代表中共中央致祝詞 (Comrade Teng Hsiao-p'ing, Representing the CPC Center, Delivers Words of Greeting to the Third National Congress of the Youth League.) PD, May 16, 1957, p. 1.
²¹ Hu Yao-pang, 團結全國青年, 建設社會主義的新中國 (Unite the Youth of the Whole Country, Build a Socialist New China) PD, May 16, 1957, pp. 2-3, p. 3.
²² Teiwes, "Provincial Purge," *loc. cit.* He does not count Ch'en Man-yuan.
²³ Communist Party Center, State Council, 嚴肅處理廣西因災餓死人事件 (Severely Deal With the Famine Resulting From Disasters in Kwangsi), PD, June 18, 1957, p. 2. The purge may have come as a surprise for Ch'en. In April he had congratulated himself for putting down left and right deviation in Kwangsi, and for the annually increasing farm income. He did, however, admit some shortcomings remained: for example, many comrades did not like to inspect actual conditions. 學習唯物辯證法, 克服工作中的片面性 (Study Dialectical Materialism, Overcome Bias in Work), *Study*, 7 (April 4, 1957), pp. 20-21. The purge of Chao Chien-min might also seem to be a special case, since it did not occur until October, 1958. Chao was a supporter of the Leap, 改革喪葬禮俗, 提倡廢棺薄葬而不墳 (Change Burial Customs, Promote Burial Without Coffin, Small Tombs, and No Mound), PD., June 17, 1958, p. 4. His proposal, to reform burial customs, was not particularly radical, but it may have been unpopular. But the accusations against the Shantung localists were on the whole the same as those levied against the other localists. See 甘肅、山東兩省黨整肅概況 (The Party Purge in Kansu and Shantung) *Bandit Affairs Monthly*, Vol. 1, No. 11 (November, 1958) pp. 91-97.

²⁴ Teiwes, "Provincial Purges," p. 14.
²⁵ Teng Hsiao-p'ing, 1958 PHB, *loc. cit.*, p. 40.
²⁶ PD, May 25, 1958, p. 1.
²⁷ Chiang Hua, 堅持黨的正確路線,爭取整風運動在戰線上全勝 (Firmly Uphold the Correct Line of the Party, Seize Victory on All Fronts in the Rectification Movement), PD, December 28, 1957, pp. 2-3. p. 2.
²⁸ *Ibid.* p. 2.
²⁹ K'o Ch'ing-shih, 乘風破浪,加速建設社會主義的新上海 (Ride the Wind and the Waves, Rapidly Build a Socialist New Shanghai), PHB, 1958, pp. 46-48, p. 46.
³⁰ *Ibid.*
³¹ *Ibid.*, p. 41.
³² In October, 1957, P'an published an essay attacking rightist thought, but this rightism was mostly manifested by cadres who were afraid of "unleashing the masses in a great blooming, great contending, great struggle debate." His position is more "liberal" than that of K'o Ch'ing-shih. The general impression is that P'an wanted to conduct a purge of his own, but was beat to the draw. P'an Fu-sheng, 目前河南農村的階級鬥爭形勢 (The Current Condition of the Class Struggle in the Rural Areas of Honan), 新華半月刊 *(New China Half-Monthly)* (NCHM), 23 (December 10, 1957) pp. 121-123.
³³ Ulanfu, in *Bandit Congress,* p. 537.
³⁴ Report of the Second Plenum, *loc. cit.* p. 148.
³⁵ Ulanfu, 在民族工作座談會上的總結合發言 (Summary Speech at the Minorities' Work Conference), 南方日報 *(Southern Daily* (Canton)=SD) August 24, 1957, p. 4.
³⁶ Teng Hsiao-p'ing, 1958 PHB, p. 39.
³⁷ Saifudin, 層層批駁地方民族主義 (Layer by Layer, Rebut Local Nationalism), PD, December 26, 1957, p. 4.
³⁸ Liu Ko-p'ing, 在少數民族中進行一次反對地方民族主義的社會主義教育 (Implement a Socialist Education Movement Among Minority Nationalities Against Local Nationalism), PD, January 11, 1958, p. 7.
³⁹ Wang Feng, 是社會主義還是民族主義? (Socialism or Nationalism?) PD, March 2, 1958, p. 2.; March 3, 1958, p. 4; at March 2.
⁴⁰ *Ibid.*, March 3.
⁴¹ Ulanfu, 思想大解放,民族大團結,生產大躍進 (Great Liberation of Thought, Great Solidarity of Nationalities, Great Leap Forward in Production), PD, May 21, 1958, p. 2. Mongolia soon shook off the Center's yoke. In May, 1959, during the first stage of the relaxation of the Leap policies, K'uei Pi, Ulanfu's deputy, wrote that the people's communes in Mongolia were "basically" like the communes elsewhere, but in fact resembled more the first stage rural co-ops (something all people's communes eventually came to do around 1962.) This is because of the "special characteristics" of Mongolia. During the past year, 1958, there had been a "deviation," a tendency to go "a little too fast," to the detriment of the welfare of the people. 人民公社制度為畜牧業的高速發展開闢了廣闊前途 (The People's Communes Open a Broad Road for the Rapid Development of the Livestock Industry), PD, May 2, 1959, p. 6.

⁴² Ezra Vogel, "Land Reform in Kwangtung, 1951-1953; Central Control and Localism," CQ 38 (April-June, 1969) pp. 27-62.

⁴³ Ou Meng-chueh, 古大存，馮白駒的錯誤在那裡？ (What Are the Mistakes of Ku Ta-ts'un and Feng Pai-chü?) NCHM, 19 (October 10) 1958, pp. 43-45, p. 43.

⁴⁴ Ibid., p. 44.

⁴⁵ Ibid., p. 43.

⁴⁶ Ou Meng-chueh, 廣東鬥爭地方主義的勝利 (Victory of the Struggle Against Localism in Kwangtung), PD, June 6, 1958, p. 4. This is probably a reference to decisions arrived at a meeting of the Kwangtung Party's provincial Control Commission, which issued a resolution on an "education in discipline" movement to be carried out in conjunction with rectification. The resolution is dated August 29. See SD, September 8, 1957, p. 1.

⁴⁷ Feng Pai-chü, 廣東工業生產建設的成就與存在問題 (The Success of the Construction of Industrial Production in Kwangtung and Remaining Problems), SD, August 10, 1957, pp. 2-3.

⁴⁸ SD, August 11, 1957, p. 1.

⁴⁹ Chou En-lai, "Report on the Establishment of the Second Five-Year Plan for the Development of the National Economy." *Eighth Congress,* pp. 189-234, p. 198.

⁵⁰ So the Red Guards once called him. See his *Bandit Affairs* biography, p. 131.

⁵¹ Ch'en Yun, "Some Problems of Reform in the Non-Socialist Sector of the Economy," *Bandit Congress,* pp. 545-559, pp. 546-547.

⁵² Ibid., p. 548.

⁵³ See, for example, Li Fu-ch'un, "For the Sake of Socialist Construction, Strengthen National Planning Work," *Bandit Congress,* pp. 560-571; Li Hsien-nien, "Enable Our Commodity Pricing to Do Even Better in Promoting the Development of Production," *Ibid.,* pp. 597-609; Yao I-lin, "Solve the Problems of Pork and Vegetable Supply," *Ibid.,* pp. 626-638; Po I-po, a P'eng Chen man, but, like much of Chou's group, a central bureaucrat, argued along similar lines: "Correctly Manage the Relationship Between Spending and Saving," *Ibid.,* pp. 572-586.

⁵⁴ Schurmann, *Ideology,* p. 143.

⁵⁵ 中共中央第三次全體會議（擴大） (Third Plenum of the Chinese Communist Center (Enlarged)), PHB, 1958, p. 182.

⁵⁶ CC CPC, 關於整頓農業生產合作社的指示 (Directive on the Rectification of Rural Co-ops); 關於作好農業合作社生產管理工作的指示 (Directive on Doing a Good Job of Production Management on the Rural Co-ops); 關於在農業合作社內部貫徹執行互利政策的指示 (Directive on Implementation of Mutual Benefit Polities Within the Rural Co-ops), PHB, 1958, pp. 517-520. The PHB also published a portion of a report delivered to the Plenum by Teng Tzu-hui in general agreement with these directives, but with perhaps somewhat less emphasis on material incentives. 關於農業合作社擴大生產及其他幾個問題 (Raising Production on the Rural Co-ops and a Few Other Problems), *Ibid.,* pp. 520-524.

⁵⁷ 1958 PHB, p. 519.

[58] *Ibid.*, pp. 519-520. The "rich" (an extremely relative term) farmers were rich mainly because of greater farming skill; hence, when priority is placed upon increasing production without regard to ideological purity, a conciliatory policy toward them is taken. This benefits production, but, from the Party's point of view, leads to politically undesirable consequences. *Cf.* Chiang Hua, *op. cit.*, on "'left' deviation."

[59] 1958 PHB, p. 182.

[60] See Liu Shao-ch'i, 中國共產黨中央委員會向第八屆全國代表大會第二次會議工作報告 (Work Report of the Central Committee of the Communist Party of China to the Second Session of the Eighth National Congress.) PD, May 27, 1958, pp. 1-2, p. 2. Also Schurmann, *Ideology,* pp. 196 ff., for a hypothesized conflict between Mao and Ch'en Yun.

[61] 1958 PHB, p. 182.

[62] Teng Hsiao-p'ing, 1958 PHB, p. 36. Teng's appetite for increased political control over the peasants may not at that time have been combined with desires for radical experimentation. He was later accused of having said in 1957, "The Chinese donkey is slow, but slowness has its good points." 人民公社的勝利和"超越了階級論"的破產 (The Victory of the People's Communes and the Bankruptcy of the Theory of "Transcending Class."), PD, February 4, 1968, p. 4.

[63] Chu Te, 在農業戰線上鼓足幹勁前進 (Drum Up Labor Enthusiasm on the Agricultural Front), PD, December 28, 1957, pp. 1, 4, p. 4.

[64] Schurmann, *Ideology,* p. 475.

[65] Union Research Institute, *The Case of P'eng Te-huai* (Kowloon, 1968) xii, 6, 494 pp., p. 24.

[66] PD, February 17, 1958, p. 1.

[67] Wu Chih-p'u, 論悲觀主義 (On Pessimism), NCHM, 19, 1958, pp. 39-42, p. 41.

[68] Vogel, *Canton,* p. 241. "Moderate" here would seem to mean "not totally stupid." These concepts should probably be treated distinctly. Liu's arguments were reasoned, but his ends were grandiose. It cannot, however, be argued there was no difference between Mao and Liu in 1958. One possible difference, on the role of the leader, was discussed in the fourth chapter. The example in that chapter also indicates a substantive difference between Mao and Liu. Mao, it will be recalled, spoke of "water control," a traditional method; whereas Liu spoke of mechanization. Some economists argue that the traditional methods for raising agricultural output have reached the point now where they are not worth the effort put into them, and that further increases in output depend upon modernization. Liu may have held this view in 1958, but it was not adopted by the Party as a whole until around 1961. See Dwight H. Perkins, *Agricultural Development in China, 1368-1968,* (Chicago, 1969) xv, 395 pp., pp. 68-70, 78.

[69] "Down with Liu Shao-ch'i: Life of Counter-Revolutionary Liu Shao-ch'i," Peking *Chingkangshan,* May, 1967; in *Current Background* (CB), August, 19, 1967, pp. 16-27, p. 17. A Tsinghua University wall poster, however, had said: "At the time of the realization of the people's communes Liu made this statement, with some secret intentions in mind: The movement to realize the people's

communes is not a project which can be realized at a word from somebody." *Mainichi,* April 6, 1967; DSJP, April 10-12, 1967, p. 36. The "secret intentions" would seem to be to cut down the pretentions of "somebody" (Mao) rather than to criticize the communes. In his report at the Ninth Congress Lin Piao includes the grotesque accusation that Liu had been a KMT agent since the 1920's, but he does not say that Liu had opposed the Leap in 1958. "Report to the Ninth National Congress of the Communist Party of China," *Peking Review,* Vol. 12, No. 8 (April 30, 1969) pp. 16-35.

[70] Liu Shao-ch'i, May 27, 1958, p. 2.

[71] 要多快好省，不要少慢差貴 (We Want Much Fast Good Cheap, Not Little Slow Inferior Expensive), PD, February 15, 1958, p. 3.

[72] The move was a wise one, as Nieh became famous for his ability to build and maintain "independent kingdoms." See, e.g., Canton *September 16 Bulletin,* August, 1968; SCMP, 4240, August 16, 1968, pp. 1-3. Nieh was thus able to keep politics from commanding defense research; China's progress in nuclear weaponry and rocketry is probably in large part Nieh's doing.

[73] Nieh Jung-chen, 科學事業必須為生產大躍進服務 (Science Must Serve the Great Leap Forward in Production), PD, March 15, 1958, p. 2.

[74] Wu Te, 解放思想，迎接技術革命 (Liberate Thought, Welcome the Technological Revolution), PD, May 24, 1958, p. 2. In August Nieh surrendered. He spoke of "experts" in quotation marks, and argued against "superstitious fear" of them. But he did maintain the core of his ideas: experts should not be deified, and more of them should be trained. 全黨抓科學技術工作，實現技術革命 (The Whole Party Grasp Science and Technology Work, Realize a Technological Revolution), PD, August 2, 1958, p. 4.

[75] Enlarged Meeting of the Central Politburo, 為生產一千零七十萬噸鋼而奮鬥 (Fight to Produce 1,000,100,000 Tons of Steel), PD, September 1, 1958, p. 1.

[76] See T'an Chen-lin, 關於一九五六年到一九六七年全國農業發展綱要(第二次修正草案)的說明 (Explanation of the Outline for National Agricultural Development, 1956-1967 (Second Revised Draft), PD, May 28, 1958, pp. 1-2; Liao Lu-yen, 在農業戰線上鼓足幹勁，力爭上游，多快好省地建設社會主義 (On the Agricultural Front, Drum up Labor Enthusiasm, Struggle Upstream, Build Socialism Much Good Fast Cheap), PD, June 10, 1958, p. 2. These men may have supported the Leap because of the emphasis it put on agriculture. T'an Chen-lin had also been a long-time proponent of decentralization. 在中央集中領導下充分發揮地方積極性 (Under the Centralized Leadership of the Center, Fully Develop the Activism of the Localities), PD, October 9, 1956, p. 4. In view of T'an's 1958 behavior, it is interesting that he was the follower Chou En-lai was most willing to abandon in 1968. Teng Tzu-hui, the apparatchik in charge of agriculture, was not a strong supporter of the Leap.

[77] 人民公社好 (People's Communes Are Good), PD, August 18, 1958; 怎樣辦好人民公社 (How to Do a Good Job of Running People's Communes), PD, August 21, 1958, p. 2. In any case, Mao had forced the issue himself in early August. The Party's decision on the communes was not published until

September 10, 關於在農村建立人民公社問題的決議 (Resolution on the Problem of Establishing People's Communes in Rural Areas), PD, September 10, 1958, p. 1. For a discussion of the propaganda buildup to the communes, see Frederick Yü, *op. cit.,* pp. 98-101.

[78] Cheng Chu-yuan, *Communist China's Economy, 1949-1962: Structural Changes and Crises* (Seton Hall: University Press, 1963) xii, 217 pp., p. 116.

[79] PD, September 1, 1958, p. 1. The economic bureaucrats may not have taken much comfort in this, since much of the steel was to be produced in "backyard furnaces."

[80] Po I-po, a non-CEL bureaucrat, gave a strong endorsement of the backyard furnaces. 打破工業的神祕觀點 (Smash the Mysterious Viewpoint in Industry), RF, 3 (July 18) 1958, pp. 18-21. *A propos* of Chou En-lai's group, Mao made an interesting statement at Lushan: "The State Planning Commission and the Central Ministries have carried on for ten years. Suddenly, at Peitaiho [the Enlarged Politburo meeting of August] they just gave up." *The Case of P'eng Te-huai,* p. 24.

[81] In September Mao complained that much of the seeming enthusiasm for the Leap was half-hearted and superficial. 在九月間的重要談話 (Important Conversations in September), RF, 10 (October 16), 1958, pp. 1-2.

[82] Chou had urged that farmers not be forced to join the co-ops. 鞏固農業生產合作社的一些問題 (A Few Problems in Consolidating Rural Co-ops), PD, September 30, 1956, p. 8.

[83] Chou Hsiao-chou, 農業大躍進促前了全面大躍進 (The Great Leap Forward in Agriculture Propels an Overall Great Leap Forward), PD, May 24, 1958, p. 2.

[84] There are so many ambiguities here. In fact, the policies Chou was at least overtly supporting were not adopted. During 1958 the area under cultivation was actually reduced. See Perkins, *Market,* p. 84.

[85] *The Case of P'eng Te-huai,* p. 24.

[86] T'ao Chu, 駁"糧食增產有限論" (Rebutting the Theory That "Increases in Food Production Are Limited"), RF, 5 (August 1) 1958, pp. 1-5, pp. 1-2. The theory behind this seems to have been to increase somehow the efficiency of photosynthesis. In 1961 T'ao told a group of intellectuals he had been wrong to try to tell the farmers their business. See Canton *Kwang-yu August 31,* Nos. 2-3, (April-May, 1968) SCMP, 42000 (June 18, 1968) pp. 6-16, p. 14.

[87] T'ao Chu, August, 1958, p. 2.

[88] Mao Tse-tung, 介紹一個合作社 (Introducing a Co-op.) RF 1 (June 1) 1958, pp. 3-4.

[89] PD, May 26, 1958, p. 1.

[90] T'an Chen-lin, 論我國今年夏季的空前大豐收 (Our Country's Unprecedentedly Rich Summer Harvest This Year) PD, August 11, 1968, pp. 1, 4.

[91] Li Hsien-nien, 人民公社所見 (A View of the People's Communes), PD, October 17, 1958, p. 3.

[92] 要注意保証農民的休息 (Attention Must Be Given to Guaranteeing the Peasants Rest), PD, November 9, 1958, p. 1.

[93] Hu Yao-pang, 發揚共產主義精神,努力建設社會主義

(Develop the Communist Spirit, Earnestly Build Socialism), PD, December 3, 1958, p. 3.; delivered November 29. Not everyone got the word. As late as December 9 (PD, p. 2) a report from Kwangtung still spoke of "building communism." This could indicate the matter was still under debate until the last day of the sixth plenum (or it could have been an effort by someone at the Center to embarass T'ao Chu).

[94] 毛主席永遠領導我們 (Chairman Mao Always Leads Us), PD, December 18, 1958, p. 2.

[95] *Mainichi,* January 5, 1967; DSJP, December 31, 1966-January 5, 1967, p. 46.

[96] *Yomiuri,* January 7, 1967; DSJP, January 7-9, 1967, p. 22.

[97] Sixth Plenum, Eighth CC, 同意毛澤東同志指出的關於他不作中華人民共和國主席候選人 (Agreeing with Comrade Mao Tse-tung's Proposal That He Not Be a Candidate for Chairman of the People's Republic of China), December 10, 1958; PD, December 18, 1958, p. 1.

[98] Peking *Chingkangshan,* April 18, 1967; SCMP, 3946, May 25, 1967, p. 1.

[99] CPC 8th CC 6th Plenum, 關於人民公社問題的決議 (Resolution on Several Problems of the People's Communes), PD, December 19, 1958, pp. 1-2, p. 1.

[100] *Ibid.,* p. 2.

[101] CPC 8th CC 6th Plenum, 公報 (Public Report), PD, December 18, 1968, p. 1.

[102] Li Hsien-nien, 積極開發多種經營,大力增產副食品 (Actively Develop Many Kinds of Management, Put Great Effort into Producing By-Products), PD, December 29, 1958, p. 2.

[103] Li Hsien-nien, 怎樣認識農村財貿管理體制的改進 (How to Look at the Reform of the Management System of Finance and Trade in the Rural Areas), PD, January 17, 1959.

[104] Ch'en Yun, 建設共產主義的偉大計劃 (The Great Plan for Building Communism), PD, January 3, 1959, p. 1.

[105] Ch'en Yun, 當前基本建設工作中的幾種大問題 (A Few Current Important Problems in Basic Construction), PD, March 1, 1959, pp. 1-2.

[106] Teng Tzu-hui, 積極辦好公共食堂,認真貫徹自願原則 (Actively Manage Well the Public Mess Halls, Sincerely Implement the Voluntary Principle), 中國青年 (*China Youth*=CY) 12 (June 1) 1959, pp. 5-6.

[107] Po I-po, 一九五九年工業戰線的任務 (The Task on the Industrial Front in 1959), PD, January 1, 1959, p. 2.

[108] K'o Ch'ing-shih, 論全國一盤棋 (The Whole Country Is a Chessboard) RF, 4 (February 16), 1959, pp. 9-12; T'ao Lu-chia, 廣泛實行全國一盤棋的教育 (Broadly Implement the Lesson of the Whole Country Is a Chessboard) RF, 5 (March 1) 1959, pp. 25-29.

[109] Chou En-lai, 政府工作報告 (Report on the Work of the Government) PD, April 19, 1959, pp. 2-4, p. 2.

[110] Ch'en Po-ta, 厚今薄古,邊幹邊學 (Stress the Present, Slight the Past, Work and Study at the Same Time) PD, March 11, 1958, p. 7.

[111] Ch'en Po-ta, 批判的繼承和新的探索 (The Continuation of Arguments and New Understandings), RF, 13 (July 1) 1959, pp. 36-45, pp. 36-37.

[112] In August Chou En-lai spoke of some severe flooding in Kwangtung in the spring. 關於一九五九年國民經濟計劃主要指示和進一步開展增產節約運動的報告 (Report on the Important Directive Rectifying the 1959 National Economic Plan and Going a Step Further to Begin an Economy in Production Movement.), PD, August 29, 1959, pp. 1-2, p. 2.

[113] T'ao Chu, 虎門公社調查報告 (Report on an Investigation of Tiger Gate Commune), PD, February 25, 1969, p. 7.

[114] Tseng Hsi-sheng, 總結去年的經驗,搞好今年的大躍進 (Sum up Last Year's Experience, Get a Good Great Leap Forward This Year) PD, March 3, 1959, p. 7.

[115] *The Case of P'eng Te-huai*, p. 16.

[116] See C. S. Chen and Charles Price Ridley, *Rural People's Communes in Lien-Chiang County, Fukien Province, 1962-1963* (Hoover Institute, 1969) xi, 243 pp., p. 6, for a general discussion of the changes in commune organization. While not promulgated, this change was referred to in scattered discussions. See, for example, Ch'en Cheng-jen. 人民公社的所有制和分配制度 (The Ownership and Distribution System on the People's Communes) PD, October 12, 1959, p. 7.

[117] Seventh Plenum, 8th CC, 公報 (Public Report) PD, April 8, 1959, p. 1.

[118] *The Case of P'eng Te-huai*, p. 27.

[119] Wang Jen-chung, 讀書,談心,想問題 (Read Books, Speak Your Mind, Think About Problems.) PD, April 9, 1959, p. 7.

[120] T'ao Chu, 太陽的光輝 (The Brilliance of the Sun), PD, June 3, 1959, p. 7. During the Cultural Revolution this was held to be a hint that Mao had some imperfections; but high ranking cadres in 1959 had not yet taken to referring to the leader as the "most red, most red, red red sun in our hearts." It is reasonable to take T'ao at his word and hold that the "sun" was meant to represent the Party as a whole. Later in June T'ao published some more explicit criticisms of the commune system. 總路線與工作方法 (The General Line and Work Methods) PD, June 18, 1959, p. 7.

[121] Li Ta-chang, 為奪取一九五九年農業豐收而奮鬥 (The Fight to Reap a Rich Harvest in 1959) PD, May 1, 1959, p. 12.

[122] For material on P'eng and the Lushan Conference, see *The Case of P'eng Te-huai; Talk About This Fellow P'eng Te-huai;* Charles, *op. cit.;* J. P. Simmonds, "P'eng Te-huai: A Chronological Re-examination," CQ, 37 (January-March, 1969) pp. 120-138.

[123] Canton *Ta P'i-p'an T'ung-hsun*, SCMP, 4124, February 19, 1968, pp. 1-6, p. 5.

[124] *Ibid.*

[125] *Talk About This Fellow P'eng Te-huai*, p. 5.

[126] "Down With P'eng Te-huai," CB, 851 (April 26, 1968). The Red Guard explanation for this was simple—P'eng was a traitor. Actually, P'eng's attitude toward the Soviet Union was probably more a function of his professionalism. He no doubt felt that the next war would be with the United States, and that it was thus not expedient to antagonize China's major ally.

[127] In 1961, to cope with the deteriorating morale within the PLA, Lin Piao ordered a campaign to "remember the bitter [of the past], talk of the sweet [of the present]." Lo Jui-ch'ing reported, "A rather common problem throughout the movement is that when talking of the sweet, there is much talk about the sweetness of land reform and cooperativization, and the talk is natural and concrete. But there is little talk about the sweetness of the people's communes, and it is forced and lacks content." WB, 11 (March 2) 1961, pp. 2-18, p. 3. Lo's report won a "I have read this; very good" from the Chairman. *Ibid.*, p. 1.

[128] For a text, see Peking *Ko-ming Huan-lien*, August 24, 1967; SCMP, October 2, 1967, pp. 1-4.

[129] Charles, *op. cit.*, p. 21.

[130] Simmonds, *op. cit.*, p. 133.

[131] Eighth CC 8th Plenum, 關於從彭德懷為首的反黨集團的決議 (Resolution on the Anti-Party Clique Headed by P'eng Te-huai) (August 16, 1959) RF, 13 (August 15, 1967) pp. 18-20.

[132] 無產階級必須牢牢掌握槍桿子 (The Proletariat Must Firmly Grasp the Barrel of the Gun) RF, 12 (August 1) 1967, pp. 43-47, p. 45.

[133] *The Case of P'eng Te-huai*, pp. 37 ff.

[134] Schurmann, *Ideology*, p. 56.

[135] At one point Mao said, "The principal members of this clique were formerly important members of the Kao Kang anti-Party clique." SCMP, 4124, p. 4. This is probably not literally true, and may simply be a general reference to the army. But some people purged around the time of P'eng had once worked for Kao Kang.

[136] Wang Chia-hsiang was spared disgrace long enough to expound on the "International Significance of the Victory of the Chinese People" (中國人民勝利的國際意義), RF, 19 (October 1) 1959, pp. 56-60.

[137] RF, 12, 1967, p. 41.

[138] "A Condensation of P'eng Te-huai's Talks," *loc. cit.*, pp. 28, 29.

[139] Canton *Chingkangshan*, August 26, 1967; SCMP, 4032 (October 2, 1967), p. 7.

[140] RF, 12, 1967, *op. cit., passim*. Those attacks on the rightists at the time which did not concentrate upon the substance of their arguments accused them of violating Party discipline. Liu Lan-t'ao, *op. cit.*, 1959; Wang Ts'ung-wu, 黨的團結和紀律 (The Unity and Discipline of the Party), RF, 24 (December 16) 1958, pp. 9-15.

[141] RF, 13, 1967, p. 18.

[142] *The Case of P'eng Te-huai*, p. 21.

[143] Peking *Chingkangshan*, April 18, 1967; SCMP, 3946 (May 25, 1967), p. 2.

[144] For a study of Wu Han's satirical writings, see James R. Pusey, *Wu Han: Attacking the Present Through the Past* (Harvard: University Press, 1969) x, 84 pp.

[145] Wu Han, 海瑞罷官反其他 ("Hai Jui Is Dismissed From Office" and Other Works), (Hong Kong, nd) 56 pp., pp. 15-56.

[146] *The Case of P'eng Te-huai*, p. 37.

[147] Simmonds, *op. cit.*, p. 138.

¹⁴⁸ Dairen *Ko-ti T'ung-hsun,* 4 September 13, 1967; SCMP, 4081 (December 15, 1967) p. 7. In his first signed article on Hai Jui, Wu Han took specific steps to disassociate his Hai Jui from P'eng Te-huai. He concludes the article with a denunciation of "self-styled" Hai Jui's who are really nothing but right opportunists. 論海瑞 (Hai Jui), PD, September 21, 1959, p. 11.
¹⁴⁹ Liu Mien-chih (Wu Han) 海瑞罵皇帝 (Hai Jui Scolds the Emperor), PD, June 16, 1959, p. 8. This is essentially a *pai-hua* translation of a portion of Hai Jui's biography in the official Ming history (明史), *Chüan* 226. Incidentally, while Wu Han cannot simply be dismissed as a tool of a group of politicians, this article is evidence that P'eng Chen was at that time disenchanted with the policies of the Leap.
¹⁵⁰ "A Condensation of P'eng Te-huai's Talks," *loc. cit.,* p. 29.
¹⁵¹ For another argument that P'eng did not intend to challenge Mao, see Teiwes, "Leadership Purges," p. 127.
¹⁵² 8th Plenum, 8th CC, CPC, 公報 (Public Report), PD, August 27, 1959, p. 1.
¹⁵³ T'ao Chu, 革命堅定性 (Revolutionary Resolution), PD, September 2, 1959, p. 7.
¹⁵⁴ *The Case of P'eng Te-huai,* p. 20. The editors of this collection think the second XX, like the third, is Ch'en Yun. However, all indications are that Ch'en Yun was not standing firm. An alternative guess for the second XX might be Hsien-nien.
¹⁵⁵ *Ibid.,* p. 18.
¹⁵⁶ According to his daughter, Lin was seriously ill for a time in the 1960's. Lin Tou-tou, 劉亞樓叔叔永遠活在我們心裡 (Uncle Liu Yao-lou Always Lives in Our Hearts), PD, May 12, 1965, p. 6. On the name of the daughter: the children of high ranking Chinese Communist cadres, for some reason, always seem to go by their baby names: Tou-tou here, K'o Ch'ing-shih's Liu-liu, Liu Shao-ch'i's P'ing-p'ing and Ting-ting.
¹⁵⁷ *Talk About This Fellow Lin Piao,* p. 11.
¹⁵⁸ Alice Langley Hsieh, *op. cit.,* p. 176.
¹⁵⁹ Chou Ching-wen, 風暴十年 (*Ten Years of Storm*) (Hong Kong, 1962), 5, 9, 2, 9, 12, 588 pp., p. 108. There are suggestions that Lin, like many other soldiers, was somewhat implicated in Kao Kang's conspiracy. *Talk About This Fellow Lin Piao,* p. 69.
¹⁶⁰ Hsieh was to claim, however, that in spite of the transfers, the ministry continued to be run by Lo's men. "Talk at a Struggle Rally Against Lo Jui-ch'ing," August 7, 1967. *Issues and Studies,* Vol. V, No. 12 (September, 1969) pp. 94-102. The claim is so obviously self-serving that it is difficult to evaluate.
¹⁶¹ Canton *Hung Wei Pao,* January 22, 1967; SCMP, 3937, May 11, 1967, p. 2.
¹⁶² Eighth Plenum, 8th CC, CPC, 關於開展增產節約運動的決議 (Resolution on Beginning an Economy in Production Movement), August 16, 1959; PD, August 27, 1959, pp. 1-2.
¹⁶³ Party Center, State Council, 關於組織農村集市貿易的指示 (Directive on Organizing Collective Markets in Rural Areas), PD, September 23, 1959, p. 1.

[164] Lin T'ieh, 為一九六零年的更大勝利而鬥爭 (Struggle for an Even Greater Leap Forward in 1960), PD, December 28, 1959, p. 7. Li Fu-ch'un, 迎接一九六零年的新躍進 (Welcome the New Leap Forward in 1960), PD, January 1, 1960, p. 2.

[165] Ch'en Cheng-jen, PD, October 18, 1959, *op. cit.*; also, his 加速農業的技術改造 (Speed Up the Reform of Agricultural Techniques), PD, February 16, 1960, p. 7, in which he urged the comrades to consider the needs of the locality before embarking upon ambitious projects. Chang Te-sheng, a major architect of the capitalist road agricultural policies, in attacking the rightists, said their mistakes were a "contradiction among the people." 用實際行動保衛總路線 (Protect the General Line with Practical Measures), RF, 21 (November 1), 1959, pp. 36-39, p. 38.

[166] Liu Shao-ch'i, 馬克思列寧主義在中國的勝利 (The Victory of Marxism-Leninism in China), PD, October 1, 1959; but it should be kept in mind that this appeared first in *Problems of Peace and Socialism*, and one of Liu's goals would thus be to try to placate the Russians.

[167] See Tseng on the anti-rightist struggle: 同右傾機會主義思想堅決作鬥爭 (Struggle Against Right Opportunist Thought), PD, October 21, 1959, p. 7; on the communes: 人民公社在安徽 (The People's Communes in Anhwei), PD, December 6, 1957, p. 5; on the Thought and general economics: 認清大好形勢千方百計地為實現今年更大躍進而奮鬥 (Recognize the Excellent Situation, in a Thousand Places with a Hundred Tricks Struggle for an Even Greater Leap Forward This Year), PD, January 7, 1960, p. 7; on newspapers: 關於黨辦報問題 (The Problem of Party Management of Newspapers), PD, June 16, 1960, p. 7.

[168] Chou En-lai, PD, August 29, 1959, p. 2.

[169] Li Ching-ch'uan, 人民公社是我國社會發展的必然產物 (The People's Communes Are a Necessary Product of Our Country's Social Development), PD, October 18, 1959, pp. 2-3; Tseng Hsi-sheng, PD, December 6, 1959, *op. cit.*

[170] Po I-po, 大搞群眾運動,使生產高潮滾滾向前 (Get With a Big Mass Movement, Let the High Tide of Production Roll Forward) PD, October 28, 1959, p. 2; K'o Ch'ing-shih, 關於工業戰線上的群眾運動 (The Mass Movement on the Industrial Front) PD, November 1, 1959, p. 2; Sung Jen-ch'iung, 無產階級領導工業的基本方針 (The Basic Direction of Proletarian Leadership of Industry), PD, January 18, 1960, p. 7. See also Ch'en Pei-hsien, 堅持政治掛帥的方針 (Firmly Uphold the Direction of Politics Takes Command), RF, 20 (October 16) 1959, pp. 47-49.

[171] *The Case of P'eng Te-huai*, p. 25.

[172] *Ibid.*, p. 26.

[173] Li Fu-ch'un, 高舉黨的總路線的紅旗,為社會主義建設事業的繼續躍進而奮鬥 (Raise High the Red Flag of the Party's General Line, Struggle for a Continued Leap Forward in the Task of Socialist Construction), PD, October 27, 1959, p. 2.

[174] Teng Tzu-hui, 中國農業的社會主義改造 (The Socialist Reform of Chinese Agriculture), PD, October 18, 1959, p. 6.

[175] Ma Ming-fang, 把銀行工作推進到新階段 (Push Banking Work to a New Stage), PD, January 15, 1960, p. 2; 把財政金融工作企業財物工作推向新發展階段 (Push Treasury Finance Work and Business Finance Work to a New Stage of Development) PD, March 29, 1960, p. 7.

[176] Ou-yang Chin, 財貿工作的政治觀點生產觀點和群眾觀點問題 (The Political, Production, and Mass View Points of Finance and Trade Work), PD, November 14, 1959, p. 7.

[177] Li Ta-chang, 把財貿工作提高到更好地為生產和生活服務 (Raise Finance and Trade Work so It Can Better Serve Production and Life), PD, April 11, 1960, p. 9.

[178] Li Hsien-nien, 更高地舉起三面紅旗,完成和超額完成今年國民經濟計劃 (Raise the Three Red Flags Even Higher, Fulfill and Over-Fulfill This Year's Economic Plan), PD, June 5, 1960, p. 2.

[179] T'ao Chu, PD, September 2, 1959.

[180] T'ao Chu, 歌頌人民公社 (Singing the Praises of the People's Communes), RF, 19 (October 1) 1959, pp. 61-68, p. 67.

[181] Lu Ting-i, 反右傾,鼓幹勁,配合增產節約運動大搞文化革命 (Oppose Rightism, Drum Up Labor Enthusiasm, Coordinate with the Economy in Production Movement, Get with a Big Cultural Revolution), PD, October 31, 1959, p. 2; also Lin Feng, 大搞文化大革命,實現工農群眾知識化,知識份子勞動化 (Get with a Big Cultural Revolution, Realize the Enlightenment of the Workers, Farmers, the Laborizing of the Intellectuals) PD, June 2, 1960, p. 2.

[182] Chang P'ing-hua, 黨的報刊要大插紅旗 (Party Publications Must Stick in the Red Flag), PD, Janury 12, 1960.

[183] T'ao Chu, 思想,"感情"文采 (Thought, 'Emotion', Style), PD, January 11, 1960, p. 7.

[184] Tseng Hsi-sheng, June 16, 1960, *op. cit.*

[185] Maoism, however, was not universal. P'eng Chen's local apparatchiks took a rather radical line at this time, but cited the authority of the Party, not of the Thought: Huang Huo-ch'ing, 大興共產主義合作作風 (Raise High the Style of Communist Cooperation), PD, January 23, 1960, p. 7; T'ao Lu-chia, 全新的時代,全新的人 (An Entirely New Age, an Entirely New Man), PD, March 16, 1960, p. 7. Surprisingly, future members of the CR Group also tended to downplay Mao at this time. Ch'en Po-ta, 無產階級世界觀和資產階級世界觀的鬥爭 (The Struggle Between the Proletarian and Bourgeois World Views), PD, November 16, 1959, p. 2; and Liu Ko-p'ing, 在工礦企業中貫徹執行黨的領導 (Firmly Uphold Party Leadership in Mining Work), PD, March 30, 1960, p. 7. Both stressed Party leadership; Liu Ko-p'ing even citing "Comrade Shao-ch'i" to this effect. Comrade Shao-ch'i had him purged later that year; perhaps Ko-p'ing had wind of this, and was trying to forestall it.

[186] The radical Maoists include: Wu Chih-p'u, PD, January 1, 1960, *op. cit.*; Tseng Hsi-sheng, PD, January 6, 1960, *op. cit.*; Yeh Fei, 為今年的繼續躍進奮勇前進 (Bravely Struggle for a Continued Leap Forward This Year), PD, February 8, 1960, p. 7; Li Ta-chang, PD, April 11, 1960, *op. cit.*; Chiang

241

Wei-ching, 學習毛澤東思想,充分發揚自覺的能動性 (Study the TMTT, Fully Develop a Self-Aware Ability to Act), PD, January 19, 1960, p. 7.

[187] Shu T'ung, 掌握不斷革命的理論武器,促使農業生產不斷躍進 (Grasp the Theoretical Weapon of Uninterrupted Revolution, Let Agricultural Production Continuously Leap Forward), PD, February 6, 1960, p. 7. There is perhaps an emotional affinity between Trotskyism and Maoism.

[188] Shu T'ung, 認真學習和運用毛澤東思想 (Sincerely Study and Use the TMTT), PD, April 12, 1960, p. 7.

[189] Chang Chung-liang, 人民公社的鞏固和發展,促進了農業的大躍進 (The Consolidation and Development of the People's Communes Propels a Great Leap Forward), PD, September 22, 1960, p. 2. Ch'en Yü, 依靠群眾,團結多數是取得革命勝利的根本保証 (Depend on the Masses and Unite With the Majority is the Basic Guarantee of the Victory of the Revolution), PD, December 6, 1960, p. 7.

[190] Ulanfu, 認真學習毛澤東思想,廣泛宣傳毛澤東思想, (Sincerely Study the TMTT, Broadly Propagate the TMTT), PD, April 7, 1960, p. 2. Immediate after Lushan Ulanfu had again renewed his allegiance to the "Party Center headed by Comrade Mao Tse-tung," praised the communes, and urged that minority cadres be educated against the perniciousness of bourgeois nationalism. 不斷發展我國各民族的大團結 (Continuously Develop the Great Unity of All Nationalities of Our Country), RF, 19 (October 1) 1959, pp. 43-50.

[191] Ma Ming-fang, PD, March 19, 1960, *op. cit.*; Lu Ting-i, 教學必須改革 (Teaching Must Be Reformed), PD, April 10, 1960, p. 2; Lin Feng, PD, June 2, 1960, *op. cit.*

[192] Ts'ai Ch'ang, 高舉毛澤東思想的旗幟,進一步發動婦女,為實現一九六零年的繼續躍進而奮鬥 (Raise High the Banner of the TMTT, Go a Step Further to Mobilize Women, Fight for a Continued Leap Forward in 1960), PD, February 25, 1960, p. 4; Li Fu-ch'un, PD, February 28, 1960, *op. cit.* Teng Ying-ch'ao, 發揚"三八"革命傳統,向婦女徹底解放的偉大目標前進 (Develop the Tradition of the "March 8" Revolution, Move Forward to the Great Goal of the Total Liberation of Women), PD, March 8, 1960, p. 2; Li Hsien-nien, PD, June 3, 1960, *op. cit.*

[193] Li Fu-ch'un, 關於一九六零年國民經濟計劃草案的報告 (Report on the Draft 1960 National Economic Plan), PD, March 31, 1960, pp. 2-3.

[194] Henry J. Lethbridge, *China's Urban Communes* (Hong Kong, 1961) xi, 74 pp., pp. 21-22.

[195] 大躍進的高速度和按比例是辯証的統一 (The Dialectical Unity of the Rapidity and Proportionality of the Great Leap Forward), PD, June 14, 1960, pp. 1, 4. In the same issue, Wu Chih-p'u published his swan song, urging the creation of an "active balance." 矛盾是社會主義社會發展的動力 (Contradictions Are the Motive Force of Socialist Social Development), *Ibid.*, p. 7. By August, those favoring adherence to the national plan had won. Li Fu-ch'un announced "The whole country is a chessboard." 高舉總路

線的紅旗,繼續前進 (Raise High the Red Flag of the General Line, Continue to Move Forward), PD, August 17, 1960, pp. 2-3.

[196] Chang P'ing-hua, 繼承和發揚"湘江評論"的光榮傳統 (Continue and Develop the Glorious Tradition of the *Hsiang River Review*), PD, June 30, 1960, p. 7.

[197] Ou-yang Ch'in, 發揚黨的優良作風 (Develop the Excellent Work Style of the Party), PD, July 4, 1960, p. 7.

[198] Tseng Hsi-sheng, 學習毛澤東同志實事求是的精神 (Study Comrade Mao Tse-tung's Spirit of Seeking Truth From Facts), PD, July 6, 1960, p. 7. Aware that he was beginning to sound like P'eng Te-huai, Tseng added that the rightists do indeed advocate seeking truth from facts, but with the motive of undermining Party leadership.

[199] T'ao Chu, 關於過渡時期的規律問題的商榷 (Discussion of the Laws of the Transitional Period), PD, August 8, 1960, p. 7.

[200] Ou-yang Ch'in, 必須把革命進行到底 (Revolution Must Be Carried Through to the End), PD, October 13, 1960, p. 7; October 14, 1960, p. 7; October 14.

[201] Lin T'ieh, 開展一個馬克思主義改進領導方法領導作風的運動 (Begin a Marxist Movement to Reform Leadership Methods and Style), PD, July 13, 1960, p. 7.

[202] Li Wei-han, 學習毛澤東著作逐步改造世界觀 (Study the Works of Chairman Mao, Step by Step Reform Your World View), PD, September 25, 1960, pp. 2-3, p. 3.

[203] Li Fu-ch'un, PD, August 17, 1960, *op. cit.*, p. 3.

[204] Chang Te-sheng, 站在最大多數勞動人民的一面 (Stand on the Side of the Greatest Number of the Laboring People), PD, October 20, 1960, p. 7.

[205] Wu Te, 必須堅決徹底地執行黨的政策 (We Must Firmly and Thoroughly Carry Out the Policies of the Party), PD, December 22, 1960.

[206] 充分發揮生產小隊的戰鬥作用 (Fully Develop the Fighting Function of the Production Team, PD, November 25, 1960, p. 1.

[207] Chang Te-sheng, 以農業為基礎,促進國民經濟的發展 (With Agriculture as the Base, Propel the Development of the National Economy), PD, December 12, 1960, p. 7.

[208] Ch'en and Ridley, *op. cit.*, p. 6. For a general discussion of the "three-tier ownership system," see Lo Keng-mo, 論我國農村人民公社的三級所有制 (The Three-Level Ownership System of Our Country's Rural People's Communes), CY, 1 (January 1) 1961, pp. 4-9. As this article makes clear, the change to emphasis on the team (about 30 families) would tend to benefit the formerly more wealthy, *i.e.,* efficient, farmers. In his confession Liu Shao-ch'i said that in 1962 he and Teng Hsiao-p'ing wanted to make the household the basic accounting unit. *Mainichi,* January 28, 1967; DSJP, January 28-30, p. 39. This would have restored the *status quo* after land reform.

[209] Hu Yao-pang, 在農業戰線上的偉大鬥爭中造就一代新人 (The Great Struggles on the Agricultural Front Create a Generation of New Men), PD, November 22, 1960, p. 7.

²¹⁰ This sending-down policy, renewed with a vengeance in 1968, was of course unpopular with the youths. It also seems to have been unpopular with the farmers, not only because of the apparently universal dislike by working people for "educated young people" not related to them, but also because state grain levies did not take into account the increased local population. CNA, 729 (October 18, 1968) p. 7.

²¹¹ PD, December 29, 1960, p. 1.

²¹² For different aspects, see Franz Schurmann, "China's 'New Economic Policy'—Transition or Beginning?" in McFarquhar, *op. cit.*, pp. 211-237; Charles Hoffman, "Industrial Work Incentives," in Francis Harper (ed) *This Is China: Analysis of Mainland Trends and Events* (Hong Kong, 1965) pp. 81-94, pp. 94 ff.; Merle Goldman, "The Unique 'Blooming and Contending' of 1961-1962," CQ, No. 37 (January-March, 1969) pp. 54-83. For a study of factors behind the change, see W. K., "Communist China's Agricultural Calamities," McFarquhar, *op. cit.*, pp. 163-174. Some contemporary Chinese writings on the new policies include: Chung Hsiao-i, 領導和組織農業生產的一些體會 (A Few Notes on Leading and Organizing Agricultural Production), PD, January 4, 1961, p. 7; Ko Chih-ta, 財政資金與信貸資金的安排和管理問題 (The Problem of Managing and Allocating Finance and Credit Capital), PD, March 31, 1961, p. 7; Kuan Tu-t'ung, 關於農村家庭副業,自留地,集市貿易問題 (The Problem of Rural Handcrafts, Retained Plots, and Collective Markets), 大公報 *(Ta Kung News)* (Peking) July 5, 1961, p. 3; Lo Keng-mo, *op. cit.*, and 關於如何正確徹底實行按勞分配原則的問題 (The Problem of Correctly and Thoroughly Implementing the Principle of Distribution on the Basis of Labor), *Ta Kung News,* April 16, 1962, p. 3. For a Maoist critique of some of the more interesting economic ideas discussed (mostly not in public) during this period, see Kung Wen-sheng, 駁孫冶方的修正主義經濟綱領 (Rebutting Sun Yeh-fang's Revisionist Economic Outline), PD, August 10, 1966, p. 4.

²¹³ One can, for that matter, gain something of the flavor of the period simply be leafing through the *People's Daily.* The paper began carrying lengthy articles on literature, many apparently with esoteric political significance. It also began carrying non-political cartoons (one series, "Papa and Children," about an old-fashioned Chinese gentleman of obviously "bourgeois" life-style and his mischievous grandchildren); the last page began featuring frequent photographs of pleasant scenery, fat, smiling babies, and pretty girls. The people, of course, were starving. Those in charge of such things may have decided to temper the harshness of life. But this also reflects the desire by the Party intelligentsia in Peking for a partial return to more human values than the regime had been wont to stress.

²¹⁴ K'o Ch'ing-shih, 工農聯盟是中國革命和建設勝利的保証 (The Alliance of Workers and Peasants is the Guarantee of the Victory of the Chinese Revolution and Construction), PD, July 20, 1961, p. 7.

²¹⁵ This is an inference drawn in part from an article by Yeh Ch'ün, Lin Piao's wife (although not so identified at the time) published in 1962 about Lu Hsun (not the 20th Century writer), a rather obscure figure from the Three Kingdoms period. According to Miss Yeh, Lu Hsun was one of China's greatest strategists.

His thinking in many respects was similar to Chairman Mao's. He was particularly good at knowing when it was best to retreat and avoid battle. The article is also fairly obviously a bit of esoteric boosting of Lin Piao. Lu, like Lin, came from Hupei, achieved a reputation for tactical brilliance at an early age, and was a loyal subordinate. 古代的一位優秀戰略家——陸遜 (An Outstanding Strategist of Our Country of Ancient Times—Lu Hsun), PD, June 3, 1962, p. 5. For the story of Lu Hsun, see the *Chronicle of the Three Kingdoms* (三國志), Wu (吳), chüan 13.

216 Chung Hsuan-tsai, 從"魏徵"的出籠看陸定一的反革命嘴臉 (Lu Ting-i's Counter-revolutionary Mug Revealed by the Hawking of the *Story of Wei Cheng*), PD, November 9, 1967, p. 4.

217 *Mainichi*, June 16, 1966; DSJP, July 1, 1966, p. 17.

218 Teng Hsiao-p'ing, *Studies on Chinese Communism, op. cit.*, p. 93.

219 Teng's economic views are fairly obscure. Prior to the Leap he is said to have opposed putting emphasis on "speed." But his main crime during the Leap seems to have been that he advocated mechanization in May, 1959. PD, February 4, 1968, *op. cit.*

220 Teng, *Studies on Chinese Communism*, p. 93.

221 The account is reprinted in Wang Hsueh-wen, 中共文化大革命與紅衛兵 (*The Chinese Communist Cultural Revolution and the Red Guards*), (Taipei, 1969) 3, 9, 714 pp., pp. 14 ff.

222 *Ibid.*, p. 17. Cf. Also Lin Piao, "Address to the Enlarged Meeting of the CCP Central Politburo," May 1, 1966, *Issues and Studies*, Vol. VI, No. 5 (February, 1970) pp. 81-92, p. 90.

223 Wang Hsueh-wen, *op. cit.*, p. 16.

224 *Ibid.*, p. 17.

225 在學術研究中堅持百花齊放,百家爭鳴的方針 (In Scholarly Research Uphold the Direction of Let a Hundred Flowers Bloom, a Hundred School Contend), PD, March 1, 1961, p. 7.

226 Goldman, "Unique Blooming," pp. 69 ff. For some criticisms of the cruder aspects of the Maoist literary line, see K'ang Chueh, 試論近年間的短篇小說 (Short Stories of the Past Few Years) 文學評論 (*Literary Review*), 5 (September, 1962), pp. 12-29; for the pre-Cultural Revolution attacks on the tendencies of that time, see, for example, Ch'eng Sheng-i, 對"文藝報"的幾點批評和建議 (Criticism and Proposals for the *Literary Gazette*), *Literary Gazette* (文藝報), 2 (February 16) 1965, pp. 26-28.

Chou Yang's role in all this is quite puzzling. To all appearances his entire career was one of an unusually mediocre and unusually repressive Party hack. But in the Cultural Revolution he was accused of a liberalism of truly Jeffersonian proportions: "Views on the Current Literary and Art Work," *Literary War News*, 17-18, (June 30, 1967); Union Research Services, Vol. 57, No. 1, 2 (October 3, 7, 1967) pp. 2-19. In 1960 Chou had given some hints of the relaxation to come: 我國社會主義文學藝術的道路 (The Socialist Road for Our Country's Socialist Literature and Art), PD, September 4, 1960, pp. 5-7. But he was also the major spokesman for the repressive policies adopted after 1962: 哲學社會科學工作者的戰鬥任務 (The Fighting Tasks of Philosophy and Social

Science Workers), PD, December 27, 1963, pp. 1-4; 高舉毛澤東思想紅旗,做又會勞動又會創作的文藝戰士 (Raise High the Red Flag of the TMTT, Be Literary Warriors Able Both to Labor and Create), PD, January 1, 1966, pp. 5-6. This last speech, made about half a year before he was purged, could have been delivered by Chiang Ch'ing. Perhaps, as one attack had it, "What Chou Yang said at large meetings was one thing, what he said in small meetings and outside talks was something else." 高舉毛澤東思想大紅旗,憤怒聲討文藝界黑幫頭子周揚 (Raise High the Great Red Banner of the TMTT, Righteously Attack the Head of the Black Gang in Literary Circles, Chou Yang), PD, July 29, 1966, pp. 1-2. p. 2. But Chou's main crime might have been simply that he carried out the policies his boss, Lu Ting-i, told him to.

[227] Teng T'o, op. cit., and 燕山夜話 (Evening Talks on Swallow Mountain), (Hong Kong, 1966) 157 pp. The Chinese term "three family village" is an equivalent of our "one horse town." The Maoists claim the name was chosen in sympathy with P'eng Te-huai, then amusing himself by breeding fish in his old home town.

[228] In 1962, P'eng's crony, Li Wei-han, published a lengthy article praising the role Mao and his Thought played in Party history. 新民主主義革命時期爭取無產階級領導權的鬥爭 (The Struggle to Obtain Proletarian Leadership Power in the Stage of the New Democratic Revolution), PD, February 9, 1962, p. 5; February 10, 1962, p. 5.

[229] PD, June 24, 1962, p. 1.

[230] This Fellow P'eng Te-huai, p. 91. This source suggests the circulation of P'eng's essay was the main occasion for the convening of the Tenth Plenum. No copy of the essay itself, as far as I know, is available outside mainland China.

[231] This section is taken from the Nihon Keizai, December 29, 1966; DSJP, December 29, 1966.

[232] Peking Ts'ao-mao Hung-ch'i, SCMP, 3899, March 15, 1967, p. 4.

[233] Liu Shao-ch'i also took the blame for this error. Mainichi, January 28, 1967; DSJP, January 28-30, 1967, p. 39.

[234] Chung Hsuan-tsao, op. cit. In his report to the Ninth Congress, Lin Piao speaks of conferences in January and August of 1962. Loc. cit., p. 19. It is not ascertained at which these exchanges took place.

[235] Li Li, 正確發揚黨內民主的幾個問題 (Some Questions on the Correct Development of Inner-Party Democracy) PD, July 3, 1962, p. 5.

[236] Teng T'o, 詩文選 Selected Prose, pp. 124-126.

[237] For the text, see PD, August 1, 1962, pp. 1-6. See also the PD, April 12, 1967, op. cit. critique. This does not mention, of course, that Liu had also added some footnotes citing works by Mao.

[238] There is an outside chance that Liu was specifically condemned at this meeting, but it seems very remote. The writer Andrew Tully claims that in November, 1962, United States intelligence sources obtained papers describing Liu Shao-ch'i, P'eng Chen, and Teng T'o as "right opportunist anti-party renegades." These men may have been so described, say, in secret Social Department memoranda; but even this would have been risky. Liu and P'eng suffered no loss in prestige after the plenum. In the texts of Mao's speech to the plenum released by

the Red Guards, Mao worries about he danger of revisionism taking hold in China, but he does not mention any potential revisionists by name. (*Mainichi,* March 9, 1967, DSJP, March 10, 1967, pp. 15-16.) As Josh Billings said, it ain't what a man doesn't know that makes him a fool, it's what he knows for sure as ain't so. But I suspect that Mr. Tully has his dates wrong, or that someone at NSA was pulling his leg. Andrew Tully, *The Super-Spies* (New York, 1969) 256 pp., pp. 172-175.

[239] Lo did say, it will be recalled, that the soldiers did not care much for the people's communes; and it is an old Chinese Communist trick for politicians to put their own more controversial opinions into the mouths of anonymous "masses." But except on humanitarian grounds, Lo would have no particular reason to object to the communes; and Lo was not a humane man. Here is a sample of his "work style": "Some of our soldiers are afraid of ghosts, afraid to die, just like a bunch of little gentlemen (像大少爺). We must give these men a good education, raise their awareness, and also apply a little pressure of public opinion. Fear of death, fear of ghosts is shameful, ridiculous...We must make these people feel they have no honor, no place to show themselves (?—沒有市場 —literally, no market place). Make those who fear death become afraid that people will say they fear death." WB, 20 (May 22, 1961) p. 12.

[240] RF, 12, 1957, *op. cit.,* pp. 43-47, *passim.*

[241] *Asahi,* January 20, 1967; DSJP, January 21-21, p. 20.

[242] CPC 8th CC 10th Plenum, 進一步鞏固人民公社集體經濟,發展農業生產 (Go a Step Further to Consolidate the Collective Economy of the People's Communes, and Develop Agricultural Production), PD, September 29, 1962, p. 1.

[243] Hsiao Shu, 〔合二而一〕論的反辯証法實質 (The Anti-Dialectical Nature of "Two Combine into One"), PD, August 14, 1964, p. 5. If the official press is to be believed, the issue was a source of grave concern for many different kinds of people. *Red Flag,* The Central Committee's theoretical journal, published the thoughts of an oil worker on the subject: Chang Tzu-ch'eng, "合二而一"就是不要革命 ("Two Combine into One" Means No Revolution), RF, 23-24 (September 15) 1964, pp. 27-28. For a summary of the "debate" see CNA, 535 (October 2, 1964).

[244] For an initial survey of the major documents, see Richard Baum and Frederick D. Teiwes, *Ssu-Ch'ing: The Socialist Education Movement of 1962-1966* (Berkeley, 1968) 128 pp. See Also Bureau of State Security (ROC) 對匪黨"中央關於農村社會主義教育運動中一些具體政策的規定"之分析 *(An Analysis of the Bandit Party's "Central Regulations on Some Concrete Policies of the Rural Socialist Education"),* (Taiwan, 1965) 11 pp., for a useful summary and comparative analysis of the first three documents.

[245] 假四清,真復俗 (False Four Cleans, True Restoration), PD, September 6, 1967, pp. 1-3, p. 1.

[246] The relevant documents have not been published by the Communists, but copies were obtained by Republic of China intelligence sources in 1965. For the first document, see 關於目前農村工作中若干問題的決定 (草案) *(Resolution on Certain Problems in Current Rural Works (Draft)),* (May 1963); published by Bureau of State Security, (ROC) (Taiwan, 1965) 19 pp. (Referred to hereafter as "May, 1963 document.") p. 1.

[247] *Ibid.*, p. 2. It is very interesting that toward the end of May the *People's Daily* carried an attack on pragmatism as a philosophy: Ch'en Yuan-hui 實用主義——真理就是一種權宜手段 (Pragmatism—Truth Is Nothing But the Expedient Way), PD, May 30, 1963, p. 5. Mao's enemies apparently had scored a point.

[248] May, 1963, Document, p. 7.

[249] *Ibid.*, p. 10.

[250] *Ibid.*, pp. 11-12.

[251] *Ibid.*, p. 13.

[252] 關於農村社會主義教育運動中的一些具體政策的規定(修正草案) (*Regulations on Some Concrete Policies in the Rural Socialist Education Movement (Draft)*), September, 1963. Released by Bureau of State Security (ROC) (Taiwan, 1965) 35 pp.

[253] *Ibid.*, p. 13.

[254] *Ibid.*, pp. 8, 10.

[255] *Ibid.*, p. 30

[256] 關於農村社會主義教育運動中的一些具體問題(草案) (*Regulations on Some Concrete Policies in the Rural Socialist Education Movement (Revised Draft)*), Released by Bureau of State Security (ROC) (Taiwan, 1965) 36 pp. Cited as September, 1964 Document.

[257] *Ibid.*, p. 7.

[258] *Ibid.*, p. 29.

[259] Baum and Teiwes, *op. cit.*, p. 36.

[260] PD, September 6, 1967, *op. cit.*, p. 1.

[261] *Ibid.*, p. 3.

[262] CC CPC, "Some Questions in the Current Socialist Education Movement," January 14, 1965. *Issues and Studies,* Vol. VIII, No. 1 (October, 1970). pp. 94-95. Cited as "23 Articles".

[263] Baum and Teiwes, *op. cit.*, p. 36.

[264] Yang Hsiu, 應該培養這樣的共產主義精神 (This is the Kind of Communist Spirit that Should Be Cultivated), *China Youth,* 5 (March 1) 1960, pp. 5-6, 36, p. 5. This "theory of docile tools" was one of the major targets of the Cultural Revolution.

[265] Washington *Post,* February 14, 1965.

[266] *China Youth Daily,* January 22, 1963, p. 1.

[267] Lo Jui-ch'ing, 學習雷鋒 (Learn from Lei Feng), PD, March 5, 1963, p. 2.

[268] 一代一代的繼承和發揚黨的革命傳統 (Generation upon Generation Continue and Develop the Revolutionary Traditions of the Party) PD, May 4, 1963, p. 1.

[269] K'o Ch'ing-shih, 向好八連學習 (Learn From the Good Eighth Company), PD, May 8, 1963, p. 2.

[270] Li Hsueh-feng, 讓千百個周明山更好地成長起來 (Let Hundreds of Thousands of Chou Ming-shan's Grow-Up Even Better), PD, May 28, 1964, p. 5.

[271] An Tzu-wen, 培養革命接班人是黨的一項戰略任務

(The Cultivation of Revolutionary Successors Is a Strategic Task of Our Party) PD, September 23, 1964, pp. 5-6.

272 PD, July 7, 1964, p. 1.

273 Hu Yao-pang, 為我國青年革命化而鬥爭 (Struggle for the Revolutionization of the Youth of Our Country), PD, July 7, 1964, pp. 2-3, p. 2.

274 Ibid., p. 3. In 1965 Hu became a secretary of Shensi, perhaps as a first step in his purge. But he also remained first secretary of the YCL until that organization was temporarily dissolved in late 1966.

275 Constitution of the Chinese Communist Youth League, PD, July 18, 1964, p. 3.

276 Ch'un Mei, 自我批判 (Self Criticism), Peking, *Ta Kung News*, December 19, 1964, p. 3. The criticisms in this article seem to be variations on a more general pattern, perhaps filed in the Propaganda Department under "idealistic young girl." Thus, the substance of the criticism here is the same as that used against Ting Ling when she was first rectified in 1942. See Frederick Yü, *op. cit.*, p. 58.

277 *Hung-i Chan Pao*, February 15, 1967; SCMP, 3908 (March 30, 1967) pp. 9-11.

278 Peking *Ching Kang Shan*, May 25, 1967; SCMP, 3996 (August 8, 1967) p. 5.

279 Ch'en Ch'i-t'ung, 在毛澤東思想哺育下的部隊文藝工作 (Literary and Art Work of the Troops Nurtured by the TMTT), PD, May 30, 1962, p. 5.

280 Lin Tou-tou, *op. cit.*

281 Her major speech delivered at that time was not published until 1967: Chiang Ch'ing, 談京劇革命 (Talk on the Peking Opera Revolution), PD, May 10, 1967; originally delivered July, 1964. There is speculation that references to the contributions of a "comrade at the Party Center" in 1964 referred to Miss Chiang. CNA, 643 (January 13, 1967) pp. 3-5. But as far as is known, she held no official Party post at that time.

282 K'o Ch'ing-shih, 大力發展和繁榮社會主義戲劇, 更好地為社會主義的經濟基礎服務 (Put Great Efforts into Developing and Making Flourish Socialist Plays, Make Them Serve the Socialist Economic Base Even Better), PD, August 16, 1964, pp. 2-3, p. 2.

283 K'o Ch'ing-shih, 反映社會主義新時代的現代劇前途燦爛 (The Brilliant Road Ahead for Modern Plays Which Reflect the New Socialist Era), PD, December 29, 1963. The "new morality" here may have some vague philosophical affinity with the concept by the same name being developed at the same time by the mod theologians in the West: it is a kind of situation ethics in which the ruler defines the situation for everyone else. But pragmatically this seems to be an answer to a Three Family Village essay urging that some aspects of traditional ethics still applied under the new order. Teng T'o, *Selected Prose*, pp. 122-123.

284 P'eng Chen, 在現代京劇觀摩演出大會上的講話 (Speech at the Meeting of Actors in the Modern Peking Operas), RF, 14 (July 31), 1964, pp. 18-24, p. 21.

285 *Ibid.*, p. 21. K'o Ch'ing-shih disputed the implications of this in *op. cit.*, August 16, 1964, p. 3.

[286] P'eng Chen, July 1964, p. 22.
[287] Chiang Ch'ing, May 10, 1967, *op. cit.*
[288] P'eng Chen, July 1964, p. 22.
[289] Po I-po, 在階級鬥爭的熔爐中鍛煉 (Tempering in the Furnace of Class Struggle), PD, May 15, 1964, p. 5.
[290] Lu Ting-i, 會勞動又會從事文藝活動的人是最好的文藝工作者 (People Who Can Both Labor and Carry on Literary and Artistic Activities Are the Best Literary and Artistic Workers), PD, November 27, 1964, pp. 1-2, p. 1.

Chapter VI

[1] Scott Boorman, *The Protracted Game: A Wei-Ch'i Interpretation of Maoist Revolutionary Strategy* (New York, 1969) xiv, 242 pp.
[2] Ou-yang Ch'in, 毛澤東思想——勞動人民手裡的尖銳武器 (The TMTT—A Sharp Weapon in the Hands of the Laboring People) PD, July 11, 1964, p. 5.
[3] Liu Shao-ch'i, 在慶祝中華人民共和國成立十五周年招待會上的講話 (Speech at the Reception in Celebration of the 15th Anniversary of the Founding of the People's Republic of China) PD, October 1, 1964, p. 1.
[4] P'eng Chen, 在慶祝中華人民共和國成立十五周年典禮上的講話 (Speech at the Ceremony Celebrating the 15th Anniversary of the Founding of the People's Republic of China) PD, October 2, 1964, p. 1.
[5] Hsu Yao-sheng, 關於如何打乒乓球 (How to Play Ping Pong) PD, January 17, 1965, pp. 1-2, p. 2.
[6] P'eng Chen, 代表中央作重要報告 (Important Report, Representing the Center.) PD, January 31, 1965, p. 1.
[7] Peking *Ching-kang Shan*, May, 1967; CB, August 17, 1967, p. 25.
[8] One assumes the coalition suffered a setback with the death of K'o Ch'ing-shih in the spring of 1965. Some Red Guards later claimed that K'o had been murdered by his doctors (CNA, 608, May 17, 1968, p. 2) but this line was never followed up. Nor was there any comment upon the coincidence of the almost simultaneous death of Lin Piao's close friend, Liu Ya-lou, that I have been able to find. The immediate effect of K'o's death was to deliver the Shanghai Party Committee over to Ch'en P'ei-hsien, who was less sympathetic to the Maoist cause. But Mao still had substantial support among the junior Shanghai secretaries, such as Chang Ch'un-ch'iao. Any inconvenience caused by K'o's death, obviously, was not decisive for the gross outcome of the struggle.
[9] Chou En-lai, 在第三屆全國人民代表大會第一次會議上的政治工作報告 (Speech on the Work of the Government to the First Session of the Third National People's Congress) PD, December 31, 1964, pp. 1-3, p. 2. This speech also seems to indicate, however, that polarization had not yet taken place along all issues. He praises the "half-work half study, half farming-half

study schools," attributing the idea to Liu Shao-ch'i. *Ibid.* An extended discussion of these schools had earlier been presented by Ou Meng-chueh of the T'ao Chu group: 從新會縣的辦學實踐看半工(農)半讀教育制度 (A Look at the Half Work (Farm) Half Study Educational System From the Experience of Hsin-hui County) PD, October 19, 1964, p. 5.

[10] Li Hsien-nien, 高舉毛澤東思想紅旗,作好社會主義商業工作 (Raise High the Red Flag of the TMTT, Do Good Socialist Commerce Work) PD, February 16, 1965, p. 2. Li's commitment to the red flag of the TMTT probably did not mean any lack of commitment to doing a proper job of finance management. In 1963 he published an article rather neatly illustrating the pressures under which experts had to operate. He told the accountants under his ministry that he hoped each "will come to have a more ardent love for his work." Perhaps realizing the work was not glamorous, he told his men it was necessary. Also, "I hope [each of you] will go a step fruther in raising his socialist political awareness." This is done by studying Marxism-Leninism, the TMTT. Each person should perform his own task well, and should obey orders ("support the system"). Also, "depend upon the leader [in this case, the Party], depend upon the masses." He concludes by saying that everyone in the Party and government should pay more attention to finance work, an ambiguous statement. It could be an invitation for wholesale politicization of the work (*cf.* Tseng Hsi-sheng on newspaper management), or it could be a bureaucratic empire builder's appeal for more funds for his office. 對財務會計人員的幾點希望 (A Few Hopes for Finance Accountants) PD, September 4, 1963, p. 2. The rhetoric of the Cultural Revolution sometimes gave the impression that "redness" was more important than competence in career advancement. This was perhaps not usually the case. Competence alone could not assure a person's survival (unless he were a nuclear physicist or the like), but no amount of redness could compensate for doing a bad job. The obvious point that there is no operational determinant of redness should be noted; anybody at any time can plausibly be found deficient in this regard. One function of the demand for redness would seem to be to keep the office holder off balance, to prevent him from enjoying life too much, to keep him from forming ambitions which might disrupt the ease of his superiors.

[11] P'an Fu-sheng 正確處理副業生產中的各種關係,大力發展農村副業生產 (Correctly Handle All the Relations in Rural By-Product Production, Put Great Energy into Developing Rural By-Product Production) PHB, 1965, pp. 533-534.

[12] Wang Jen-chung, 認真學習和運用"矛盾論" (Sincerely Study and Use "On Contradictions") PD, July 25, 1965, p. 5.

[13] T'ao Chu, 一定要演好革命現代戲 (We Certainly Want to Show Good Modern Plays) PD, July 29, 1965, p. 5.

[14] T'ao Chu, 革命現代戲要迅速地全部地佔領舞臺 (Revolutionary Modern Plays Should Quickly and Completely Occupy the Stage) PD, August 28, 1965, p. 2.

[15] Ho Lung, 中國人民解放軍的民主傳統 (The Democratic Tradition of the Chinese People's Liberation Army) PD, August 1, 1965, pp. 1-2, p. 1.

[16] *Ibid.*, p. 2.
[17] *Ibid.*
[18] *This Fellow Ho Lung*, p. 7.
[19] Lin Tou-tou, *op. cit.*
[20] *Mainichi*, May 24, 1967; DSJP, May 26, 1967, p. 28. This sounds like the mutterings of a stage villain in a 19th century melodrama, but probably mainly because of the damages done in translation—from Chinese to Japanese to English. Whether Lo ever in fact uttered these words, according to the consensus of unofficial sources these words describe the facts.
[21] Canton *Ching Kang Shan and Kwangtung Wen-i Chan-pao*, 7-8 (Setpember 5, 1967) SCMP, 4046 (October 24, 1967) p. 4. This is perhaps a reference to the training program described in the MAC summons, 號召全軍學習郭興福教學方法，提高訓練工作水平 (Summons to the Whole Army to Study the Kuo Hsing-fu Teaching Methods and Raise the Level of Training Work), PD, February 16, 1964, p. 1, which, on its face, at least, does not neglect political work. Lo was closely associated with this, as were Yeh Chien-ying, Chang Tsung-hsun, Chang Ai-p'ing, Yang Te-chih, and Liu Chen; all were either not in Lin's group, or were his more conservative regional followers. *Ibid.*, p. 2. There is no evidence that Lin Piao is unaware of the value of professional competence. He says morale is more important, but that is not the same thing. In 1961, when both proficiency and ideology were at an ebb, Lin talked a lot about ideology, but allocated more time to professional training. Lo's crime, despite what the Red Guards might have thought, was not that he promoted military training. (*Cf.* note 10 on previous page.) This may simply have been a convenient stick to beat Lo with; or, while he was pushing his own training program, Lo may have let drop some hints that he thought Lin's emphasis on political work tended to undermine training.
[22] *Mainichi*, May 24, 1967, *loc. cit.*
[23] Donald S. Zagoria, *Vietnam Triangle: Moscow, Peking Hanoi* (New York, 1967) xiv, 286 pp., pp. 67-83; and Uri Ra'anan, "Peking's Foreign Policy 'Debate,' 1965-1966," in Tang Tsou, *China in Crisis*, Vol. II, pp. 23-71. These works raise questions about my interpretation of the alignment of Lo Jui-ch'ing at that time; yet the Cultural Revolution materials do definitely place Lo with P'eng Chen, who, in 1966, seems to have followed Lin Piao in foreing policy matters. Matters were then rather complex; several hypotheses may help explain Lo's behavior: 1) Lo may not have broken with Lin Piao until late 1964, althought he never may have been in Lin's inner circle, in the manner of, say, Hsiao Hua; 2) No other soldier publicly endorsed Lo's call for a more conventional army; I have interpreted Ho Lung's 1965 article as an attack on Lin Piao, while Ra'anan thinks he was criticizing Lo Jui-ch'ing; both interpretations are probably correct; 3) I am inclined to think (mostly on the basis of gossip given out by the Red Guards), that Ho was lined up with P'eng Chen at the time he wrote his article; 4) Lo probably saw Lin Piao as his main opponent, while P'eng Chen was probably more worried about Teng Hsiao-p'ing. As Zagoria and Ra'anan point out, Teng wanted some kind of partial reconciliation with the Soviet Union; 5) the P'eng-Lo-Ho alliance probably formed after November, 1965, when Lo had been purged,

P'eng Chen was under attack, and it was obvious that Lin Piao was now the man to beat.

[24] Lo Jui-ch'ing, 紀念戰勝德國法西斯,把反對美帝國主義鬥爭進行到底 (Commemorate the Victory Over German Fascism, Carry the Struggle Against U.S. Imperialism Through to the End), PD, May 11, 1965, pp. 1-2.

[25] Zagoria, op. cit., pp. 67-68, 70.

[26] Lin Piao, 人民戰爭勝利萬歲 (Long Live the Victory of People's War), KMD, September 3, 1966, pp. 1-4.

[27] Zagoria, op. cit., pp. 78-83. Lin's "moderation," however, should not be exaggerated. This was, after all, an announcement that the People's Republic intended to support actively subversive movements in other countries.

[28] He explicitly exalted Mao's "personality" as well as his Thought, something rather rare prior to the Cultural Revolution. Yeh said: "Besides studying Chairman Mao's works, we also want to study Chairman Mao's life—a life of war, a great life—study his great practice. His life is our living model." WB, 10 (February 20, 1961) p. 8.

[29] Yeh Chien-ying, 偉大的戰略決定戰爭 (Great Strategy Decides the War) PD, August 30, 1965, p. 2.

[30] Lo Jui-ch'ing, 人民戰勝了日本法西斯,人民也一定能夠戰勝美帝國主義 (The People Defeated Japanese Fascism, the People Will Certainly Be Able to Defeat U.S. Imperialism) KMD, September 4, 1965, pp. 2-3.

[31] Zagoria, op. cit., p. 92.

[32] Obviously, this does not mean that the non-Maoists were not attacked for their foreign policy views. See Daniel Tretiak, "The Chinese Cultural Revolution and Foreign Policy," *Current Scene,* Vol. VIII, No. 7 (April, 1970) 25 pp. Rather, the continuity in Chinese foreign policy before and after the Cultural Revolution leads one to suspect that the attitudes for which the non-Maoists were attacked were not substantially different from those held by many in the Maoist camp.

[33] P'eng Chen, 在慶祝中華人民共和國成立十六周年典禮上的講話 (Speech at the Ceremony Celebrating the 16th Anniversary of the Founding of the People's Republic of China), KMD, October 3, 1965, p. 1.

[34] Twenty-three Articles, loc. cit., p. 96.

[35] P'eng Chen, PD, January 31, 1965, op. cit.

[36] Chu Te-hai, 廣泛開展群眾性的農業科學實驗活動,掀農業生產的新高潮 (Broadly Begin Mass Agricultural Scientific Experiment Activities, Propel a New High Tide in Agricultural Production), PD, January 31, 1965, p. 5.

[37] Twenty-three Articles, loc. cit., p. 96. During the Cultural Revolution the "Triple Alliance" became: army, revolutionary masses, revolutionary cadres.

[38] PD, March 28, 1965, p. 2.

[39] Huang Huo-ch'ing, 關於農村支部培養接班人問題 (The Problem of Cultivating Successors in the Countryside), PD, May 21, 1965, p. 5.

[40] Baum and Teiwes, op. cit., p. 42.

[41] T'ao Chu, 五億農村人民沿著社會主義道路前進的南針 (The Compass for 500 Million Peasants Going Forward Along the Socialist Road), PD, August 2, 1965, p. 5.

[42] Wang Jen-chung, PD, July 25, 1965, op. cit.

⁴³ Chang P'ing-hua, 一定要依靠貧農中農 (We Must Certainly Depend on the Poor and Middle Peasants), PD, November 2, 1964, p. 5.

⁴⁴ Martin King Whyte, "The Tachai Brigade and Incentives for the Peasant" *Current Scene,* Vol. VII, No. 16 (August 15, 1969) 13 pp., p. 6.

⁴⁵ T'ao Chu, 人民公社在前進 (The Future of the People's Communes) PD, February 28, 1964, pp. 5-6.

⁴⁶ T'ao Lu-chia, 讓大寨精神遍地開花結果 (Let the Spirit of Taichai Bloom Forth and Bear Fruit Everywhere) PD, October 5, 1965, p. 5.

⁴⁷ Chiang Wei-ching, 運用樣板,推動全盤是領導農業生產的好方法 (Use the Template, Mobilize the Whole Board Is a Good Method for Leading Agricultural Production) PD, January 28, 1966, pp. 5-6, p. 5.

⁴⁸ Chang P'ing-hua, 論辦點 (Managing the Spot) PD, March 7, 1966, p. 5.

⁴⁹ Pusey, *op. cit.,* p. 54.

⁵⁰ Wang Jen-chung, 突出政治,用毛澤東思想統帥一切 (Politics to the Fore, Use the TMTT to Command Everything.) PD, April 7, 1966, pp. 2-3.

⁵¹ 高舉毛澤東思想紅旗,把無產階級文化大革命進行到底 (Raise High the Great Red Banner of the TMTT, Carry Out the Great Proletarian Cultural Revolution Through to the End) PD, June 6, 1966, pp. 1-2, p. 1.

⁵² Yao Wen-yuan, 評新編歷史劇《海瑞罷官》 (Criticism of the New Historical Play, *Hai Jui Is Dismissed From Office*) PD, November 30, 1965, pp. 5-6.

⁵³ *Ibid.,* p. 5.

⁵⁴ 關於海瑞罷官問題各種意見的簡介 (Short Introduction to Different Opinions on the Question of *Hai Jui Is Dismissed From Office*) PD, December 15, 1965, p. 5.

⁵⁵ Wu Han, 關於"海瑞罷官"的自我批評 (Self Criticism on *Hai Jui Is Dismissed From Office*) PD, December 30, 1965, pp. 5-6.

⁵⁶ For a survey of the Wu Han debate, see Pusey, *op. cit.,* pp. 51-53.

⁵⁷ Union Research Institute, *CCP Documents of the Great Proletarian Cultural Revolution, 1966-1967* (Hong Kong, 1968) vi, 692 pp., p. 7.

⁵⁸ Chang Man, *op. cit.,* p. 8.

⁵⁹ CC CPC, 通知 (Announcement) May 16, 1966; PD, May 17, 1967, pp. 1-2, p. 1. This document, in fact, claims that P'eng Chen did all the work himself. See below.

⁶⁰ URI, *CCP Documents,* pp. 7-10, p. 9.

⁶¹ PD, May 17, 1967, *op. cit.,* p. 1.

⁶² *Nihon Keizai,* February 1, 1967; DSJP, February 1, 1967, pp. 36-37.

⁶³ *This Fellow Ho Lung,* p. 96.

⁶⁴ *Yomiuri,* May 8, 1967; DSJP, May 9, 1967, p. 5.

⁶⁵ Li Ching-ch'üan was not officially removed from office until May, 1967. URI *CCP Documents,* pp. 434-435.

⁶⁶ Lin Piao, "Speech at Enlarged Meeting," *Loc. cit.,* pp. 84-86.

⁶⁷ 毛主席暢游長江 (Chairman Mao Joyously Swims the Yangtze.) PD, July 25, 1966, pp. 1-2. In October, 1966, T'an Chen-lin published a short article, 毛主席身體這樣健康是全國人民的幸福

which is translated, "That Chairman Mao Is so Healthy Is the Happiness of the People of the Whole Country." PD, October 8, 1966, p. 1. One usually does not make a fuss about another's health unless he is really unhealthy, or is suspected by some to be unhealthy.

[68] Hsiao Hua, 高舉毛澤東思想偉大紅旗,堅決執行突出政治的五項原則 (Raise High the Great Red Flag of the TMTT, Firmly Carry Out the Five Principles of Politics to the Fore.) PD, January 25, 1966, pp. 1-2.

[69] PD, May 29, 1967, pp. 1-2.

[70] Chang Man, *op. cit.*, p. 9.

[71] 毛澤東思想的新勝利 (A New Victory of the TMTT) PD, June 4, 1961, p. 1.

[72] PD, May 7, 1967, p. 1.

[73] Lin Piao, "Speech at Enlarged Meeting," *loc. cit.*, p. 82.

[74] Juan Ming, Juan Jo-ying, 周揚顛倒歷史的一枝暗箭 (Some Sneaky Business by Chou Yang in Distorting History) PD, July 4, 1966, pp. 2-3.

[75] Lin Piao, "Speech at Enlarged Meeting," *loc cit.*, p. 87.

[76] 毛澤東思想萬歲 (Long Live the TMTT) PD, July 1, 1966, pp. 1, 3, p. 3.

[77] PD, July 31, 1966, p. 2.

[78] Yeh Chien-ying, 高舉毛澤東思想偉大紅旗,以抗大為榜樣,辦抗大式的學校 (Raise High the Great Red Banner of the TMTT, Use Resistance University as the Model for Running Resistance University-Type Schools) PD, August 2, 1966, p. 2.

[79] *Tokyo Shimbun,* January 12, 1967; DSJP, January 13, 1967, p. 9.

[80] CB, 819 (March 10, 1967) report of an August 2, 1966 speech by Teng Hsiao-p'ing, p. 4.

[81] *Nihon Keizei,* January 5, 1967; DSJP, January 6, 1967, p. 22.

[82] *Mainichi,* January 29, 1967; DSJP, January 31, 1967, p. 39.

[83] Peking *Ching Kang Shan.* CB 821 (March 16, 1967) p. 2. Liu is consistent in thinking of the opponents of the work teams as "bourgeois." After August, however, the Red Guards liked to boast of their "proletarian" backgrounds. In fact there seem to have been few children of workers or poor peasants in the high schools and universities, and the "proletarian" Red Guards seem to have been members of the privileged class, the children of the communist cadres. Thus, a Red Guard leaflet attacked the "bourgeois little gentlemen and ladies" in these terms: "You abuse us in this way doubtless because our parents are officials." CNA 636 (November 11, 1966) p. 3. Despite the enormous publicity the Red Guards have received, there is, as far as I know, as yet no satisfactory systematic study of the organization, composition, political opinions, and political affiliations of the various groups. But see Wang Hsueh-wen, *op. cit.;* and for puerile, if sometimes entertaining, efforts, Li Chin-wei, 紅衛兵實錄 *(True Account of the Red Guards)* (Hong Kong, 1967) 10, 2, 462 pp.; and Wang En, 紅衛兵造反記 *(Record of the Red Guards Rebellion)* (Hong Kong, 1967) Two volumes; 32, 135, 6, 16, 422, 7 pp. An extended discussion of the "mass

movement," of course, is beyond the scope of this study, but a few random speculations may be in order. The most active groups in Peking in 1967 (e.g., the Ching Kang Shan) seem to have affiliations reaching up to the Cultural Revolution Group, were the most radical, and had the least contact with the formal Party establishment. It is possible that the "proletarians" of the fall of 1966 were actually the "moderate" wing of the Red Guard movement.

[84] SCMP, 3855 (January 9, 1967) p. 1-4, p. 2. I understand, however, that Mr. Bogunovic has since denied having written this story, which was printed in Chinese by papers in Hong Kong and Taipei.

[85] Ibid., p. 3.

[86] Ibid., p. 4.

[87] CB, 819 (March 10, 1967) p. 3.

[88] Ibid., p. 5.

[89] Mao Tse-tung, 炮打司令部 (Bombard the Headquarters), August 5, 1966; PD, August 5, 1967, p. 1. For a time during the Cultural Revolution there was the custom of publishing documents in the official press a year after they had been written.

[90] CC, CPC, 關於無產階級文化大革命的決定 (Resolution on the Great Proletarian Cultural Revolution), August 8, 1966; PD, August 9, 1966, pp. 1-2, p. 1.

[91] Ibid., p. 2.

[92] Ibid., p. 1.

[93] Mainichi, January 29, 1967; (DSJP, January 31, 1967), p. 39.

[94] 毛主席會見首都革命群眾 (Chairman Mao Receives the Revolutionary Masses of the Capital), PD, August 12, 1967, p. 1. According to Japanese reporters this story had first appeared in the PD of August 11, but issues containing the story were withdrawn. The following day the story reappeared, with minor alterations praising Mao "more conspicuously." Sankai, August 30, 1966; DSJP, September 30, 1966, p. 12. This implies, if nothing else, that some of the routine mechanisms of the Party were beginning to break down.

[95] Eighth CC, CPC, 11th Plenum, 公報 (Public Report), PD, August 14, 1966, p. 1.

[96] PD, August 19, 1966, p. 2. For some reason (a bit of cattyness on the part of T'ao Chu, then controlling that paper?) Ch'en Po-ta was not included in the PD listings, but his presence was noted by observers; thus, he is placed in parentheses above.

[97] Mainichi, September 14, 1966; DSJP, September 16, 1966, p. 28.

[98] Lin Piao, 在慶祝無產階級文化大革命群眾大會上的講話 (Speech at the Mass Meeting Celebrating the Great Proletarian Cultural Revolution), PD, August 19, 1966, p. 2.

[99] 革命青少年要向解放軍學習 (Revolutionary Youths Must Learn From the Liberation Army), PD, August 28, 1966, p. 1.

[100] Hsiao Hua, 把活學活用毛主席著作群眾運動推向新階段 (Push the Mass Movement for Living Study Living Use of the Works of Chairman Mao to a New Stage), PD, October 10, 1966, p. 1.

[101] Yomiuri, January 7, 1967; DSJP, January 7-9, 1967, pp. 22-24.

[102] *Ibid.*, January 8, 1967; p. 30.

[103] *Ibid.* This tends to confirm the hypothesis that by the early 1960's P'eng had replaced Teng as effective head of the Secretariat. One may still be permitted to think that Teng did not exactly "have" P'eng take over his job.

[104] *Mainichi*, January 5, 1967; DSJP, January 6, 1967, p. 17.

[105] Ch'en Po-ta, 無產階級文化大革命的兩條路線 (The Two Lines in the Great Proletarian Cultural Revolution), October 24, 1966; transcript in collection of the Institute of International Relations, Republic of China, 14 pp.

[106] Lin Piao, "Address at the CCP Central Committee Working Conference," *Issues and Studies*, Vol. VI, No. 1 (October, 1969) pp. 101-105; and *ibid.*, Vol. VI, No. 2 (November, 1969) pp. 93-98.

[107] Chou En-lai, 在接見外地來京革命師生大會上的講話 (Speech at the Reception of Revolutionary Teachers and Students Who Have Come to Peking) PD, September 1, 1966, p. 2.

[108] Lin Piao, 在接見外地來京革命師生大會上的講話 (Speech at the Reception of Revolutionary Teachers and Students Who Have Come to Peking) PD, September 1, 1966, p. 2.

[109] 用文鬥，不用武鬥 (Use Civil Struggle, Not Armed Struggle) PD, September 5, 1966, p. 2.

[110] 抓革命，促生產 (Grasp Revolution, Promote Production) PD, September 7, 1966, p. 1.

[111] Chou En-lai, 講話 (Speech), PD, September 16, 1966, p. 2.

[112] Lin Piao, 講話 (Speech), PD, November 4, 1966, p. 2.

[113] Chou En-lai, 讚揚長征小將樹立全程步行串連的好榜樣 (Approving the Good Example of the Long March Little Generals Who Have Established the Practice of Engaging in Roving Solidarity Entirely on Foot), PD, November 16, 1966, pp. 1-2.

[114] 以毛主席為代表的無產階級革命路線的勝利 (The Victory of the Proletarian Revolutionary Line Represented by Chairman Mao), PD, November 2, 1966, p. 1. This recapitulates some of Ch'en's October 24 report.

[115] Ch'en Po-ta, October 24, 1966, *op. cit.*, p. 13. This opposition to the "blood system," however, does not necessarily imply moderation.

[116] For the texts of these harangues, see PD, December 4, 1966, pp. 1-3.

[117] *Mainichi*, December 1, DSJP, December 10-12, 1966, pp. 21-22.

[118] *Asahi*, December 13, 1966; DSJP, December 13, 1966, p. 11.

[119] For overt indications of this, see 奪取新的勝利 (Snatch New Victories), PD, December 13, 1966, p. 1.

[120] See Tokyo *Shimbun*, January 6, 1967; DSJP, January 7-9, 1967, p. 32. *Yomiuri*, January 14, 1967; DSJP, January 18, 1967, p. 30.

[121] CB, 830 (June 26, 1967) pp. 1-2.

[122] CB, 819 (March 10, 1967) pp. 11-15.

[123] CNA, 637 (November 18, 1966) pp. 2-6. The relations between T'ao and Wang are unclear. In 1958 Wang wrote an attack on localism: Wang K'uang, 反對地方主義 (Oppose Localism), PD, February 25, 1958, p. 7. The Kwangtung purge of that year almost certainly was T'ao's own show. But a

biography of Wang, basing itself upon a refugee report, says Wang was purged for localism himself in 1958, and spent three years getting himself rectified. Institute of International Relations, *op. cit.*, p. 18. In this case, Wang would have been one of T'ao's opponents in 1958, and his anti-localism article a self-criticism. But he and T'ao may have made up after Wang got out of jail.

[124] *Mainichi*, November 8, 1966; DSJP, November 8, 1966, p. 8.

[125] *Asahi*, November 23, 1966; DSJP, November 26-28, 1966.

[126] *Yomiuri*, December 15, 1966; DSJP, December 15, 1966, pp. 13-14.

[127] *Mainichi*, December 19, 1966; DSJP, December 17-19, 1966, p. 14.

[128] *Yomiuri*, December 29, 1966; DSJP, December 30, 1966, p. 13.

[129] *Asahi*, January 7, 1967; DSJP, January 10, 1967, p. 191.

[130] For general surveys, see Philip Bridgham, "Mao's Cultural Revolution in 1967: The Struggle to Seize Power," CQ, 34 (April-June, 1969) pp. 6-37; Vogel, "The Structure of Conflict," *loc. cit.*

[131] 迎接工礦企業文化大革命的高潮 (Welcoming the High Tide of Great Cultural Revolution in Mining and Industry), PD, December 26, 1966, p. 1.

[132] 把無產階級文化大革命進行到底 (Carry Out the Great Proletarian Cultural Revolution to the End), PD, January 1, 1967, pp. 1-2, p. 2.

[133] *Mainichi*, January 11, 1967; DSJP, January 12, 1967, p. 5.

[134] *Ibid.*, January 4, 1967; DSJP, December 31, 1966-January 5, 1967, p. 24.

[135] *Yomiuri*, January 22, 1967; DSJP, January 21-23, 1967, p. 21.

[136] *Yomiuri*, January 22, 1967; DSJP, January 26, 1967, p. 19.

[137] *Sankei*, January 26, 1967; DSJP, January 26, 1967, p. 10. I have heard there were also wall posters attacking Mao himself, but have not come across any.

[138] *Yomiuri*, January 8, 1967; DSJP, January 12, 1967, p. 12. The delineation of groups in this study does not show any support for T'ao in Nanking. The link was possibly one Hsiao Wang-tung, a "faithful jackel" of T'ao's, who had been transferred from Nanking to the Ministry of Culture in 1965. *Chan-tou Pao*, February 15, 1967; SCMP, 3901, (March 17, 1967) p. 17.

[139] *Tokyo Shimbun*, January 13, 1967; DSJP, January 13, 1967, p. 29.

[140] Teiwes, "Leadership Purges," p. 130.

[141] URI, *CCP Documents*, p. 181.

[142] LAD, January 14, 1967; NCNA English, January 14, 1967; SCMP, 3862, January 18, 1967, p. 3. This, of course, contradicts Ho Lung's 1965 statement.

[143] 無產階級革命派大聯合,奪走資本主義當權派的權! (The Proletarian Revolutionary Faction Form a Great Alliance, Seize Power From the Power Holders Walking the Capitalist Road!), PD, January 22, 1967, p. 1.

[144] URI, *CCP Documents*, p. 196; 解放軍最最堅定地站在革命造反派的一邊,堅決支持奪走資本主義當權派的權 (The Liberation Army Should Most Firmly Stand on the Side of the Revolutionary Rebels, Firmly Support the Seizure of Power From the Power Holders Walking the Capitalist Road), PD, January 24, 1967, p. 1.

[145] See Gerald Tannenbaum, "The 1967 Shanghai Revolution Recounted," *Eastern Horizon*, Vol. VII, No. 3 (May-June, 1968) pp. 7-25, for an eye-witness account from a Maoist viewpoint, written mainly in "Peking English." The flavor

of the account is captured in the first sentence: "To the growing and glorious list of cataputic social changes, class struggles on a grand scale which are known as 'turning points of history,' must now be added the 1967 Shanghai January Revolution." p. 7. This deserves to rank with "For God, for country, and for Yale" in any anthology of anticlimaxes.

[146] 無產階級革命派大聯合萬歲 (Long Live the Great Alliance of the Proletarian Revolutionary Faction), PD, January 15, 1967; from KMD, January 14.

[147] 無產階級革命派聯合起來 (The Proletarian Revolutionary Faction Form an Alliance), PD, January 16, 1967, pp. 1-2; from RF, 2, 1967.

[148] See Ch'en Po-ta, October 24, 1966, op. cit., p. 5; also his remarks reported in Asahi, January 27, 1967; DSJP, January 27, 1967, p. 5.

[149] 上海人民公社今天宣告誕生 (The Shanghai People's Commune Proclaims Its Birth), Shanghai Wen Hui News (文匯報) February 5, 1967, pp. 1, 3.

[150] Nihon Keizai, March 4, 1967; DSJP, March 6, 1967, p. 36.

[151] 堅決捍衛"三結合"的正確方針 (Firmly Protect the Correct Line of the 'Triple Unity.'), PD, February 17, 1967, p. 1. Either Han was more even-handed than his detractors gave him credit for, or the situation was very complex. The following day the LAD carried an attack from Fukien on the "adverse current," as far as I know the first mention of that phrase. 堅決粉碎反革命逆流 (Thoroughly Smash the Counter-Revolutionary Adverse Current), PD, February 19, 1967, p. 1. From LAD, February 18. For more on the difference between the "commune" and Revolutionary Committee forms, see Jürgen Domes, "The Role of the Military in the Formation of Revolutionary Committees, 1967-1968", CQ 44 (October-December, 1970) pp. 112-145, pp. 113-114.

[152] 必須正確地對待幹部 (Cadres Must Be Treated Correctly), PD, February 23, 1967, pp. 1-2, p. 1.

[153] 論革命"三結合" (The Revolutionary 'Triple Unity'), PD, March 10, 1967, p. 1.

[154] For the speeches, see PD, February 2, 1967, p. 2. Heilungkiang was probably the exception. The situation in other provinces was not so neat. Most of the "revolutionary cadres" were not Chou En-lai men. In the technical terminology of Peking, for example, P'an Fu-sheng was also a revolutionary cadre. The "revolutionary cadres" affiliated with the CR Group in effect had the same political position as the mass representatives. Others probably were former associates of the condemned factions whose purge the radicals found inexpedient or impossible. These men may have come to look to Chou En-lai for leadership; but the umbrella of the CR Group also soon became large enough to admit those who were not ultra-radicals.

[155] In 1971, however, P'an was out once again, and Wang Chia-tao became first secretary of Heilungkiang.

CONCLUSION

[1] Whitson, *op. cit.,* pp. 23 ff.

[2] After 1969 this consideration may have also ceased to hold true for the army—a factor which might help explain the fall of Lin Piao in 1971. In general, the charismatic leader will fear any group which threatens to achieve supremacy; and that group will fear the leader.

[3] An objection has been made to this picture of Chinese politics, to the effect that such a fragmented elite would have been hard put to hold the country together for so long. It is, of course, beyond the scope of this study to deal with this problem, but a few comments are probably in order. 1) This picture of fragmentation is derived from the events of 1966 and 1967, when the country was not being held together very well. I am sure that many of the ties discovered in this study predate this period, but am also sure that the factional structure was not static. 2) The existence of factions does not by itself imply that the factions will, at all times and on all issues, be in conflict with each other. The evidence of Chapter V would indicate that there was a great deal of attention paid to coalition formation by the leaders of the various factions, and that many policies were the results of compromise. 3) The same evidence indicates that differences of opinion could be limited, and that until the Cultural Revolution the dissidents were willing to accept at least a minimum of Party discipline.

[4] *Cf.* Franz Schurmann on the Party of the mid-1960's: "It may be an exaggeration to say so, but in effect these 17,000,000 party members had nothing to do except what they had to do otherwise in their practical roles (for example, as factory directors)." "The Attack of the Cultural Revolution on Ideology and Organization," in Ho and Tsou, *op. cit.,* vol. I, Book 2, pp. 525-564, p. 543.

[5] Thus, the pragmatic uses of the Thought in 1960, which might have worked prior to Lushan (and which might have been working in 1971), came to nothing.

[6] Eg, Towsand, *Participation,* p. xiii: "The Cultural Revolution...implied a willingness among some elites to place higher priority on their own policy objectives than on the institutional integrity of the CCP." Since the policy in the wake of the Cultural Revolution was, if anything, more conservative than what went before, perhaps "general tendency" or "political style" would be better than "policy objectives."

[7] Also, to be thorough, there should be a systematic analysis of the various personal characteristics and relationships among the elite, an aspect neglected in this study except for a few *obiter dicta.* Thus, it would appear: P'eng Te-huai was chronically unable to get along with people; Chiang Ch'ing was an unusually vindictive woman; Mao's senior colleagues regarded the later development of his cult with amused contempt...A full study of Chinese politics would have to consider such factors. The present study, reducing the argument to its bare bones, tends to consider the actors as automatons programmed to display ambition, acting rationally in accord with their political opportunities. In defense, one can cite the maxim that any "model" should be judged by its explanatory power, not the realism of its assumptions. It would appear that the hypotheses proposed in this study explain behavior sufficiently, and so there is no need to bring in personal

characteristics; to do so would make the study longer and more complex, but not substantially add to understanding. Also, data on personal characteristics is hard to evaluate, and there is the danger of doing someone an injustice.

[8] *The Case of P'eng Te-huai,* p. 411 (English on p. 25.)

[9] This struggle, I think, would be very hard to explain purely on policy grounds.

[10] Along, apparently, with Li Hsueh-feng and P'an Fu-sheng—which is evidence of the correctness of their group assignment in this study.

[11] See Alexander Eckstein, "Economic Fluctuations in Communist China's Economic Development," Ho and Tsou, *op. cit.,* Vol. 1, Book 2, pp. 691-729. Eckstein, accepting the hypothesis of Mao's radicalism, believes the cycle cannot be broken in Mao's life-time. The theory in this study makes Mao's radicalism a function of the political opportunities; when the opportunities change, it is possible that Mao's radicalism will also change.

[12] For a discussion of the virtues of turmoil (which I do not find very convincing) see Maurice Meisner, "Leninism and Maoism: Some Populist Perspectives on Marxism-Leninism in China," CQ, 45 (January-March, 1971) pp. 2-36.

[13] Such periods might include: the T'ung-chih reign; the period between the end of the Northern Expedition and the beginning of the Japanese invasion; the period between 1949-1955 (or even 1958); the capitalist road; the period following the Ninth Congress; and, on Taiwan, the period since 1949.

[14] L. LaDany, "China: Period of Suspense," *Foreign Affairs,* Vol. 48, No. 4 (July, 1970) pp. 701-711.

[15] Jan Myrdal, "A New Look at Mao's China," *Look,* Vol. 34, No. 3 (February 10, 1970) pp. 19-26, p. 26.

[16] Rush, *op. cit., passim,* esp. p. 72.

Appendix

MEMBERS AND ALTERNATE MEMBERS
OF THE EIGHTH CENTRAL COMMITTEE, COMMUNIST PARTY
OF CHINA, ALIVE IN 1965.

The marginal numbers indicate party rank as listed in U.S. Department of State, *op. cit.* Also listed are the jobs held by the member in 1965, and his group and fate during the Cultural Revolution. For the most part, changes after the Ninth Congress are not noted.

080. An Tzu-wen 安子文 Dir., Organization Department. P'eng Chen group. Purged.
179. Chang Ai-p'ing 張愛萍 Deputy CoS, PLA. Liu-Teng group. Purged.
052. Chang Chi-ch'un 張際春 Dept. Dir., Propaganda Department; Dir., SC Culture and Education Staff Office. T'ao Chu group. Purged.
128. Chang Ch'i-lung 張啟龍 Dept. Dir., Organization Department. T'ao Chu group. Purged.
173. Chang Ching-fu 張勁夫 V. Chmn., SC Technical Planning Commission. Liu-Teng group. Purged.
095. Chang Ching-wu 張經武 V. Chmn., UF Dept. Secretariat, Tibet. Cultural Revolution Group. Purged.
158. Chang Chung-liang 張仲良 Secretary, Kiangsu (late 1965?) P'eng Te-huai faction. Purged.
099. Chang Han-fu 章漢夫 V. Min., Foreign Affairs. Chou En-lai group (*via* Ch'en Yi). Purged.
130. Chang Lin-chih 張霖之 Min. of Coal Industry. Chou En-lai group. Died, Feb., 1967, after undergoing struggle.
172. Chang P'ing-hua 張平化 1st Secretary, Hunan, Commissar, Hunan. Later Deputy Dir., Prop. Dept. T'ao Chu group. Purged.
155. Chang Su 張蘇 Deputy Procurator General. Anti-revolutionary revisionist, P'eng Chen group. Purged.
134. Chang Ta-chih 張達志 Secretary, NW Bureau; Commander, Lanchow. Lin Piao faction; promoted to full membership, CC.

025. Chang Ting-ch'eng 張鼎丞 Control Commission; Procurator General. Liu-Teng group; still full member, CC
108. Chang Tsung-hsun 張宗遜 Dept. CoS, PLA. Lin Piao headquarters group. Purged.
062. Chang Wen-t'ien 張聞天 Alt. memb., PB. Peng Te-huai group. Purged.
139. Chang Yun 張蘊 Female. Secretary, Woman's Work Committee, CC. P'eng Chen group. Purged.
040. Chang Yun-i 張雲逸 Alt. Sect., Control Commission; Cultural Revolution group. Still full member, CC.
148. Chao Chien-min 趙建民 Secretary, Yunnan. 1958 localist, no role in Cultural Revolution. Purged.
075. Chao Ehr-lu 趙爾陸 V. Chmn., State Ec. Comm.; Dir., CC Defense Industry Work Dept. P'eng Chen group. Died 6 February, 1967, probably of natural causes.
161. Chao I-min 趙毅敏 V. Dir., CC International Liason Dept. Chou En-lai group. Purged.
177. Chao Po-p'ing 趙伯平 Formerly governor of Shensi, purged in 1964. Inactive during Cultural Revolution. Purged.
156. Ch'en Cheng-jen 陳正人 Dept. Dir., SC Agriculture and Forrestry Staff Office; Min., 8th Min. Machine Building; V. Dir., CC Rural Work Department. Chou En-lai group, *via* T'an Chen-lin. Purged.
112. Ch'en Ch'i-han 陳奇涵 Control Comm.; V. Pres., Supreme Court. Cultural Revolution Group. Purged.
106. Ch'en Hsi-lien 陳錫聯 Sect., N.E. Bureau; Commander, Mukden. Lin Piao regional faction; promoted to full member, CC.
019. Ch'en I 陳毅 PB; V. Premier, SC; Dir., Foreign Affairs Staff Office; Minister of Foreign Affairs. Chou En-lai group. Removed from PB; following Ninth Congress inactive as foreign minister.
113. Ch'en Man-yuan 陳漫遠 V. Min., State Farms and Land Reclamation. Ho Lung faction. Purged.
147. Ch'en Pei-hsien 陳丕顯 Sect., E. China Bureau; 1st Sect., Shang-hai; Commissar, Shanghai. P'eng Chen group. Purged.
010. Ch'en Po-ta 陳伯達 PB(A); Dept. Dir., Propaganda Department; V. Chmn., State Planning Commission; Chmn., CC Party Newspaper Comm.; Ed., *Red Flag;* V. Chmn., CC Rural Work Department. Cultural Revolution Group. Promoted to PBSC.
065. Ch'en Shao-min 陳少敏 Control Commission; V. Chmn., All China Federation of Trade Unions. Liu-Teng group. Purged.

089. Ch'en Shao-yu 陳紹禹, or Wang Ming 王明 Inactive, probably in Moscow since 1957. Purged.
054. Ch'en Yü 陳郁 3rd Sect., CS Bureau; Gov., Kwangtung; Sect., Kwangtung. Chou En-lai group. V. Chmn., Kwangtung Revolutionary Committee; still on CC.
007. Ch'en Yun 陳雲 V. Chmn., CC, PBSC; V. Prem., SC; Chmn., CC Economics and Finance Committee. Chou En-lai group. Removed as V. Chmn., also removed from PB.
053. Ch'eng Tzu-hua 程子華 Sect., SW Bur.; V. Chmn., State Planning Commission. P'eng Chen group. Purged.
071. Cheng Wei-san 鄭位三 Very old; inactive; possibly Cultural Revolution Group; re-elected to CC.
081. Chia T'o-fu 賈拓夫 Purged 1959; P'eng Te-huai faction. Purged.
152. Chiang Hua 江華 Sect., E. China; 1st Sect., Chekiang; Commissar, Chekiang; Chou En-lai group. Purged.
151. Chiang Nan-hsiang 蔣南翔 Min. Higher Education; Pres., Tsinghua U. P'eng Chen group. Purged.
141. Chiang Wei-ch'ing 江渭清 Sect., E. China; 1st Sect., Kiangsu; Commissar, Kiangsu; Liu-Teng group. Purged.
149. Ch'ien Chün-jui 錢俊瑞 Purged in 1963; inactive. Purged.
158. Ch'ien Ying 錢瑛 Female; Alt. Sect., Control Commission; Chou En-lai group. Purged.
005. Chou En-lai 周恩來 V. Chmn., CC; PBSC; Premier, SC; removed as V. Chmn.; Chou En-lai group.
168. Chou Hsiao-chou 周小舟 Purged in 1959 as 1st Sect., Hunan; P'eng Te-huai group.
145. Chou Huan 周桓 Sect., Liaoning; may have sided with P'eng Te-huai. Liu-Teng group in Cultural Revolution. Purged.
109. Chou Yang 周揚 Dept. Dir., Propaganda Dept. P'eng Chen faction. Purged.
004. Chu Te 朱德 V. Chmn., CC; PBSC. Chou En-lai faction. Removed as V. Chmn., CC, and from Standing Committee; elected to Politburo.
125. Chu Te-hai 朱德海 1st Sect., Yenpen; V. Gov., Kirin. Probably P'eng Chen faction. Purged.
146. Chung Ch'i-kuang 鐘期光 Commissar, Nanking Mil. Acad. Probably Lin Piao group. Purged.
124. Fan Wen-lan 范文瀾 Dir., History Institute, China Academy of Sciences. P'eng Chen group. Elected full member CC. Died between April-October, 1969.

169. Fang I 方毅 Dept. Dir., Foreign Affairs Staff Office; Chmn., SC Comm. for Economic Relations with Foreign Countries. Member, State Planning Commission. Chou En-lai group. Re-elected alternate member, CC.

120. Feng Pai-chü 馮白駒 V. Gov., Chekiang. 1958 localist, no role in Cultural Revolution. Purged.

153. Han Kuang 韓光 V. Chmn., SC Science and Technology Commission. Chou En-lai group. Purged.

174. Han Hsien-ch'u 韓先楚 Dept. CoS, PLA. Cmdr., Fukien front; Chmn., Fukien RC. Lin Piao regional faction. Elected full member, CC.

033. Ho Lung 賀龍 PB; V. Chmn. MAC; V. Prem., SC. Chmn., SC Physical Culture and Sports Commission. Ho-Lung group. Purged.

077. Hsi Chung-hsun 習仲勳 Purged 1962; may have been associated with P'eng Te-huai. Purged.

030. Hisao Ching-kuang 蕭勁光 Dir., General Office, Ministry of Defense; Commander, Naval HQ, PLA. Lin Piao headquarters faction. Re-elected to CC.

073. Hsiao Hua 蕭華 Alt. Sect., Control Commission; Dept. Sect.-Genl., MAC. Dir., PLA GPD. Lin Piao Headquarters faction. Purged.

057. Hsiao K'o 蕭克 V. Min., State Farms and Land Reclamation. Probably associated with P'eng Te-huai; Ho Lung faction during Cultural Revolution. Purged.

096. Hsieh Chüeh-tsai 謝覺哉 Retired. Probably Cultural Revolution Group. Purged; or possibly gravely ill. Died 1971.

079. Hsieh Fu-chih 謝富治 V. Prem., SC; Min. Public Security; Commander, Public Security Forces, PLA; Dir., Internal Affairs Staff Office, SC. Made Chmn., Peking Rev. Comm. Promoted to Politburo. Chou En-lai group.

072. Hsu Hai-tung 徐海東 Retired. No attacks on him, possibly Cultural Revolution group. Re-elected to CC.

016. Hsu Hsiang-ch'ien 徐向前 V. Chmn., MAC. Chou En-lai group. Re-elected to CC.

067. Hsu Kuang-ta 徐光達 V. Min. Defense; Commander, Armored Force, PLA. Ho Lung group. Purged.

140. Hsu Ping 徐冰 Dir., CC UF Dept. Liu-Teng group. Purged.

102. Hsu Shih-yu 許世友 V. Min. Defense; Commander, Nanking. Lin Piao regional faction; elected full member, CC.

013. Hsu T'e-li 徐特立 Dept. Dir., Prop. Dept. Died December, 1968. CR Group.

114. Hsu Tzu-jung 徐子榮 Dept. Dir., SC Internal Affairs Staff Office; V. Min. Public Security. Liu-Teng group. Purged.
049. Hu Ch'iao-mu 胡喬木 Alt. Member, Secretariat; Dept. Dir., Propaganda Department. P'eng Chen group. Purged.
074. Hu Yao-pang 胡耀邦 1st Sect., CC Youth Work Comm.; 3rd Sect. NW China Regional Bureau. Liu-Teng group. Purged.
110. Huang Huo-ch'ing 黄火青 Sect., NE China; 1st Sect., Liaoning; Commissar, Liaoning; P'eng Chen group. Purged.
028. Huang K'o-ch'eng 黄克誠 V. Gov., Shansi; purged 1959 as CoS, PLA P'eng Te-huai group. Purged.
115. Huang Ou-tung 黄歐東 Sect., NE China; 2nd Sect., Liaoning; Gov., Liaoning. P'eng Chen group. Purged.
127. Huang Yung-sheng 黄永勝 Sect., CS China; Commander, Canton. Later, Chmn., Kwangtung Rev. Comm.; CoS PLA; Politburo. Lin Piao regional faction.
138. Hung Hsueh-chih 洪學智 Purged 1959 as head, PLA Rear Services Department. P'eng Te-huai group.
044. K'ang Sheng 康生 Alt. Memb., PB; Secretariat. CR Group, promoted to PBSC.
135. Kao K'o-lin 高克林 Control Commission; Sect., NW China; Ho Lung group. Purged.
116. Ku Ta-ts'un 古大存 V. Gov., Kwangtung. 1958 localist. Died November, 1966.
122. Ku'ei Pi 奎壁 Sect., Inner Mongolia; V. Chmn., SC Nationalities Commission; V. Gov., Inner Mongolia. Probably Liu-Teng. Purged.
162. K'ung Yuan 孔原 Probably V. Chmn., CC Foreign Affairs Dept.; SC Foreign Affairs Staff Office. Chou En-lai group. Purged.
154. Li Ch'ang 李昌 V. Chmn., SC Comm. for Cultural Relations with Foreign Countries. Chou En-lai group. Purged.
175. Li Chieh-po 李頡伯 Dept. Dir., CC Genl. Office; V. Chmn., All China Federation of Trade Unions. T'ao Chu group. Purged.
128. Li Chien-chen 李堅真 Female. Control Commission; Sect., Kwangtung; T'ao Chu group. Purged.
117. Li Chih-min 李志民 Commissar, PLA Mil. Acad.; Ho Lung group. Purged.
083. Li Ching-ch'üan 李井泉 PB; 1st Sect., SW China; Commissar, Chengtu; Ho Lung group. Purged.
012. Li Fu-ch'un 李富春 PB; Sect.; V. Prem., SC; Chmn., State Planning Comm.; V. Dir., CC Economics and Finance Dept.; Chou En-lai group; removed from PB.

022. Li Hsien-nien 李先念 PB; Sect.; V. Prem., State Council; Dir., SC Finance and Trade Office; V. Chmn., State Planning Commission; Min. Finance; V. Dir., CC Economics and Finance Dept. Chou En-lai group; retained position.
064. Li Hsueh-feng 李雪峯 Sect.; 1st Sect., N. China. Originally probably Liu-Teng Group, later CR Group. Made 1st Sect., Peking; then Chmn., Hopei Rev. Comm.; promoted to Politburo.
082. Li Li-san 李立三 Sect., N. China. Faction not ascertained; may have hanged himself prior to August, 1967. In any case, "purged."
066. Li Pao-hua 李葆華 3rd Sect., E. China; 1st Sect., Anhwei; 1st Commissar, Anhwei. T'ao Chu group. Purged.
101. Li Ta-chang 李大章 Sect., SW China; Sect., Szechuan; Gov., Szechuan. Probably P'eng Chen group, but became V. Chmn., Szechuan Rev. Comm.; promoted to full member, CC.
111. Li T'ao 李濤 Head, Military Intelligence. Lin Piao headquarters group. Purged.
042. Li Wei-han 李維漢 Former head, CC UF Work; purged 1964. P'eng Chen group.
021. Liao Ch'eng-chih 廖承志 Dept. Dir., SC Foreign Affairs Staff Office; Chmn., Overseas Chinese Affairs Committee; Dept. Dir., CC UF Work Dept.; 1st Sect., CC Overseas Chinese Work Comm. Chou En-lai group. Purged.
176. Liao Chih-kao 廖志高 Sect., SW China; 1st Sect., Szechuan; Commissar, Szechuan. Ho Lung group. Purged.
137. Liao Han-sheng 廖漢生 Sect., N. China; V. Min. Defense. Ho Lung group. Purged.
142. Liao Lu-yen 廖魯言 Dept. Dir., SC Agriculture Staff Office; Min. Agriculture; Dept. Dir., CC Rural Work Dept. Chou En-lai group. Purged.
024. Lin Feng 林楓 Pres., Higher Party School; Dir., CC Political Work Department (?). P'eng Chen group. Purged.
008. Lin Piao 林彪 PBSC; V. Chmn., MAC; V. Prem., SC; Min. Defense. Lin Piao group; promoted to second rank, CC.
070. Lin T'ieh 林鐵 3rd Sect., N. China; 1st Sect., Hopeh; Commissar, Hopeh. Liu-Teng group. Purged.
055. Liu Ch'ang-sheng 劉長勝 V. Chmn., All China Federation of Trade Unions. Died Jan., 1967, in good graces. Not classified.
171. Liu Chen 劉震 Dept. Commander, Air Force. Ho Lung group. Purged.
160. Liu Chien-hsün 劉建勳 Sect., CS China; 1st Sect., Honan;

Commissar, Honan. Cultural Revolution group; V. Chmn., Peking Rev. Comm.; later, Chmn., Honan Rev. Comm. Promoted to full member, CC.

041. Liu Hsiao 劉曉 V. Min. Foreign Affairs; later, Ambassador, Albania. Chou En-lai group. Purged.

105. Liu Jen 劉仁 2nd Sect., Peking; Judge, Supreme Court; Sect., N. China Regional Bureau; 1st Commissar, Peking Police. P'eng Chen group. Purged.

078. Liu Ko-p'ing 劉格平 Purged 1960; later V. Gov., Shansi, CR Group; Chmn., Shansi Rev. Comm. Re-elected to CC.

118. Liu Lan-po 劉瀾波 V. Min. Water Conservancy and Electric Power; purged. Liu-Teng group.

048. Liu Lan-t'ao 劉瀾濤 Alternate, Secretariat; 1st Sect. NW China. Ho Lung group. Purged.

047. Liu Ning-i 劉寧一 Dept. Dir., SC Foreign Affairs Staff Office; 1st Sect., CC Labor Work Committee; Chmn., All China Federation of Trade Unions. Cultural Revolution group. Purged.

018. Liu Po-ch'eng 劉伯承 PB; V. Chmn., MAC. Probably CR group, but inactive. Removed from PB.

002. Liu Shao-ch'i 劉少奇 PBSC; V. Chmn., CC. Chmn., People's Republic of China. Liu-Teng group. Purged.

164. Liu Tzu-hou 劉子厚 Sect., N. China; 2nd Sect. Hopei, Gov., Hopei. Liu-Teng group; promoted to CC.

015. Lo Jui-ch'ing 羅瑞卿 V. Chmn., MAC; V. Prem., SC; V. Min. Defense; CoS, PLA. Link between P'eng Chen and Ho Lung. Purged.

094. Lo Kuei-po 羅貴波 V. Min., Forn. Aff. Probably CR group. Purged from CC, but remained active in Min. Foreign Affairs.

085. Lü Cheng-ts'ao 呂正操 Min. Railroads. Ho Lung group. Purged.

014. Lu Ting-i 陸定一 PB(A); Secretariat; Dir., Propaganda Dept.; Sect., CC Cultural Work Committee; V. Prem., SC; Min. Culture. P'eng Chen group. Purged.

061. Ma Ming-fang 馬明方 Control Commission; 3rd. Sect., NE China. P'eng Chen group. Purged.

129. Ma Wen-jui 馬文瑞 Min. Labor; Chou En-lai group. Purged.

001. Mao Tse-tung 毛澤東 Chmn., CC; PBSC; Chmn., MAC. Same.

023. Nieh Jung-chen 聶榮臻 V. Chmn., MAC; V. Prem., SC; Chmn., SC Scientific and Technological Comm. Chou En-lai group; Same.

123. Ou Meng-chüeh 區夢覺 Alt. Sec., CS China; Sect., Kwantung; T'ao Chu group. Purged.

076. Ou-yang Ch'in 歐陽欽 2nd Sect., NE China; 1st Sect., Heilung-Kiang; Commissar, Heilungkiang. Liu-Teng group. Purged.

150. P'an Fu-sheng 潘復生 Dir., All China Federation of Marketing and Supply Cooperatives. Purged in 1958 for localism and "pessimism." Later, 1st Sect., Heilungkiang; 1st commissar; Heilungkiang; Chmn., Heilungkiang Rev. Comm. CR group, promoted to CC.

100. P'an Tzu-li 潘自力 Ambassador, USSR. CR group? Purged.

026. P'eng Chen 彭真 PB; Secretariat; 1st Sect., Peking; Mayor, Peking. P'eng Chen group. Purged.

020. P'eng Te-huai 彭德懷 PB; purged, 1959, as Minister of Defense, V. Chmn., MAC. P'eng Te-huai group. Purged.

049. Po I-po 薄一波 PB(A); V. Prem., SC; Dir., SC Industry and Communications Staff Office; Chmn., State Ec. Comm.; V. Chmn., State Planning Comm. P'eng Chen group. Purged.

136. Sai Fu-ting 賽福鼎 (Saifudin) Sect., Sinkiang; Gov., Sinkiang; later, V. Chmn., Sinkiang Rev. Comm.; CR group, promoted to CC.

051. Shu T'ung 舒同 Sect., Shensi; Sect., NW. China; probably member of P'eng Te-huai group; in Cultural Revolution, Liu-Teng group. Purged.

103. Shuai Meng-ch'i 帥孟奇 Female. Dept. Dir., Organization Dept. CR group. Purged.

119. Su Chen-hua 蘇振華 Commissar, Naval HQ, PLA; Ho Lung group. Purged.

032. Su Yü 粟裕 V. Min. Defense; V. Gov., Liaoning; Lin Piao Headquarters group; same.

178. Sun Chih-yüan 孫志遠 Min., 3rd Min. Machine Building; Ho Lung group. Died October, 1966, of natural causes.

039. Sung Jen-ch'iüng 宋任窮 1st Sect., NE China. Commissar, Mukden; Probably Chou En-lai group. Purged.

143. Sung Shih-lun 宋時輪 V. Chmn., State Sci. & Tech. Comm.; Chou En-lai group. Purged.

031. T'an Cheng 譚政 Purged 1959 as Dir., GPD. Late 1965 became Vice Gov. Fukien. P'eng Te-huai group. Purged.

063. T'an Chen-lin 譚震林 PB; Sect.; V. Prem., SC; Dir., Agriculture and Forestry Staff Office., SC; V. Chmn., State Planning Comm. Chou En-lai group. Purged.

144. T'an Ch'i-lung 譚啟龍 Sect., E. China; 1st Sect., Shantung; Commissar, Tsinan. T'ao Chu group; re-elected alternate member, CC. Inactive.

163. T'ang Liang 唐亮 Commissar, Nanking Military Academy. Lin Piao group. Re-elected alternate member, CC.

027. T'ao Chu 陶鑄 1st Sect., CS China; V. Prem., SC; Commissar, Kwangtung. Later, Dir., Propaganda Dept.; possibly Sect. Genl., CC; PBSC. T'ao Chu group. Purged.

159. T'ao Lu-chia 陶魯笳 V. Chmn., State Ec. Comm. Dir., CC Industry and Communications Pol. Dept. P'eng Chen group. Purged.

003. Teng Hsiao-p'ing 鄧小平 Sect. Genl., CC; PBSC; V. Prem. SC; Liu-Teng group. Purged.

060. Teng Hua 鄧華 V. Gov. Szechuan; P'eng Te-huai group. Purged.

029. T'eng Tai-yuan 滕代遠 No position; probably P'eng Te-huai group; but may later have joined Chou En-lai. Re-elected to CC.

036. Teng Tzu-hui 鄧子恢 V. Chmn., State Planning Comm. Dir., CC Rural Work Dept. Chou En-lai group; re-elected to CC.

017. Teng Ying-ch'ao 鄧穎超 Female; V. Chmn. Women's Federation; 2nd Sect., CC Women's Work Dept.; wife of Chou En-lai; re-elected to CC.

133. T'ien Pao 天寶 A Tibetan; V. Gov., Szechuan; probably CR group; promoted to CC.

011. T'sai Ch'ang 蔡暢 Female; Chmn., Women's Federation; 1st Sect. CC Women's Work Dept.; wife of Li Fu-ch'un; Chou En-lai group; same.

086. Tseng Hsi-sheng 曾希聖 Sect., SW China; purged prior to Cultural Revolution; faction not determined.

069. Tseng Shan 曾山 Min. Interior; Chou En-lai group; same.

006. Tung Pi-wu 董必武 PB; 1st Sect. Control Commission; probably Chou En-lai group. Same.

107. Wan I 萬毅 Purged 1959, P'eng Te-huai group.

068. Wang Chen 王震 Min. State Farms and Land Reclamation; Chou En-lai group; same.

043. Wang Chia-hsiang 王稼祥 Secretariat; P'eng Te-huai group. Purged.

091. Wang En-mao 王恩茂 Sect., NW China; 1st Sect., Sinkiang; Commander, Sinkiang; Commissar, Sinkiang. Ho Lung group; demoted to alternate member, CC. Inactive.

167. Wang Feng 汪鋒 Sect., NW China; 1st Sect., Kansu; V. Chmn., SC Nationality Affairs Comm.; Commissar, Kansu; Liu-Teng group. Purged.

155. Wang Ho-shou 王鶴壽 Purged c. 1964; became 1st Sect., An Shan county, Liaoning; purged, but faction not determined.

157. Wang Jen-chung 王任重 2nd Sect., CS China; 1st Sect.,

Hupehi; Commissar, Wuhan. Later 1st Sect., CS China; Dept. Dir., Cultural Revolution Group. T'ao Chu group. Purged.

170. Wang Shang-jung 王尚榮 Dir., Operations Subdept., PLA. Ho Lung group. Purged.

131. Wang Shih-tai 王世泰 Sect., Kansu; member of P'eng Te-huai group; later Liu-Teng group. Purged.

034. Wang Shou-tao 王首道 Sect., CS China. Possibly supported P'eng Te-huai. Later, probably CR group. Made V. Chmn., Kwangtung Revolutionary Committee; re-elected to CC.

085. Wang Shu-sheng 王樹聲 V. Min. Defense; Lin Piao Headquarters group; re-elected to CC.

059. Wang Ts'ung-wu 王從吾 Alt. Sect., Control Commission; purged 1963, inactive in Cultural Revolution.

035. Wang Wei-chou 王維舟 Control Commission; possibly CR group. Purged (dead?).

093. Wei Kuo-ch'ing 韋國清 1st Sect., Kwangsi; Gov., Kwangsi; Commissar, Kwangsi. Lin Piao regional group; became Chmn., Kwangsi Rev. Comm.; promoted to CC.

084. Wu Chih-p'u 吳芝圃 Sect., SC China; purged in early 1960's. Faction not determined.

056. Wu Hsiu-ch'üan 伍修權 Dir., CC International Liason Dept. P'eng Chen group. Purged.

037. Wu Lan-fu 烏蘭夫 (Ulanfu) PB(A); 2nd Sect., N. China, 1st Sect., Innter Mongolia; V. Prem., SC; Chmn., Nationality Affairs Comm.; Gov., Inner Mongolia; Commander, Inner Mongolia, Sect., CC Minorities Work Comm. Liu-Teng group. Purged.

121. Wu Te 吳德 Sect., NE China; 1st Sect., Kirin; Commissar, Kirin. Later, V. Chmn., Peking Rev. Comm.; CR group, promoted to CC.

009. Wu Yü-chang 吳玉章 Retired; died December, 1966; natural death.

098. Yang Ch'eng-wu 楊成武 Dept. CoS, PLA; V. Chmn., MAC. Later Acting CoS, PLA. Lin Piao Headquarters faction. Purged.

090. Yang Hsien-chen 楊獻珍 V. Dir., Higher Party School. P'eng Chen group, purged; under attack prior to Cultural Revolution.

050. Yang Hsiu-feng 楊秀峯 Dir., SC Sect.; Pres., Supreme Court. Liu-Teng group, purged. Committed suicide, c. spring, 1968.

166. Yang I-ch'en 楊一辰 V. Gov., Hupei; probably P'eng Te-huai group. Purged.

087. Yang Shang-k'un 楊尚昆 Alt. memb., Sect.; Dir., CC Genl.

Office; Dir., CC Comm. on Organs Under Direct Control of the Center; P'eng Chen group. Purged.

092. Yang Te-chih 楊德志 Commander, Tsinan; Lin Piao regional faction. Promoted to CC.

104. Yang Yung 楊勇 Dept. CoS, PLA; Commander, Peking. Lin Piao regional group. Purged.

180. Yao I-lin 姚依林 Dir., CC Finance and Trade Pol. Dept.; Min. Commerce; purged; Chou En-lai faction.

045. Yeh Chi-chuang 葉季壯 Dept. Dir., SC Finance and Trade Office; Min. Forn. Trade. Died June 1967; faction not determined.

038. Yeh Chien-ying 葉劍英 V. Chmn., MAC; Chou En-lai group; promoted to PB.

097. Yeh Fei 葉飛 Sect., E. China; 1st Sect., Fukien; Commissar, Foochow; Commander, Foochow. Liu-Teng group. Purged.

132. Yen Hung-yen 閻紅彥 1st Sect., Yunnan; Commissar, Kunming; Sect., SW China. Ho Lung group; suicide, January, 1967.

ABBREVIATIONS

Acad.—Academy
Alt.—Alternate
CC—Central Committee
Chmn.—Chairman
CoS—Chief of Staff
CR—Cultural Revolution
CS—Central South
Dept.—Deputy
Dir.—Director
E—East
Ed.—Editor
Gov.—Governor
GPD—General Political Department
HQ—Headquarters
MAC—Military Affairs Commission
Memb.—Member
Mil.—Military
Min.—Ministry, Minister
N—North
NE—Northeast
NW—Northwest
PB—Politburo
PB(A)—Alternate Member of the Politburo
PBSC—Politburo Standing Committee
Pol.—Political
Rev. Comm.—Revolutionary Committee
SC—State Council
Sect.—Secretary, Secretariat
Sect. Genl.—Secretary General
SW—Southwest
U—University
UF—United Front
V—Vice

BIBLIOGRAPHY

I. Biographical and Documentary Compilations, Organizational Charts, Non-Communist Serial Publications.

American Consulate General, Hong Kong, *Current Background* (CB) *Selections from China Mainland Magazines.* *Survey of the China Mainland Press* (SCMP).

American Embassy, Tokyo, Political Section, Translation Services Branch, *Daily Summary of the Japanese Press* (DSJP).

Asia Research Centre, *The Great Cultural Revolution in China* (Hong Kong, 1967) 507 pp.

Bandit Affairs (匪情研究) (Taiwan)' "Important Bandit Chiefs" (重要匪酋事略), series, biographies of:
Ch'en Yun, Vol. 11, No. 6 (June, 1968) pp. 123-131.
Huang Yung-sheng, Vol. 11, No. 11 (November, 1968) pp. 133-141.
Hsiao Ching-kuang, Vol. 12, No. 2 (February, 1969) pp. 141-149.
Wang En-mao, Vol. 12, No. 3 (March, 1969) pp. 135-144.
Li Hsueh-feng, Vol. 12, No. 8 (August, 1969) pp. 127-36.
Wei Kuo-ch'ing, Vol. 12, No. 9 (September, 1969) pp. 125-133.
Liu Chien-hsun, Vol. 12, No. 11 (November, 1969) pp. 111-120.
Liu Ko-p'ing, Vol. 12, No. 12 (December, 1969) pp. 137-144.
Han Hsien-ch'u, Vol. 13, No. 3 (March, 1970) pp. 141-150.

Bandit Affairs Special Report, 匪情研究專報 , *General Study of the Resolutions and Documents of the Bandit Party's Eighth Congress* (匪黨八全大會決議案之綜合研究) (Taipei, 1956) 4, 674 pp.

Bandit Affairs Monthly (匪情月報) (Taiwan).

Albert P. Balustein, *Fundamental Legal Documents of Communist China* (South Hackensack, 1962) xxix, 603 pp.

Conrad Brandt, Benjamin Schwartz, John King Fairbank, *A Documentary History of Chinese Communism* (Harvard: University Press, 1959) 552 pp.

C. S. Ch'en, Charles Price Ridley, *Rural People's Communes in Lien-Chiang: Documents Concerning Communes in Lien-Chiang County, Fukien Province,* 1962-1963 (Hoover Institution, 1969) xi, 243 pp.

Chiang I-shan (江一山) 中共軍事文件彙編 *(Collection of Chinese Communist Military Documents)* (Hong Kong 1965) 4, 24, 845, 21 pp.

China News Analysis (CNA) (Hong Kong).

Collection of Reports and Resolutions of the Bandit Party's Eighth Congress (匪黨八全大會報告與決議彙編) (Yangmingshan, 1956) 306 pp.

Collections of Special Studies for Recognition of the Enemy; (認識敵人專題研究彙編) *The Bandit Party's Organizational and Strategic Line* (匪黨的組織與策略路線 (Taipei, 1952) 176 pp.

Boyd Compton, *Mao's China: Party Reform Documents, 1942-194* (University of Washington Press, 1952) lii, 278 pp.

The Eighth National Congress of the Communist Party of China (共產黨第八次全國代表大會) (Peking, 1956) 236 pp.

Enemy Intelligence Research Office, War College (Republic of China), *Problems of Internal Struggle Among the Communist Bandits: Important Source Materials* (共匪內部鬥爭問題：重要原始資料彙編) (Taipei, 1967) 2, 8, 439 pp.

Hsiao Tso-liang, *Power Relations Within the Chinese Communist Movement, 1930-1934: A Study of Documents* (University of Washington Press, 1960) x, 401 pp.

Huang Chen-hsia (黃震遐) 中共軍人誌 *("Mao's Generals")* (Kowloong 1968) 790, 13 pp.

Institute of International Relations, Republic of China, (中共人名錄) *("Chinese Communist Who's Who")* (Taipei, 1967) 4, 24, 756 pp.

Intelligence Staff Office, Ministry of Defense (Republic of China), *Collection of Communist Bandit Documents* (共匪文件彙編) (Taiwan, 1962) 1, 240 pp.

"Talk About This Fellow..." (談談...這個人) series, biographies of:
P'eng Te-huai (1968) 3, 139 pp.
Lin Piao (1968) 2, 4, 142 pp.
Ho Lung (1968) 4, 160 pp.
Ch'en Yi (1968) 1, 2, 120 pp.
Chu Te (1969) 2, 4, 153 pp.
Nieh Jung-chen (1969) 2, 133 pp.

Collection of Important Documents on the Communist Bandits' Great Cultural Revolution (共匪文化大革命重要文件彙編) (1968) 2, 12, 338 pp.

Bandit Affairs Year Book, 1968 (一九六八匪情年報) (1968) 23, 1102, 34 pp.

News Office, Ministry of National Fefense (Republic of China), *Collection of Communist Bandit Reactionary Documents* (共匪反動文件彙編), Vol. I, (np, nd—probably compiled early 1940's) 279 pp.

Pao Ching-an (鮑靜安), *Bandit Affairs Handbook* (匪情手冊) (Taipei, 1968) 2, 2, 16, 494 pp.

Organization Charts, Collection of Material on Bandit-Puppet

Personnel (匪偽人事資料彙編, 組織表) Vol. 6 (Taipei, 1962) 1, 8, 238, 2, 56, 124 pp.

Ibid., Vol. 9 (Taipei, 1968) 7, 39, 56, 56, 89 pp.

Stuart Schram, *The Political Thought of Mao Tse-tung* (New York, 1963), ix, 319 pp.

Seminar for Examination of Bandit-Puppet Personnel Materials (匪偽人事資料調查研究會) *Changes in the Communist Bandits' Party, Government, and Military Organizational Structures* (共匪黨政軍組織機構之演變) (Taipei, 1965) 2, 78 pp. plus charts.

Supplementary Revision, 56th Year of the Republic, on Collection of Materials on Personnel Rosters of the Bandit-Puppets (匪偽人事資料彙編人物誌部分,民國五十六年度補充修正資料) (Taipei, 1968) Vol. I, pp. 1-252; Vol. II, pp. 253-453. 47.

Union Research Institute, *Who's Who in Communist China* (Hong Kong, 1966) v, 754 pp.

CCP Documents of the Great Proletarian Cultural Revolution, 1966-1967 (Hong Kong, 1968) vi, 692 pp.

The Case of P'eng Teh-huai (Kowloon, 1968) xiii, 6, 494 pp.

Collected Works of Liu Shao-ch'i Before 1944 (Kowloon, 1969) xiv, 471 pp.

Union Research Translation Services.

US Department of State, Division of Biographical Information, *Directory of Chinese Communist Officials* (Washington, D.C., 1966) xii, 621 pp.

II. **Chinese Communist Serial Publications.**

Chekiang Daily (浙江日報) (Hangchow)

China Youth (中國青年) (CY)
China Youth Daily (中國青年報) (Peking)
Daily Worker (工人日報) (DW) (Peking)
Kuang Ming Daily (光明日報) (KMD) (Peking)
Liberation Army Daily (解放軍報) (LAD) (Peking)
Literary Gazette (文藝報)
Literary Review (文藝評論)
New China Half-Monthly (新華半月刊) (NCHM)
Peking Review
People's Daily (人民日報) (PD) (Peking)
People's Handbook (人民手冊) (PHB)
People's Literature (人民文學)
Red Flag (紅旗) (RF)
Southern Daily (南方日報) (SD) (Canton)
Study (學習)
Ta Kung News (大公報) (Peking)
Wen Hui News (文滙報) (Shanghai)

III. **Official Documents of the Communist Party of China, the Chinese People's Republic, and Their Agencies.**
(Note: Documents taken from the collections listed in Part I of this bibliography are not listed here.)

Central Committee, Comunist Party of China (or "Party Center"):

"Public Report" (公報) of Second Plenum, Eighth Central Committee, PHB, 1957, pp. 147-148.
"Directive on the Rectification Movement" (關於整風運動的指示) April 27, 1957, PHB, 1958, pp. 20-30.
"Directive on the Participation in Collective Labor by Leading Personnel at all Levels." (關於各級領導人員參加體力勞動的指示) PHB, 1958, pp. 43-44.
"Directive on Implementing Large Scale Socialist Education Among the Entire Rural Population" (關於向全體農村人口進行一次大規模的社會主義教育的指示) (August 8, 1957) PD, August 10, 1957, p. 1.
"Directive on Implementing a Rectification and Socialist Education Movement in Enterprises." (關於在企業中進行整風和社會主義教育運動的指示) September 12, 1957; PHB, 1958, pp. 44-45.

"Directive on Rectifying the Agricultural Production Cooperatives" (關於整頓農業生產合作社的指示) September 14, 1957; PHB, 1958, pp. 517-518.

"Directive on Doing Good Work in the Management of Production on the Agricultural Production Cooperatives" (關於做好農業合作社管理的指示) September 14, 1957; PHB, 1958, pp. 518-519.

"Directive on the Thorough Implementation of Mutual Benefit Policies Within the Agricultural Production Cooperatives." (關於在農業合作社內部貫澈執行互利政策的指示) September 14, 1957, PHB, 1958, pp. 519-520.

"Public Report" of the Third Plenum (Enlarged) of the Eighth CC, CPC, PHB, 1958, p. 182.

"Outline Program for National Development of Agricultural Production, 1956-1967 (Revised Draft)" (一九五六年到一九六七年全國農業發展綱要(修正草案)) (October 25, 1957) PD, October 26, 1957, pp. 1-2.

"The Cadres of the Whole Party Must Actualize the Unity of Politics and Technology." (全黨幹部必須實現政治和技術的統一) February 14, 1958, PD, February 15, 1958, p. 1.

"Reform All State Work, Promote the Work Enthusiasm of All the People" (改進整個國家工作, 促進全民大幹勁) March 3, 1958; PD, March 4, 1958, p. 1.

"Resolution on the Problem of Establishing People's Communes in Rural Areas" (關於在農村建設人民公社問題的決議) August 29, 1958; PD, September 10, 1958, p. 1.

"Public Report" of the Sixth Plenum of the Eighth CC CPC, PD, December 18, 1958, p. 1.

Sixth Plenum: "Decision Agreeing with Comrade Mao Tse-tung's Proposal That He Not Be a Candidate for the Chairmanship of the People's Republic of China in the Coming Term." (同意毛澤東同志提出的關於他不作下屆中華人民共和國主席候選人的建議的決定) December 10, 1958; PD, December 18, 1958, p. 1.

Sixth Plenum: "Resolution on Certain Problems Concerning the People's Communes" (關於人民公社若干問題的決議) PD, December 19, 1958, pp. 1-2.

"Public Report" of the Seventh Plenum, Eighth CC, CPC, PD, April 8, 1959, p. 1.

"Public Report" of the Eighth Plenum of the Eighth CC CPC, PD, August 27, 1959, p. 1.

Eighth Plenum: "Resolution on the Anti-Party Clique Headed by P'eng Te-huai" (關於從彭德懷為首的反黨集團的決議) August 16, 1959; RF, 13 (August 15) 1967, pp. 18-20.

Eighth Plenum: "Resolution on Starting an Economy in Production Movement (關於發展增產節約運動的決議) August 16, 1959; PD, August 27, 1959, pp. 1-2.

"Public Report" of the Ninth Plenum of the Eighth CC, CPC; PD, Kanuary 21, 1961, p. 1.

Tenth Plenum, CC CPC, "Go a Step Further to Consolidate the Collective Economy of the People's Communes and Develop Agricultural Production" (進一步鞏固人民公社集體經濟發展農業生產) PD, September 29, 1962, p. 1.

"Decision on Several Current Problems in Rural Work (Draft)" (關於目前農村工作中若干問題的決定(草案)) May, 1963; published by Bureau of State Security, Republic of China (Taipei, 1965) 19 pp.

"Regulations on Some Concrete Policies in the Rural Socialist Education Movement (Draft)" (關於農村社會主義教育運動中一些具體政策的規定(草案)) September, 1963; published by the Bureau for State Security, Republic of China, (Taipei, 1965) 35 pp.

"Regulations on Some Concrete Policies in the Rural Socialist Education Movement (Revised Draft)" (關於社會主義教育運動中一些具體政策的規定(修正草案)) September, 1964; published by Bureau of State Security, Republic of China (Taipei, 1965) 36 pp.

"Some Questions in the Current Rural Socialist Education Movement", January 14, 1965; *Issues and Studies,* Vol. VII, No. 1 (October, 1, 1970) pp. 94-95.

"Announcement" (通知) May 16, 1966; PD, May 17, 1967, pp. 1-2.

Eleventh Plenum, Eighth CC CPC, "Decision on the Great Proletarian Cultural Revolution" (關於無產階級文化大革命的決定) August 8, 1966; PD, August 9, 1966, pp. 1-2.

"Public Report" of Eleventh Plenum, PD, August 14, 1966 p. 11.

Central Politburo, Enlarged Meeting, "Fight to Produce 100,700,000 Tons of Steel" (為生產一千零七十萬噸鋼而奮鬥) PD, September 1, 1958, p. 1

Constitution of the Chinese Communist Youth League (中國共產主義青年團的章程) PD, July 18, 1964, p. 3.

Constitution of the Communist Party of China (中國共產黨章程) PHB, 1957, pp. 49-55.

General Political Department of the Chinese People's Liberation Army, *Work Bulletins* (工作通訊) (WB). Twenty-nine bulletins, Nos. 1-8, 10-30, January-August, 1961.

Military Affairs Commission, "Summons to the Whole Army to Study the Kuo Hsing-fu Teaching Method and Raise the Level of Training Work." (號召全軍學習郭興福教學方法,提高訓練工作水平) PD, February 18, 1964, p. 1.

Ministry of National Defense, "Military Forms of Address, According to the New Regulations" (軍人之間按照新的規定互相稱呼) PD, June 27, 1965, p. 1.

National Conference of the Communist Party of China, "Resolution on the Establishment of a Central and Local Control Commissions" (關於成立黨的中央和地方監察委員會的決議) PHB, 1956, pp. 79-80.

"Party Center," State Council, "Directive on Wiping Out the Four Pests and Paying Attention to Hygiene" (關於除四害講衛生的提示) February 11, 1958; PD, February 18, 1958, p. 1.

"Announcement of the Convening This Winter of Representatives of Advanced Units in Agricultural Production" (今冬召開農業先進單位代表會議的通知) April 7, 1958; PD, April 9, 1958, p. 1.

"Directive on Educational Work" (關於教育工作的提示) September 19, 1958; PD, September 20, 1958, p. 1.

"All Cadres Must Engage in Physical Labor for One Month Every Year," (全體幹部每年體力勞動一個月) PD, September 30, 1958, p. 1.

"Decision Reforming the Management of the Rural Finance and Trade System to Make It Conform to the Form of People's Communization" (關於適應人民公社化的形勢改進農村的財政貿易管理體制的決定) December 20, 1958; PD, December 23, 1958, p. 1.

"Urgent Directive on Beginning a Struggle to Resist Disasters" (關於展開抗災鬥爭的緊急提示) PD, August 14, 1959, p. 1.

"Directive on Organizing Collective Trade in Rural Areas" (關於組織農村集市貿易的提示) PD, September 25, 1959, p. 1.

Propaganda Department, CC CPC, "Report to the Center on the Setting Up of a Curriculum for Socialist Education" (關於設立社會主義教育課程向中央的報告) October 21, 1957; PHB, 1958, p. 46.

State Council, "Decision on the Participation by Working Personnel in State Organs in the Rectification Movement and the Struggle Against the Bourgeois Rightists" (關於國家機關工作人員參加整風運動和反對資產階級右派鬥爭的決定) July 26, 1957; PHB, 1958, p. 71.

"Decision on Cultivation Through Labor" (關於勞動教養問題的決定) August 1, 1957, PD, August 4, 1957, p. 1.

"Order" (任命) PD, November 9, 1962, p. 1.

IV. Works by Members of the Eighth Central Committee, Communist Party of China.
(Note: This list, not exhaustive, includes the more important speeches and articles by the members during the tenure of the Eighth CC. Some more important earlier works are also included. Works taken from the collections in Part I of this bibliography are not included here. For the Chinese names of the authors alive in late 1965, see Appendix.)

An Tzu-wen, 共產黨能夠領導科學、文化、和教育工作 (The Communist Party Is Able to Lead Work in Science, Culture, and Education.) CY, 13 (July 1) 1957, pp. 5-6.

進一步加強人民公社黨組織的領導作用 (Go a Step Further to Strengthen the Leadership Function of the Party Organization on the People's Communes) PD, December 17, 1959, p. 7.

培養革命接班人是黨的一項戰畧任務 (The Cultivation of Revolutionary Successors Is a Strategic Task of the Party) PD, September 23, 1964, pp. 5-6.

Chang Ai-p'ing, 少奇同志在淮北敵後 (Comrade Shao-ch'i Behind Enemy Lines North of the Huai) PD, August 15, 1965, p. 5.

Chang Ching-wu, 正確貫徹黨在西藏民主改革中的方針反政策 (Correctly Carry Through the Party's Direction and Policy on the Democratic Reforms in Tibet) PD, May 25, 1962, p. 5.

Chang Chung-liang, 人民公社的鞏固和發展促進了農業的大躍進 (The Consolidation and Development of the People's Communes Propels a Great Leap Forward in Agriculture) PD, September 22, 1960, p. 7.

Chang P'ing-hua, 工業企業中的整風運動與技術革命 (The Rectification Movement in Industrial Enterprise and the Technological Revolution) PD, May 28, 1958, p. 3.

黨的報刊要大插紅旗 (Party Publications Must Stick in the Red Flag) PD, January 12, 1960, p. 7.

繼承和發揚"湘江評論"的光榮傳統 (Continue and Develop the Glorious Tradition of the *Hsiang River Review*) PD, June 30, 1960, p. 7.

一定要依靠貧下中農 (We Must Certainly Depend upon the Poor and Lower-Middle Farmers) PD, November 2, 1964, p. 5

論辦點 (Managing the Spot) PD, March 7, 1966, p. 5.

Chang Te-sheng, (張德生), 用實際行動保衛黨的總路線 (Protect the Party's General Line with Practical Activities) RF 21 November 1, 1959, pp. 38-39.

站在最大多數勞動人民的一面 (Stand on the Side of the Great Majority of the Laboring People) PD, October 20, 1960, p. 7.

以農為基礎促進國民經濟的發展 (With Agriculture as the Base, Propel the Development of the National Economy) PD, December 12, 1960, p. 7.

Chang Ting-ch'eng, 整風在延安中央黨校 (The Rectification in the Yenan Central Party School) PD, August 17, 1961, p. 7.

最高人民檢察院工作報告 (Report on the Work of the Supreme People's Procuratorate) PD, January 1, 1965, p. 1.

Chao Chien-min, 改革喪葬禮俗,提倡薄棺薄葬,墓而不墳 (Change Burial Customs, Promote Burial Without Coffin, Small Tombs, and No Mound) PD, June 17, 1958, p. 4.

Ch'en Cheng-jen 論人民公社的所有制和分配制度 (The Ownership and Distribution Systems of the People's Communes) PD, October 18, 1959, p. 7.

加速農業的技術改造 (Speed up the Technological Reform in Agriculture) PD, February 18, 1960, p. 7.

Ch'en I, 對北京高等院校應屆畢業學生的講話 (Speech to the Graduating Students at Higher Level Schools in Peking) KMD, September 3, 1961, p. 2.

Ch'en Man-yuan, 實行多種經營,全面發展農業生產 (Implement All Kinds of Management, Develop Agricultural Production in an Overall Way) PD, September 28, 1956, p. 6.

學習唯物辯證法,克服工作中的片面性 (Study Dialectical Materialism, Overcome Bias in Work) *Study*, 7 April 4, 1957, pp. 20-21.

Ch'en Pei-hsien, 貫徹依靠工人群眾辦好企業的方針 (Carry out the Direction of Depending upon the Working Masses to Do a Good Job in Managing Enterprises) PD, September 19, 1956, p. 8.

堅持政治掛帥的方針 (Uphold the Direction of Politics Takes Command) RF, 20 October 16, 1959, pp. 47-49.

Ch'en Po-ta, 厚今薄古,邊幹邊學 (Stress the Present, Slight the Past, Work and Study at the Same Time) PD, March 11, 1958, p. 7.

建設共產主義的新北大 (Build a New Communist Peking University) PD, May 5, 1958, pp. 1-2.

全新的社會, 全新的人 (An Entirely New Society, an Entirely New Man), RF, 3, July 1, 1958, pp. 9-12.

在毛澤東同志的旗幟下 (Under the Banner of Comrade Mao Tze-tung) RF 4, July 15, 1958, pp. 1-12.

批評的繼承和新的探索 (The Continuation of Arguments and New Understandings) RF 13, July 1, 1959, pp. 36-45.

無產階級世界觀和資產階級世界觀的鬥爭 (The Struggle Between the Proletarian and Bourgeois World Views) PD, November 16, 1959, p. 2.

在大風大浪裏成長 (Grow in the Big Wind and Waves) PD, August 22, 1966, p. 1.

無產階級文化大革命的兩條路線 (The Two Lines in the Great Proletarian Cultural Revolution). Transcript in Collection of the Institute of International Relations, Republic of China; dated October 24, 1966; 14 pp.

在紀念魯迅大會上的開幕詞 (Opening Words at the Meeting Commemorating Lu Hsun) PD, November 1, 1966, p. 1.

開幕詞 (Opening Words) PD, December 4, 1966, p. 1.

紀念毛主席"在延安文藝座談會上的講話"二十五周年 (Commemorating the 25th Anniversary of Chairman Mao's "Speech at the Yenan Forum of Literature and Art) PD, May 24, 1967, pp. 1-2.

Ch'en Yü, 依靠羣眾, 團結多數是取得革命勝利的根本保證 (Depend upon the Masses, Unite with the Majority Is the Basic Guarantee of Victory in Revolution) PD, December 6, 1960, p. 7.

Ch'en Yun, 建設共產主義的偉大計劃 (The Great Plan for Building Communism) PD, January 3, 1959, p. 1.

當前基本建設工作中的幾個重大問題 (A Few Important Questions on Current Basic Construction Work) PD, March 1, 1959, pp. 1-2.

Chiang Hua, 一次實際的教育 (A Practical Education) PD, September 25, 1956, p. 4.

堅持黨的正確路線,爭取整風運動在各戰線上全勝 (Firmly Uphold the Correct Line of the Party, Struggle Through to Victory on All Fronts in the Rectification Movement) PD, December 28, 1957, pp. 2-3.

Chiang Nan-hsiang, 黨的教育方針促進了高等學校的革命 (The Party's Line on Education Propels a Revolution in High Level Schools) RF, 8 September 16, 1958, pp. 18-23.

學習一二·九運動的歷史經驗,做無產階級革命事業的接班人 (Study the Historical Experience of the December 9 Movement, Be Successors to the Work of the Proletarian Revolution) PD, December 10, 1965, p. 3.

Chiang Wei-ching, 政治掛帥,以生產為中心,帶動各項工作一道前進 (Politics Takes Command, With Production as the Center, Lead Forward All Kinds of Work) PD, May 14, 1958, p. 2.

學習毛澤東思想,充分發揚自覺的能動性 (Study the Thought of Mao Tse-tung, Fully Develop a Self-Aware Ability to Act) PD, January 19, 1960, p. 7.

廣泛開展支援農業的群眾運動 (Begin a Broad Mass Movement to Aid Agriculture) PD, July 16, 1960, p. 7.

運用樣板,推動全盤,是領導農業生產的好方法 (To Use the Template, Act Over the Whole Board Is a Good Method for Leading Agricultural Production) PD, January 28, 1966, pp. 5-6.

Ch'ien Ying, 堅決向官僚主義作鬥爭 (Firmly Struggle With Bureaucratism) PD, September 30, 1956, p. 5.

Chou En-lai, 關於知識分子問題的報告 (Report on the Problem of Intellectuals) PD, January 30, 1956, pp. 1-3.

政府工作報告 (Report on the Work of the Government) PD, April 19, 1959, pp. 2-4.

關於調整一九五九年國民經濟計劃主要提示和進一步開展增產節約運動的報告 (Report on the Important Directive Rectifying the 1959 National Economic Plan and Going a Step Further to Begin an Economy in Production Movement) PD, August 29, 1959, pp. 1-2.

偉大的十年 (Ten Great Years) PD, October 6, 1959, pp. 2-3.

在國慶招待會上的講話 (Speech at the National Day Reception) PD, October 1, 1962, p. 2.

在第三屆全國代表大會第一次會議上(的)政府工作報告 (Report on the Work of the Government at the First Session of the Third National People's Congress) PD, December 31, 1964, pp. 1-3.

在慶祝無產階級文化大革命群眾大會上...的講話 (Speech at the Mass Meeting Celebrating the Great Proletarian Cultural Revolution) PD, August 19, 1966, p. 2.

在接見外地來京革命師生大會上...的講話 (Speech While Meeting Revolutionary Teachers and Students Who Have Come to the Capital From Elsewhere) PD, September 1, 1966, p. 2.

講話 (Speech) PD, September 16, 1966, p. 2.

(Speech) PD, October 1, 1966, p. 2.

讚揚長征小將樹立全程步行串連的好榜樣 (Approving the Good Example of the Long March Little Generals

Who Have Established the Practice of Engaging in Roving Solidarity Entirely on Foot) PD, November 16, 1966, pp. 1-2.

(Speech) PD, December 4, 1966, p. 2.

"Chou En-lai Talks About the 'February Adverse Current' ", *Issues and Studies*, Vol. V, No. 12 (September, 1969) pp. 103-104 (Delivered in February or March, 1967).

(Speech) PD, April 21, 1967, p. 2.

Chou Hsiao-chou, 鞏固農業生產合作社的一些問題 (A Few Problems in Consolidating Agricultural Production Co-operatives) PD, September 20, 1956, p. 6.

農業大躍進促進了全面大躍進 (The Great Leap Forward in Agriculture Propels an All-Around Great Leap Forward) PD, May 24, 1958, p. 2.

Chou Yang, 讓文學藝術在建設社會主義偉大事業中發揮巨大的作用 (Let Literature and Art Perform a Huge Function in the Great Task of Building Socialism) PD, September 26, 1956, p. 4.

文藝戰線上的一場大辯論 (A Big Debate on the Literature and Art Front) PD, February 28, 1958, pp. 2-3.

新民歌開拓了詩歌的新道路 (The New Folk Songs Open a New Road in Poetry) RF, 1, (June 1,) 1958, pp. 33-38.

我國社會主義文學藝術的道路 (Our Country's Socialist Literature and Art Road) PD, September 4, 1960, pp. 5-7.

哲學社會科學工作者的戰鬥任務 (The Fighting Tasks of Philosophy and Social Science Workers) PD, December 27, 1963, pp. 1-4.

高舉毛澤東思想紅旗, 做又會勞動又會創作的文藝戰士 (Raise High the Red Banner of the Thought

289

of Mao Tse-tung, Become Literary and Art Warriors Who are Able Both to Labor and Create) PD, January 1, 1966, pp. 5-6.

Chu Te, 加張团結,建設社會主義　　(Strengthen Unity, Build Socialism) PHB, 1957, pp. 65-67.

在農業戰線上鼓足幹勁前進 (Drum Up Work Enthusiasm on the Agricultural Front and Move Forward) PD, December 28, 1957, pp. 1-4.

人民軍隊,人民戰爭 (People's Troops, People's War) PD, August 1, 1958, p. 4.

Chu Te-hai, 廣泛開展羣象性的農業科學實驗活動促 農業生產新高潮 (Open on a Broad Scale Scientific Experiment Activities of a Mass Nature, Propel a New High Tide in Agricultural Production) PD, January 31, 1965, p. 5.

Fan Wen-lan, 砍除迷信 (Root Out Superstition) RF, 2 (June 16,) 1958, pp. 1-4.

Feng Pai-chü, 廣東生產建設的成就與存在問題 (The Results of Industrial Production Construction in Kwangtung and Remaining Problems) SD, August 10, 1957, pp. 2-3.

Ho Lung, 南昌起義與我軍建設 (The Nanchang Uprising and the Establishment of Our Army) PD, August 1, 1958, p. 4.

中國人民解放軍的民主傳統 (The Democratic Traditions of the Chinese People's Liberation Army) PD, August 1, 1965, pp. 1-2.

Hsiao Hua, 培養三八作風是我軍建設的重要任務 (Cultivation of the Three Eight Work Style is an Important Task in Our Army Building) PD, May 24, 1960, p. 7.

以毛澤東思想為指針,作好連隊政治工作 (With the Thought of Mao Tse-tung as the Compass, Do a Good Job in Company-Level Political Work) PD, November 15, 1961, p. 1.

我軍指戰員怎樣學習毛澤東著作 (How Our Army's Battle Leaders Should Study the Works of Mao Tse-tung) PD, May 23, 1964, p. 5. (Note: Hsiao's name in this article is written 肖, not the usual way. This is probably just some trial simplified character that was not adopted; but conceivably there was another man named "Hsiao Hua" who was concerned with political work in the army, but was not the one on the CC, the director of the GPD).

高舉毛澤東思想偉大紅旗,堅決實行突出政治的五項原則 (Raise High the Great Red Banner of the Thought of Mao Tse-tung, Firmly Uphold the Five Principles of Politics to the Fore) PD, January 25, 1966, pp. 1-2.

把活學活用毛主席著作的羣眾運動推向新階段 (Push the Mass Movement of the Living Study Living Use of Chairman Mao's Works to a New Stage) PD, October 10, 1966, p. 1.

Hsieh Chueh-tsai, 我們要重視檔案工作,做好檔案工作 (We Must Treat Documentary Work as Important Do It Well) PD, September 6, 1959, p. 7.

最高人民法院工作報告 (Report of the Supreme People's Court) PD, January 1, 1965, p. 3.

Hsieh Fu-chih, 講話 (Speech) PD, April 21, 1967, pp. 3-4.

"Hsieh Fu-chih's Talk at a Struggle Rally Against Lo Jui-ch'ing" August 7, 1967; *Issues and Studies,* Vol. V, No. 12 (September, 1969) pp. 94-102.

Hsu Hsiang-ch'ien, 鄂豫皖紅軍的反圍攻鬥爭 (The Red Army's Counter-Encirclement Campaign in Hupei, Honan, and Anhwei) PD, July 29, 1961, p. 7.

Hsu Kuang-ta, Wang Chen, Wang Shang-jung, 湘鄂西和湘鄂川黔的武裝鬥爭 (The Armed Struggle in Hunan-Hupeh-Shansi and in Hunan-Hopeh-Szuchwan-Kweichow) PD, February 1, 1962, p. 5.

Hu Ch'iao-mu, *Thirty Years of the Communist Party of China,* (Peking, 1952) 93 pp.

Hu Yao-pang, 引導我國青年向最偉大的目標前進 (Leading the Youth of Our Country Forward Toward the Greatest Goal) PD, September 25, 1956, p. 6.

團結全國青年建設社會主義的新中國 (Unite the Youth of the Whole Country to Build a Socialist New China) PD, May 16, 1957, pp. 2-3.

發揚共產主義精神，努力建設社會主義 (Make the Communist Spirit Flourish, Energetically Build Socialism) PD, December 3, 1958, p. 3.

中國人民有力量維護祖國的統一 (The Chinese People Have the Strength to Maintain the Unity of the Fatherland) PD, May 5, 1959, p. 3.

在農業戰線的偉大鬥爭中造就一代新人 (Create a Generation of New Men in the Great Struggle on the Agricultural Front) PD, November 22, 1960, p. 7.

為我國青年革命化而鬥爭 (Struggle for the Revolutionization of the Youth of Our Country) PD, July 7, 1964, pp. 2-3.

Huang Huo-ch'ing, 對改造資本主義工商業和資本家的體會 (The Reform of Capitalist Industry and Commerce and of the General Attitude of Capitalists) PD, September 30, 1956, p. 6.

認真克服領導工作人員的官僚主義 (Sincerely Overcome the Bureaucratism of Leading Personnel) PD, April 28, 1957, p. 2.

大興共產主義協作之風 (Raise Up the Great Wind of Communist Cooperation) PD, January 23, 1960, p. 7.

關於農村支部培養接班人問題 (The Problem of Cultivation of Successors by Rural Branches) PD, May 21, 1965, p. 5.

Huang Ou-tung, 遼寧省農業戰線的新任務 (The New Duty on the Agricultural Front in Liaoning) PD, February 1, 1960, p. 7.

K'ang Sheng, 中國革命是偉大十月革命的繼續 (The Chinese Revolution Is the Continuation of the Great October Revolution) PD, November 7, 1957, p. 7.

南斯拉夫的修正主義恰恰適合美帝國主義者的需要 (Yugoslav Revisionism Neatly Fits the Requirements of the US Imperialists) PD, June 14, 1958, p. 5.

高舉馬克思列寧主義的紅旗前進 (Raise High the Red Banner of Marxism-Leninism and Move Forward) PD, May 5, 1959, p. 3.

K'o Ch'ing-shih (柯慶施) 黨對資本主義工商業的改造政策的偉大勝利 (The Great Victory of Party Policy Toward the Reform of Capitalist Industry and Commerce) PD, September 21, 1956, p. 6.

乘風破浪加速建設社會主義的新上海 (Ride the Wind and the Waves to Speed Up the Construction of a Socialist New Shanghai) PHB, 1958, pp. 46-58.

論全國一盤棋 (On the Whole Country Is One Chess Board) RF, 4 (February 16, 1959) pp. 9-12.

關於工業戰線的群眾運動 (The Mass Movement on the Industrial Front) PD, November 1, 1959, p. 2.

工農聯盟是中國革命和建設勝利的保證 (The Worker-Peasant Alliance is the Guarantee of the Victory of the Chinese Revolution and Construction) PD, July 20, 1961, p. 7.

向好八連學習 (Learn From the Good Eight Company) PD, May 8, 1963, p. 2.

反映社會主義新時代的現代劇前途燦爛 (The Brilliant Road Ahead for Modern Plays Which Reflect the New Socialist Era) PD, December 29, 1963, p. 2.

大力發展和繁榮社會主義戲劇，更好地為社會主義的經濟基礎服務 (Put Great Efforts into Developing and Making Flourish Socialist Plays, Make Them Serve the Socialist Economic Base Even Better) PD, August 16, 1964, pp. 2-3.

K'uei Pi, 人民公社制度為畜牧業的高速發展開闢了廣闊的進途 (The People's Commune System Opens a Broad Road for the Rapid Development of the Livestock Industry) PD, May 2, 1959, p. 6.

Lai Jo-yü, (賴若愚) 進一步發揮工會組織在社會主義建設中的作用 (Move a Step Further in Developing the Function of Trade Union Organizations in Socialist Construction) PD, September 24, 1956, p. 4.

Li Ching-ch'üan, 不斷改進國家和農民的關係 (Continue to Improve the Relations Between the State and the Peasants) PD, September 19, 1956, p. 7.

人民公社是我國社會發展的必然產物 (The People's Communes Are a Necessary Product of Our Country's Social Development) PD, October 18, 1959, pp. 2-3.

Li Fu-ch'un, 關於一九五九年國民經濟計劃草案的報告 (Report on the Draft 1959 National Economic Plan) PD, April 22, 1959, pp. 2-4.

高舉黨的總路線的紅旗為社會主義建設事業的繼續躍進而奮鬥 (Raise High the Red Banner of the Party's General Line, Fight for the Continuation of the Leap Forward in the Task of the Construction of Socialism) PD, October 27, 1959, p. 2.

迎接一九六零年的新躍進 (Welcome the Continuing New Leap Forward in 1960) PD, January 1, 1960, p. 1.

毛澤東思想指導下的羣衆運動 (The Mass Movement Under the Direction of the Thought of Mao Tse-tung) PD, February 28, 1960, p. 2.

關於一九六零年國民經濟計劃草案報告 (Report on the 1960 Draft Economic Plan) PD, March 31, 1960, pp. 2-3.

高舉總路線的紅旗繼續前進 (Raise High the Red Flag of the General Line and Continue to Move Forward) PD, August 17, 1966, pp. 2-3.

Li Hsien-nien, 人民公社所見 (A Look at the People's Communes) PD, October 17, 1958, p. 3.

積極開展多種經營,大力增產副食品 (Actively Undertake Many Kinds of Management, Put Great Effort into Producing By-Products) PD, December 29, 1958, p. 2.

怎樣認識農村財貿體制的改進 (How to Look at the Reform of the Management System of Finance and Trade in the Rural Areas) PD, January 17, 1959, p. 2.

關於一九五八年國家決算和一九五九年國家預算草案的報告 (Report on the State Budget for 1958 and the 1959 Draft on Expected Expenditures) PD, April 22, 1959, p. 3.

關於一九五九年國家決算和一九六零年國家預算的報告 (Report on the State Budget for 1959 and the Expected Expenditures for 1960) PD, April 1, 1960, pp. 2-3.

更高地舉起三面紅旗,完成和超額完成今年國民經濟計劃 (Raise Even Higher the Three Red Flags, Fulfill and Overfulfill This Year's National Economic Plan) PD, June 5, 1960, p. 2.

對財務會計人員的幾點希望 (A Few Hopes for the State Accountants) PD, September 4, 1963, p. 2.

高舉毛澤東思想紅旗,做好社會主義商業工作 (Riase High the Red Banner of the Thought of Mao Tse-tung, Do a Good Job in Socialist Commerce) PD, February 16, 1965, p. 2.

Li Hsueh-feng, 加強黨對企業的領導,貫徹執行群眾路線 (Strengthen Party Leadership Over Enterprise, Fully Carry Out the Mass Line) PD, September 25, 1956, p. 5.

關於企業管理方法的群眾路線的問題 (The Problem of the Mass Line in Business Management Methods) RF, 5 (August 1,) 1958, pp. 12-15.

讓千萬個周明山更好地成長起來 (Let Ten Million Chou Ming-shans Grow Up Even Better) PD, May 28, 1964, p. 5.

Li Ta-chang, 為奪取一九五九年農業大豐收而奮鬥 (Fight to Reap a Bumper Harvest in 1959) PD, May 1, 1959, p. 12.

把財貿工作提高到更好地為生產和生活服務的新階段 (Raise Finance and Trade Work to a New Level So It Can Serve Production and Life Even Better) PD, April 11, 1960, p. 9.

堅持幹部參加集體生產勞動的制度 (Firmly Uphold the System Whereby Cadres Participate in Collective Labor) PD, January 16, 1965, p. 5.

Li Wei-han, 社會主義是長期共存的政治基礎 (Socialism Is the Political Base for Long-Term Coexistence) PD, June 4, 1957, p. 1.

學習毛主席著作,逐步改造世界觀 (Study the Works of Chairman Mao, Gradually Reform Your World View) PD, September 25, 1960, pp. 2-3.

中國人民民主統一戰線的特點 (The Special Characteristics of the Democratic United Front of the Chinese People) PD, June 16, 1961, p. 7; June 17, 1961, p. 7.

新民主主義革命的時期爭取無產階級領導權的鬥爭 (The Struggle of the Proletariat to Obtain Leading Power in the Period of the New Democratic Revolution) PD,

February 9, 1962, p. 5; PD, February 10, 1962, p. 5; PD, February 11, 1962, p. 5.

Liao Lu-yen, 在農業戰線上, 鼓足幹勁, 力爭上游, 多快好省地建設社會主義 (On the Agricultural Front Drum Up Labor Enthusiasm, Struggle Up Stream, Build Socialism Much Fast Good Cheap) PD, June 10, 1958, p. 2.

一九五九年農業戰線的任務 (The Task on the Agricultural Front in 1959) PD, January 1, 1959, p. 3.

鼓足幹勁, 力爭豐收 (Drum Up Work Enthusiasm, Struggle For a Bumper Harvest) RF, 3-4 (February 1, 1961) pp. 26-32.

Lin Feng, 大搞文化革命, 實現工農群眾知識化, 知識份子勞動化 (Make a Big Cultural Revolution, Actualize the Enlightenment of the Working and Farming Masses, the Laborizing of the Intellectuals) PD, June 2, 1960, p. 3.

Lin Piao, 高舉黨的總路線和毛澤東軍事思想的紅旗闊步前進 (Raise High the General Line of the Party and the Military Thought of Mao Tse-tung and Advance with Great Steps.) RF, 19 (October 1,) 1959, pp. 16-25.

中華人民共和國國防部命令 (Order of the Ministry of National Defense, the People's Republic of China) PD, October 2, 1959, p. 2.

中國人民革命戰爭的勝利是毛澤東思想的勝利 (The Victory of the Chinese People's Revolutionary War Is the Victory of the Thought of Mao Tse-tung) PD, September 30, 1960, pp. 3-4.

人民戰爭勝利萬歲 (Long Live the Victory of People's War) PD, September 3, 1965, pp. 1-4.

"Address at the Enlarged Meeting of the CCP Central Politburo" May 10, 1966; *Issues and Studies,* Vol. VI, No. 5 (February, 1970) pp. 81-92.

毛主席天才地把馬克思列寧主義提高到嶄新
的階段；思想灌輸到工農中能轉化為巨大的
物質力量 (Chairman Mao, by Dent of Genius, Has Raised Marxism-Leninism to a Brand New Stage; the Thought of Mao Tse-tung, Flowing Down Among the Workers and Farmers, Is Transformed into a Gigantic Material Strength) KMD, June 19, 1966, p. 1.

在慶祝無產階級文化大革命羣衆大會上⋯的
講話 (Speech at the Mass Meeting Celebrating the Great Proletarian Cultural Revolution) PD, August 19, 1966, p. 2.

在接見外地來京革命師生大會上的講話
(Speech at the Meeting Welcoming the Revolutionary Students and Teachers Who Have Come to the Capital from Elsewhere) PD, September 1, 1966, p. 2.

講話 (Speech) PD, September 16, 1966, p. 2.

(Speech) PD, October 2, 1966, p. 2.

"Address to the CCP Central Committee Working Conference" October 25, 1966; *Issues and Studies,* Vol. VI, No. 1 (October, 1969); pp. 101-105; *Ibid.,* Vol. VI, No. 2 (November, 1969) pp. 93-98.

(Speech) PD, November 4, 1966, p. 2.

"毛主席語錄"再版前言 (Forward to the Second Edition of *Quotations from Chairman Mao*) PD, December 17, 1966, p. 1.

"Report to the Ninth National Congress of the Communist Party of China" *Peking Review,* Vol. 12, No. 18 (April 30, 1969) pp. 16-35.

Lin Po-chü (林伯渠) 中國革命的歷史教訓 (The Historical Lessons of the Chinese Revolution) PHB, 1957, pp. 92-93.

Lin T'ieh, 共產主義思想的大躍進 (The Great Leap Forward in Communist Thought) PD, May 13, 1958, p. 2.

河北省的人民公社運動 (The People's Commune Movement in Hopei) RF, 9 (October 1, 1958) pp. 16-21.

為一九六零年的更大勝利鬥爭 (Struggle for Even Greater Victories in 1960) PD, December 28, 1959, p. 7.

開展一個馬克思主義的改進領導方法，領導作風的運動 (Begin a Marxist Reform Movement in Leadership Methods and Leadership Style) PD, July 13, 1960, p. 7.

Liu Ko-p'ing, 在少數民族中進行一次反對地方民族主義的社會主義教育 (Implement a Socialist Education Against Local Nationalism Among Minority Nationalities) PD, January 11, 1958, p. 7.

在工礦企業中堅決貫徹執行黨的領導 (Firmly Carry Through Party Leadership in Industrial and Mining Enterprises) PD, March 30, 1960, p. 7.

Liu Lan-t'ao, 正確執行黨的紀律，加強黨的監察工作 (Correctly Implement Party Discipline, Strengthen Party Control Work) PD, September 29, 1956, p. 5.

中國共產黨是中國人民建設社會主義的最高統帥 (The Communist Party of China Is the Supreme Commander of the Chinese People in Building Socialism) PD, September 28, 1959, p. 2.

Liu Ning-i, 高舉毛澤東旗幟，樹雄心，立大志，為實現一九六零年更好的躍進而奮鬥 (Raise High the Banner of Mao Tse-tung, With a Heroic Heart and a Firm Will Fight to Realize an Even Better Leap Forward in 1960) PD, March 5, 1960, pp. 2-3.

Liu Shao-ch'i, "The Class Character of Man" appendix to *How to Be a Good Communist* (Peking, 1951) pp. 113-120.

論共產黨員修養 *(The Self-Cultivation of a Communist Party Member)* (np, 1947) 68 pp.

論黨內鬥爭 *(Inner-Party Struggle)* (np, 1947) 49 pp.

"Liquidate the Menshevist Ideology Within the Party" (1943); appendix to English translation of *On Inner-Party Struggle* (Peking, 1951) pp. 71-87.

論黨 *(The Party)* (Peking, 1952) 2, 154 pp.

中國共產黨中央委員會向第八屆全國代表大會第二次會議的工作報告 (Report of the Work of the Central Committee of the Communist Party of China to the Second Session of the Eighth National Congress of the Communist Party of China) PD, May 27, 1958, pp. 1-3.

代表黨中央致詞 (Words of Greeting, Representing the Party Center) PD, December 26, 1958, p. 1.

馬克思列寧主義在中國的勝利 (The Victory of Marxism-Leninism in China) PD, October 1, 1959, pp. 2-3.

在慶祝中國共產黨成立四十周年大會上的講話 (Speech at the Meeting Celebrating the 40th Anniversary of the Founding of the Communist Party of China) PD, July 1, 1961, pp. 2-3.

"The Self-Cultivation of a Communist Party Member" (revised edition) PD, August 1, 1962, pp. 1-6.

在慶祝中華人民共和國成立十五周年大會上的講話 (Speech at the Reception in Celebration of the 15th Anniversary of the Founding of the People's Republic of China) PD, October 1, 1964, p. 1.

Liu Ya-lou (劉亞樓) 回憶天津戰役更好地學習毛澤東思想 (Remembering the Tientsin Campaign, Study Even Better the Thought of Mao Tse-tung) PD, October 28, 1960, p. 7.

偉大的第一步 (The Great First Step) PD, July 4, 1961, p. 7.

橫掃七百里 (The 700 *Li* Vicious Sweep) PD, July 22, 1961, p. 7.

Lo Jui-ch'ing, 中華人民共和國治安管理處罰條例草案的說明 (Explanation of the Draft Law of the People's Republic of China on the Handling of Criminal Cases) PD, October 3, 1957, p. 4.

我國肅反鬥爭的成就和今後的任務 (The Success of Our Country's Purge Struggle and the Task Ahead) *Study*, 1 (January 3) 1958, pp. 2-9.

公安工作必須進一步地貫徹群眾路線 (Public Security Work Must Go a Step Further in Carrying Out the Mass Line) PD, June 3, 1958, p. 3.

在慶祝中國人民解放軍建軍三十五周年大會上的講話 (Speech at the Reception for the Celebration of the 35th Anniversary of the Founding of the Chinese People's Libration Army) PD, August 2, 1962, p. 2.

學習雷鋒 (Learn From Lei Feng) PD, March 5, 1963, p. 2.

一個極其重要的政治原則 (An Extremely Important Political Principle) PD, August 3, 1964, p. 2.

紀念戰勝德國法西斯,把反對美帝國主義鬥爭進行到底 (Commemorate the Victory Over German Fascism, Carry the Struggle Against US Imperialism Through to the End) KMD, May 11, 1965, pp. 1-2.

人民戰勝了日本法西斯,人民也一定能夠戰勝美帝主義 (The People Were Able to Defeat Japanese Fascism, the People Also Certainly Will Be Able to Defeat US Imperialism) KMD, September 4, 1965, pp. 2-3.

Lu Ting-i, 百花齊放,百鳥爭鳴 (Let a Hundred Flowers Bloom, a Hundred Schools Contend) PHB, 1957, pp. 565-571.

紀念整風運動十五周年 (Comemorating the 15th Anniversary of the Rectification Movement) PD, March 5, 1957, pp. 2-3.

我們同資產階級右派的根本分歧 (Our Fundamental Divergence with the Bourgeois Rightists) PD, July 12, 1957, p. 2.

教育必須與生產勞動相結合 (Education Must Become Coordinated with Productive Labor) PD, September 2, 1958, p. 2.

工農羣衆學哲學的意義 (The Significance of the Study of Philosophy by the Working and Farming Masses) PD, October 11, 1958, p. 7.

反右傾, 鼓幹勁, 配合增產節約運動, 大搞文化革命 (Oppose Right Deviation, Drum Up Labor Enthusiasm, Join the Economy in Production Movement, Make a Big Cultural Revolution) PD, October 31, 1959, p. 2.

教學必須改革 (Teaching Must Be Reformed) PD, April 10, 1969, p. 2.

在全國文教羣英大會上的祝詞 (Words of Congratulations at the National Meeting of Mass Heroes in Culture and Education) PD, June 2, 1960, p. 1.

會勞動會從事文藝活動的人是最好的文藝工作者 (People Who Can Both Labor and Carry On Literary and Artistic Activities Are the Best Literary and Artistic Workers) PD, November 27, 1964, pp. 1-2.

Ma Ming-fang, 財貿戰線上的職工, 鼓足幹勁奮勇向前 (The Task on the Finance and Trade Front Is to Drum Up Labor Enthusiasm and Fight Forward) PD, June 23, 1958, p. 3.

把財政金融工作, 企業財務工作推向一個新的發展階段 (Push Treasury Finance Work and Business

Finance Work to a New Stage of Development) PD, March 29, 1960, p. 7.

把銀行工作推進到新的階段 (Push Banking Work to a New Stage) PD, June 15, 1960, p. 2.

Ma Wen-jui, 我國社會主義建設中的勞動力問題 (The Problem of Labor Power in Our Country's Socialist Construction) RF, 5 (March 1,) 1961, pp. 6-16.

Mao Tse-tung, "Combat Liberalism" *Selected Works*, Vol. 11 (Peking, 1965) pp. 31-34.

"Problems of War and Strategy" *Ibid.*, pp. 219-236.

關於農業合作社問題 (The Problem of Agricultural Cooperativization) PHB, 1956, pp. 80-86.

論十大關係 (Ten Great Relations) 中共研究 (*Studies on Chinese Communism*) Vol. 4, No. 2 (February, 1970) pp. 116-124.

關於正確處理人民內部矛盾問題 (The Problem of the Correct Handling of Contradictions Among the People) PHB, 1958, pp. 9-20.

介紹一個合作社 (Introducing a Cooperative) RF, 1, (June 1,) 1958, pp. 3-4.

在九月間的重要談話 (Important Conversations in September) RF, 10 (October 16,) 1958, pp. 1-2.

炮打司令部 (Bombard the Headquarters) PD, August 5, 1967, p. 1.

Nieh Jung-chen, 堅決保衛社會主義的科學事業 (Firmly Protect the Scientific Tasks of Socialism) PHB, 1958, pp. 159-160.

科學事業必須為生產大躍進服務 (Scientific

Work Must Serve the Great Leap Forward in Production) PD, March 15, 1958, p. 2.

全黨抓科學技術工作,實現技術革命 (The Whole Party Grasps Science and Technology to Realize a Technological Revolution) PD, August 2, 1958, p. 4.

在走上工作崗位以後 (After Walking the Work Beat) CY, 11 (June 1,) 1962, pp. 2-6.

聽毛主席的話,向白求恩學習 (Listen to Chairman Mao's Words, Learn From Bethune) PD, May 31, 1966, p. 4.

Ou Meng-chueh, 廣東反地方主義鬥爭勝利 (The Victory of the Anti-Localist Struggle in Kwangtung) PD, June 6, 1958, p. 4.

古大存,馮白駒的錯誤在哪裏 (Where Did Ku Ta-ts'un and Feng Pai-chü Go Wrong) *New China Half-Monthly*, 19 (October 10,) 1958, pp. 43-45.

從新會縣的辦實踐者半工(農)半讀教育制度 (A Look at the Half Work (Farm) Half Study Educational System From the Experience of Hsin-hui County) PD, October 19, 1964, p. 5.

Ou-yang Ch'in, 同削弱黨的領導作用的傾向作鬥爭 (Struggle Against the Deviation of Weakening the Leadership Function of the Party) PD, September 21, 1956, p. 4.

財貿工作的政治觀點,生產觀點,和羣眾觀點問題 (The Problem of the Political Viewpoint, the Production Viewpoint, and the Mass Viewpoint in Finance and Trade Work) PD, November 14, 1959, p. 7.

關於農業機械的幾個問題 (A Few Problems of Agricultural Mechanization) PD, December 21, 1959, p. 7.

新形勢,新階段,新任務 (The New Form, the New Stage, the New Task) PD, January 4, 1960, p. 7.

發揚黨的優良作風 (Make Flourish the Excellent Party Work Style) PD, July 4, 1960, p. 7.

必須把革命進行到底 (It Is Necessary to Carry Out Revolution to the End) PD, October 13, 1960, p. 7; October 14, 1960, p. 7.

加強黨的建設,不斷提高黨的領導水平 (Strengthen the Construction of the Party, Continuously Raise the Party's Leadership Level) PD, July 21, 1961, p. 7.

毛澤東思想——勞動人民手裏的尖銳武器 (The Thought of Mao Tse-tung—a Sharp Weapon in the Hands of the Laboring People) PD, July 11, 1964, p. 5.

P'an Fu-sheng, 目前河南農村的階級鬥爭形勢 (The Present Condition of Class Struggle in the Rural Areas of Honan) *New China Half-Monthly,* 23 (December 10) 1957, pp. 121-123.

正確處理副業生產中的各種關係,大力發展農村副業生產 (Correctly Handle All the Relations in Side-Line Production, Put Great Effort into Developing Agricultural Side-Line Production) PHB, 1965, pp. 533-534.

講話 (Speech) PD, February 2, 1967, p. 2.

跟著毛主席革命到底 (Make Revolution with Chairman Mao to the End) PD, March 21, 1967, pp. 1, 3.

堅定同無產階級革命派站在一起 (Staunchly Stand on the Side of the Proletarian Revolutionary Faction) PD, May 13, 1967, pp. 2-3.

P'eng Chen, 在北京市宣傳工作會議上作報告 (Report at a Meeting of Propaganda Workers of Peking) PD, April 22, 1957, p. 1.

談堅持和風細雨的方法 (Talk About Upholding the Method of Gentle Breeze and Light Rain) PD, May 10, 1957, p. 1.

"五一"講話 (May Day Speech) PD, May 2, 1958, p. 1.

在慶祝中華人民共和國成立十二周年典禮上的講話 (Speech at the Ceremony Celebrating the 12th Anniversary of the Founding of the People's Republic of China) PD, October 2, 1961, p. 2.

講話 (Speech) PD, October 3, 1962, p. 4.

在慶祝中華人民共和國成立十四周年大會上的講話 (Speech at the Ceremony Celebrating the 14th Anniversary of the Founding of the People's Republic of China) PD, October 2, 1963, p. 2.

在京劇現代觀摩演出大會上的講話 (Speech at the Meeting of Actors in the Modern Peking Operas) RF, 14 (July 31,) 1964, pp. 18-24.

在慶祝中華人民共和國成立十五周年大會上的講話 (Speech at the Ceremony Celebrating the 15th Anniversary of the Founding of the People's Republic of China) PD, October 2, 1964, p. 2.

代表黨中央作重要報告 (important Report, Representing the Party Center) PD, January 31, 1965, p. 1.

在慶祝中華人民共和國成立十六周年大會上的講話 (Speech at the Ceremony Celebrating the 16th Anniversary of the Founding of the People's Republic of China) KMD, October 3, 1965, p. 1.

P'eng Te-huai, "A Condensation of P'eng Te-huai's Talks at the Lushan Conference in 1959", *Facts and Features*, Vol. II, No. 9 (February, 1969) pp. 27-29.

Po I-po, 打破辦工業的神秘觀點 (Destroy the Fetishist Outlook in Industrial Management) RF, 3 (July 18,) 1958, pp. 18-21.

一九五九年工業戰線的任務 (The Task on the Industrial Front in 1959) PD, January 1, 1959, p. 2.

大搞羣衆運動,使生産高潮滾滾向前 (Get with the Big Mass Movement, Let the High Tide of Production Roll Forward) PD, October 28, 1959, p. 2.

爭取我國工業生產建設的新勝利 (Fight Through to New Victories in Our Country's Construction of Industrial Production) RF 3-4 (February 1,) 1961, pp. 19-25.

鼓足幹勁,爭取一九六二年工業生產的更大成就 (Drum Up Work Enthusiasm, Struggle for Even Greater Results in Industrial Production in 1962) Peking *Daily Worker*, December 31, 1961, p. 1.

在階級鬥爭的熔爐中鍛煉 (Tempering in the Furnace of Class Struggle) PD, May 15, 1964, p. 5.

Saifudin, 層層批駁地方民族主義 (Rebutting Point by Point Local Nationalism) PD, December 26, 1957, p. 4.

毛澤東文藝思想在新疆的偉大勝利 (The Great Victory of the Literary Thought of Mao Tse-tung in Sinkiang) PD, July 27, 1960, p. 7.

Shu T'ung, 掌握不斷革命的理論武器,促使農業生產不斷躍進 (Grasp the Theoretical Weapon of Uninterrupted Revolution, Propel an Uninterrupted Leap Forward in Agricultural Production) PD, February 6, 1960, p. 7.

認真地學習和運用毛澤東思想 (Sincerely Study and Use the Thought of Mao Tse-tung) PD, April 12, 1960, p. 7.

Sung Jen-ch'iung, 無產階級領導工業基本方針 (The Basic Direction of Leadership of Industry by the Proletariat) PD, January 18, 1960, p. 7.

講話 (Speech) PD, February 2, 1967, p. 2.

T'an Chen-lin, 在中央集中領導下充分發揮地方積極性 (Under the Centralized Leadership of the Center,

Fully Develop the Activism of the Locality) PD, October 9, 1956, p. 4.

關於一九五六年到一九六七年全國農業發展綱要（第二次修正草案）的說明 (Explanation of the Outline Program for National Agricultural Development, 1966-1967 "Second Revised Draft") PD, May 28, 1958, pp. 1-2.

論我國今年夏季的空前大豐收 (Our Country's Unprecedented Summer Bumper Harvest of this Year) PD, August 11, 1958, pp. 1, 4.

現代化的大規模農業建設開始了 (Large Scale Agricultural Modernization Has Begun) PD, October 29, 1959, p. 7.

為提前實現全國農業發展綱要而奮鬥 (Struggle to Realize the National Program of Agricultural Development) PD, April 7, 1960, p. 2.

毛主席身體這樣健康是全國人民的幸福 (That Chairman Mao Is So Healthy is the Happiness of the People of the Whole Country) PD, October 8, 1966, p. 1.

T'an Ch'i-lung, 還是辦人民公社好 (Let's Do a Good Job in Running People's Communes) RF, 9 (October 1), 1958 pp. 21-24.

T'ao Chu, 更全面的,更有效地執行以農村為重點的方針 (On an Even More Overall Basis and Even More Effectively Implement the Direction of Agriculture as the Point of Emphasis) PD, September 21, 1956, p. 9.

當前農村整頓鬥爭是農業社會主義改造的繼續 (The Current Rectification Struggle in the Rural Areas Is the Continuation of Agricultural Socialist Reform) SD, September 9, 1957, pp. 1-2.

駁"糧食增產有限"論 (Refuting the Theory That "There Is a Limit to the Amount of Food that Can Be Produced") RF, 5 (August 1,) 1958, pp. 1-5.

虎門公社調查報告 (Investigation Report on the Tiger Gate Commune) PD, February 25, 1959, p. 7.

太陽的光輝 (The Brilliance of the Sun) PD, June 3, 1959, p. 7.

總路線與工作方法 (The General Line and Work Methods) PD, June 18, 1959, p. 7.

革命的堅定性 (Revolutionary Resolution) PD, September 2, 1959, p. 7.

歌頌人民公社 (Singing the Praises of the People's Commune) RF, 19 (October 1,) 1959, pp. 61-66.

思想,"感情",文采 (Thought, "Emotion," Style) PD, January 11, 1960, p. 7.

關於過渡時期的規律問題的商榷 (Discussion of the Problem of the Laws of the Transitional Period) PD, August 5, 1960, p. 7.

人民公社在前進 (The Future of the People's Communes) PD, February 28, 1964, pp. 5-6.

一定要演好革命現代戲 (We Certainly Want to Show Good Modern Revolutionary Plays) PD, July 29, 1965, p. 5.

五億人民沿着社會主義道路前進的南針 (The Compass for the Future Socialist Road to Be Followed by Five Hundred Million Peasants) PD, August 2, 1965, p. 5.

革命現代戲要迅速地全部地佔領舞台 (Revolutionary Modern Plays Must Rapidly and Utterly Occupy the Stage) PD, August 28, 1965, p. 2.

T'ao Lu-chia, 廣泛地進行"全國一盤棋"的教育 (Broadly Implement the Lesson of the Whole Country Is One Chess Board) RF, 5 (March 1,) 1959, pp. 25-29.

全新的時代,全新的人 (A Wholly New Era, a Wholly new Man) PD, March 16, 1960, p. 7.

工廠大辦學校的偉大意義 (The Great Significance of Factories Managing Schools) PD, June 11, 1960, p. 7.

讓大寨精神遍地開花結果 (Let the Spirit of Tachai Bloom Forth and Bear Fruit Everywhere) PD, October 5, 1965, p. 5.

Teng Hsiao-p'ing, 關於修改黨的章程的報告 (Report on the Revision of the Party Constitution) PHB, 1956, pp. 26-37.

在青年團第三次全國代表大會上---代表中共中央致祝詞 (Words of Congratulations, Representing the Chinese Communist Party Center, to the Third National Congress of the Youth League) PD, May 16, 1957, p. 1.

關於整風運動的報告 (Report on the Rectification Movement) PHB, 1958, pp. 33-42.

中國人民大團結和世界人民大團結 (The Great Solidarity of the Chinese People and the Great Solidarity of the Peoples of the World) PD, October 2, 1959, pp. 2-3.

在中央工作會議上的檢討 (Examination at a Central Work Conference) *Studies on Chinese Communism,* Vol. 3, No. 11 (November, 1969) pp. 90-94.

Teng Tzu-hui, 論農業合作社內部矛盾與民主辦社 (Internal Contradictions in the Agricultural Cooperatives and Democratic Coop Management) PD, May 7, 1957, p. 4.

關於農業合作社擴大再生產及其他幾個問題 (On the Expansion, Production, and Other Problems of the Agricultural Cooperatives) PHB, 1958, pp. 520-524.

全國農業社會主義建設先進單位代表會議上的開幕詞 (Opening Words at the National Meeting of

Representatives of Advanced Units in Agricultural Socialist Construction) PD, December 26, 1958, p. 2.

農業戰線的光榮任務 (The Glorious Task on the Agricultural Front) PD, April 27, 1959, p. 5.

積極辦好公共食堂,認真貫徹自願原則 (Actively Do a Good Job in Managing Public Mess Halls, Sincerely Carry Through the Principle of Voluntariness) China Youth, 12 (June 1,) 1959, pp. 5-6.

中國農業的社會主義改造 (The Socialist Reform of Chinese Agriculture) PD, October 18, 1959, p. 6.

關於知識青年到農村去的幾個問題 (A Few Problems in Educated Youths Going to the Countryside) CY, 13 (July 1,) 1962, pp. 2-5.

Teng Ying-ch'ao, 黨更要加強婦女工作領導,團結和發揮廣大婦女群眾的力量 (The Party Must Strengthen Its Leadership of Women's Work, Unite with and Make Flourish the Strength of the Broad Female Masses) PHB, 1957, pp. 94-95.

發揚"三八"革命傳統,向婦女徹底的解放的目標前進 (Develop the Revolutionary Traditions of "March 8", Advance to the Great Goal of the Thorough Liberation of Women) PD, March 8, 1960, p. 2.

Ts'ai Ch'ang, 積極培養和提拔更多更好的女幹部 (Actively Cultivate and Promote Even More and Better Female Cadres) PD, September 25, 1956, p. 3.

高舉毛澤東思想的旗幟,進一步發動婦女,為實現一九六零年繼續躍進而奮鬥 (Raise High the Banner of the Thought of Mao Tse-tung, Move a Step Further in Mobilizing Women, Fight for a Continued Leap Forward in 1960) PD, February 25, 1960, p. 4.

Tseng Hsi-sheng, 巨大的勝利,深刻的教訓 (A Giant Victory, A Deep Lesson) PD, March 10, 1958, pp. 2-3.

總結去年的經驗，搞好今年的大躍進 (Sum Up Last Year's Experience, Get a Good Great Leap Forward This Year) PD, March 3, 1959, p. 7.

同右傾機會主義堅決作鬥爭 (Firmly Struggle Against Right Opportunist Thought) PD, October 21, 1959, p. 7.

人民公社在安徽 (The People's Communes in Anhwei) PD, December 6, 1959, p. 5.

認清大好形勢，千方百計地為實現今年的更大躍進而奮鬥 (Clearly Recognize the Excellent Conditions, Fight in a Hundred Places with a Thousand Tricks to Realize an Even Greater Leap Forward this Year) PD, January 7, 1960, p. 7.

關於全黨辦報問題 (The Problem of the Whole Party's Management of Newspapers) PD, June 16, 1960, p. 7.

學習毛澤東同志實事求是的精神 (Learn From Comrade Mao Tse-tung's Spirit of Seeking Truth From Facts) PD, July 6, 1960, p. 7.

Tung Pi-wu, 關於工農群眾生活及其他 (The Problem of the Working and Farming Masses and Other Matters) *China Youth Daily,* April 13, 1957, p. 3.

Ulanfu, 在民族工作座談會上的總結發言 (Summary Words at the Nationalities Work Meeting) SD, August 24, 1957, p. 4.

思想大解放，民族大團結，生產大躍進 (A Big Liberation of Thought, the Big Solidarity of the Nationalities, a Big Leap Forward in Production) PD, May 21, 1958, p. 2.

不斷發展我國各民族的團結 (Continually Develop the Great Unity of All Nationalities of Our Country) RF, 19 (October 1,) 1959, pp. 43-50

認真學習毛澤東思想, 廣泛宣傳毛澤東思想 (Sincerely Study the Thought of Mao Tse-tung, Broadly Propagate the Thought of Mao Tse-tung) PD, April 6, 1960, p. 2.

Wang Chia-hsiang, 中國人民勝利的國際意義 (The International Significance of the Victory of the Chinese People) RF, 19 (October 1,) 1959, pp. 56-60.

Wang Ts'ung-wu, 黨的團結和紀律 (Party Solidarity and Discipline) RF, 24 (December 16,) 1959, pp. 9-15.

Wang En-mao, 為新疆維吾爾自治區各民族人民和全國各民族人民同過渡到社會主義而奮鬥 (The People of All Nationalities in the Sinkiang-Uighur Autonomous District and the Peoples of the Nationalities of the Whole Country Are Fighting Together for the Transition to Socialism) PD, September 28, 1956, p.

Wang Feng, 是社會主義還是民族主義? (Socialism or Nationalism?) PD, March 2, 1958, p. 2; March 3, 1958, p. 4.

Wang Jen-chung, 集體領導的原則是不是適用於工礦企業 (Is the Principle of Collective Leadership Suited to the Management of Factories and Mines?) PD, September 19, 1956, p. 7.

大轉變和大躍進 (A Big Change and a Great Leap Forward) PD, February 15, 1958, p. 4.

依靠群眾, 勢如破竹 (Depend Upon the Masses, Whose Strength Is Like That of Bamboo Sprouts) RF, 1 (June 1,) 1958, pp. 39-46.

讀書, 談心, 想問題 (Read Books, Speak Your Mind, Think About Problems) PD, April 29, 1959, p. 7.

領導農業生產的幾點經驗 (A Few Experiences in Leading Agricultural Production) RF, 1 (January 1,) 1961, pp. 17-21.

認真學習和運用"矛盾論" (Sincerely Study and Use "On Contradictions") PD, July 25, 1965, p. 5.

突出政治,用毛澤東思想統帥一切 (Politics to the Fore, Use the Thought of Mao Tse-tung to Command Everything) PD, April 7, 1966, pp. 2-3.

Wang Shou-tao, 繼續發展交通運輸事業,更好的為生產和生活服務 (Continue to Develop Transportation, Let It Serve Production and Life Even Better) PD, May 26, 1961, p. 7.

Wu Chih-p'u, 由農業生產合作社到人民公社 (From the Agricultural Cooperatives to the People's Communes) RF, 8 (September 15,) 1958, pp. 5-12.

論悲觀主義 (On Pessimism) *New China Half-Monthly,* 19 (October 10,) 1958, pp. 39-42.

學習毛澤東同志的著作 (Study the Works of Comrade Mao Tse-tung) PD, January 1, 1960, p. 7.

矛盾是社會主義社會發展的動力 (Contradictions Are the Motive Force of Socialist Social Development) PD, June 14, 1960, p. 7.

Wu Te, 工業建設中的一個突出的矛盾 (An Emerging Contradiction in Industrial Construction) PD, September 28, 1956, p. 3.

解放思想迎接技術革命 (Liberate Thought, Greet the Technological Revolution) PD, May 24, 1958, p. 2.

必須堅決徹底地執行黨的政策 (It Is Necessary Firmly and Thoroughly to Uphold the Policy of the Party) PD, December 22, 1960, p. 7.

發言 (Speech) PD, December 4, 1966, p. 2.

Wu Yü-chang, 漢語拼音方案在各方面應用 (How

the Phonetic System Ought to Be Used) PD, February 17, 1964, p. 5.

Yang Ch'eng-wu, 大樹特樹偉大統帥毛主席絕對權威, 大樹特樹偉大毛澤東思想的絕對權威 (Very Particularly Establish the Absolute Authority of the Great Generalissimo Chairman Mao, Very Particularly Establish the Absolute Authority of the Great Thought of Mao Tse-tung) PD, November 3, 1967, pp. 2-3.

Yang Hsien-chen, 捍衛馬列主義，粉碎現代修正主義 (Protect Marxism-Leninism, Smash Modern Revisionism) PD, May 5, 1958, p. 1.

Yang I-ch'en, 論建立商品生產基地網 (Establishing a Nexus of Local Markets) PD, February 12, 1960, p. 7.

Yang Te-chih, 學習王杰同志，做徹底革命派 (Learn from Comrade Wang Chieh, Be a Complete Revolutionist) PD, November 18, 1965, p. 5.

Yeh Chien-ying, 偉大的戰畧決議 (Great Strategy Decides the War) PD, August 30, 1965, p. 2.

高舉毛澤東思想偉大紅旗，以抗大為榜樣辦各式學校 (Raise High the Great Red Banner of the Thought of Mao Tse-tung and Manage Schools After the Style of Resist Japan University) PD, August 2, 1966, p. 2.

Yeh Fei, 思想解放，工作躍進 (A Liberation of Thought, a Leap Forward in Work) May 22, 1958, p. 2.

為今年的繼續躍進奮勇前進 (Bravely Advance in a Continuing Leap Forward this Year) PD, February 8, 1960, p. 7.

V. **Other Chinese Communist Sources.**

Chang Hsiao-i (張孝義) 領導和組織農業生產的一些體會 (A Few Notions on Leading and Organizing Agricultural Production) PD, January 4, 1961, p. 7.

Chang Tzu-ch'eng (張子成) "合二為一"就是不要革命 ("Two Combine Into One" Means No Revolution) RF, 23-24, (September 15,) 1964, pp. 27-28.

Chao Han (趙 漢) 遵守黨章,增強黨性 (Obey the Party Constitution, Strengthen Party Nature) PD, October 17, 1961, p. 7.

做好黨的基層組織的經常工作 (Do a Good Job in Routine Work at the Basic Level Party Organizations) PD, March 30, 1963, p. 5.

Chao Shou-i (趙守一) 在毛澤東思想領導下,加強農業科學技術工作 (Under the Guidance of Mao Tse-tung's Thought, Strengthen Agricultural Science and Technological Work) PD, March 19, 1960, p. 7.

Ch'en Ch'i-t'ung (陳其通) 在毛澤東思想哺育下的部隊 (Literary and Art Work by the Troops Under the Nurture of the Thought of Mao Tse-tung) PD, May 30, 1962, p. 5.

Ch'en Yuan-hui (陳元暉) 實用主義—真理就是一種權宜手段 (Pragmatism: Truth Is Nothing But the Expedient Way) PD, May 30, 1963, p. 5.

Ch'eng Sheng-i (程生義) 對"文藝報"的幾點批評和建議 (A Few Criticisms and Suggestions for *Literary Gazette*) *Literary Gazette*, 2 (February 16,) 1965, pp. 26-28.

Cheng Yuan (鄭遠) 學習黨的發展國民經濟的總方針 (Study the Party's General Direction for the Development of the National Economy) PD, October 16, 1962, p. 5.

發展農業生產的必由之路 (The Necessary Road for Agricultural Development) PD, November 11, 1962, p. 5.

Chi Pen-yü (戚本禹) "海瑞罵皇帝"和"海瑞罷官"的反動實質 (The Reactionary Nature of "Hai Jui Scolds the Emperor" and "Hai Jui Is Dismissed From Office") PD, April 2, 1966, pp. 5-6.

評"前線""北京日報"的資產階級立場 (Criticizing the Bourgeois Standpoint of *Front Line* and the *Peking Daily*) PD, April 16, 1966, pp. 1-2.

愛國主義還是賣國主義 (Patriotism or Treason?) PD, April 1, 1967, pp. 1-3.

Chiang Ch'ing (江青) 講話 (Speech) PD, December 4, 1966, pp. 1-2.

(Speech) PD, April 21, 1967, p. 2.

談京劇革命 (Talk About the Revolution in Peking Opera) PD, May 10, 1967, p. 1.

Chou Kuo-ch'üan (周國全) 實行集體領導是實現正確領導的重要保證 (To Implement Collective Leadership Is an Important Guarantee of Implementing Correct Leadership) PD, May 18, 1963, p. 5.

Ch'un Mei (春梅) 自我批判 (Self-Criticism) *Ta-Kung News*, (Peking) December 19, 1964, p. 3.

Chung Hsuan-tsao (鐘宣造) 從"魏徵傳"的出籠看陸定一的反動嘴臉 (Lu Ting-i's Counter-Revolutionary Mug Revealed by the Hawking of *The Story of Wei Cheng*) PD, November 9, 1967, p. 4.

Hsiao Shu (蕭述) "合二為一"論的反辯證法實質 (The Anti-Dialectical Nature of the Theory of "Two Combine into One") PD, August 14, 1965, p. 5.

Hsiao Tung (曉東), Hou Tso-ch'ing (侯作卿), 中國赫魯曉夫和所謂"三十年代文藝" (China's Khrushchev and the So-Called "Literature of the Thirties") PD, September 16, 1967. p. 3.

Hsu Fei-kuang (徐非光) 革命的幹勁和小資產階級的狂熱 (Revolutionary Work Enthusiasm and Petty Bourgeois Fanaticism) PD, September 12, 1959, p. 7.

Hsu Li-ch'ün (許立羣) 關於黨的幹部理論教育工作 (The Theoretical Education Work for Party Cadres) PD, September 26, 1956, p. 3.

Hsu Pang-i (許邦儀) 更好地發揮農村基層組織的領導核心作用 (Develop Even Better the Nuclear Leadership Function of the Rural Basic Level Party Organizations) RF, 20 (October 16) 1961, pp. 21-25.

Hsu Yen-sheng (徐寅生) 關於如何打乒乓球 (How to Play Ping-Pong) PD, January 17, 1965, pp. 1-2.

Juan Ming (阮銘), Juan Jo-ying (阮若英), 周揚顛倒歷史的一支暗箭 (Some Sneaky Business by Chou Yang in Distorting History) PD, July 4, 1966, pp. 2-3.

K'ang Chuoh (康濯) 劉少奇同志在徐水 (Comrade Liu Shao-ch'i at Hsu Shui) PD, September 18, 1958, p. 2.

試論近年間的短篇小說 (Short Stories of the Past Few Years) *Literary Review* 5 (September, 1962) pp. 12-29.

Kao Chü (高炬) 向反黨反社會主義的黑線開火 (Open Fire on the Anti-Party Anti-Socialist Black Line) PD, May 9, 1966, p. 1.

Ko Chih-ta (葛致達) 財政資金和信貸資金的安排和管理問題 (The Problem of Managing and Allocating Finance Capital and Credit Capital) PD, March 31, 1961, p. 7.

K'o Liu-liu (柯六六) 懷爸爸,做堅強的革命接班人 (Remember Papa, Be a Staunch Revolutionary Successor) PD, June 8, 1965, p. 6.

Kuan Feng (關鋒), Lin Chieh (林杰), "海瑞罵皇帝"和"海瑞罷官"是反黨反社會主義的兩株大毒草 (Hai Jui Scolds the Emperor and *Hai Jui Is Dismissed From Office* Are a Couple of Anti-Party Anti-Socialist Poisonous Weeds) PD, April 5, 1966, pp. 5-6.

Kuan Ta-t'ung (管大同) 關於農村家庭副業,自留地,集市貿易問題 (Rural Handicrafts, Retained Plots, and Collective Markets.) *Ta Kung News* (Peking) July 5, 1961, p. 3.

Kung Wen-sheng (貢文聲) 駁孫冶方的修正主義"經濟綱領" (Rebutting Sun Ye-fang's Revisionist "Economic Outline") PD, August 10, 1965, p. 4.

Kuo Mo-jo (郭沫若) 替曹操翻案 (Reversing the Verdict on Ts'ao Ts'ao) PD, March 23, 1959, p. 7.

Li Li (李立) 正確發揚黨內民主的幾個問題 (A Few Questions on the Development of Inner Party Democracy) PD, July 3, 1962, p. 5.

Lin Chieh (林杰) 打倒奴隸主義,嚴格遵守無產階級的紀律 (Down With Slavism, Strictly Obey Proletarian Revolutionary Discipline) PD, June 16, 1967, p. 3.

Lin Mo-han (林默涵) 一篇引起爭論的小說 (A Story that Has Aroused a Controversy) PD, March 12, 1957, p. 7.

Lin Tou-tou (林豆豆) 劉亞樓叔叔永遠活在我們心裏 (Uncle Liu Ya-lou Will Always Live in Our Hearts) PD, May 12, 1965, p. 6.

Liu Ch'ung (柳冲), 加強集中統一,發揚黨內民主 (Strengthen Centralized Unity, Develop Inner-Party Democracy) PD, April 3, 1962, p. 5.

Liu Mien-chih (劉勉之) (Wu Han), 海瑞罵皇帝 (Hai Jui Scolds the Emperor) PD, June 16, 1959, p. 8.

Lo Keng-mo (駱耕漠), 論我國農村人民公社的三級所有制 (The Three Tier Ownership System in Our Country's People's Communes) *China Youth*, 1 (January 1) 1961, pp. 4-9.

關於如何正確徹底地實行按勞分配原則的問題 (The Problem of Correctly and Thoroughly

Implementing the Principle of Allocation on the Basis of Labor) *Ta Kung News,* (Peking) April 16, 1962, p. 3.

Lu Hsueh-fu (陸學斌), 試談曹操戲 (The Discussion About Ts'ao Ts'ao Plays) PD, June 9, 1959, p. 7.

Lu Li (魯力), 領導農業生產必須從實際出發 (The Leadership of Agricultural Production Must Begin from Reality) PD, November 12, 1960, p. 7.

Lung Wen (龍文), 全面規劃, 加強領導 (Overall Planning, Strengthen Leadership) RF, 10 (September 19) 1970, pp. 35-37.

Miao Chu-huang (繆楚黃), 中國共產黨簡要歷史 *(A Short History of the Communist Party of China)* (Peking, 1963) 214 pp.

P'an Chün (潘俊), "人的階級性" 是一株反毛澤東思想的毒草 ("The Class Character of Man" Is an Anti-Thought of Mao Tse-tung Poisonous Weed) PD, April 30, 1967, p. 4.

Teng T'o (鄧拓), 燕山夜話 *(Evening Talks on Swallow Mountain)* (Hong Kong, 1966) 157 pp.

鄧拓詩文選 *(Selected Prose and Poetry of Teng T'o)* (Hong Kong, 1966) 151 pp.

T'ien Ch'ing-hsiang (田慶祥), 無聲的教育 (A Voiceless Education) PD, July 30, 1963, p. 1.

Tseng San (曾三), 讓檔案工作更好地為國家建設服務 (Let Documentary Work Serve National Construction Even Better) PD, October 2, 1956, p. 6.

Wang Chia-tao (汪家道), 講話 (Speech) PD, February 2, 1967, p. 2.

Wang Chih-hsiang (王之襄), 我怎樣下了決心參加

勞動 (How I Decided to Participate in Labor) August 19, 1963, p. 2.

Wang K'uang (王匡), 反對地方主義 (Oppose Localism) PD, February 25, 1958, p. 7.

Wang Meng (王蒙), 組織部新來的青年 (The Young Newcomer at the Organization Department) *People's Literature,* September, 1956, pp. 29-43.

Wu Han (吳晗), 論海瑞 (Hai Jui) PD, September 21, 1959, p. 11.

海瑞罷官及其他 ("Hai Jui Is Dismissed From Office" and Other Works) (Hong Kong, 1966 (?)) 56 pp.

關於"海瑞罷官"的自我批評 (Self Criticism Concerning Hai Jui Is Dismissed From Office) PD, December 30, 1965, pp. 5-6.

Yang Hsiu (楊秀), 應該培養這樣的共產主義精神 (This Is the Kind of Communist Spirit We Must Cultivate) *China Youth,* 5 (March 1) 1960, pp. 5-6, 35.

Yang P'ing (楊柄), 曹操應當肯定嗎 (Should Ts'ao Ts'ao Be Affirmed?) PD, April 21, 1959, p. 7.

Yao Wen-yuan (姚文元), 評新歷史劇"海瑞罷官" (Criticizing the New Historical Play, *Hai Jui Is Dismissed From Office*) PD, November 30, 1965, pp. 5-6.

評三家村 (Criticizing the "Three Family Village") PD, May 11, 1966, pp. 1, 3-4.

評陶鑄的兩本書 (Criticism of Two Books by T'ao Chu) PD, September 8, 1967, pp. 1-3.

Yeh Ch'ün (葉羣), 古代的一位優秀戰畧家——陸遜 (An Excellent Strategist of Ancient Times—Lu Hsun) PD, June 3, 1962, p. 5.

Yü Kuang-yuan (于光遠), 進一步加強黨對科學工作的領導 (Move a Step Further to Strengthen the Leadership of the Party over Scientific Work) PD, September 27, 1956, p. 5.

VI. Some Other Sources.

Herman Akhminov, "On Methods of Analyzing Soviet Politics" *Bulletin* (of the Institute for the Study of the USSR), Vol. XIV, No. 10 (October, 1967), pp. 3-15.

David Apter, *The Politics of Modernization* (University of Chicago Press, 1967) xvi, 481 pp.

Asian People's Anti-Communist League, *Factional Struggles Within the Chinese Communist Party* (Taipei, 1960) 88 pp.

A. Doak Barnett, *China After Mao* (Princeton: University Press, 1967) 287 pp.

(With a contribution by Ezra Vogel) *Cadres, Bureaucracy, and Political Power in Communist China* (Columbia: University Press, 1967) xxix, 563 pp.

"History's Logic Weighs Against Maoism" *Life* Vol. 62 (January 20, 1967) p. 32.

Richard Baum and Frederick C. Teiwes, *Ssu-Ch'ing: The Socialist Education Movement of 1962-1966* (Berkeley, 1968) 128 pp.

Hubert M. Blalock, *Social Statistics* (New York, 1960) xiv, 465 pp.

Howard L. Boorman, "Liu Shao-ch'i: A Political Profile" *China Quarterly*, 10 (April-June, 1962) pp. 1-22.

Scott A. Boorman, *The Protracted Game: A Wei-ch'i Interpretation of Maoist Revolutionary Strategy* (New York, 1969) xiv, 242 pp.

Conrad Brandt, *Stalin's Failure in China*, 1924-1927 (New York, 1966) xiv, 226 pp.

Philip Bridgham, "Mao's Cultural Revolution in 1967: The Struggle to Seize Power" *China Quarterly*, 34 (April-June, 1969) pp. 6-37.

Crane Brinton, *The Anatomy of Revolution* (New York, 1958) x, 300, viii pp.

Bureau of State Security (Republic of China), 對匪黨"中央關於農村社會主義教育運動中一些具體政策的規定"之分析 *(An Analysis of the Bandit Party's "Central Regulations on Some Concrete Policies in the Rural Socialist Education Movement")* Taiwan, 1965) 11 pp.

Robert Burrows, "Totalitarianism: The Revised Standard Version" *World Politics,* Vol. XXI, No. 2 (January, 1969) pp. 272-294.

David W. Chang, "The Military and Nation-Building in Korea, Burma, and Pakistan" *Asian Survey,* Vol. IX, No. 11 (November, 1969) pp. 818-830.

Wang Gung-wu, *The Structure of Power in North China During the Five Dynasties* (Stanford: University Press, 1967) vii, 257 pp.

Chang Kuo-t'ao: "Mao: A New Portrait by an Old Colleague" New York *Times Magazine,* August 2, 1953, pp. 5, 45-47.

Chang Man, *The* People's Daily *and the* Red Flag *Magazine During the Cultural Revolution* (Kowloon, 1969) 126 pp.

Parris H. Chang, "The Changing Loci of Decision in the CCP," *China Quarterly,* 44 (October-December, 1970) pp. 169-194.

Chao Kuo-chün, "Leadership in the Chinese Communist Party," *Annals of the American Academy of Political and Social Science,* Vol. 321 (January, 1959) pp. 40-50.

David A. Charles, "The Dismissal of Marshal P'eng Teh-huai," in Roderick MacFarquhar, *China Under Mao: Politics Takes Command* (MIT Press, 1966) pp. 20-33.

Jerome Ch'en, *Mao and the Chinese Revolution* (New York, 1965) 419 pp.

"Resolutions of the Tsunyi Conference," *China Quarterly,* 40 (October-December, 1969) pp. 1-38.

Ch'en Kuang (陳光) 對中共八屆中央委員,候補中央委員之調查分析 (Investigation Analysis of the Members and Alternates of the Eighth Central Committee, Communist Party of China" *Bandit Affairs,* Vol. 3, No. 3 (March, 1969) pp. 11-33.

Cheng Chu-yuan, *Communist China's Economy, 1949-1962: Structural Changes and Crises* (Seaton Hall: University Press, 1963) xii, 217 pp.

Ch'ien Tuan-sheng, *The Government and Politics of China* (Harvard: University Press, 1961) pp. xviii, 526.

Chien Yu-shan, *China's Fading Revolution: Army Dissent and Military Divisions, 1967-1968* (Hong Kong, 1969) 405 pp.

Chin Szu-k'ai, "The Party," in Union Research Institute, *Communist China, 1949-1959.* Vol. I (Kowloon, 1961) pp. 1-52.

Chou Ching-wen (周鯨文) 風暴十年 *(Ten Years of Storm)* (Hong Kong, 1962) 5, 19, 2, 9, 12, 588 pp.

Chow Tse-tsung, *The May Fourth Movement: Intellectual Revolution in Modern China* (Stanford: University Press, 1967) xiii, 486 pp.

H.C. Chung, *The Great Proletarian Cultural Revolution: A Terminological Study* (Berkeley, 1967) vii, 72 pp.

Chung Hua-min, Arthur C. Miller, *Madame Mao: A Profile of Chiang Ching* (Hong Kong, 1968) v. 314 pp.

Robert Conquest, *Power and Policy in the USSR: The Struggle for Stalin's Succession, 1945-1960.* (New York, 1967) x, 484.

Richard K. Diao, "The Impact of the Cultural Revolution on China's Economic Elite" *China Quarterly*, 42 (April-June, 1970) pp. 65-87.

Milovan Djilas, *The New Class: An Analysis of the Communist System* (New York, 1957) vii, 214 pp.

Jürgen Domes, "The Role of the Military in the Formation of Revolutionary Committees, 1967-1968" *China Quarterly*, 44 (October-December, 1970) pp. 112-145.

Dennis J. Doolin, *Communist China: The Politics of Student Opposition* (Hoover Institution, 1964) 70 pp.

Anthony Downs, *An Economic Theory of Democracy* (New York, 1957) x, 310 pp.

Inside Bureaucracy (Boston, 1967) xv, 294 pp.

S.N. Eisenstadt, "Bureaucracy and Political Development," in Joseph LaPalombara (ed), *Bureaucracy and Political Development* (Princeton: University Press, 1963) pp. 96-119.

中國共產黨反毛聯盟非常委員會 (Extraordinary Committee of the Anti-Mao Alliance of the Communist Party of China), 誰是馬列主義的叛徒？ *(Who Is the Renegade to Marxism-Leninism?* (Np, 1956) 63 pp.

Merle Fainsod, *How Russia Is Ruled* (revised edition, Harvard: University Press, 1964), ix, 698 pp.

Fang Chun-kuei (方君歸), 從北平"五一節"集會看共匪領導集團現況 (The Current Condition of the Communist Bandit Leadership Clique as Viewed From the May Day Meetings in Peiping) *Bandit Affairs*, Vol. 11, No. 5 (May, 1968), pp. 1-11.

從"十一"偽慶活動看共匪領導集團現況 (The Current Condition of the Communist Bandit Leadership

Clique as Seen From the Activities in the Phony National Day Celebration) *Bandit Affairs,* Vol. 11, No. 11 (November, 1968) pp. 5-12.

Fang Ning (方寧), 共匪"文化大革命"以來被整肅或受批判重要匪幹調查 (Study of the Important Bandit Cadres Who Have Been Purged or Criticized Since the Start of the Communist Bandits' "Great Cultural Revolution") *Bandit Affairs,* Vol. 11, No. 1 (January, 1968) pp. 77-92.

近半年來被整肅或受批判之重要匪幹調查 (Study of the Important Bandit Cadres Who Have Been Purged or Criticized in the Half Past Year).

Herbert Feith, *The Decline of Constitutional Democracy in Indonesia* Cornell, 1962) xx, 618 pp.

W.E. Fernside and W.B. Holther, *Fallacy: The Counterfeit of Argument* (Englewood Cliffs, 1959) 218 pp.

Michel P. Gehlen and Michael McBride, "The Soviet Central Committee: An Elite Analysis" *American Political Science Review,* Vol. LXII, No. 4 (December, 1968) pp. 1234-1241.

Alexander L. George, *The Chinese Communist Army in Action: The Korean War and Its Aftermath* (Columbia: University Press, 1967) xii, 255 pp.

John R. Gillis, "Political Decay and the European Revolutions, 1789-1848" *World Politics,* Vol. XXII, No. 3 (April, 1970) pp. 344-370.

John Gittings, *The Role of the Chinese Army* (Oxford: University Press, 1967) xx, 331 pp.

Merle Goldman, *Literary Dissent in Communist China* (Harvard: University Press, 1967) xvii, 343 pp.

"The Unique 'Blooming and Contending' of 1961-1962" *China Quarterly,* 37 (January-March, 1969) pp. 54-83.

Hans Grandquist, *The Red Guard: A Report on Mao's Revolution* (New York, 1967) ix, 159.

Jack Gray, "Mao's Economic Thoughts" *Far Eastern Economic Review,* Vol. LXVII, No. 3 (January 15, 1970) pp. 16-18.

John C. Harsanyi, "Rational Choice Models of Political Behavior vs. Functionalist and Conformist Theories," *World Politics,* Vol. XXI, No. 4 (July 1969) pp. 513-536.

Charles Hoffmann, "Industrial Work Incentives," in Francis Harper (ed), *This is China: Analysis of Mainland Trends and Events* (Hong Kong, 1965) pp. 81-99.

Alice Langley Hsieh, *Communist China's Strategy in the Nuclear Era,* (Englewood Cliffs, 1962) xx, 204 pp.

Hsu Kai-yu, *Chou En-lai: China's Gray Eminence* (New York, 1968) xviii, 294.

Hsuan Mo (玄 默), 楊匪成武事件的幕前幕後 (The Open and the Hidden Story of the Bandit Yang Ch'eng-wu Incident) *Bandit Affairs* Vol. 11, No. 8 (August, 1968) pp. 43-56.

Huang T'ien-chien (黃天健), 匪偽政權十八年 *(Eighteen Years of Bandit-Puppet Power)* (Taipei, 1967) 7, 11, 908 pp.

Samuel P. Huntington, *The Soldier and the State* (Cambridge, 1957) xiii, 534 pp.

Political Order in Changing Societies (Yale: University Press, 1968) xii, 488 pp.

Ronald Inglehart, "An End to European Integration?" *American Political Science Review,* Vol. LXI, No. 1 (March, 1967) pp. 91-105.

Institute on China Mainland Problems, *The Bandit Party's Control Methods and Work Methods* (匪黨控制方式與工作方式) (Taipei, 1956) 172 pp.

Investigation Bureau, Legal Administrative Ministry (Republic of China) *The Communist Bandits' Special Work* (共匪特務工作) (Taipei, 1963) 4, 206 pp.

Andrew C. Janos, "Authority and Violence", in Harry Eckstein (ed) Internal War (New York, 1964) pp. 130-141.

Chalmers A. Johnson, *Peasant Nationalism and Communist China: The Emergence of Revolutionary China, 1937-1945* (Stanford: University Press, 1962) pp. vii, 256.

Kan Yu-lan (甘友蘭), 毛澤東及其集團 *(Mao Tse-tung and His Clique* (Kowloon, 1954) 8, 250, 3 pp.

Donald W. Klein, "The 'Next Generation' of Chinese Communist Leadership," in MacFarquhar, *op. cit.,* pp. 69-86.

Kuo Hua-lun (郭華倫) (Warren Kuo), 遵義會議 (The Tsunyi Conference) 匪情月報 *(Bandit Affairs Monthly)* Vol. 10, No. 7 (September, 1968) pp. 95-102; No. 8, (October, 1968) pp. 101-111.

L. LaDany, "China: Period of Suspense" *Foreign Affairs,* Vol. 48, No. 4 (July, 1970) pp. 701-711.

V.I. Lenin, *What Is to Be Done: Burning Questions of Our Movement* (New York, 1929) 176 pp.

"Left-Wing" Communism, an Infantile Disorder (New York, 1940) 95 pp.

Henry J. Lethbridge, *China's Urban Communes* (Hong Kong, 1961) ii, 74 pp.

Marion J. Levy, *The Family Revolution in Modern China* (New York, 1968) xvi, 390 pp.

John Wilson Lewis, *Leadership in Communist China* (Cornell: University Press, 1966) xiii, 305 pp.

"China's Secret Military Papers: 'Continuities' and 'Revelations' " MacFarquhar, *op. cit.*, pp. 58-68.

"Leader, Commissar, and Bureaucrat: The Chinese Political System in the Last Days of the Revolution" in Ping-ti Ho and Tang Tsou (eds) *China in Crisis,* (Chicago: University Press, 1968) Vol. I, Book 2, pp. 449-461.

Daniel Lerner, *The Passing of Traditional Society: Modernizing the Middle East* (Glencoe, 1958) xii, 466 pp.

Li Chien-hung, *The Political History of China, 1840-1928* (Translated and edited by Ssu-yu Teng and Jeremy Ingalls) (Stanford: University Press) xii, 545 pp.

Li Chin-wei (黎晉偉), 紅衛兵實錄 *(Facts About Red Guards)* (Hong Kong, 1967) 10, 2, 462 pp.

Robert Jay Lifton, *Revolutionary Immortality: Mao Tse-tung and the Chinese Cultural Revolution* (New York, 1968) xviii, 178 pp.

W.J.M. Mackenzie, *Politics and Social Science* (Baltimore, 1967) 424 pp.

(毛匪澤東的黨務工作) *Bandit Mao Tse-tung's Party Work* (Taipei, 1953) 130 pp.

Klaus Mehnert, *Peking and Moscow* (New York, 1964) 559 pp.

Peking and the New Left: At Home and Abroad (Berkely, 1969) 156 pp.

Maurice Meisner, *Li Ta-chao and the Origins of Chinese Communism* (Harvard: University Press, 1967) xvii, 326 pp.

Robert Michels, *Political Parties: A Sociological Study of the*

Oligarchical Tendencies of Modern Democracy (New York, 1959) ix, 416 pp.

Barrington Moore, *Social Origins of Dictatorship and Democracy,* (Boston, 1966) xix, 559 pp.

Jan Myrdal, "A New Look at Mao's China" *Look,* Vol. 34, No. 3 (February 10, 1970) pp. 19-26.

Charles Neuhauser, "The Chinese Communist Party in the 1960's: Prelude to the Cultural Revolution" *China Quarterly,* 32 (October-December, 1967) pp. 2-36.

Robert C. North, with Ithael deSola Pool, "Kuomintang and Chinese Communist Elites," in Daniel Lerner and Harold D. Lasswell (eds) *World Revolutionary Elites: Studies in Coercive Ideological Movements* (MIT Press, 1966) pp. 319-455.

Moscow and Chinese Communists (Second edition, Stanford: University Press, 1965) viii, 310 pp.

Joseph Nyomarkay, *Charisma and Factionalism in the Nazi Party* (University of Minnesota Press, 1967) 161 pp.

Michael Oksenberg, "Occupational Groups in Chinese Society and the Cultural Revolution" *The Cultural Revolution in 1967 in Review* (Ann Arbor, 1968) pp. 1-44.

A.F.K. Organski, *The Stages of Political Development* (New York, 1967) xii, 229, vi pp.

Dwight H. Perkins, *Market Control and Planning in Communist China* (Harvard: University Press, 1966) x, 291 pp.

Agricultural Development in China, 1368-1968 (Chicago, 1969) xv, 395 pp.

Amos Perlmutter, "The Arab Military Elite," *World Politics,* Vol. XXII, No. 2 (January, 1970) pp. 269-300.

Richard M. Pfeffer, "The Pursuit of Purity: Mao's Cultural Revolution" *Problems of Communism,* Vol. XVII (November, 1969) pp. 12-25.

Nelson W. Polsby, *Community Power and Political Theory* (Yale: University Press, 1963) xiv, 141 pp.

Ralph L. Powell, "The Military Affairs Committee and Party Control of the Military in China" *Asian Survey,* Vol. III, No. 7 (July, 1963) pp. 347-356.

"The Increasing Power of Lin Piao and the Party Soldiers, 1959-1966" *China Quarterly,* 34 (April-June, 1968) pp. 38-65.

James R. Pussey, *Wu Han: Attacking the Present Through the Past* (Harvard: University Press, 1969) x, 84 pp.

Lucian Pye, *Aspects of Political Development* (Boston, 1966) xiii, 205 pp.

The Spirit of Chinese Politics: A Psychocultural Study of the Authority Crisis in Political Development (MIT Press, 1968) xxii, 255 pp.

Fred W. Riggs, *Administration in Developing Countries: The Theory of Prismatic Society* (Boston, 1964) xvi, 477 pp.

William H. Riker, *The Theory of Political Coalitions* (Yale: University Press, 1962) xii, 300 pp.

John E. Rue, *Mao Tse-tung in Opposition, 1927-1935* (Stanford: University Press, 1966) vii, 387 pp.

Myron Rush, *Political Succession in the USSR* (Second edition, Columbia: University Press, 1968) xi, 281 pp.

Giovanni Sartori, "Politics, Ideology, and Belief Systems" *American Political Science Review*, Vol. LXIII, No. 2 (June, 1969) pp. 398-411.

Leonard Schapiro, *The Communist Party of the Soviet Union* (New York, 1960) xiv, 631 pp.

and John W. Lewis, "The Roles of the Monolithic Party Under the Totalitarian Leader," *China Quarterly*, 40 (October-December, 1969) pp. 39-64.

Joseph A. Schlesinger, *Ambition and Politics* (Chicago, 1966) xv, 226 pp.

Stuart Schram, *Mao Tse-tung* (Harmondsworth, 1967) 272 pp.

"The Party in Chinese Communist Ideology" *China Quarterly*, 38 (April-June, 1969) pp. 1-26.

Franz Schurman, *Ideology and Organization in Communist China* (Berkeley, 1966) xlvi, 540 pp.

"Organizational Principles of the Chinese Communists," in MacFarquhar, *op. cit.*, pp. 37-98.

"China's 'New Economic Policy'—Transition or Beginning" *Ibid.*, pp. 211-237.

Benjamin T. Schwartz, *Chinese Communism and the Rise of Mao* (Harvard: University Press, 1966) x, 258 pp.

Communism and China: Ideology in Flux (Harvard: University Press) 1968, v. 253 pp.

James E. Sheridan, *Chinese Warlord: The Career of Feng Yü-hsiang* (Stanford: University Press, 1966) v, 386 pp.

J.P. Simmonds, "P'eng Te-huai: A Chronological Re-examination" *China Quarterly*, 37 (January-March, 1969) pp. 120-134.

Agnes Smedley, *The Great Road: The Life and Times of Chu Teh* (New York, 1956) xviii, 461.

Edgar Snow, *Red Star Over China* (New York, 1961) 529 pp.

Richard Solomon, "On Activism and Activists" *China Quarterly*, 39 (July-September, 1969) pp. 76-114.

"One Party and 'One Hundred Schools': Leadership, Lethargy, or *Luan?*" *Current Scene*, Vol. VII, Nos-19-20 (October 1, 1969) 49 pp.

John W. Spanier, *The Truman-MacArthur Controversy and the Korean War* (Cambridge, 1959) xii, 311 pp.

Stanley Specter, *Li Hung-chang and the Huai River Army: A Study in Nineteenth Century Regionalism* (University of Washington Press, 1964) xliii, 359 pp.

Peter S. H. Tang, *Communist China Today* (New York, 1957) 516 pp.

Tang Tsou, "The Cultural Revolution and the Chinese Political System" *China Quarterly*, 38, (April-June, 1969) pp. 63-91.

Gerald Tannenbaum, "The 1967 Shanghai January Revolution Recounted" *Eastern Horizon*, Vol. VII, No. 3 (May-June, 1968) pp. 7-25.

T'ao Hsi-sheng (陶希聖), Shen Jen-yuan (沈任遠), 明清政治制度 *(The Ming and Ch'ing Political Systems* (Taipei, 1967) 4, 6, 244, 200 pp.

Frederick C. Teiwes, "The Purge of Provincial Leaders, 1957-1958" *China Quarterly*, 27 (July-September, 1966) pp. 14-32.

Provincial Party Personnel in Mainland China, 1956-1966 (New York, 1967) vi, 114 pp.

"The Evolution of Leadership Purges in Communist China" *China Quarterly*, 41 (January-March, 1970) pp. 122-135.

Sir Robert Thompson, *Defeating Communist Insurgency* (London, 1967) 171 pp.

Ting Wang (丁望) (ed) 牛鬼蛇神集 *(Anthology of Cow Devils Snake Spirits)* (Hong Kong, 1967) 8, 209 pp.

James R. Townsend, *Political Participation in Communist China* (University of California Press, 1969) xviii, 233 pp.

Daniel Tretiak, "The Chinese Cultural Revolution and Foreign Policy" *Current Scene,* Vol. VIII, No. 7 (April 1, 1970) 25 pp.

Leon Trotsky, "The Revolution Betrayed" in Samuel Hendel (ed) *The Soviet Crucible: The Soviet System in Theory and Practice,* (Princeton: University Press, 1963) pp. 283-296.

Robert C. Tucker, "The Dictator and Totalitarianism" *World Politics,* Vol. XVII, No. 4, July, 1965, pp. 555-583.

Andrew Tully, *The Super-Spies,* (New York, 1969) 256 pp.

V.I. Ulianov ("N. Lenin") "The State and Revolution," in *The Essential Left* (London, 1960) pp. 147-255.

Sidney Verba, *Small Groups and Political Behavior: A Study of Leadership* (Princeton: University Press, 1961) 273 pp.

Ezra F. Vogel, "The Structure of Conflict: China, 1967" *The Cultural Revolution in 1967 in Review,* (Ann Arbor, 1968) pp. 97-125.

"Land Reform in Kwangtung, 1951-1953: Central Control and Localism" *China Quarterly,* 38, (April-June, 1969) pp. 27-62.

Canton Under Communism: Programs and Politics in a Provincial Capital, 1949-1968 (Harvard: University Press, 1969) xviii, 448 pp.

W.K., "Communist China's Agricultural Calamities," in MacFarquhar, *op. cit.,* pp. 163-174.

Richard L. Walker, *China Under Communism: The First Five Years* (Yale: University Press, 1955) xv, 403 pp.

Immanuel Wallerstein, "The Decline of the Party in Single-Party African States" in Joseph LaPalombara and Myron Weiner, *Political Parties and Political Development* (Princeton: University Press, 1962) pp. 201-214.

Wan Yan-kang, *The Rise of Communism in China* (1920-1950) (Hong Kong, 1952) 77 pp.

Wang En (王恩) 紅衛兵造反記 *(Record of the Red Guard Rebellion)* (Hong Kong, 1967) Two volumes: 32, 135, 6, 16, 422, 7 pp.

Wang Hsiao-t'ang (王曉堂) 共匪最近宣佈成立六個省"革命委員會"之研析 (Study of the Communist Bandits' Recent Proclamation of the Establishment of Six 'Revolutionary Committees') *Bandit Affairs,* Vol. 11, No. 2 (February, 1968) pp. 1-10.

Wang Hsueh-wen (汪學文) 中共文化大革命與紅衛兵 *(The Chinese Communists' Cultural Revolution and the Red Guards)* (Taipei, 1969) 3, 9, 714 pp.

Max Weber, *The Theory of Social and Economic Organization* (translated by A. M. Henderson and Talcott Parsons, edited with an introduction by Talcott Parsons) (New York, 1947) pp. x, 436.

Allen S. Whiting, *Soviet Policies in China, 1917-1924* (Stanford: University Press, 1968) viii, 360 pp.

William Whitson, "The Field Army in Chinese Communist Military Politics" *China Quarterly,* 37 (January-March, 1969) pp. 1-30.

Martin King Whyte, "The Tachai Brigade and Incentives for the Peasant" *Current Scene,* Vol. VII, No. 16 (August 15, 1969) 13 pp.

Richard W. Wilson, Amy A. Wilson, "The Red Guards and the World Student Movement" *China Quarterly,* 42 (April-June, 1970) pp. 88-104.

Mary C. Wright, *The Last Stand of Chinese Conservatism: The T T'ung-Chih Restoration, 1862-1874* (New York, 1966) xii, 429 pp.

Wu Chin-yin (吳錦蔭) 匪軍總政治部的癱瘓與蕭匪華被整肅 (The Paralysis of the Bandit Army's General Political Department and the Purge of Bandit Hsiao Hua) *Bandit Affairs,* Vol. 11, No. 3 (March, 1968) pp. 13-18.

Frederick T. C. Yu, *Mass Persuasion in Communist China* (New York, 1964) viii, 186 pp.

Donald S. Zagoria, *Vietnam Triangle: Moscow, Peking, Hanoi* (New York, 1967) xiv, 286 pp.

INDEX

Members of Eighth Central Committee, Communist Party of China, denoted by *

African politics: 54
Agricultural and Forestry Department (State Council): 35
Akimov, Herman: 214, 215
Alabama: 49
All-China Federation of Marketing and Supply Cooperatives: 169
All-China Federation of Trade Unions: 44
All-China Federation of Women: 44
ambition theory: 9, 194
An Tzu-wen*: 40, 63, 224, 226, 248; member of P'eng Chen group, 62, 69; on people's communes, 104; on youth, 162
Anhwei: 137
apparatchiks, apparatus: 36, 51ff, 193-194; definted, 30; as members of CC, 30-32; structure of apparatus, 39-44; and 100 Flowers, 94ff; relations with army, 107ff; as commissars, 112-113
Apter, David: 4, 202

"base areas and military Party": 25
Basic Construction Political Department: 40
Barnett, A. Doak: 48, 49, 202, 204, 211, 214, 219
Baum, Richard: 160, 161, 174, 247, 248, 253
Billings, Josh (Shaw, Henry Wheeler): 247
Blalock, Hubert M.: 219
Bogunovic, B.: 182, 256
"Bolshevik" faction: 19, 22, 140
Boorman, Howard: 207
Boorman, Scott: 167, 250
Brandt, Conrad: 205, 206, 208, 210
Bridgham, Philip: 258
Brinton, Crane: 2, 3, 201, 209
Bureau for the Translation of Works by Marx, Engels, and Lenin: 40

bureaucratism: 91ff.
"bureaucrats": defined, 51ff.
Burrows, Robert: 209

Caesar, Julius Gaius: 209
Canton (Kuangchou): 74, 114, 117, 119, 174
capitalist road: 16, 104-106, 151-157
Catholic Church: 49
Central Committee (CC): as a political institution, 29-55, *passim;* membership characteristics, 29; structure, 32-47; as a policy-making body, 47-48; group and "factional" structure, 56 ff.; powers under 1956 constitution, 89; Eighth CC, second plenum, 95; Eighth CC, eighth (Lushan) plenum, 103, 139-146; Eighth CC, ninth plenum, 104; Eighth CC, tenth plenum, 110; Eighth CC, third plenum, 126; Eighth CC, third plenum, 126; Eighth CC, sixth plenum, 134; Eighth CC, seventh plenum, 138; Eighth CC, ninth plenum, 151-152, 213; Eighth CC, tenth plenum, 157-158; Eighth CC, eleventh plenum, 183-184
Central Work Conferences: 83, 156, 185; described, 48
Chang Ai-p'ing*: 217; classified in LT group, 58, 64; and Kuo Hsing-fu method, 252
Chang Ch'i-lung*: member of T'ao Chu group, 65
Chang Chi-ch'un*: 40; member of T'ao Chu group, 65
Chang Chia-jen: 99
Chang Ching-fu*: member of LT group, 64
Chang Ching-wu*: 40; member of CR group, 68; and capitalist road, 152

333

Chang Ch'un-ch'iao: 56, 250; and CR group, 74; and Shanghai Commune, 191
Chang Chung-liang*: 149, 242; member of P'eng Te-huai group, 69, 141
Chang Han-fu*: member of Chou En-lai group, 66
Chang Kuo-t'ao: 20, 21, 207
Chang Lin-chih*: member of Chou En-lai group, 66
Chang Man: 217, 254, 255
Chang, Parris H.: 48, 214
Chang P'ing-hua*: 241, 243, 254; member of T'ao Chu group, 65; supports Leap, 128; becomes first secretary, Hunan, 145; on ghost stories, 147; seeks truth from facts, 149; on mass mobilization, 174; and Tachai model, 175
Chang Su*: member of P'eng Chen group, 62
Chang Ta-chih*: 220; member of Lin Piao group, 67
Chang Te-sheng*: 150, 240, 243; and capitalist road, 152
Chang Ting-ch'eng*: member of LT group, 64; survives Cultural Revolution, 86
Chang Tsung-hsun*: member of Lin Piao group, 67; and Kuo Hsing-fu method, 252
Chang Tzu-ch'eng: 247
Chang Wen-t'ien*: 35, 140; member of P'eng Te-huai group, 69, 141
Chang Yun*: 40, 44; member of P'eng Chen group, 62
Chang Yun-i*: member of CR group, 68
Changsha: 19
Chao Chien-min*: 69, 230; purged for localism, 122; supports Leap, 128
Chao Ehr-lu*: 40; member of P'eng Chen group, 62
Chao Han: 110-111, 226, 228
Chao I-min*: member of Chou En-lai group, 66
Chao Kuo-chün: 210
Chao Po-p'ing*: 69
charisma, charismatic authority: 5-7, 203
Charles, David A.: 139, 227, 237, 238
Chekiang: 120-121
Ch'en, C. S.: 237, 243

Ch'en Cheng-jen*: 40, 237, 240; member of Chou En-lai group, 66
Ch'en Ch'i-han*: member of CR group, 68
Ch'en Ch'i-t'ung: 249
Ch'en Hsi-lien*: member of CR group, 67; enemy of Yang Ch'eng-wu, 73
Ch'en I*: 34, 35, 40, 53, 81, 130, 120; member of Chou En-lai group, 66, 71; and capitalist road, 152; esteem for Liu Shao-ch'i, 218
Ch'en, Jerome: 206, 207
Ch'en Kuang: 215, 216
Ch'en Man-yuan*: 230; member of Ho Lung group, 63
Ch'en Pei-hsien*: 240; member of P'eng Chen group, 62; becomes first secretary, Shanghai, 250
Ch'en Po-ta*: 34, 35, 40, 53, 54, 60, 79, 163, 164, 184, 216, 217, 235, 236, 237, 241, 256, 257, 259; possible conflict with Lu Ting-i, 41; leader of CR group, 57, 68, 74; attacks Hsiao Hua, 72; revives "Thought of Mao Tse-tung," 102; supports Leap, 128; becomes editor of Red Flag, 132; on past and present, 137; on bourgeois reactionary line, 185; takes a mild line, 186; on reactionaries, 187; critic of T'ao Chu, 188; a fanatic, 190; and Shanghai Commune, 191; purged, 198
Ch'en Shao-min*: member of LT group, 64
Ch'en Shao-yü-(Wang Ming)*: 69, 142, 207
Ch'en Tu-hsiu: 17
Ch'en Yü*: 194; member of Chou En-lai group, 66
Ch'en Yuan-hui: 248
Ch'en Yun*: 10, 15, 34, 35, 40, 43, 53, 129, 132, 140, 144, 157, 168, 184, 210, 232, 233, 236, 239; member of Chou En-lai group, 66, 71, 72; arch-moderation of, 125-126; return of, 136; and capitalist road, 155, 156
Cheng Chu-yuan: 235
Ch'eng Sheng-i: 245
Ch'eng Tzu-hua*: member of P'eng Chen group, 62
Cheng Wei-san*: member of CR group, 68

334

Ch'i Pen-yü: 216; and CR group, 74
Chia T'o-fu*: member of P'eng Te-huai group, 69, 141
Chiang Ch'ing: 56, 66, 86, 168, 184, 216, 217, 218, 246, 249, 250, 260; leader of CR group, 57, 74; on Hsieh Fu-chih, 58; attacks Hsiao Hua, 72; and opera reform, 164-167; attacks various villains, 186; a fanatic, 190; and purge of Yang Ch'eng-wu, 219
Chiang Hua*: 231, 233; member of Chou En-lai group, 66; attacks localists, 120-121
Chiang Kai-shek: 6, 18, 22, 155, 203
Chiang Nan-hsiang*: member of P'eng Chen group, 62; supports Leap, 127, 128
Chiang Wei-ch'ing*: 224, 241-242, 254; member of LT group, 64; on Leap, 99-100, 128; on Tachai model, 175
Ch'ien Chün-jui*: 69
Ch'ien Tuan-sheng: 203
Ch'ien Ying*: in Chou En-lai group, 58, 66
Ch'ien Yu-shen: 215, 218
Ch'in Shih Huang-ti: 209
China Youth Daily: 161
Chingkangshan: 19, 76, 77, 82
Chou Ching-wen: 145, 239
Chou En-lai*: 20, 26, 34, 35, 51, 53, 56, 58, 67, 117, 121, 123, 133, 168, 180, 184, 190, 194, 200, 217, 222, 229, 232, 236, 237, 240, 250, 257; supporter of Li Li-san, 19; on founding of political offices, 46; leader of Chou En-lai group, 66, 71-72; and Wuhan Incident, 73; on bureaucratism, 92; on intellectuals, 166; supports 100 Flowers, 118; on blind adventures, 125; attitude toward Leap, 129-130; on mass movement, 137; at Lushan, 144-145; on voluntary mess halls, 146; and capitalist road, 155, 156; speech to Third National People's Congress, 169; on February coup, 178; sends work teams, 182; urges weakening of Red Guard movement, 186; sings, 186; criticized by radicals, 189; on Mao's modesty, 209; and adverse current, 216, 217; supports Huang Yung-sheng and criticizes Su Yü, 219

Chou En-lai group: 56-87; 113, 115, 116, 118, 128, 149, 153, 192, 232, 235, 259; members, 66; described, 71-72; characteristics, 74-81; and the purge, 84; and 1958 alternates, 132
Chou Hsiao-chou*: 140, 235; member of P'eng Te-huai group, 69, 141; supports Leap, 128, 131
Chou Huan*: member of LT group, 64; member of P'eng Te-huai group, 141
Chou Kuo-ch'üan: 228
Chou Ming-shan: 162
Chou Yang*: 40, 164, 212, 229; member of P'eng Chen group, 62, 69; on 100 Flowers, 117; supports Leap, 128; and capitalist road, 154; purged, 180; paradoxical nature of career, 245-246
Chow Tse-tsung: 206
Chu Te*: 34, 35, 81, 133, 210, 233; joins Mao Tse-tung, 19; member of Chou En-lai group, 66, 71; announces "huge leap forward," 126; and adverse current, 218
Chu Te-hai*: 253; member of P'eng Chen group, 62; on agricultural experimentation, 173
Chuang, H. C.: 216, 235
Ch'un Mei: 249
Chung Ch'i-kuang*: member of Chou En-lai group, 66
Chung Hsiao-i: 244
Chung Hsuan-tsai: 245, 246
Chung Hua-min: 229
Comintern (Communist International): 17, 18, 31
commissars: defined, 31; local apparatchiks serving as, 112-113
Committee on Organizations Under the Direct Control of the Center: 40
Communist Party of China (CPC): 17; founded, 18; Sixth Congress, 18; Seventh Congress, 23-24; Eighth Congress, 29, 88-91, 114-116; use of term, "Party," 30; variations in Party control, 88-113; 1956 constitution, 88-89; control of courts, 97; functions during Leap, 99-101; second session, Eighth Congress, 102; retrenchment of, 104 ff; age composition of, 110

335

Communist Party of the Soviet Union (CPSU): 8, 33; composition of CC, 52
Communist Youth League: 44, 95, 119, 134, 163, 249
Compton, Boyd: 207
Confucius: 198, 225
Conquest, Robert: 203, 225
Control Commission: 33, 35, 36, 44, 47, 83; described, 38-39
Cult of Mao, cult of the individual: 22 ff, 101-104, 167, criticized by Teng Hsiao-p'ing, 89; revival after Lushan, 148
Cultural Revolution (Great Proletarian Cultural Revolution): 44, 46, 48, 49, 54, 56, 57, 59, 70 ff, 81, 102, 112, 143, 153, 164, 167, 197, 207, 213, 225, 248; as abortion of Thermidor, 2; ideology during, 26-27; phases of, 60-61; resolutions on, 183-184
Cultural Revolution Group (CR group): 56-87, 113, 115, 116, 122, 128, 153, 187, 192, 194, 218, 259; members, 68; described, 74; characteristics, 74; and the purge, 84; and 1958 alternates, 132, loses control, 190
Culture, Ministry of: 35, 41, 164, 168
Culture Work Committee: 35, 40, 41
Czechoslovakia: 199, 202

Defense Industry Political Department: 40
democratic centralism: 24, 27
"democratic parties": 49
Democratic Party: 49
Diao, Richard K.: 220
Disciplinary Supervision Committee: 38
Djilas, Milovan: 3, 16, 202, 204
"docile tools": 99, 164, 248
dogmatism: 106
Domes, Jürgen: 259
Doolin, Dennis J.: 223
Downs, Anthony: 202, 204
Dulles, John Foster: 162

East China Regional Bureau: 47, 164; group membership from, 80-81
Eckstein, Alexander: 261
Eckstein, Harry: 202

Economics and Commerce Department: 47
Economics and Finance Committee: 35, 36, 40; described, 43
Education Political Department: 40
Eisenstadt, S. N.: 4, 202
Employees' Work Committee: 40; described, 42
Engels, Friederick: 21, 109, 167, 186, 228
Erickson, Eric: 12
Extraordinary Committee of the Anti-Mao Alliance of the Communist Party of China: 221

factions: 56; relation to groups, 51
Fainsod, Merle: 203
Fairbank, John King: 203
Fan Wen-lan*: member of P'eng Chen group, 62; survives Cultural Revolution, 85; supports Leap, 128
Fang I*: member of Chou En-lai group, 66
Fang Ning: 215-216
February Adverse Current (1967): 57, 59, 66, 71
February coup; 62, 63, 69, 178-179
Feith, Herbert: 203
Feng Pai-chü*: 69, 232; purged for localism, 122, 124-125
Fernside, W. W.: 210
Finance, Ministry of: 35, 36
Finance and Trade Department: 40, 155; described, 42-43
Foreign Affairs, Ministry of: 35, 54, 72, 83
Foreign Affairs Staff Office: 42, 71
Forestry Political Department: 40
Fukien: power struggle in, 73, 259

Gehlen, Michael: 214
General Office: 39, 40
General Political Department: 39, 40, 52, 107, 117, 184, 218, 227; described, 44-45
George, Alexander L.: 227, 228
Gillis, John R.: 209
Gittings, John: 226-227
Goldman, Merle: 212, 222, 223, 229, 244, 245
Grandquist, Hans: 204, 209
Gray, Jack: 204, 226
Great Britain: 18

Great Leap Forward (Leap): 10, 108; criticized by Liu Chien-hsun, 59; Party control during, 98-101; political support for, 127-133
Great Purge: 30

Hai Jui: 137, 143, 147, 164, 177, 239
Hainan Island: 124
Han Kuang*: member of Chou En-lai group, 66
Han Hsien-ch'u*: 191, 210, 219, 259; member of Lin Piao group, 67; attacked by Red Guards, 73
Harsanyi, John C.: 14, 15, 204, 205
Heilungkiang: 122, 167, 192, 259
Higher Party School: 40, 41, 158
Hitler, Adolph: 6, 203, 205
Ho Lung*: 3, 20, 23, 34, 35, 44, 45, 56, 62, 79, 168, 210, 251, 252; leader of Ho Lung group, 63, 70; commander of First Field Army, 82; on military democracy, 170; and February coup, 178-179; purged, 190
Ho Lung group: 56-87, 113, 115, 116, 122; membership, 63; described, 70; characteristics, 74-81; and the purge, 84; and 1958 alternates, 132
Ho Meng-hsiung: 19
Hobbes, Thomas: 7, 13
Hoffman, Charles: 244
Holther, W. B.: 210
Honan: 100, 103; a leftist province, 131, 137
Hopei: 111; CC members from, 76
Hsi Chung-hsun*: member of P'eng Te-huai group, 69, 141
Hsiao Ching-kuang*: 53, 210; member of Lin Piao group, 67
Hsiao Hua*: 39, 40, 44, 45, 157, 190, 218, 226, 228, 255, 256; member of Lin Piao group, 67, 72; purged, 73; on Lin Piao's greatness, 179, 185
Hsiao K'o*: 83; member of Ho Lung group, 63; member of P'eng Te-huai group, 141
Hsiao Shu: 247
Hsiao Tso-liang: 205, 206
Hsiao Wang-tung: 258
Hsieh, Alice Langley: 106, 145, 227, 239
Hsieh Chueh-tsai*: 168; member of CR group, 68

Hsieh Fu-chih*: 40, 64, 67, 70, 122, 212, 217, 239; member of Chou En-lai group, 58, 66; and Wuhan Incident, 73; on 100 Flowers, 117, 118; becomes Minister of Public Security, 145
Hsu Hai-tung*: member of CR group, 68
Hsu Hsiang-ch'ien*: 44, 45; member of Chou En-lai group, 66
Hsu Kai-yu: 206
Hsu Kuang-ta*: member of Ho Lung group, 63
Hsu Li-ch'ün: 212
Hsu Ping*: 40, 43; member of P'eng Chen group, 62; becomes head of United Front Work Department, 168
Hsu P'ing-i: 226
Hsu Shih-yu*: member of Lin Piao group, 67; enemy of Yang Ch'eng-wu, 73
Hsu T'e-li*: 40; member of CR group, 68
Hsu Tzu-jung*: member of Liu-Teng group, 64
Hsu Yao-sheng: 250
Hsuan Mo: 216, 217, 218
Hu Ch'ao-mu*: 37, 40, 205, 207; member of P'eng Chen group, 62
Hu Yao-pang*: 40, 44, 161, 230, 235, 243, 249; member of LT group, 64; on building socialism, 134; sending-down of youths, 151; on revolutionary successors, 162-163
Huang Chen-hai: 210
Huang Huo-ch'ing*: 221, 241, 253; member of P'eng Chen group, 62; supports 100 Flowers, 118; on cadre cultivation, 173
Huang K'o-ch'eng: 36, 106, 140; member of P'eng Te-huai group, 69, 141; removed from Secretariat, 157
Huang Ou-tung*: member of P'eng Chen group, 62
Huang T'ien-chien: 214
Huang Yung-sheng*: 65, 80, 192, 210, 218; member of Lin Piao group, 67; enemy of Yang Ch'eng-wu, 73; appointed Chief of Staff, 73
Hunan: 29, 69, 131; CC members from, 75-76
Hundred Flowers: 94 ff, 100, 101, 116-123, 222; conspiracy theory of, 97

337

Hung Hsueh-chih*: member of P'eng Te-huai group, 69, 141
Hungary, Hungarian rebellion: 97, 223
Huntington, Samuel P.: 1, 7 ff, 54, 201, 203, 227
Hupei: CC members from, 76; a leftist province, 131, 137

independent kingdoms: 25, 38, 39
Indonesia: 203
Industry and Communications Department: 36, 40
Inglehart, Ronald: 220
Inner Mongolia: 34, 35, 122 ff, 231
institutionalization: 32
institutionalized Party control: defined, 49 f; at Eighth Congress, 88-91
International Liason Department: 40; described, 42

Jacobins: 2
Janos, Andrew C.: 202
Jao Shu-shih: 25, 38
Japan: 18
Johnson, Chalmers: 205
Julius Caesar: 229

Kan Yu-lan: 206
K'ang Chüeh: 245
K'ang Sheng*: 34, 35, 36, 37, 40, 167, 185, 211, 225, 229; head of Social Department, 41-42, 212; leader of CR group, 57, 68; on Mao, 101; demoted, 115; supports Leap, 128; appointed to Secretariat, 157; and (first) cultural revolution group, 177; absolved from coup plot, 180, criticizes work teams, 183; attacked, 189
Kao Kang: 24 ff, 38, 93, 116, 140, 208, 209, 238; and one-man management, 90; linked with P'eng Te-huai, 142
Kao K'o-lin*: member of Ho Lung group, 63
"Kendall's Q" coefficient of correlation: 74 ff, 84, 113
Khrushchev, Nikita S.: 8, 136, 137, 176, 214, 223
Kiangsi: CC members from, 76
Kiangsi Soviet: 20, 76, 77
Kiangsu: 99; CC members from, 76
Klein, Donald W.: 32, 210

K'o Ch'ing-shih*: 34, 46-47, 133, 163, 231, 236, 244, 248, 249; on 100 Flowers, 117, 118; on anti-rightist campaign, 121-122; supports Leap, 128; promoted to Politburo, 132; the whole country is a chessboard, 137; on the mass movement, 146; and capitalist road, 152, 153; on PLA, 162; and opera reform, 164-165; death, 250
K'o Liu-liu: 229
Ko Ta-chih: 244
Ku Ta-ts'un*: 69; purged for localism, 122, 124-125
Kuan Ta-t'ung: 244
K'uei Pi*: classified in Liu-Teng group, 58, 64; on communes, 231
Kung Wen-sheng: 244
K'ung Yuan*: member of Chou En-lai group, 66
Kuo Mo-jo: 103, 225
Kuo, Warren: 207
Kuomintang (KMT; Nationalist Party): 6, 17, 31, 49; alliance with CPC, 18
Kwangsi: 60
Kwangtung: 47, 65, 71, 137, 236; anti-localist purge in, 124
Kweichou: 156

LaDany, L.: 261
LaPalombara, Joseph: 202, 205
Leap: SEE Great Leap Forward
Lei Feng: 161, 174
Lenin, Vladmir Illich (Ulianov, V. I.; N. Lenin): 8, 21, 24, 109, 117, 167, 186, 203, 225, 228
Leninism: 54; notion of "Party," 4-5; as a form of institutionalized authority, 7 ff; "formalistic Leninism," 17 ff; and Liu Shao-ch'i, 21
Lerner, Daniel: 201
Lethbridge, Henry J.: 242
Levy, Marion J.: 208
Lewis, John Wilson: 8, 10, 11, 12, 203, 204, 208, 211, 212, 214
Li Ch'ang*: member of Chou En-lai group, 66
Li Chieh-po*: 40; member of T'ao Chu group, 65
Li Chien-nung: 206
Li Chien-chen*: member of T'ao Chu group, 65
Li Chien-nung: 206

Li Chien-chen*: member of T'ao Chu group, 65
Li Chih-min*: member of Ho Lung group, 63
Li Chin-wei: 255
Li Ching-ch'üan*: 34, 35, 46-47, 64, 133, 217, 240; member of Ho Lung group, 63, 70; and Leap, 131; promoted to Politburo, 132; on mess halls, 146; and coup, 178-179
Li Fu-ch'un*: 34, 35, 36, 37, 40, 43, 58, 129, 232, 240, 242, 243; member of Chou En-lai group, 66, 71; appointed to Secretariat, 132; shows enthusiasm, 146; on urban communes, 149; on mass line, 150
Li Hsien-nien*: 34, 35, 36, 40, 43, 129, 137, 146, 225, 232, 235, 236, 239, 241, 242; founding of political offices, 46; member of Chou En-lai group, 66, 71, 72; on commune management, 100-101, 133-134; promoted to Secretariat, 132; on private ownership on communes, 136; cites the Thought, 147; on politics takes command, 169; on politics and accounting, 251
Li Hsueh-feng*: 36, 37, 47, 182, 210, 221, 248, 261; member of CR group, 68, 71, 74; supports Leap, 128; on Chou Ming-shan, 162; appointed to Peking Party Committee, 180
Li K'o-nung*: 212
Li Li: 156, 246
Li Li-san*: 19, 21, 206
Li Pao-hua*: member of T'ao Chu group, 65
Li Ta-chang*: 237, 241; member of P'eng Chen group, 62; survives Cultural Revolution, 86; on farming, 138; on finance work, 147
Li Ta-chao: 17; influence on Mao, 18
Li T'ao*: member of Lin Piao group, 67
Li Wei-han*: 43, 57, 212, 214, 221, 243, 246; on United Front Work Department, 50; member of P'eng Chen group, 62; criticizes blind adventures, 150; and capitalist road, 152; removed as head of United Front Work Department, 168
Liao Ch'eng-chih*: 40, 42, 53; member of Chou En-lai group, 66

Liao Chih-kao*: member of Ho Lung group, 63
Liao Han-sheng*: member of Ho Lung group, 63; and February coup, 178-179
Liao Lu-yen*: 40, 234; member of Chou En-lai group, 66; supports Leap, 126, 128; and capitalist road, 152, 155
Liao Mo-sha: 155
"liberalism": 19, 20
Lifton, Robert Jay: 12, 13, 204, 205
"Lin Chen": 92-93, 98, 99
Lin Chieh: 26-27, 99, 188, 209, 216, 219; and CR group, 74
Lin Feng*: 40, 241, 242; member of P'eng Chen group, 62
Lin Mo-han: 230
Lin Piao*: 26, 34, 35, 44, 45, 53, 56, 58, 60, 65, 66, 68, 69, 70, 71, 79, 101, 104, 110, 112-113, 132, 140, 144, 161, 163, 164, 167, 168, 176, 178, 184, 190, 195, 203, 209, 210, 213, 216, 217, 227, 228, 238, 244, 245, 250, 252, 253, 254, 255, 256, 257, 260; on Thermidor, 5; defends Liu Ko-p'ing, 59-60; leader of Lin Piao group, 67, 72 ff; and role of army, 106-110; use of Thought of Mao, 107 ff; on human factor in war, 108; promoted to PBSC, 132; replaces P'eng Te-huai, 145; attitude during capitalist road, 155; becomes first vice-premier, 168; challenges to, 170-172; on people's war, 171-172; on February coup, 179, 180; criticizes Liu and Teng, 185; purged, 198; on Liu Shao-ch'i and the KMT, 234; Yang Ch'eng-wu's backstage boss, 219; illness, 239
Lin Piao group: 56-87; 113, 115, 116, 122, 192, 220; members, 67; described, 72-74; characteristics, 74-81; compared with other soldiers on CC, 81-83; and the purge, 84; and 1958 alternates, 132
Lin T'ieh*: 240, 243; member of LT group, 64; supports Leap, 128; opposes bureaucratic attitude, 150
Lin Tou-tou: 164, 23, 249, 252
Lipset, Seymore Martin: 205, 208
Liu-Teng group (LT): 56-87; 113, 115, 116, 122, 128, 153, 167, 175, membership, 64; described, 70-71;

characteristics, 74-81; and the purge, 84; and 1958 alternates, 132
Liu Ch'ang-sheng*: 69
Liu Chen*: member of Ho Lung group, 63; and Kuo Hsing-fu training method, 252
Liu Chien-hsun*: 112, 210; member of CR group, 59, 68, 74
Liu Ch'ung: 226
Liu Hsiao*: member of Chou En-lai group, 66
Liu Jen*: member of P'eng Chen group, 62, 69; supports 100 Flowers, 118; and capitalist road, 154
Liu Ko-p'ing*: 210, 217, 231; member of CR group, 58, 68; attacks local nationalism, 124; purged, 241
Liu Lan-po*: member of LT group, 64
Liu Lan-t'ao*: 36, 37, 38, 47, 62, 104, 211, 214, 226, 238; on institutionalized Party control, 49-50; member of Ho Lung group, 63; on the Thought, 103; supports Leap, 128
Liu Mien-chih: SEE Wu Han
Liu Ning-i*: 40, 42, 43, 77; member of CR group, 68; under attack, 189
Liu Po-cheng*: 34, 35, 53; member of CR group, 68
Liu Shao-ch'i*: 2, 27, 34, 35, 54, 57, 58, 59, 61, 62, 71, 72, 83, 86, 115, 117, 133, 157, 166, 167, 173, 180, 184, 207, 208, 212, 217-218, 221, 224, 230, 233, 234, 240, 241, 243, 246, 250, 251; supports Mao, 19; builds Party, 20-22; builds cult of Mao, 22 ff; on "special work," 41; leader of LT group, 64; backstage manipulator, 70; links with P'eng Chen, 77; on 1956 constitution, 89-91; on bureaucratism, 91; goes on tour, 101; and 100 Flowers, 118-119; supports Leap, 128 ff; becomes state chairman, 135; at Lushan Conference, 142, 143, 144; on left and right deviation, 146; and capitalist road, 152, 154; advocates opposition faction, 156; republishes *Self-Cultivation,* 157; and socialist education campaign, 159 ff; 1964 National Day speech, 168; and Tachai model, 175; and 50 days, 181-183; purged, 185, 220;
on blind obedience, 209; attitude toward Red Guards, 255
"Liu Shih-wu": 92-93; 230
Liu Tzu-hou*: member of LT group, 64; survives Cultural Revolution, 86
Liu Ya-lou*: 250
Lo Chang-lung: 19
Lo Jui-ch'ing*: 36, 37, 44, 63, 83, 198, 212, 221, 224, 239, 248, 252, 253; member of P'eng Chen group, 62, 69; link between P'eng Chen and Ho Lung, 70; at 1956 congress, 91; on rightists, 97-98; becomes chief of staff, 145; appointed to Secretariat, 157; on Lei Feng, 161; opposes Lin Piao, 170-172; and February coup, 178-179; his problem solved, 180; on the bitter and the sweet, 238; on fearing ghosts, 247
Lo Jung-huan*: 228; on Mao, 109-110
Lo Keng-mo: 243, 244
Lo Kuei-po*: 83; member of CR group, 68
local nationalism: 122-124
localism: 59; 120-122
Long March: 20, 76, 77, 82
Lü Cheng-ts'ao: member of Ho Lung group, 63
Lu Hsueh-fu: 226
Lu Hsun: 244
Lu Ting-i*: 34, 35, 36, 37, 40, 65, 71, 79, 164, 222, 223, 230, 241, 242, 246, 250; possible conflict with Ch'en Po-ta, 41; member of P'eng Chen group, 62, 69; on 100 Flowers, 94, 117-118; on rectification, 95; supports Leap, 128; calls for "cultural revolution", 147; and capitalist road, 154, 156; appointed to Secretariat, 157; on literature, 166; becomes Minister of Culture, 168; and (first) cultural revolution group, 177; and February coup, 178-179; purged, 180
Lushan Conference: 10, 101, 138 ff, 196, 225, 237, 242, 260; SEE also, Eighth CC, eighth plenum, under "Central Committee"

Ma Ming-fan*: 212, 241, 242; on CC Finance and Trade Department, 42-43; member of P'eng Chen group, 62; supports Leap, 128; on finance work, 147

340

Ma Wen-jui*: member of Chou En-lai group, 66; and capitalist road, 152
MacArthur, Douglas: 206
MacBride, Michael: 214
Mackenzie, W. J. M.: 201
Malenkov, Georgi: 55
Manchuria: 25
Mao Tse-tung*: 8, 10, 12, 30, 33, 35, 44, 57, 59, 64, 66, 67, 68, 69, 70, 76, 86, 95, 100, 110, 115, 126, 131, 133, 159, 165, 167, 184, 186, 195, 202, 205, 207, 209, 221, 223, 229, 233, 245, 248, 256, 259; rise to power, 17 ff; denounces liberalism, 20; Chairman of MAC, 45; on independent kingdoms, 54-55; says Liu and Teng did not band together, 70; on bureaucratism, 91 ff; advocates agricultural cooperatives, 93-94; on 100 Flowers, 94 ff, 116 ff, 222; goes on tour, 101-102; era of, 103; opposes Great Han chauvinism, 123; on Wu Chih-p'u, 127; supports Leap, 128; retires as state chairman, 134-135; on wind of communism, 137; criticized by P'eng Te-huai, 141; at Lushan Conference, 144 ff; criticizes Li Fu-ch'un, 146; position during capitalist road, 155; attacked, 156-157; 1962 attitude on transition to communism, 158; on socialist education, 159 ff; doubts younger generation, 161; on men on the capitalist road, 172-173; criticizes Wu Han, 176 ff; takes a swim, 179; returns to Peking, 183; on Liu and Teng, 185; on Shanghai Commune, 190; on his posterity, 198; on mistakes, 225; on superficial support for Leap, 235; on Kao Kang and P'eng Te-huai, 238
"Maoism": 56, 99, 223, 235, 241; and Cultural Revolution, 26-27; pragmatic version, 149-150; libertarian elements in, 163
"Maoist mainstream": 77
Marx, Karl: 21, 109, 167, 186, 228
Marxism-Leninism: 14, 109; in 1956 constitution, 89-90
mass line: 98; pragmatic version, 150
masses: 110; control of, 43-44; principled distinction between Party and the, 111; hostility to cadres, 112

May Fourth movement: 17
May 16 Corps: 57, 59, 216
Meisner, Maurice: 205, 206, 261
Mehnert, Klaus: 223
Mencius: 24
Miao Chu-huang: 205
Michels, Robert: 4, 16, 187, 202
Military Affairs Committee (MAC): 33, 35, 52, 170, 184, 213, 252; described, 44-45; as example of "multiple-hat policy," 48-49; and group membership, 78-79; Mao becomes head of, 20
Miller, Arthur C.: 229
Minorities Work Commission: 35, 40; lobbying function of, 43
Moore, Barrington: 204
Moscow: 18
Myers, James T.: 225
Myrdal, Jan: 261

Nanchang Rebellion: 82
Nanking: 258
National Conference of the Communist Party of China: 38
National Defense, Ministry of: 35, 44
National People's Congress: 168
Nationality Affairs Commission: 35
Nazi Party, Nazis: 6
Neuhauser, Charles: 229
Nieh Jung-chen*: 44, 45, 210, 217, 219; attacked in Cultural Revolution, 60; member of Chou En-lai group, 66, 71; supports Leap, 127-128; on scientists, 130, 234; and capitalist road, 152
North China Bureau (old): 70, 77
North China Regional Bureau: 35, 47, 162; group members from, 80-81
North, Robert C.: 205, 210
Northeast Regional Bureau: 47; group membership from, 80-81
Northwest Regional Bureau: 38, 47; group membership from, 80-81
Nyomarkay, Joseph: 6, 203, 205

Oksenberg, Michael: 214, 215, 219
opera reform: 164-166, 169-170
Organization Department: 39-40, 104
Organsky, A. F. K.: 4, 201, 202, 204
Orgburo: 39, 40
Ou Meng-chüeh*: 232, 250; member of T'ao Chu group, 57, 65; on localism, 124-125

Ou-yang Ch'in*: 221, 226, 241, 243, 250; member of LT group, 64; on inner-Party democracy, 105; on finance work, 147; recognizes objective laws, 149; on stages of development, 150; and capitalist road, 152; on Mao's works, 167
Ou-yang Hai: 174
Overseas Work Committee: 40; described, 42

P'an Fu-sheng*: 122, 251, 259, 261; member of CR group, 59, 68, 74; a pessimist, 127, 129; chairman of All-China Federation of Marketing and Supply Cooperatives, 169; in Heilungkiang, 172; on rightist thought, 231
P'an Tzu-li*: member of CR group, 68
Pao Ching-an: 33
Paris Commune: 183, 190
Party Newspaper Work Committee: 35, 40, 41
Peach Garden: 160
Peiping: 21; SEE also Peking
Peking: 35, 58, 59, 60, 73, 178, 183, 188
Peking Daily: 98, 154
P'eng Chen*: 34, 35, 36, 37, 54, 56, 60, 61, 64, 70, 71, 83, 133, 145, 174, 175, 185, 194, 226, 232, 239, 246, 250, 252, 253, 257; leader of P'eng Chen group, 62, 69; link with Liu Shao-ch'i, 70, 77; heads early Cultural Revolution Group, 74; demoted (1956), 115; and 100 Flowers, 117, 118; and capitalist road, 153 ff; on opera reform, 165-166; on Mao and youth, 168; on foreign policy, 172; on the sins of the fathers, 173; and February coup, 178-179; purged, 180; struggled, 187
P'eng Chen group: 46, 56-87, 113, 115, 116, 118, 121, 128, 147, 149, 153, 168, 175, 241; membership, 62; described, 69; characteristics, 74-81; and the purge, 84; and 1958 alternates, 132
P'eng Te-huai*: 34, 35, 36, 45, 69, 83, 168, 196, 209, 210, 217, 227, 228, 237, 238, 239, 243, 246, 260; commander of First Field Army, 82; on left and right errors, 101; and the role of the army, 106-107; purged, 139-146; attempts comeback, 155
P'eng Te-huai group: 114, 115, 116, 122, 128; members, 69, 141; and 1958 alternates, 132
"people": 43; contradictions among, 95
people's communes: and Party control, 100-101; structural reforms of, 138
People's Daily: 94, 96, 97, 98, 111, 117, 121, 123, 131, 149, 151, 170, 175, 184
People's Liberation Army (PLA): 142; factions in, 81-83; Party organization in, 44-45; political status of, 106-110; politicization of, 108 ff; elimination of NCO ranks, 109; whole country should learn from, 110; and model heroes, 161; and proletarian literature, 164; debate over organization of, 171; supports left, 190
people's war: 171-172
Perkins, Dwight H.: 224, 233, 235
Perlmutter, Amos: 227
Peter I (the Great): 209
Physical Culture and Sports Committee: 35, 44, 45
Po I-po*: 34, 35, 232, 235, 236, 240, 250; and founding of political offices, 46; member of P'eng Chen group, 62, 69; supports 100 Flowers, 118; supports Leap, 127-128; on man and matter, 136-137; on mass movement, 146; and capitalist road, 152; on literature, 166
Politburo: 33, 36, 37, 39, 40, 52, 53, 59, 71, 83, 214; membership, 33, 34; role in decision-making, 47-48; and group membership, 78-79
Politburo Standing Committee (PBSC): 33, 37, 54, 184; membership, 33, 34
Political Committee: 40
political culture: 14
political development: 1; and bureaucracy, 5-8
political offices: 36; described, 45-46
political opportunities: 13 ff; in China, 16 ff
Political Studies Office: 40
Political Work Department: 40, 42
Polsby, Nelson: 9, 204

342

Pool, Ithael de Sola: 210
Powell, Ralph L.: 48-49, 213, 214, 227
power, problem of measuring, 9 ff
pragmatism: 159, 248
"principle": 22
professional military ethic: 107
proletarian revolutionary road: 16
Propaganda Department: 35, 40, 50, 74, 164, 249; described, 41; and capitalist road, 154
Provincial Proletarian Alliance: 72
Pusey, James R.: 238, 254
Pye, Lucien: 201

Ra'anan, Uri: 171 ff, 252
Red Flag: 35, 74, 104, 186; as theoretical organ of CC, 41; temporary closure, 60
Red Guards: 70, 74, 84, 99, 112, 139, 143, 164, 178, 184 ff, 207, 215, 232, 247, 250; antagonism against military, 72-73; nature of, 255-256
regional bureaus: 33; formed, 46; SEE also entries under individual regional bureaus
Revolutionary Great Alliance: 190
Richelieu, Armand Jean du Plessis, Cardinal de: 209
Ridley, Charles Price: 237, 243
Riggs, Fred: 206
rightism: 96 ff
Riker, William: 54, 215
Robespierre, Maximillian: 2
Rue, John E.: 205, 206, 208
Rural Work Department: 35, 40
Rush, Myron: 203, 261

Saifudin (Sai Fu-ting)*: 31, 80, 110, 231; member of CR group, 68; attacks local nationalism, 123
Sartori, Giovanni: 202
Schapiro, Leonard: 8, 11, 203, 204
Schlesinger, Joseph: 9, 13, 204, 205
Schram, Stuart: 204, 205, 206
Schurmann, Franz: 45, 47, 126, 140, 204, 207, 208, 213, 214, 224, 232, 233, 238, 244, 260
Schwartz, Benjamin I.: 18, 205, 206, 208, 223
Science and Technology Commission: 44
Second Ministry of Machine Building: 47

Secretariat (new): 33, 34, 35, 39, 40, 45, 48, 74, 83; structure and membership, 34, 36-37; and the P'eng Chen group, 69; and group membership, 78-79; 1962 changes in, 157
Secretariat (old): 33
Secretary General: 33
sending down *(hsia-fang)*: 98; of military officers, 107
Shanghai: 18, 34, 47, 121, 162, 250
Shanghai People's Commune: 191
Shansi: 59, 69, 174; CC members from, 76
Shantung: 42, 83
Shen Jen-yuan: 212
Shensi: 69, 249; CC members from, 75-76
Sheridan, James E.: 206
Shu T'ung*: 242; member of LT group, 64; member of P'eng Te-huai group, 141; on uninterrupted revolution and the Thought, 148
Shuai Meng-ch'i*: 40; member of CR group, 68
Simmonds, J. P.: 139, 143, 227, 237, 238
Sinkiang: 20, 83, 126
"slavism": 27
Smedley, Agnes: 206, 207
Snow, Edgar: 12, 161
Social Department (Inspection Department): 40, 212, 246; described, 41-42; change of name, 42
socialist education campaign: 159-161
socialist legality: 38, 97
Socialist Youth Corps: 20
Solomon, Richard: 94, 117-118, 222, 229, 230
South Central Regional Bureau: 47, 65, 71; group members from, 80-81
Southwest Regional Bureau: 35, 47, 71; group members from, 80-81
Spanier, John W.: 206
special work: 36; described, 41-42
Spector, Stanley: 206
Sputnik Commune: 100
Stalin, Joseph D.: 3, 8, 18, 21, 39, 52, 109, 142, 157, 167, 186, 195, 203, 204, 205, 223, 238
Stalinist politics: 4
State Council: 35, 37, 42, 44, 52, 100; SEE also entries under specific divisions, or under specific members

343

State Economic Commission: 35
State Planning Commission: 35
Su Chen-hua*: member of Ho Lung group, 63
Su Yü*: 140; member of Lin Piao group, 67; criticized by Chou En-lai, 219
Sukarno: 203
Sun Chih-yuan*: member of Ho Lung group, 63
Sun Yat-sen: 18
Sung Jen-ch'iung: 47, 240; member of Chou En-lai group, 66; on mass movement, 146; in Heilungkiang, 192
Sung Shih-lun*: member of Chou En-lai group, 66
systems: 36, 37; and group membership, 79
Szechuan: 20, 47; CC members from, 75-76; a leftist province, 131, 137

Tachai model: 174-175
Taiwan: 49, 261
T'an Chen-lin*: 34, 35, 36, 37, 121, 216, 234, 235; member of Chou En-lai group, 66, 72; supports Leap, 127, 128; promoted to Politburo, 132; on 1958 harvest, 133; and adverse current, 218; on Mao's health, 254-255
T'an Cheng*: 36, 45, 107, 168; member of P'eng Te-huai group, 69, 141; removed from Secretariat, 157; on military modernization, 227
T'an Ch'i-lung*: 83, 112; member of T'ao Chu group, 65; survives Cultural Revolution, 86; supports Leap, 128
T'ang Liang*: member of Lin Piao group, 67
Tang, Peter H. S.: 206, 208
Tannenbaum, Gerald: 258
T'ao Chu*: 2, 10, 46, 47, 56, 57, 67, 79, 117, 140, 145, 184, 197, 235, 236, 237, 239, 241, 243, 250, 253, 254, 256, 257-258; leader of T'ao Chu group, 65, 71; and the Kwangtung purge, 125; supports Leap, 128, 131-132; discontent with Leap, 137; "The Brilliance of the Sun," 138; at Lushan, 144; after Lushan, 147; on newspapers, 148; on building communism, 150; becomes vice-premier, 168; on opera reform, 169-170; on the mass movement, 174; on the distribution system, 175; promoted, 181; sends work teams, 182; activities during Cultural Revolution, 188; purged, 189; and May 16 Corps, 216
T'ao Chu group: 56-87, 113, 115, 116, 122, 128, 251; membership, 65; described, 71; relations with CR group, 74; characteristics, 74-81; and the purge, 84; and 1958 alternates, 132; joins Maoist coalition, 169 ff
T'ao Hsi-sheng: 212
T'ao Lu-chia*: 40, 241, 254; member of P'eng Chen group, 62; supports Leap, 127, 128; the whole country is a chessboard, 137; on Tachai model, 175
Teiwes, Frederick C.: 160, 161, 174, 204, 208, 211, 224, 230, 231, 239, 247, 248, 253, 258
"Ten Great Relationships": 93-94, 223
Teng Hsiao-p'ing*: 2-3, 34, 35, 37, 52, 53, 54, 56, 58, 63, 66, 79, 94, 107, 111, 117, 118, 122, 125, 133, 135, 145, 149, 157, 163, 180, 184, 194, 208, 209, 211, 214, 212, 220, 221, 223, 224, 226, 230, 231, 243, 245, 252, 255, 257; attacks Kao Kang and Jao Shu-shih, 25; on institutionalized Party control, 50, 51; leader of LT group, 64, 70-71; on 1956 constitution, 89; on bureaucratism, 91-92; on rightists, 98; cult of, 102; possible opposition to 100 Flowers, 119-120; opposes local nationalism, 123; on class struggle in countryside, 127; possible loss of power to P'eng Chen, 181; sends work teams, 182; criticizes work teams, 183; purged, 185; on the Chinese donkey, 233
Teng Hua*: 85; member of P'eng Te-huai group, 69, 141
T'eng T'ai-yuan*: member of Chou En-lai group, 66, 217; member of P'eng Te-huai group, 141
Teng T'o: 154, 177, 201, 246, 249
Teng Tzu-hui*: 40, 79, 168, 232, 234, 240; member of Chou En-lai group, 66, 71, 72; supports 100 Flowers,

118; on voluntary mess halls, 136; on communes, 146; and capitalist road, 153, 154; a bound-foot woman, 222
Teng Ying-ch'ao*: 40, 44, 212, 214, 242; on women, 50; member of Chou En-lai group, 58, 66
Thermidor: 1, 8, 182, 197, 198-199, 202; described, 2-3; and bureaucracy, 3-5; and the purge, 84-87; at time of Eighth Congress, 88 ff
Thompson, Robert: 207
Thought of Mao Tse-tung: 73, 147, 149, 153, 167, 177, 199, 266; in 1945 constitution, 23; and Cultural Revolution, 26-27; omitted from 1956 constitution, 89; 1958 revival, 102; used by Lin Piao, 107-110; and the left line, 144; and youth, 161 ff
Three Family Village: 3, 156-157, 246, 249
Three Kingdoms: 103, 244
T'ien Pao*: 80; member of CR group, 68
Ting Ling: 139, 249
Ting Wang: 210
Townsend, James R.: 201, 213, 215, 223, 260
Tretiak, Donald: 253
Trotsky, Leon: 3, 16, 55, 142, 202, 204
Truman, Harry: 206
truth: 27, 105, 163, 226
Ts'ai Ch'ang*: 40, 44, 212, 242; member of Chou En-lai group, 58, 66
Ts'ao Ts'ao: 103, 137, 226
Tseng Hsi-sheng*: 10, 47, 69, 237, 240, 241, 243, 251; supports Leap, 128, 137; sets trends, 146; on journalism, 148; seeks truth from facts, 149
Tseng San*: 211; member of Chou En-lai group, 66
Tsinghua University: 201, 233
Tsou Tang: 204
Tsunyi Conference: 20, 21, 45, 145, 207
Tucker, Robert: 11, 204
Tully, Andrew: 246-247
Tung Pi-wu*: 34, 35, 39, 53, 58, 119, 211, 221, 230, advocates socialist legality, 38, 91; member of Chou En-lai group, 66

Ulanfu (Wu Lan-fu)*: 34, 35, 40, 131, 133, 137, 149, 213, 231, 242; member of LT group, 58, 64; purged, 61; and local nationalism, 122-124; supports Leap, 128; trusted?, 211
Union of the Soviet Socialist Republics (Soviet Union): 7, 30, 31, 39, 52
United Front Work Department: 40, 168; described, 43
United States of America: 9

Verba, Sidney: 208
Vietnam: 171
Vogel, Ezra: 211, 229, 230, 232, 233, 259

W. K.: 244
Walker, Richard: 205, 208
Wallerstein, Emmanuel: 215
Wan I*: member of P'eng Te-huai group, 69, 141
Wan Yah-hang: 205
Wang Chen*: member of Chou En-lai group, 66
Wang Chia-hsiang*: 20, 36, 37, 238; member of P'eng Te-huai group, 69, 141
Wang Chia-tao: 192, 259
Wang Chih-hsiang: 111-112, 207, 229
Wang En: 255
Wang En-mao*: 83, 210; member of Ho Lung group, 63; survives Cultural Revolution, 86; promoted to full CC membership, 132
Wang Feng*: 231; member of LT group, 64; on local nationalism, 124
Wang Gung-wu: 206
Wang Ho-shou*: 69
Wang Hsueh-wen: 245, 255
Wang Jen-chung*: 179, 184, 237, 251, 253, 254; member of T'ao Chu group, 65; supports Leap, 128; on communist style, 138; and capitalist road, 152; on Marxist theory, 169; on the complexity of the struggle, 174; on politics and other matters, 175-176
Wang K'uang: 188, 257-258
Wang Kuang-mei: 59, 135, 160
Wang Li: 73, 216; and CR group, 74
Wang Meng: 222, 230
Wang Shang-jung*: member of Ho Lung group, 63

345

Wang Shih-tai*: member of LT group, 64; member of P'eng Te-huai group, 141
Wang Shou-tao*: member of CR group, 68; and capitalist road, 152
Wang Shu-sheng*: member of Lin Piao group, 67
Wang Ts'ung-wu*: 69, 238; supports Leap, 128
Wang Wei-chou*: member of CR group, 68
warlordism: 17, 106, 107
Weber, Max: 5 ff, 202, 203
Wei Cheng: 156
Wei Kuo-ch'ing*: 65, 80, 81, 112, 210, 217; member of Lin Piao group, 60, 67
wei-ch'i: 167
Whampoa Military Academy: 82
"white areas Party": 25
white terror: 182, 183, 190
Whiting, Allen S.: 205
Whitson, William: 81-82, 193, 220, 260
Whyte, Martin King: 254
Women's Work Committee: 40, 44
Work Bulletins: 108-110, 157
Work Conference: SEE Central Work Conference
Wright, Mary: 206
Wu Chih-p'u*: 10, 47, 69, 226, 233, 241, 242; on Mao, 103-104; purged, 104; on P'an Fu-sheng, 127, 129; supports Leap, 128
Wu Han: 143, 147, 155, 176-177, 238, 239, 254
Wu Hsiu-ch'üan*: 40, 53; member of P'eng Chen group, 62
Wu Leng-hsi: 177
Wu Te*: 112, 234, 243; member of CR group, 59, 68; on red and expert, 130, 221; on mass line, 150; appointed to Peking Party Committee, 180
Wuhan Incident: 60, 73, 192, 218

Yale University: 259
Yang Ch'eng-wu*: 44, 59, 192, 209, 220; and cult of Mao, 26; member of Lin Piao group, 67; purged, 73, 219; becomes acting chief of staff, 172

Yang Hsien-chen*: member of P'eng Chen group, 62; promoted to full CC membership, 132; on "two combine into one," 158
Yang Hsiu: 248
Yang Hsiu-feng*: 53; member of Liu-Teng group, 64; becomes president of supreme court, 168
Yang I-ch'en*: member of P'eng Te-huai group, 141
Yang Ping: 226
Yang Shang-k'un*: 37, 40; member of P'eng Chen group, 62, 69; and (first) cultural revolution group, 177; and February coup, 178-179; purged, 180
Yang Te-chih*: member of Lin Piao group, 67; enemy of Yang Ch'eng-wu, 73-74; and Kuo Hsing-fu method, 252
Yang Yung*: 182, 218; member of Lin Piao group, 67; purged, 72
Yao I-lin*: 40, 232; member of Chou En-lai group, 66
Yao Wen-yuan: 56, 216, 254; and CR group, 74; criticizes Wu Han, 176-177; and Shanghai Commune, 191
Yeh Chi-chuang*: 40, 53, 69
Yeh Chien-ying*: 44, 45, 218, 255; member of Chou En-lai group, 66, 72; on Liberation War, 172; on Resist Japan University, 181; and Kuo Hsing-fu method, 252; on Mao's great life, 253
Yeh Ch'ün: 244
Yeh Fei*: 225, 241; member of LT group, 64; purged, 73; supports Leap, 128
Yen Hung-jen*: member of Ho Lung group, 63
Yenan: 20
Youth Work Committee: 40, 44
Yü, Frederick C. T.: 212, 235, 249
Yü Kuang-yuan: 214
Yugoslavia: 202

Zagoria, Donald: 171 ff, 252, 253